100 CONTEMPORARY WOOD BUILDINGS

IMPRINT

PROJECT MANAGEMENT
Florian Kobler and
Inga Hallsson, Berlin

COLLABORATION
Harriet Graham, Turin

DESIGN
Sense/Net Art Direction,
Andy Disl and Birgit Eichwede,
Cologne, www.sense-net.net

PRODUCTION
Ute Wachendorf, Cologne

GERMAN TRANSLATION
Caroline Behlen, Berlin; Christiane Court, Frankfurt; Karin Haag, Vienna; Kristina Brigitta Köper, Berlin; Nora von Mühlendahl, Ludwigsburg; Gregor Runge, Berlin; Holger Wölfle, Berlin

FRENCH TRANSLATION
Jacques Bosser, Montesquiou;
Claire Debard, Freiburg;
Yves Minssart, Saint-Avertin;
Blandine Pélissier, Paris

Hohenzollernring 53
D–50672 Cologne
www.taschen.com

This book is in part a compilation from TASCHEN's previously published **ARCHITECTURE NOW!** series.

EACH AND EVERY TASCHEN BOOK PLANTS A SEED!
TASCHEN is a carbon neutral publisher. Each year, we offset our annual carbon emissions with carbon credits at the Instituto Terra, a reforestation program in Minas Gerais, Brazil, founded by Lélia and Sebastião Salgado. To find out more about this ecological partnership, please check: www.taschen.com/zerocarbon
Inspiration: unlimited.
Carbon footprint: zero.

PRINTED IN CHINA
ISBN 978–3–8365–4281–4

Philip Jodidio

100 CONTEMPORARY WOOD BUILDINGS

100 Zeitgenössische Holzbauten
100 Bâtiments contemporains en bois

VOL 2

TASCHEN

CONTENTS VOLUME I

CONTENTS VOLUME II

LI XIAODONG

Li Xiaodong Atelier
School of Architecture, Tsinghua University
Room 401, New Building
Beijing 100084
China

Tel: +86 139 0100 9654
Fax: +86 10 6277 031
E-mail: akilixd@126.com
Web: www.lixiaodong.net

LI XIAODONG graduated from the School of Architecture at Tsinghua University in Beijing in 1984 and received his Ph.D. at the School of Architecture, Delft University of Technology (1989–93). He is currently the Chair Professor of the Architecture program at the School of Architecture, Tsinghua University. He is a practicing architect, educator, and researcher on architecture. Li Xiaodong's design ranges from interior architecture to urban spaces. His Yuhu Elementary School and Community Center (Lijiang, China, 2004) was widely praised and published and his Bridge School in Xiashi (Fujian, China, 2008–09, published here) was the winner of the 2009 AR Emerging Architecture Award and winner of a 2010 Aga Khan Award for Architecture.

LI XIAODONG schloss sein Architekturstudium 1984 an der Universität Tsinghua in Peking ab und promovierte an der Architekturfakultät der Technischen Universität Delft (1989–93). Gegenwärtig ist er leitender Professor der Studiengangs Architektur an der Universität Tsinghua. Er ist praktizierender Architekt, Lehrer und Wissenschaftler. Li Xiaodongs Entwürfe reichen von Innenarchitektur bis hin zu urbanen Räumen. Großes Lob erntete seine Grundschule mit Gemeindezentrum in Yuhu (Lijiang, China, 2004), die weithin publiziert wurde. Seine Brückenschule in Xiashi (Fujian, China, 2008–09, hier vorgestellt) wurde 2009 mit dem AR Emerging Architecture Award und 2010 mit dem Ag-Khan-Architekturpreis ausgezeichnet.

LI XIAODONG, diplômé de l'École d'architecture de l'université Tsinghua à Pékin en 1984 et docteur de l'École d'architecture de l'Université de technologie de Delft (1989–93), est actuellement professeur titulaire du programme d'architecture de l'université Tsinghua. Il est architecte praticien, enseignant et chercheur en architecture. Il intervient aussi bien en architecture intérieure qu'en urbanisme. Son école élémentaire et centre communal de Yuhu (Lijiang, Chine, 2004) a été saluée et largement publiée et son école-pont à Xiashi (Fujian, Chine, 2008–09, publiée ici) a remporté le prix 2009 de l'architecture émergente de l'Architectural Review et un prix Aga Khan pour l'architecture en 2010.

BRIDGE SCHOOL

Xiashi, Fujian, China, 2008–09

Area: 200 m². Client: Xiashi Village
Cost: $100 000

This structure connects the two parts of a small village that are divided by a creek. Two steel trusses span the creek with the space between them housing a school. A pedestrian bridge for the people of the village is suspended beneath the school. Stages can be created for performances at either end of the bridge, and a public library is located between classrooms. Though its style is not specifically related to the region, the **BRIDGE SCHOOL** serves evident public functions for the village. The jury of the Aga Khan Award stated: "The Bridge School achieves unity at many levels: temporal unity between past and present, formal unity between traditional and modern, spatial unity between the two riverbanks, social unity between one-time rival communities, as well as unity with the future."

Der Bau verbindet zwei Teile eines Dorfes, das durch einen kleinen Fluss geteilt ist. Zwei Stahlträger überspannen den Fluss, zwischen ihnen befindet sich das Schulgebäude. Unter dem Schulgebäude verläuft eine Fußgängerbrücke für die Dorfbewohner. An beiden Seiten der Brücke lassen sich Bühnen für Theateraufführungen nutzen; zwischen den Klassenräumen liegt eine öffentliche Bibliothek. Zwar knüpft die **BRÜCKENSCHULE** nicht spezifisch an regionale Baustile an, ist jedoch offensichtlich von öffentlichem Nutzen für das Dorf. Die Jury des Aga-Khan-Preises schrieb: „Die Brückenschule schafft Einheit auf zahlreichen Ebenen: zeitliche Einheit zwischen Vergangenheit und Gegenwart, formale Einheit zwischen Tradition und Moderne, räumliche Einheit zwischen den beiden Flussufern, soziale Einheit zwischen den einst rivalisierenden [Dorf-]Gruppen und schließlich Einheit mit der Zukunft."

Cette construction relie les deux parties d'un petit village séparées par un ruisseau. Deux poutres d'acier ont été jetées entre les deux rives, sur lesquelles a été construite l'école. Une passerelle piétonnière pour les villageois a été suspendue en dessous. Deux scènes ont été aménagées en plein air de chaque côté du pont tandis qu'une bibliothèque publique était installée entre les salles de classe. Si son style n'est pas vraiment proche de celui des bâtiments de la région, l'**ÉCOLE-PONT** répond à des fonctions qui sont utiles pour le village. Le jury du prix Aga Khan a écrit : « L'école-pont réussit à atteindre à l'unité à de nombreux niveaux : unité temporelle entre le passé et le présent, unité formelle entre la tradition et la modernité, unité spatiale entre les deux rives, unité sociale entre des communautés jadis rivales, ainsi qu'unité avec le futur. »

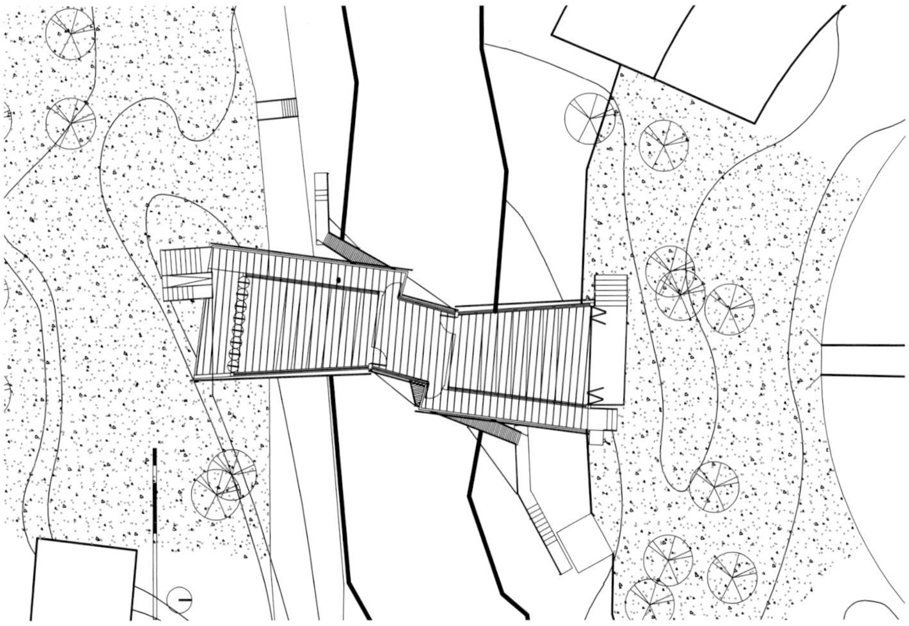

This bridge-like structure spans not only a creek but also two distinct parts of a village. Despite its location in China, it was singled out for one of the 2010 Aga Khan Awards for Architecture.

Die brückenähnliche Konstruktion überspannt nicht nur einen kleinen Fluss, sondern verbindet auch zwei separate Teile eines Dorfs. Obwohl der Bau in China liegt, wurde er 2010 für den Aga-Khan-Architekturpreis ausgewählt.

La construction conçue comme un pont franchit un ruisseau et réunit les deux parties d'un village. Projet réalisé en Chine, il n'en a pas moins reçu un des prix Aga Khan d'architecture 2010.

Drawings show the simple, elegant design of the Bridge School. In the photo below, the light, airy architecture is seen in the context of a classroom space.

Zeichnungen veranschaulichen die schlichte, elegante Gestaltung der Brückenschule. Auf der Ansicht unten ist ein Klassenraum zu sehen, Teil der leichten, luftigen Architektur.

Plans illustrant le dessin simple et élégant de l'école en forme de pont. Dans la photo ci-dessous, une classe a naturellement trouvé sa place dans cette architecture légère et aérienne.

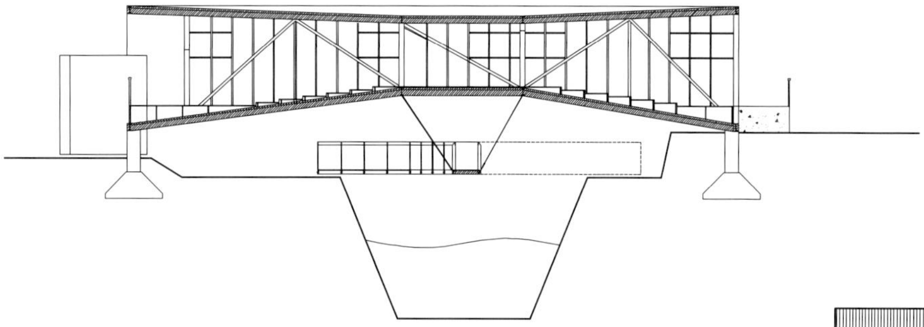

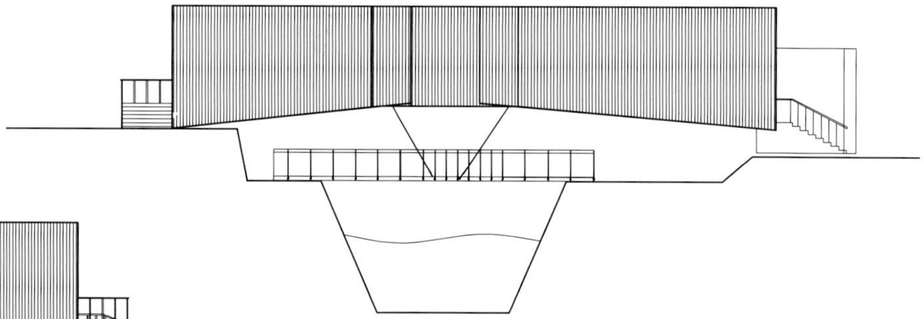

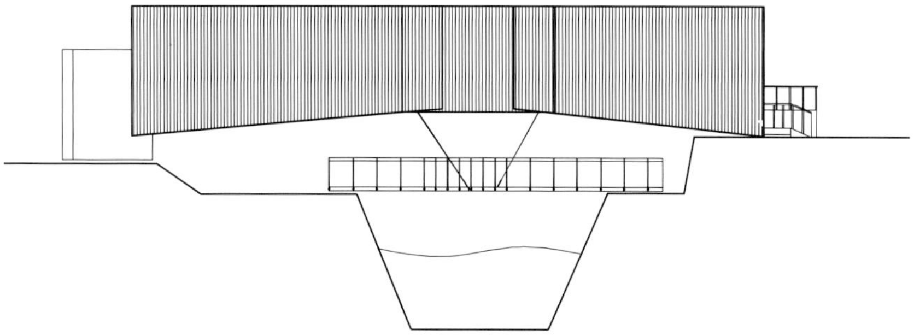

The light wooden cladding is mounted on a more solid steel structure, but the whole seems almost to float above the site and the creek.

Die leichte Holzverkleidung wurde auf einer stabileren Stahlkonstruktion befestigt. Trotzdem scheint der Bau über dem Grundstück und dem Fluss zu schweben.

Le bardage léger en bois est fixé sur une structure en acier. L'ensemble paraît flotter au-dessus du sol et du ruisseau.

BEL LOBO

be.bo.
Rua Marechal Pires Ferreira 66
Cosme Velho
22241–080 Rio de Janeiro, RJ
Brazil

Tel: +55 21 3235 2000
E-mail: contato@bebo.etc.br
Web: www.bebo.net.br

BEL LOBO was born in Rio de Janeiro in 1960. She graduated in 1984 from the Architecture and Urbanism School of Rio de Janeiro Federal University (UFRJ). She has worked on Salinas (beach fashion stores, Brazil, since 1994); Livraria da Travessa (bookstore chain, Rio de Janeiro, Rio de Janeiro, since 1995); Elle et Lui (fashion stores, Rio de Janeiro, Rio de Janeiro, since 2000); Farm (fashion stores, Brazil, since 2004); and completed the Elle et Lui Maison (furniture stores, Rio de Janeiro, Rio de Janeiro, 1999); H. Stern Home (jewelry store, Rio de Janeiro, Rio de Janeiro, 2004); and the Elle et Lui Home (gift stores, Rio de Janeiro, Rio de Janeiro, 2006). She has also completed the Zuka Restaurant (Rio de Janeiro, Rio de Janeiro, 2002); Bazzar Restaurant (Rio de Janeiro, Rio de Janeiro, 2003); the Cláudio Paiva Residence (Rio de Janeiro, Rio de Janeiro, 2007); and the Estação Cinema (Rio de Janeiro, Rio de Janeiro, 2007), all in Brazil. Although she works with her husband, the architect Bob Neri, two projects were designed entirely by Bel Lobo—the Stravaganze Restaurant (Ipanema, Rio de Janeiro, Rio de Janeiro, 2004–05) and the Quadrucci Restaurant (Búzios, Rio de Janeiro, 2008, published here), both in Brazil.

BEL LOBO wurde 1960 in Rio de Janeiro geboren. Sie beendete 1984 ihr Studium in der Abteilung für Architektur und Städtebau an der Universidade Federal do Rio de Janeiro (UFRJ). Sie hat für die Firmen Salinas (Läden für Bademoden, Brasilien, seit 1994), Livraria da Travessa (Buchladenkette, Rio de Janeiro, seit 1995), Elle et Lui (Modegeschäfte, Rio de Janeiro, seit 2000), Farm (Modegeschäfte, Brasilien, seit 2004) gearbeitet und folgende Bauten ausgeführt: Elle et Lui Maison (Möbelgeschäfte, Rio de Janeiro, 1999), H. Stern Home (Schmuckgeschäft, Rio de Janeiro, 2004) und Elle et Lui Home (Läden für Geschenkartikel, Rio de Janeiro, 2006). Zu ihren weiteren Arbeiten zählen die Restaurants Zuka (Rio de Janeiro, 2002) und Bazzar (Rio de Janeiro, 2003), das Wohnhaus Cláudio Paiva (Rio de Janeiro, 2007) und das Kino Estação (Rio de Janeiro, 2007), alle in Brasilien. Obgleich Bel Lobo mit ihrem Ehemann, dem Architekten Bob Neri, zusammenarbeitet, stammen die Restaurants Stravaganze (Ipanema, Rio de Janeiro, 2004–05) und Quadrucci (Búzios, Rio de Janeiro, 2008, hier vorgestellt) von ihr allein.

BEL LOBO, née à Rio de Janeiro, Brésil, en 1960, est diplômée de l'École d'architecture et d'urbanisme de l'Université fédérale de Rio de Janeiro (UFRJ, 1984). Elle a travaillé pour les marques Salinas (boutiques de maillot de bain, Brésil, depuis 1994) ; la chaîne de librairies Livraria da Travessa (Rio de Janeiro, depuis 1995) ; les boutiques de mode Elle et Lui (Rio de Janeiro, depuis 2000) ; Farm (boutiques de mode, Brésil, depuis 2004), a conçu les magasins de meubles Elle et Lui Maison (Rio de Janeiro, 1999) ; la bijouterie H. Stern Home (Rio de Janeiro, 2004) et les magasins de cadeaux Elle et Lui Home (Rio de Janeiro, 2006). Elle a également réalisé, à Rio de Janeiro, le restaurant Zuka (2002) ; le restaurant Bazzar (2003) ; la résidence Cláudio Paiva (2007) et le cinéma Estação (2007). Bien qu'elle travaille avec son mari, l'architecte Bob Neri, elle a accompli seule les restaurants Stravaganze (Ipanema, Rio de Janeiro, 2004–05) et Quadrucci (Búzios, Rio de Janeiro, 2008, publié ici).

QUADRUCCI RESTAURANT

Búzios, Rio de Janeiro, Brazil, 2008

Address: Av. Bento Ribeiro Dantas s/n, Centro Gastronômico Porto da Barra, 28950–000 Armação dos Búzios, RJ, Brazil, +55 22 2623 6303. Area: 240 m². Clients: Mario Fonseca, Eduardo Bellizzi, and Eduardo Sidi. Cost: $100 000. Collaboration: Mariana Travassos (Designer), Carla Dutra (Architect)

The **QUADRUCCI RESTAURANT** opened in September 2008 in the beach town of Búzios, located 180 kilometers east of Rio. It is built on a mangrove swamp, near a beach called Manguinhos. "As for the materials," explains Bel Lobo, "it has a lot of mirrors and glass in order to bring the beautiful scenery from the surroundings inside the restaurant. It is quite a simple project," she states, "that aims to allow the natural beauty of the area to play the main role, as the reflections of the mirrors and glass participate in creating a magical place." A main concern in this project was to keep the existing trees as they were, not only preserving them, but also making them part of the project. The roof is made of wood and painted white to reflect the light. A deck follows the mangrove swamp along the side of the restaurant. An effort was made to use natural, locally fabricated materials.

Das **RESTAURANT QUADRUCCI** wurde im September 2008 in der 180 km östlich von Rio am Meer gelegenen Stadt Búzios eröffnet. Es wurde an einem Mangrovesumpf nahe einer Bucht namens Manguinhos errichtet. „Die Materialien", erklärt Bel Lobo, „bestehen zum großen Teil aus Spiegeln und Glas, um die schöne Landschaft der Umgebung in das Restaurant hereinzuholen. Es ist ein ganz schlichter Entwurf, welcher der natürlichen Schönheit des Gebiets die Hauptrolle zuweist, da die Reflexionen der Spiegel und des Glases dazu beitragen, einen zauberhaften Ort zu erzeugen." Hauptanliegen bei diesem Projekt war die Erhaltung des vorhandenen Baumbestands – und ihn nicht nur zu erhalten, sondern ihn zu einem Teil des Entwurfs zu machen. Das Dach besteht aus Holz und wurde weiß gestrichen, um das Licht zu reflektieren. Eine Terrasse führt am Restaurant entlang über den Mangrovesumpf. Soweit möglich, wurden natürliche, vor Ort produzierte Materialien verwendet.

Le **RESTAURANT QUADRUCCI** a ouvert en septembre 2008 dans la ville balnéaire de Buzios, à 180 km à l'est de Rio. Il a été construit dans la mangrove, près de la plage de Manguinhos. « Pour les matériaux », explique Bel Lobo, « nous avons utilisé beaucoup de miroirs et de verre qui permettent au luxuriante environnement de pénétrer dans le restaurant. C'est un projet assez simple qui laisse le rôle principal à la beauté naturelle de l'endroit, et les reflets des miroirs et du verre participent à la création d'un lieu magique. » L'une des préoccupations principales a été de conserver les arbres existants tout en les faisant participer au projet. Le toit est en bois peint en blanc pour réfléchir la lumière. Une terrasse suit le profil de la mangrove sur un côté de l'établissement, et un effort a été fait sur le choix des matériaux naturels, travaillés localement.

The flowing decks of the restaurant run into its natural surroundings. Synthetic fiber poufs are designed by Bel Lobo as are the wooden benches.

Die auskragenden Terrassen des Restaurants leiten in die natürliche Umgebung über. Bel Lobo gestaltete die Hocker aus synthetischem Fasermaterial sowie die hölzernen Bänke.

Les terrasses suspendues du restaurant epousent le cadre naturel. Les poufs en fibre synthétique et les bancs de bois ont été dessinés par Bel Lobo.

LOCALARCHITECTURE

Localarchitecture Sàrl
Rue de la Vigie 3
1003 Lausanne
Switzerland

Tel: +41 21 310 68 98
E-mail: local@localarchitecture.ch
Web: www.localarchitecture.ch

Manuel Bieler, Antoine Robert-Grandpierre, and Laurent Saurer created Localarchitecture in Lausanne, Switzerland, in 2002. **MANUEL BIELER** was born in 1970 and received his degree in Architecture from the EPFL (Federal Polytechnic Institute, Lausanne) in 1996. He received a postgraduate diploma in the economy and management of construction from the EPFL in 2002. **ANTOINE ROBERT-GRANDPIERRE** was born in 1972 and also received his degree in Architecture from the EPFL in 1996. **LAURENT SAURER**, born in 1971, obtained his degree from the EPFL in 1998. They won Second Prize in the 2005 competition for the new Lausanne Museum of Modern Art. They have completed an opthamologist's office (Saint-Gallen, 2004); a widely published Cow Barn (Lignières, Neuchâtel, 2003–05, published here); the Guyot House (Colombier, 2003–05); the Maison du Villaret (Colombier, 2004–05); the Temporary Chapel of St. Loup (Pompaples, 2008, also published here); as well as housing in Corsy-sur-Lutry (Vaud, 2007–09), all in Switzerland. They are currently working on the Fédération Internationale de Motocyclisme (Mies, 2006–), and the Verdeil Foundation / Pierrefleur School (Lausanne, 2006–), both in Switzerland.

Manuel Bieler, Antoine Robert-Grandpierre und Laurent Saurer gründeten ihr Büro Localarchitecture 2002 in Lausanne. **MANUEL BIELER** wurde 1970 geboren und schloss 1996 sein Architekturstudium an der EPFL (École Polytechnique Fédérale de Lausanne) ab. 2002 machte er sein Diplom in Bauökonomie und -management an der EPFL. **ANTOINE ROBERT-GRANDPIERRE** wurde 1972 geboren und beendete sein Architekturstudium ebenfalls 1996 an der EPFL. **LAURENT SAURER**, 1971 geboren, absolvierte 1998 seinen Studienabschluss an der EPFL. 2005 gewann das Team den zweiten Preis im Wettbewerb für den Neubau des Museums für moderne Kunst in Lausanne. Realisierte Projekte sind u. a. ein Ladenlokal für einen Augenoptiker (St. Gallen, 2004), ein vielfach publizierter Kuhstall (Lignières, Neuchâtel, 2003–05, hier vorgestellt), das Haus Guyot (Colombier, 2003–05), die Maison du Villaret (Colombier, 2004–05), eine temporäre Kapelle in St. Loup (Pompaples, 2008, ebenfalls hier vorgestellt) sowie ein Wohnbauprojekt in Corsy-sur-Lutry (Waadt, 2007–09), alle in der Schweiz. Aktuell arbeitet das Büro an einem Projekt für die Fédération Internationale de Motocyclisme (Mies, seit 2006) sowie die Schule der Fondation Verdeil/Pierrefleur (Lausanne, seit 2006), beide in der Schweiz.

Manuel Bieler, Antoine Robert-Grandpierre et Laurent Saurer ont fondé Localarchitecture à Lausanne, en Suisse, en 2002. **MANUEL BIELER**, né en 1970, a obtenu son diplôme d'arcitecture à l'EPFL (École polytechnique fédérale de Lausanne) en 1996 ainsi qu'un diplôme de 3e cycle en économie et management de la construction de l'EPFL en 2002. **ANTOINE ROBERT-GRANDPIERRE**, né en 1972, a également obtenu son diplôme d'architecte à l'EPFL en 1996. **LAURENT SAURER**, né en 1971, a obtenu son diplôme de l'EPFL en 1998. Ils ont gagné le deuxième prix au concours pour le nouveau musée d'Art moderne de Lausanne en 2005. Ils ont réalisé un cabinet d'ophtalmologie (Saint-Gallen, 2004) ; une étable, largement publiée, à Lignières (Neuchâtel, 2003–05, publiée ici) ; la maison Guyot (Colombier, 2003–05) ; la maison du Villaret (Colombier, 2004–05) ; une chapelle provisoire à Saint-Loup (Pompaples, 2008, également publiée ici) ; ainsi que deux immeubles d'habitation à Corsy-sur-Lutry (Vaud, 2007–09), tous situés en Suisse. Leurs projets en cours incluent le nouveau siège de la Fédération internationale de motocyclisme (Mies, 2006) et la fondation de Verdeil, École Pierrefleur (Lausanne, 2006–), tous deux situés en Suisse.

VER

COW BARN

Lignières, Neuchâtel, Switzerland, 2003–05

Address: not disclosed. Floor area: 470 m²
Clients: Juan Daniel and Cuche Fernand. Cost: €201 000

This barn was designed to house 30 cows and their offspring. It includes 130 square meters of stockpiling space for hay, an exterior courtyard of 150 square meters, and other related facilities. The precise program was established by the client and the Canton's Department of Agricultural Economy. As the architects explain, the client wanted a contemporary design that would nevertheless fit within the budget allocated by Swiss federal authorities for this type of building. The farmers further wished to have a facility fully adapted to organic production. Part of a large agricultural estate called the Cerisier, the site is located in an idyllic rural Swiss landscape. The barn had to be located near the existing farm, and the architects engaged in a careful analysis of local farm building types before finalizing their design. The wooden design that they came up with is both respectful of its function, the site, and the shared goal of "sustainability." The movement of earth on the site was minimized during construction and local wood was used. The architects proved that a barn can be improved by the thoughtful use of modern design.

In diesem Stall sollen 30 Kühe und ihr Nachwuchs untergebracht werden. Darüber hinaus umfasst er 130 m² Lagerraum für Heu, einen 150 m² großen Außenhof und andere zugehörige Vorrichtungen. Der genaue Bauauftrag wurde vom Bauherrn und dem kantonalen Amt für Landwirtschaft vorgegeben. Die Architekten erläutern, dass der Auftraggeber eine zeitgenössische Gestaltung wünschte, die gleichwohl im Rahmen des von der Schweizer Bundesbehörde für diese Art von Bauwerk vorgegebenen Budgets blieb. Die Betreiber wollten darüber hinaus eine völlig der ökologischen Landwirtschaft entsprechende Einrichtung. Das Gelände gehört zu einem großen landwirtschaftlichen Betrieb mit Namen Cerisier und liegt in einer typischen idyllischen schweizerischen Landschaft. Der Stall sollte in der Nähe des Bauernhauses errichtet werden und die Architekten beschäftigten sich eingehend mit den örtlichen Hoftypen, ehe sie ihren Entwurf abschlossen. Der von ihnen entwickelte Holzbau berücksichtigt gleichermaßen Funktion, Standort und das Ziel der Nachhaltigkeit. Die Erdbewegungen auf dem Baugelände wurden auf das Minimum beschränkt und heimisches Holz verwendet. Die Architekten konnten beweisen, dass sich auch ein Stall durch die durchdachte Anwendung modernen Designs verbessern lässt.

Cette étable a été conçue pour un troupeau de trente vaches et leurs veaux. Elle comprend 130 m² pour le stockage du foin, une cour de 150 m² et divers locaux techniques. Un programme très précis avait été établi par le client et le département de l'économie agricole du canton. Le client souhaitait un bâtiment contemporain qui puisse entrer dans les conditions des subventions allouées par les autorités fédérales suisses pour ce type de construction ainsi que des installations adaptées à la production biologique. Appartenant à un vaste domaine agricole, Le Cerisier, le terrain est situé dans un paysage idyllique typiquement suisse. L'étable devait être implantée près de la ferme et les architectes ont étudié avec soin les divers types de bâtiments locaux avant de finaliser leur projet. La construction en bois respecte à la fois la fonction, le site et les objectifs de développement durable. Les déplacements de terre pendant le chantier ont été réduits au maximum et un bois local a été utilisé. Les architectes ont prouvé que même une étable pouvait bénéficier de principes de conception modernes et réfléchis.

Applying the principles of contemporary architecture to a traditional building type, such as the barn, is an interesting exercise in the reconciliation of two different worlds.

Die Prinzipien moderner Architektur auf einen traditionellen Bautypus wie einen Stall anzuwenden, ist ein interessanter Versuch, zwei verschiedene Welten in Einklang zu bringen.

Appliquer les principes de l'architecture contemporaine à un type de construction traditionnel comme une étable est un intéressant exercice de réconciliation.

The shapes of the barn are outwardly quite simple, with angles introduced to render it somewhat more dynamic than it might have been had the form of an undifferentiated shed been used.

Abgesehen von einigen Schrägen, die den Stall etwas dynamischer gestalten sollen, sind seine äußeren Formen recht einfach.

Les formes de l'étable sont assez simples vues de l'extérieur. Les pans coupés apportent un peu de dynamisme par rapport à la forme classique de ce type de construction.

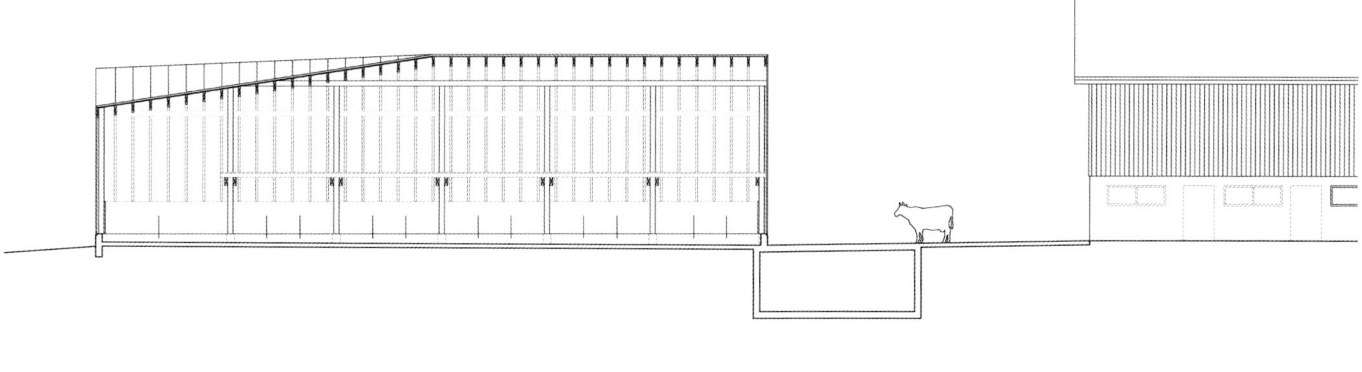

The simple wooden shapes are adapted to their intended use in farming. The Swiss maintain a high standard of workmanship in wooden architecture.

Die schlichten hölzernen Formen sind an die landwirtschaftliche Verwendung angepasst. In der Schweiz wird im Holzbau ein hoher handwerklicher Standard gepflegt.

Les formes simples en bois sont adaptées à leur usage agricole. Les Suisses ont conservé le savoir-faire de la construction en bois.

TEMPORARY CHAPEL OF ST. LOUP

Pompaples, Switzerland, 2008

Area: 130 m². Client: Deaconesses of St. Loup. Cost: not disclosed
Collaboration: in association with Bureau d'architecture Danilo Mondada and Shel Hani Buri,
Yves Weinand, Architecture, Engineering, and Production Design

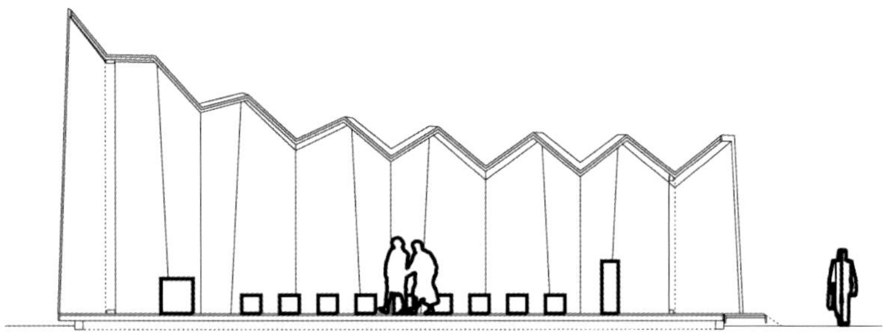

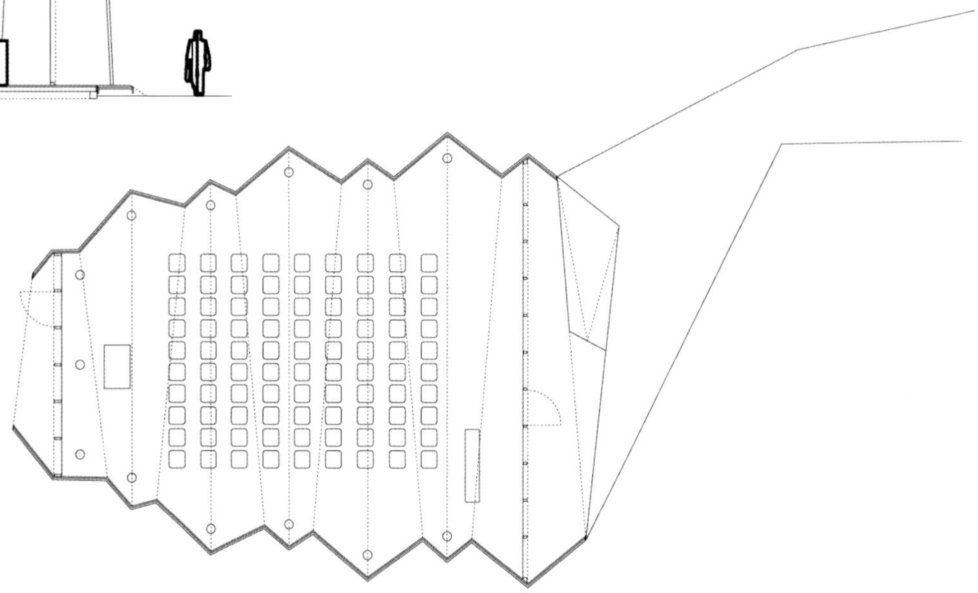

The architects were awarded the commission to renovate the home of the Community of the Deaconesses of St. Loup in the Canton of Vaud in 2007. Since this required that the facility be closed for 18 months, beginning in the summer of 2008, the architects proposed to erect a temporary chapel near the existing facilities. Localarchitecture is interested in wooden structures, and this one was designed using CAD software that was directly transferred to CNC milling to cut the four-centimeter-thick (walls) and six-centimeter-thick (roof) timber panels. Open at each end, the chapel is set directly on the ground, and is described by Localarchitecture as interpreting "the traditional layout of Protestant churches with their variations in width and height between transept and nave," and they explain that "the design creates a space whose horizontal and vertical dimensions vary via a series of origami-like folds that give rhythm to the interior and exterior of the building." Light is admitted in part through transparent plastic panels covered with fabric.

2007 erhielten die Architekten den Auftrag, das Mutterhaus der Diakonissengemeinschaft in St. Loup im Kanton Waadt zu sanieren. Da dies die Schließung der Einrichtung für 18 Monate ab Sommer 2008 bedeutete, schlugen die Architekten vor, eine temporäre Kapelle in der Nähe des Altbaus zu errichten. Localarchitecture beschäftigt sich mit Holzkonstruktionen und entwarf diesen Holzbau mithilfe von CAD, das unmittelbar auf eine CNC-Fräse übertragen wurde, mit der die 4 bzw. 6 cm starken Holzpaneele für die Wände und das Dach zugeschnitten wurden. Die an beiden Enden offene Kapelle steht unmittelbar auf der Erde und ist laut Localarchitecture eine Interpretation des „traditionellen Grundrisses protestantischer Kirchenbauten mit Höhen- und Breitenunterschieden zwischen Querhaus und Hauptschiff". Weiter führen sie aus: „Der Entwurf schafft einen Raum, dessen horizontale und vertikale Abmessungen dank der origamiartigen Faltungen variieren, die dem Inneren und Äußeren des Gebäudes Rhythmus verleihen." Licht fällt teilweise durch transparente, stoffbespannte Kunststoffpaneele ein.

Les architectes ont remporté le projet de rénovation du bâtiment de la communauté des diaconesses de Saint-Loup, dans le canton de Vaud en 2007. Comme cela impliquait la fermeture du bâtiment pendant dix-huit mois, à partir de l'été 2008, les architectes ont proposé une chapelle provisoire près des installations existantes. Localarchitecture s'intéresse aux bâtiments en bois, et celui-ci a été conçu à l'aide d'un logiciel de CAO envoyant directement les données à la fraiseuse CNC pour la coupe des panneaux de bois de 4 cm (murs) et de 6 cm (toit) d'épaisseur. Ouverte à chaque extrémité, la chapelle est posée directement au sol, elle réinterprète, selon Localarchitecture « l'espace traditionnel des églises protestantes et les variations des largeurs et hauteurs de la nef, du transept jusqu'au chœur », et crée un espace « qui varie d'une échelle horizontale à une échelle verticale en passant par une succession de plis qui rythment les volumes intérieur et extérieur du bâtiment ». La lumière pénètre en partie par des panneaux de plastique transparent recouvert de textile.

Although the structure is meant to be temporary, its form echoes the much more permanent cliff behind the Community of the Deaconesses of St. Loup. Above, a section drawing and a roof plan.

Obwohl es sich um einen temporären Bau handelt, wirkt er wie ein Echo der weitaus beständigeren Steilwand hinter dem Diakonissenmutterhaus von St. Loup. Oben: eine Schnittzeichnung und ein Plan des Dachs.

Bien qu'il s'agisse d'un bâtiment provisoire, sa forme évoque la paroi rocheuse bien plus pérenne précaire, derrière la communauté des diaconesses de Saint-Loup. Ci-dessus, une coupe et un plan du toit.

An interior view, and a night image of the structure's low, open end.

Ein Blick in den Innenraum der Kapelle und eine nächtliche Ansicht ihrer niedrigeren, transparenten Rückseite.

Une vue intérieure et une vue de nuit de l'extrémité basse et ouverte du bâtiment.

Based on an accordion-like folding of paper, the completed building nonetheless assumes a look of some permanence, and, in any case, remains quite original.

Das realisierte Gebäude basiert formal im Grunde auf einem zur Ziehharmonika gefalteten Blatt Papier. Dennoch wirkt es beständig und in jedem Fall außergewöhnlich.

Reproduisant la forme d'une feuille de papier pliée en accordéon, le bâtiment n'en revêt pas moins une certaine permanence et reste, en tout cas, vraiment original.

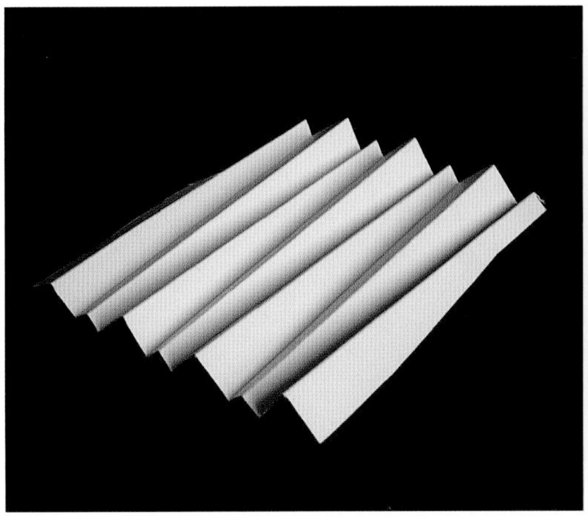

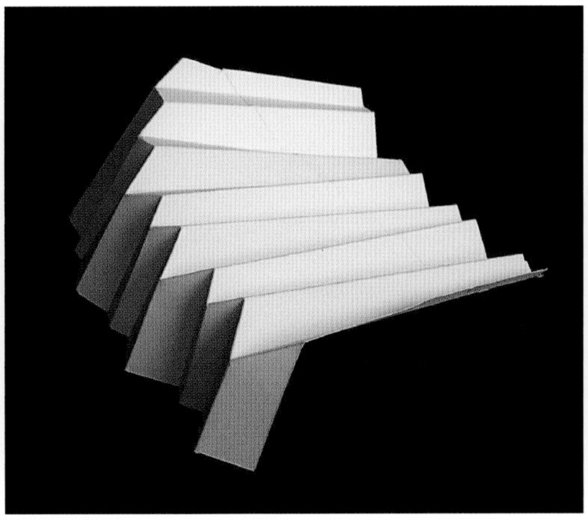

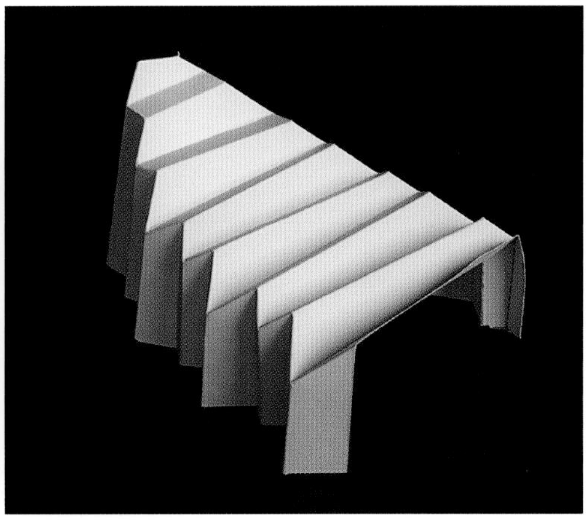

MACKAY-LYONS SWEETAPPLE

MacKay-Lyons Sweetapple Architects Ltd.
2188 Gottingen Street
Halifax, Nova Scotia B3K 3B4
Canada

Tel: +1 902 429 1867 / Fax: +1 902 429 6276
E-mail: info@mlsarchitects.ca / Web: www.mlsarchitects.ca

BRIAN MACKAY-LYONS was born in Arcadia, Nova Scotia. He received his B.Arch from the Technical University of Nova Scotia in 1978 and his Master of Architecture and Urban Design from UCLA. After studying in China, Japan, California, and Italy, working with Charles Moore, Barton Myers, and Giancarlo De Carlo, MacKay-Lyons returned to Nova Scotia in 1983. In 1985 he founded the firm Brian MacKay-Lyons Architecture Urban Design in Halifax. Twenty years later, he created a partnership with Talbot Sweetapple under the name MacKay-Lyons Sweetapple Architects Ltd. **TALBOT SWEETAPPLE** was born in St. John's, Newfoundland. He graduated with a M.Arch from Dalhousie University. He worked with Shin Takamatsu in Berlin, Germany, and the firm KPMB in Toronto. MacKay-Lyons is a Professor of Architecture at Dalhousie University. Talbot Sweetapple is a Professor of Practice at Dalhousie University's Faculty of Architecture. Significant projects, all in Canada, include Danielson House (Cape Breton Island, Nova Scotia, 1998); House on the Nova Scotia Coast #22 (Nova Scotia, 1998); Howard House (Nova Scotia Coast, 1999); Messenger House 2 (Kingsburg, Nova Scotia, 2003); Hill House (Nova Scotia Coast, 2004); Dalhousie Faculty of Computer Science (Halifax, Nova Scotia, 1999); Academic Resource Centre, University of Toronto (Scarborough, Ontario, 2003); and Office for MacKay-Lyons Sweetapple Architects (Halifax, Nova Scotia, 2003). Current work includes the Colchester–East Hants Public Library (Truro, Nova Scotia, 2015). The area occupied by the "Ghost Lab" projects (published here) is now called the Shobac Cottages and Studios.

BRIAN MACKAY-LYONS wurde in Arcadia, Nova Scotia, geboren. Er erhielt 1978 von der Technical University of Nova Scotia den Grad eines B. Arch. An der UCLA erwarb er den Master of Architecture and Urban Design. Nach Studien in China, Japan, Kalifornien und Italien sowie nach Tätigkeiten in den Büros von Charles Moore, Barton Myers und Giancarlo De Carlo kehrte MacKay-Lyons 1983 nach Nova Scotia zurück. 1985 eröffnete er in Halifax das Büro Brian MacKay-Lyons Architecture Urban Design. 20 Jahre später ging er mit Talbot Sweetapple eine Partnerschaft unter dem Namen MacKay-Lyons Sweetapple Architects Ltd. ein. **TALBOT SWEETAPPLE** wurde in St. John's in Neufundland geboren. Er verließ die Dalhousie University, Halifax, mit dem Grad eines M. Arch. und arbeitete mit Shin Takamatsu in Berlin und dem Büro KPMB in Toronto. MacKay-Lyons lehrt als Architekturprofessor an der Dalhousie University. Talbot Sweetapple ist dort Dozent an der Architekturfakultät. Zu den sämtlich in Kanada befindlichen, bedeutenden Projekten zählen: Danielson House (Cape Breton Island, Nova Scotia, 1998), Haus an der Küste von Nova Scotia #22 (Nova Scotia, 1998), Howard House (Nova Scotia Coast, 1999), Messenger House 2 (Kingsburg, Nova Scotia, 2003), Hill House (Nova Scotia Coast, 2004), Dalhousie University, Fakultät für Computerwissenschaft (Halifax, Nova Scotia, 1999), Academic Resource Centre, University of Toronto (Scarborough, Ontario, 2003) und das Büro für MacKay-Lyons Sweetapple Architects (Halifax, Nova Scotia, 2003). Zu den aktuellen Projekten Zu den laufenden Projekten zählt die Colchester-East Hants Public Library (Truro, Nova Scotia, 2015). Das Areal, auf dem die „Ghost-Lab"-Projekte stehen (hier vorgestellt), heißt nun Shobac Cottages and Studios.

BRIAN MACKAY-LYONS est né en Arcadie, Nouvelle-Écosse, Canada. Il est titulaire d'un B.Arch. de l'Université technique de Nouvelle-Écosse (1978) et d'un M.Arch. en urbanisme de l'UCLA. Après des études en Chine, au Japon, en Californie et en Italie, il a travaillé pour Charles Moore, Barton Myers et Giancarlo De Carlo. De retour en Nouvelle-Écosse en 1983, il fonde l'agence Brian MacKay-Lyons Architecture Urban Design à Halifax en 1985. Vingt ans plus tard, il s'associe avec Talbot Sweetapple sous le nom de MacKay-Lyons Sweetapple Architects Ltd. **TALBOT SWEETAPPLE** est né à St. John, Terre-Neuve. Il est titulaire d'un M.Arch. de l'université de Dalhousie et a travaillé avec Shin Takamatsu à Berlin et l'agence KPMB à Toronto. MacKay-Lyons est professeur d'architecture à l'université de Dalhousie. Talbot Sweetapple est professeur à la faculté d'architecture de l'université de Dalhousie. Parmi leurs projets les plus significatifs, tous au Canada : Danielson House (île du Cap-Breton, Nouvelle-Écosse, 1998) ; maison sur la côte de Nouvelle-Écosse n° 22 (Nouvelle-Écosse, 1998) ; Howard House (côte de Nouvelle-Écosse, 1999) ; Messenger House 2 (Kingsburg, Nouvelle-Écosse, 2003) ; Hill House (côte de Nouvelle-Écosse, 2004) ; faculté des sciences de l'informatique de l'université de Dalhousie (Halifax, Nouvelle-Écosse, 1999) ; Academic Resource Centre de l'université de Toronto (Scarborough, Ontario, 2003) et des bureaux pour Mackay-Lyons Sweetapple Architects (Halifax, Nouvelle-Écosse, 2003). Un chantier actuel est la bibliothèque publique Colchester–East Hants (Truro, Nouvelle-Écosse, 2015). Le site occupé par le *Ghost Lab* (publié ici) s'appelle désormais Shobac Cottages and Studios.

"GHOST LAB"

Nova Scotia, Canada, 1994–1997, 2002–

The unusual wooden tower seen here was built as part of "Ghost 6" in the summer of 2004.

Der hier abgebildete, ungewöhnliche Holzturm wurde im Sommer 2004 als Teil von „Ghost 6" errichtet.

Cette curieuse tour en bois, qui fait partie du projet « Ghost 6 », a été construite pendant l'été 2004.

Brian MacKay-Lyons describes his invention of the **"GHOST LAB"** as follows: "As an architectural student in my early 20s, I quickly became suspicious of the nature of the architectural education that I was receiving. While daydreaming in the classroom and looking out of the window at the life on the street outside, I felt a recurring desire to knock down the massive brick wall of the building and let the sounds and fresh air outside fill the academy. In 1994, as a Professor in that same school, I saw an opportunity to take architectural education out of the classroom and into the landscape. The Ghost Laboratory has been conducted on the nearby 400-year-old ruins on the back of my farm on the southwest coast of Nova Scotia ever since. At first (1994–97) it began as a Dalhousie University summer studio called a 'free lab.' From 2002 to 2004 it has been an international summer internship offered by my practice in partnership with Dalhousie." The "Ghost Labs" have created their own structures where "each project is a study in light wood framing which is temporary, recycled, and biodegradable, resulting in an ephemeral quality." The emphasis of the summer programs under the direction of MacKay-Lyons is "on issues of landscape, material culture, and community." The two-week sessions consist of one week of design and one week of construction.

Brian MacKay-Lyons beschreibt seine Erfindung des **„GHOST LAB"** wie folgt: „Als Architekturstudent von Anfang 20 wurde mir die Art der Architekturausbildung, die ich erhielt, schnell suspekt. Während ich tagträumend im Unterricht saß und aus dem Fenster das Leben auf der Straße draußen beobachtete, empfand ich wieder und wieder das Bedürfnis, die massiven Backsteinmauern des Gebäudes einzureißen, auf dass die Akademie mit den Geräuschen und der frischen Luft von draußen erfüllt würde. Als ich dann 1994 an derselben Schule als Professor tätig war, sah ich die Gelegenheit, die Architektenausbildung aus dem Hörsaal in die Landschaft zu verlegen. Seither wird das Ghost Laboratory auf den fast 400 Jahre alten Ruinen auf dem rückwärtigen Gelände meiner Farm an der Südwestküste von Nova Scotia durchgeführt. Zu Anfang, in den Jahren 1994 bis 1997, fand es unter der Bezeichnung ‚free lab' als Sommerkurs der Dalhousie University statt. Von 2002 bis 2004 wurde es unter Beteiligung der Universität von meinem Büro als internationales Sommerpraktikum angeboten." Während der „Ghost Labs" entstanden jeweils eigene Bauten, von denen „ein jeder eine Studie zum Leichtholzrahmen darstellt, der temporär, recyclebar, biologisch abbaubar und damit von einer kurzlebigen Qualität geprägt ist". In den von MacKay-Lyons geleiteten Sommerprogrammen werden schwerpunktmäßig „Fragen von Landschaft, Materialkultur und Gemeinschaft" behandelt. Die zweiwöchigen Veranstaltungen setzen sich aus einer Woche Entwerfen und einer Woche Bauen zusammen.

Brian MacKay-Lyons décrit ainsi ce **« GHOST LAB »** ou « labo fantôme » : « Étudiant en architecture d'une vingtaine d'années, je me suis vite posé des questions sur la nature de l'enseignement que je recevais. Tout en rêvassant pendant les cours et en regardant par la fenêtre ce qui se passait dans la rue, je ressentais le besoin récurrent de faire tomber le mur massif du bâtiment et de laisser les sons et l'air frais du dehors emplir la faculté. En 1994, professeur dans la même école, j'ai trouvé une opportunité de faire sortir l'enseignement architectural de la salle de classe et de l'attirer vers le paysage. Le Ghost Laboratory a été mis en œuvre sur des ruines datant de près de 400 ans, qui se trouvaient derrière ma ferme sur la côte sud-ouest de la Nouvelle-Écosse. » Initialement (1994–97), l'expérience débuta sous forme de stage d'été de l'université de Dalhousie appelé « free lab ». « De 2002 à 2004, il s'est transformé en stage international d'été proposé par mon agence en partenariat avec Dalhousie. » Ces « Ghost Labs » ont créé leurs propres structures dans lesquelles « chaque projet est une recherche sur les principes de l'ossature légère en bois temporaire, recyclée et biodégradable, d'où une certaine qualité d'éphémère. » L'accent mis par ces programmes d'été sous la direction de MacKay-Lyons porte « sur les enjeux du paysage, de culture matérielle et de communauté ». Les sessions d'une durée de quinze jours se répartissent entre la conception et la construction.

"Each project," says Brian MacKay-Lyons, "acts as a landscape measuring device, reading natural and settlement patterns through a built proposition. Each project is a study in light wood framing, which is temporary, recycled, and biodegradable, resulting in an ephemeral quality."

„Jedes Projekt", sagt Brian MacKay-Lyons, „fungiert als ein Messinstrument, das naturgegebene und siedlungsabhängige Muster anhand eines Bauvorhabens liest. Jedes Projekt ist ein Beispiel für das Bauen mit Leichtholzrahmen, die temporär, recycelbar, biologisch abbaubar sind und vergänglich wirken."

« Chaque projet, a déclaré Brian MacKay-Lyons, agit comme une mesure du paysage qui facilite la lecture de ses caractéristiques naturelles et de l'implantation à travers une proposition de construction. Chaque projet est une étude sur l'ossature légère en bois, temporaire, recyclée et biodégradable, et sa qualité éphémère. »

The cabins above were created for "Ghost 7" in 2005.

Die Holzhäuser oben entstanden 2005 für „Ghost 7".

Les huttes (ci-dessus) ont été créées pour le projet « Ghost 7 », en 2005.

To the right, a view showing the "Ghost 7" cabins in the background and the structure built for "Ghost 8" in 2006, in the foreground. Below, two pictures of the cabins built during "Ghost 7."

Auf der Abbildung rechts sind im Hintergrund die Holzhäuser von „Ghost 7" und im Vordergrund der 2006 für „Ghost 8" errichtete Bau zu sehen. Unten zwei Bilder der während „Ghost 7" entstandenen Holzhäuser.

À droite, vue des huttes de « Ghost 7 », en arrière-plan, et de la structure édifiée pour « Ghost 8 », en 2006, au premier plan. En bas, deux vues des huttes de « Ghost 7 ».

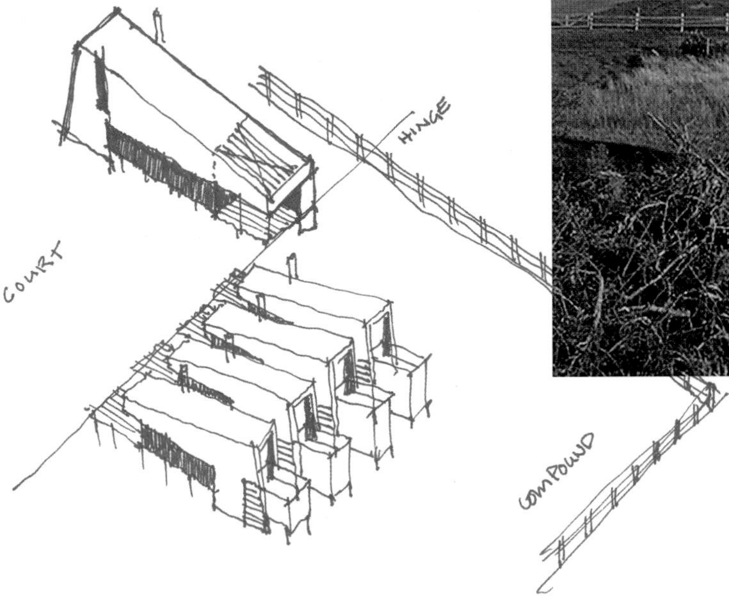

MADA S.P.A.M.

MADA s.p.a.m.
No. 2, Lane 134, Xinle Road
Xuhui District
Shanghai 200031
China

Tel: +86 21 5404 1166
Fax: +86 21 5404 6646
E-mail: marketing@madaspam.com
Web: www.madaspam.com

MA QINGYUN graduated from Tsinghua University with a degree in Civil Engineering and Architecture in 1988. He worked briefly in a government historic preservation and urban planning office, before attending the Graduate School of Fine Art at the University of Pennsylvania. He obtained his M.Arch there in 1991. He then worked in the office of KPF in New York (1991–95), before establishing MADA s.p.a.m. (for strategy, planning, architecture, and media) in Shanghai. The firm now also has offices in Xi'an, China, and Pasadena, USA. Since 2006, Ma Qingyun has been the Dean of the School of Architecture at the University of Southern California. The firm's projects include the Ningbo Culture Center (Ningbo, 2000); their own offices in Shanghai (2003–04); Father's House (Xi'an, 2004); Chunshen Floating Street (Shanghai, 2005); Xi'an TV Media Center (2005); Ningbo Y-Town (Ningbo, 2001–06); and the Comprehensive Office Building, Zhujiajiao Administration Center (Qingpu, Shanghai, 2004–06, published here). More recent work includes the Xi'an Chanba Horticultural Exposition Garden VIP Resort (Xi'an, 2009); Asian Pacific Museum (Pasadena, California, USA, 2009); Glen Oaks Residence (Pasadena, California, USA, 2009–11); and the Luneng International Exchange Center (Beijing, 2013), all in China unless stated otherwise.

MA QINGYUN schloss sein Studium 1988 an der Tsinghua University mit einem Diplom in Bauingenieurwesen und Architektur ab. Er arbeitete zunächst in einem Regierungsbüro für Denkmalschutz und Stadtplanung, ehe er an der University of Pennsylvania ein Studium an der Graduate School of Fine Art aufnahm. Dieses schloss er 1991 mit einem M.Arch. ab. Er arbeitete für KPF in New York (1991–95) und gründete anschließend sein Büro MADA s.p.a.m. (kurz für „strategy, planning, architecture, and media") in Schanghai. Das Büro hat inzwischen Niederlassungen in Xi'an, China, und Pasadena, USA. Seit 2006 ist Ma Qingyun Dekan an der Fakultät für Architektur an der University of Southern California. Zu seinen Projekten zählen das Kulturzentrum Ningbo (Ningbo, 2000), das eigene Büro in Schanghai (2003–04), das Father's House (Xi'an, 2004), Chunshen Floating Street (Schanghai, 2005), das Xi'an TV Media Center (2005), die Ningbo Y-Town (Ningbo, 2001–06) und der hier vorgestellte Bürogroßbau, die Behördenzentrale von Zhujiajiao (Quingpu, Schanghai, 2004–06). Jüngere Entwürfe sind der VIP Resort der Gartenausstellung Xi'an Chanba (Xi'an, 2009), das Asian Pacific Museum (Pasadena, Kalifornien, 2009), die Glen Oaks Residence (Pasadena, 2009–11) sowie das Luneng International Exchange Center (Peking, 2013), alle in China, sofern nicht anders angegeben.

MA QINGYUN est diplômé en ingénierie civile et architecture de l'université de Tsinghua (1988). Il a brièvement travaillé dans une agence gouvernementale de conservation historique et d'urbanisme avant d'étudier à l'École supérieure des beaux-arts de l'université de Pennsylvanie où il a obtenu son diplôme de M.Arch. en 1991. Il a ensuite travaillé pour l'agence KPF à New York (1991–95) avant de créer MADA s.p.a.m. (stratégie, programmation, architecture et médias) à Shanghai. L'agence possède aujourd'hui des bureaux à Xi'An (Chine) et à Pasadena (États-Unis). Depuis 2006, Ma Qingyun est doyen de l'école d'architecture de l'USC (University of Southern California). Parmi les réalisations de l'agence : le Centre culturel de Ningbo (Ningbo, 2001–06), leurs bureaux à Shanghai (2003–04) ; la Father's House (Xi'an, 2004) ; Chunshen Floating Street (Shanghai, 2005) ; le Xi'an TV Media Center (2005), le Ningbo Y-Town (Ningbo, 2001–06) et l'immeuble de bureaux, centre administratif de Zhujiajiao (Quingpu, Shanghaï, 2004–06, publié ici). Plus récemment, elles comprennent : le jardin-exposition d'horticulture et hôtel VIP de Xi'an (Xi'an, 2009) ; l'Asian Pacific Museum (Pasadena, Californie, 2009) ; la résidence Glen Oaks (Pasadena, Californie, 2009–11) et le Centre d'échanges internationaux de Luneng (Pékin, 2013), toutes en Chine, sauf mention contraire.

COMPREHENSIVE OFFICE BUILDING

Zhujiajiao Administration Center, Qingpu, Shanghai, China, 2004–06

Site area: 40 500 m². Floor area: 20 598 m²
Client: Zhujiajiao Invest Development Co. Ltd. Cost: not disclosed
Collaboration: Sunny Zhanhui Chen, Rong Huang

Qingpu is located approximately one hour's drive west of Shanghai, an area where MADA s.p.a.m. also built the Qio Zi Wan Shopping District and the Thumb Island Community Center. The local government asked the architects to design a new government complex, of which the so-called **COMPREHENSIVE OFFICE BUILDING** is the main project. The architects explain: "Its characteristic Jiangnan architectural form makes it also an emotionally accessible government center to the local workers. The project combined traditional gardens with modern architectural concepts: the plan is compact and orderly; it utilizes natural lighting, ventilation and makes complete use of the surrounding courtyard landscape." The building is 12 meters high and occupies three stories. As is the case in a number of other projects lead by Ma Qingyun, the materials used here—bricks, concrete, and patterned brick—are quite austere. One of the most striking elements in the large complex is a round pavilion situated near the water. Extensive use of wood was made in the complex. Here, the architects write, in almost poetic terms, "The wooden curtain wall follows the construction procedure for classical Chinese checkered windows. The wooden shutters in the curtain wall are made visible by the light that leaks in through the windows."

Quingpu liegt rund eine Stunde Autofahrt westlich von Schanghai. Hier hat MADA s.p.a.m bereits den Einkaufsdistrikt Qio Zi Wan und das Gemeindezentrum von Thumb Island gebaut. Auf Anfrage der Lokalverwaltung entwarf das Büro einen neuen Verwaltungskomplex, mit dem sogenannten **BÜROGROSSBAU** als Hauptprojekt. Zum Entwurf erklären die Architekten: „Durch seine für die Architektur in Jiangnan charakteristische Gestalt finden die örtlichen Angestellten leicht einen emotionalen Zugang zu dem Gebäude. Das Projekt kombiniert traditionelle Gärten mit einem modernen architektonischen Konzept: Der Grundriss zeigt eine kompakte, regelmäßige Aufteilung, Beleuchtung und Belüftung erfolgen auf natürlichem Weg und der Bau fügt sich vorzüglich in die Umgebung mit ihren Hofgebäuden ein." Das Gebäude ist 12 m hoch und hat drei Geschosse. Wie bei einer Reihe weiterer Projekte unter Leitung von Ma Qingyun kamen auch hier recht einfache Materialien zum Einsatz – Ziegel, Beton und gemusterete Backsteine. Eines der auffälligsten Elemente des großangelegten Komplexes ist ein runder Pavillon in Wassernähe. Eine herausragende Rolle spielt in der gesamten Anlage die Verwendung von Holz. Hierzu führen die Architekten aus: „Die hölzerne Vorhangfassade folgt der baulichen Anordnung klassischer schachbrettartiger chinesischer Fenster. Sickert Licht hindurch, werden die in die Wand eingelassenen Holzblenden sichtbar."

Quingpu se trouve à une heure de voiture environ de Shanghaï, région où MADA s.p.a.m. a également réalisé le quartier commercial de Qio Zi Wan et le centre communal de Thumb Island. L'administration locale avait demandé aux architectes de concevoir un nouveau complexe administratif dont cet **IMMEUBLE DE BUREAUX** est le composant principal. Les architectes expliquent : « Sa forme architecturale caractéristique de la région du Jiangnan facilite l'appropriation de ce centre administratif par les travailleurs locaux. Le projet combine des jardins traditionnels à des concepts architecturaux modernes : le plan compact et ordonné utilise l'éclairage et la ventilation naturels et tire le meilleur parti de l'environnement de la cour paysagée. » Le bâtiment de trois niveaux mesure 12 m de haut. Comme souvent dans d'autres projets de Ma Qingyun, les matériaux utilisés – brique, béton et brique à motif – sont assez austères. L'un des éléments les plus frappants de ce vaste complexe est un pavillon circulaire au bord de l'eau. Le bois est largement utilisé sur l'ensemble du complexe, ce que l'architecte décrit en termes presque poétiques : « Le mur-rideau en bois suit le mode de construction des fenêtres chinoises classiques. Les volets de bois dans le mur-rideau sont rendus visibles par la lumière qui filtre à travers les fenêtres. »

The emergence of contemporary Chinese architecture on the world scene is related to changes in local laws that allowed individuals like Ma Qingyun of MADA s.p.a.m. to create their own practice.

Der Einzug zeitgenössischer chinesischer Architektur auf die internationale Bühne hat mit der Änderung gesetzlicher Regelungen zu tun, die es Einzelpersonen wie Ma Qingyun von MADA s.p.a.m. erlaubten, eigene Büros zu eröffnen.

L'émergence de l'architecture chinoise contemporaine sur la scène mondiale est liée à des changements législatifs qui ont permis à des individus comme Ma Qingyun de MADA s.p.a.m. de créer leur propre agence.

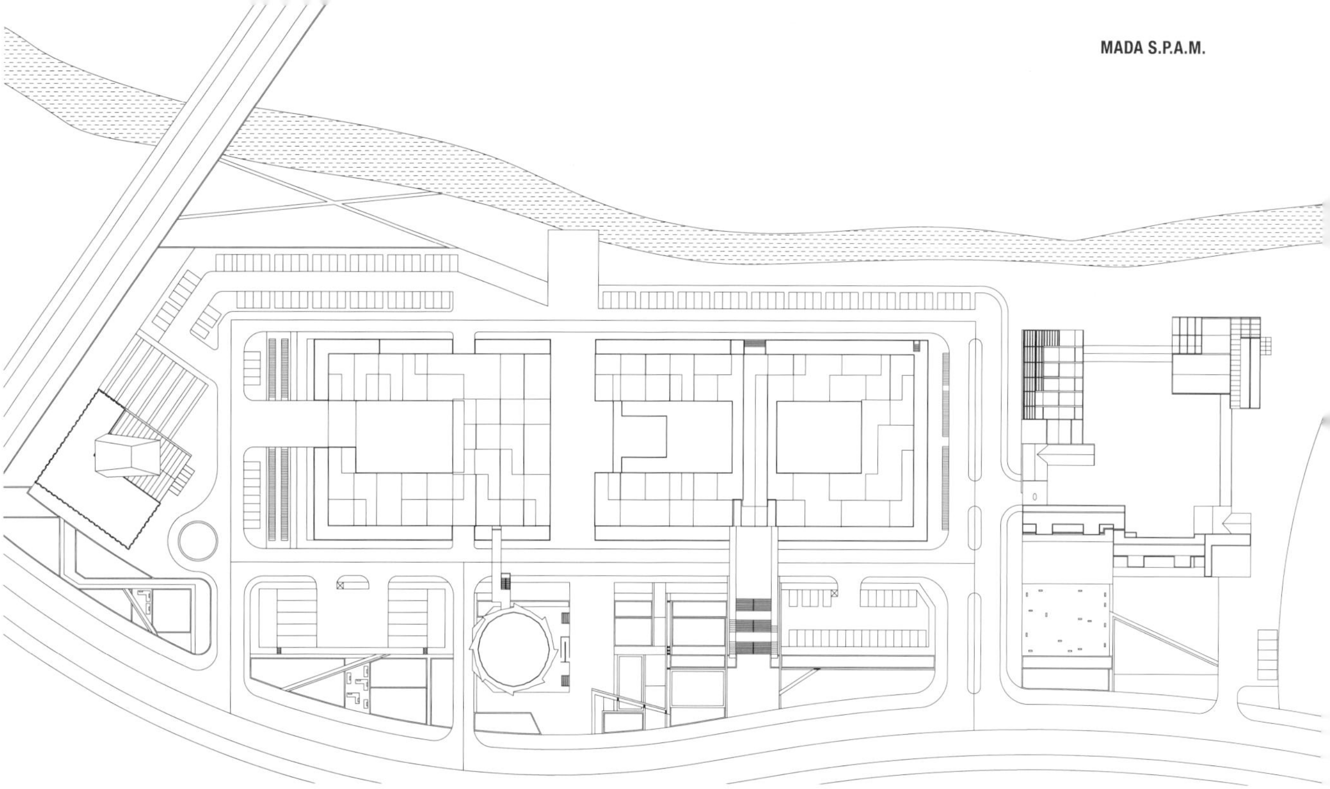

The unexpected and usually rather austere forms of MADA s.p.a.m. confer a strong originality even in the context of an office building.

Die ungewöhnlichen und häufig recht kargen Formen von MADA s.p.a.m. sind ausgesprochen originell, selbst wenn es sich um ein Bürogebäude handelt.

Les formes surprenantes et généralement assez austères de MADA s.p.a.m. confèrent une certaine originalité à ce projet, même dans le contexte de la problématique d'un immeuble de bureaux.

Generous openings usually shielded by wooden shutters characterize the design, which makes allusion to "classical Chinese checkered windows."

Charakteristisch für den Entwurf sind großzügige Gebäudeöffnungen, die in der Regel mit Holzläden verschlossen werden können und auf „klassische schachbrettartige chinesische Fenster" Bezug nehmen.

Les généreuses ouvertures, généralement protégées par des volets de bois qui font allusion aux « fenêtres chinoises classiques », sont caractéristiques de ce projet.

MARCH STUDIO

March Studio
134 Langford Street
North Melbourne
3051 Victoria
Australia

Tel: +61 3 9348 9199
Fax: +61 3 9348 9499
E-mail: info@marchstudio.com.au
Web: www.marchstudio.com.au

RODNEY EGGLESTON, born in 1981, is an Australian architect and a founding Director of March Studio. Eggleston was trained at RMIT (1999–2005). Toward the end of his study, Eggleston completed a two-year internship with OMA / Rem Koolhaas in Rotterdam. He returned to Australia and in 2007 set up March Studio with Parisian graphic artist **ANNE-LAURE CAVIGNEAUX** (born in 1980). March Studio has completed Aesop Saint-Honoré (Paris, France, 2010, published here); Aesop Westfield City (Sydney, NSW, 2011); and the bakery Baker D. Chirico (Carlton, Victoria, 2011). Current projects include the O'Keefe Residence (Ivanhoe East, Victoria, 2012); Rose Street Market, restaurant and bar alterations and addition (Fitzroy, Victoria, 2012); and Aesop (New York, New York, USA, 2012), all in Australia unless stated otherwise.

Der australische Architekt **RODNEY EGGLESTON**, geboren 1981, ist einer der Gründer von March Studio. Eggleston studierte am RMIT (1999–2005). Nach Ende seines Studiums absolvierte er ein zweijähriges Praktikum bei OMA/Rem Koolhaas in Rotterdam. 2007 kehrte er nach Australien zurück und gründete mit der Pariser Grafikdesignerin **ANNE-LAURE CAVIGNEAUX** (geboren 1980) March Studio. Das Team realisierte Aesop Saint-Honoré (Paris, 2010, hier vorgestellt), Aesop Westfield City (Sydney, NSW, 2011) und die Bäckerei Baker D. Chirico (Carlton, Victoria, 2011). Laufende Projekte sind u. a. die O'Keefe Residence (Ivanhoe East, Victoria, 2012), Um- und Anbauten eines Restaurants und einer Bar am Rose Street Market (Fitzroy, Victoria, 2012) und Aesop (New York, 2012), alle in Australien, sofern nicht anders angegeben.

L'architecte australien **RODNEY EGGLESTON**, né en 1981, est directeur fondateur de March Studio. Formé à la RMIT (1999–2005), il a fait un stage de deux ans à la fin de ses études chez OMA/Rem Koolhaas à Rotterdam. De retour en Australie, il a créé March Studio en 2007 avec la graphiste parisienne **ANNE-LAURE CAVIGNEAUX** (née en 1980). March Studio a réalisé les boutiques Aesop Saint-Honoré (Paris, 2010, publiée ici) ; Aesop Westfield City (Sydney, 2011) et la boulangerie Baker D. Chirico (Carlton, Victoria, 2011). Leurs projets en cours comprennent la résidence O'Keefe (Ivanhoe East, Victoria, 2012) ; Rose Street Market, variations et extension de restaurant et bar (Fitzroy, Victoria, 2012) et Aesop (New York, 2012), tous en Australie, sauf mention contraire.

Aesop
PARSLEY SEED

AESOP SAINT-HONORÉ

Paris, France, 2010

Address: 256 Rue Saint-Honoré, 75001 Paris, +33 1 40 20 96 14, sainthonore@aesop.com, www.aesop.com
Area: 100 m². Client: Aesop. Cost: not disclosed
Collaboration: Julian Canterbury, Sam Rice, CBD Contracting

The description given by March Studio of this project conveys its spirit and execution as clearly as any other text. "We began by looking at the possibilities of plaster, but soon became intrigued by the parquet floors one sees throughout Paris. We wanted to explore inhabiting the space with one material, used in one encompassing way. We envisaged using cut wood in such a fashion that it covered the floor, walls, and ceiling, lending a cohesive texture and warmth to the room. The wood of choice for this store is Victorian ash, a timber grown in renewable forests across Australia. The wood was cut in a factory in Melbourne's inner-city suburb of Richmond, then each of the approximately 3500 pieces was hand-cut, hand-sanded, sealed, and numbered according to meticulously drafted plans, before being strategically packed in shipping crates." Created in 1987 in Melbourne, Aesop markets products for skin, hair, and body, presented here on an accumulation of ash planks.

Die Beschreibung von March Studio erklärt die Philosophie und Entstehungsgeschichte des Projekts besser als jeder andere Text: „Anfangs überlegten wir, welche Möglichkeiten Putz bieten könnte, begeisterten uns dann aber bald für Parkettböden, die es überall in Paris gibt. Wir wollten sehen, wie man den Raum mit einem einzigen Material gestalten könnte und suchten nach einer Gesamtlösung. Wir dachten daran, Holz zuschneiden zu lassen und Böden, Wände und Decken damit zu verkleiden, sodass der Raum eine geschlossene Textur und Wärme gewinnen würde. Wir entschieden uns hier für Riesen-Eukalyptus, ein Holz, das überall in Australien in nachhaltiger Forstwirtschaft angebaut wird. Das Holz wurde in einer Fabrik in Richmond, einem innerstädtischen Bezirk von Melbourne, zugesägt. Anschließend wurde jeder der fast 3500 Abschnitte von Hand zugeschnitten, geschliffen und versiegelt, dann nach genauesten Plänen nummeriert und schließlich strategisch in Transportkisten verpackt." Aesop, 1987 in Melbourne gegründet, vertreibt Kosmetikprodukte zur Haut-, Haar- und Körperpflege, die hier auf einer Vielzahl von Eukalyptusholzbrettchen präsentiert werden.

La description que fait March Studio de ce projet en donne mieux que toute autre l'esprit et l'exécution : « Nous avons commencé par chercher des possibilités en plâtre, mais avons vite été intrigués par les sols en parqueterie qu'on voit partout à Paris. Nous voulions essayer une occupation de l'espace avec un seul matériau. Nous avons pensé couper le bois de manière à ce qu'il couvre le sol, les murs et le plafond, ce qui donne une texture cohérente et de la chaleur à la pièce. Le bois choisi est du sorbier des oiseleurs, cultivé dans des forêts renouvelables en Australie. Il a été découpé dans une usine de Richmond, une banlieue défavorisée de Melbourne, puis chacun des 3500 morceaux a été taillé et poncé à la main, collé et numéroté selon un plan méticuleux avant d'être emballé stratégiquement dans des caisses à claire-voie pour expédition. » Fondé en 1987 à Melbourne, Aesop distribue des produits pour la peau, les cheveux et les soins du corps présentés ici sur d'innombrables étagères de sorbier.

The interior of the store is reminiscent of stacks of wood—projecting from the walls just enough to allow for the display of a wide range of Aesop products.

Der Innenausbau des Ladens erinnert an gestapeltes Holz – das gerade weit genug aus der Wand herausragt, um darauf die ganze Bandbreite des Aesop-Sortiments zu präsentieren.

L'intérieur de la boutique fait penser à des piles de bois – qui dépassent juste assez des murs pour permettre d'y présenter une large gamme de produits Aesop.

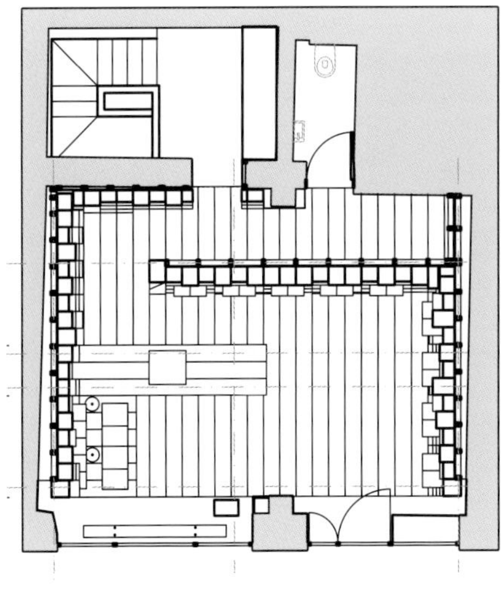

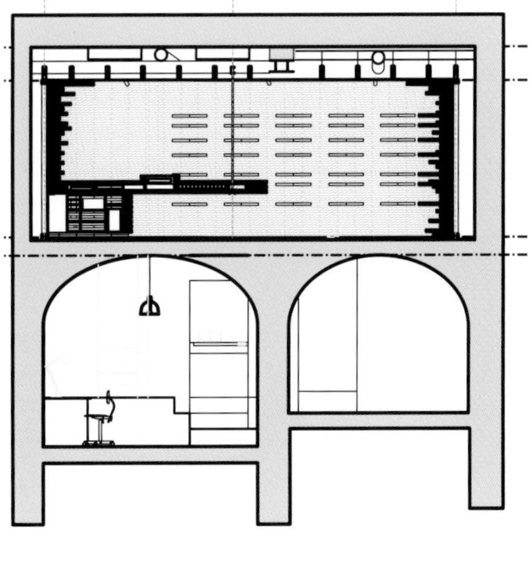

SEBASTIAN MARISCAL

Sebastian Mariscal Studio
35 Medford Street 211
Somerville, MA 02143
USA

Tel: +1 617 395 1210
E-mail: info@sebastianmariscal.com
Web: www.sebastianmariscal.com

SEBASTIAN MARISCAL was born in Mexico City in 1970. He studied at ETSAB School of Architecture in Barcelona and the Universidad Nacional Autónoma de México. After gaining early experience in the office of his father, he opened a studio in Mexico City in 1988. He then worked with Tonet Sunyer (Barcelona, 1995–96), and Jonathan Segal (San Diego, 1997–2000), before creating his own practice, Sebastian Mariscal Studio, in San Diego in 2000. He has taught at the Woodbury School of Architecture in San Diego in the Master of Real Estate Development program. Recent work includes the Wabi House (Carlsbad, California, 2008); Centro de Aprendizaje (Tijuana, Mexico, 2009); Casa Vista (La Jolla, California, 2009); the Pio Pio Restaurant (New York, New York, 2009, published here); and the Phoenix House (Cardiff, California, 2012), all in the USA unless stated otherwise. He is currently working on two apartment complexes in Boston.

SEBASTIAN MARISCAL wurde 1970 in Mexiko-Stadt geboren. Er besuchte die Escola Tècnica Superior d'Arquitectura de Barcelona (ETSAB) und die Universidad Nacional Autónoma de México. Nachdem er bereits früh im Büro seines Vaters gearbeitet hatte, eröffnete er 1988 in Mexiko-Stadt ein Studio. Er arbeitete anschließend mit Tonet Sunyer (Barcelona, 1995–96) und Jonathan Segal (San Diego, 1997–2000) zusammen, bevor er 2000 mit Sebastian Mariscal Studio in San Diego eine eigene Firma gründete. Mariscal hat in San Diego an der Woodbury School of Architecture im Rahmen des Masterstudiengangs Immobilienentwicklung unterrichtet. Zu seinen jüngeren Arbeiten gehören u. a. das Wabi House (Carlsbad, Kalifornien, 2008), das Centro de Aprendizaje (Tijuana, Mexiko, 2009), die Casa Vista (La Jolla, Kalifornien, 2009), das Pio Pio Restaurant (New York, 2009, hier vorgestellt) und das Phoenix House (Cardiff, Kalifornien, 2012). Derzeit arbeitet er zudem an zwei Apartmenthäusern in Boston.

SEBASTIAN MARISCAL est né à Mexico City en 1970. Il a étudié à l'École technique supérieure d'architecture de Barcelone (ETSAB) et à l'Université nationale autonome du Mexique (UNAM). Après une première expérience dans l'agence de son père, il a ouvert la sienne à Mexico City en 1988. Il a par la suite travaillé avec Tonet Sunyer (Barcelone, 1995–96) et Jonathan Segal (San Diego, 1997–2000), avant de fonder sa propre agence, Sebastian Mariscal Studio, à San Diego en 2000. Il a enseigné à la Woodbury School of Architecture à San Diego dans le cadre du master de développement de projets immobiliers. Parmi ses œuvres récentes figurent la Wabi House (Carlsbad, Californie, 2008) ; le Centro de Aprendizaje (Tijuana, Mexique, 2009) ; la Casa Vista (La Jolla, Californie, 2009) ; le restaurant Pio Pio (New York, 2009, publié ici) et la Phoenix House (Cardiff, Californie, 2012), toutes aux États-Unis sauf mention contraire. Il travaille actuellement sur deux ensembles résidentiels à Boston.

PIO PIO RESTAURANT

New York, New York, USA, 2009

Address: 604 Tenth Avenue, New York, New York, USA, +1 212 459 2929, www.piopio.com/locations/hells-kitchen. Area: 372 m²
Client: Pio Pio Restaurant. Cost: not disclosed

The architect plays on a willful contrast of materials with wood playing the main role. Dark or muted colors are chosen, with simple furniture and lighting. Below, section drawings show the two levels.

Der Architekt setzt bei der Wahl der Materialien auf Kontraste, wobei Holz im Vordergrund steht. Zum Einsatz kommen dunkle, gedämpfte Farben sowie schlichte Möbel und Leuchten. Die Querschnitte unten zeigen die beiden Ebenen.

L'architecte joue sur un contraste volontaire entre les matériaux, le bois tenant le rôle principal. Le choix s'est porté sur des couleurs foncées ou douces avec un mobilier et un éclairage sobres. Ci-dessous, des dessins en coupe montrent les deux niveaux.

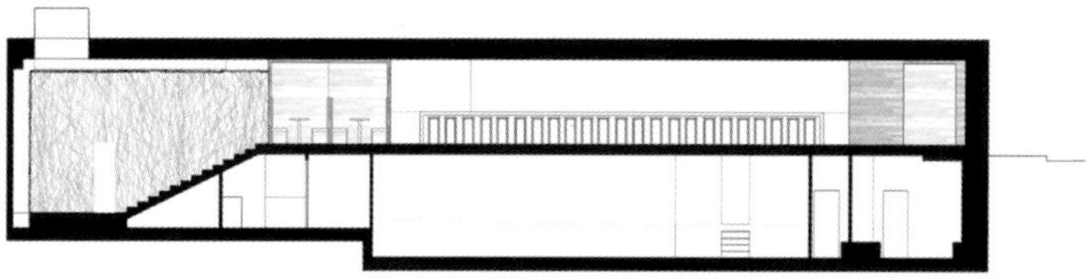

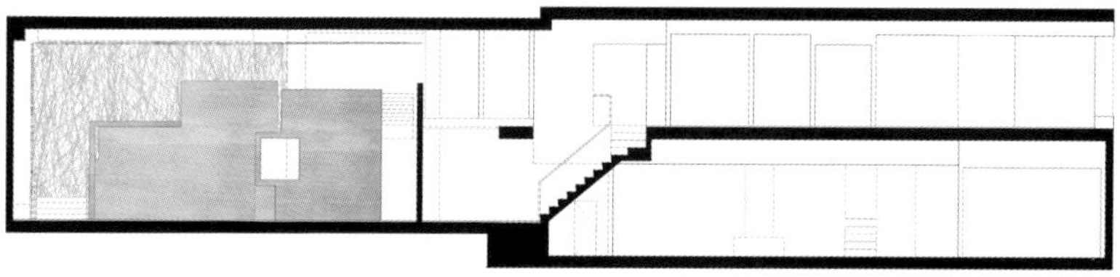

Located at 604 Tenth Avenue, the so-called Hell's Kitchen area of Manhattan, **PIO PIO** makes extensive use of reclaimed wood. The architect writes: "Conceptually, the focus was to transport the visitor into a magical architectural experience that references an intangible influence of Latin culture. With this approach, the design was detached from the ideas of traditional interior design; instead, a series of architectural installations define the atmosphere and path of travel." Willful contrasts mark the choice of materials ranging from old wood boxes to a marble host table, or a brass vestibule. A 12-meter monolithic marble bar, a concrete floor, and a "large box made of woven Ocotillo canes" are among the other surprises in this unusual installation, which might be considered to be at the juncture between architecture, interior design, and art.

Das **PIO PIO** ist in Manhattans sog. Hell's Kitchen auf der 604 Tenth Avenue gelegen und macht extensiv Gebrauch von recyceltem Holz. Der Architekt schreibt: „Der Schwerpunkt des Entwurfs lag darauf, den Gästen ein magisches Architekturerlebnis mit sehr subtilen Anklängen an lateinamerikanische Kultur zu ermöglichen. Folglich hat der Entwurf wenig mit traditionellen Vorstellungen von Innenarchitektur zu tun. Vielmehr handelt es sich um eine Reihe architektonischer Installationen, welche die Atmosphäre und die Erkundungswege beeinflussen." Die Materialien bestechen durch bewusst gesetzte Kontraste und reichen von alten Holzkisten über einen Marmoresstisch bis hin zu einem messingenen Eingangsbereich. Zu den Überraschungen dieses ungewöhnlichen Projekts, das als Verbindung aus Architektur, Raumgestaltung und Kunst verstanden werden kann, gehören eine 12 m lange Marmorbar, ein Betonboden und ein „großer Raum aus Ocotillo-Flechtwerk".

Situé au 604 Tenth Avenue dans le Hell's Kitchen (ou « cuisine du diable ») de Manhattan, **PIO PIO** est en grande partie aménagé avec du bois de récupération. L'architecte écrit : « Notre parti consistait à plonger le visiteur dans une expérience architecturale magique qui révèle une influence impalpable de la culture latine. Suivant cette approche, l'aménagement se détachait des idées de l'aménagement d'intérieur traditionnel ; ici au contraire, toute une série d'installations architecturales définissent l'atmosphère et le chemin du voyage. » Le choix des matériaux est marqué par des contrastes volontaires : anciennes caisses en bois, table d'hôte en marbre et vestibule en laiton. Un bar en marbre monolithique de 12 m de long, un sol en béton et une « grande boîte en tiges d'ocotillo tressées » figurent parmi les autres surprises de cette installation inhabituelle qui peut être considérée comme à la jonction entre architecture, aménagement intérieur et art.

Above, the 12-meter-long marble bar. Hanging bulb lights and candles provide points of light in the otherwise relatively dark space.

Oben die 12 m lange Bar aus Marmor. Glühbirnen und Kerzen setzen Lichtakzente in dem ansonsten eher dunklen Raum.

Ci-dessus, le bar en marbre de 12 m de long. Des ampoules suspendues et des bougies ajoutent des points lumineux dans cet espace sinon plutôt sombre.

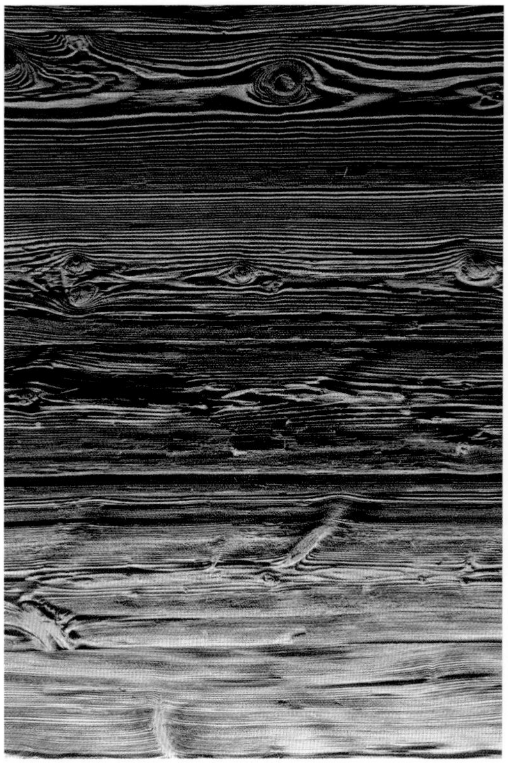

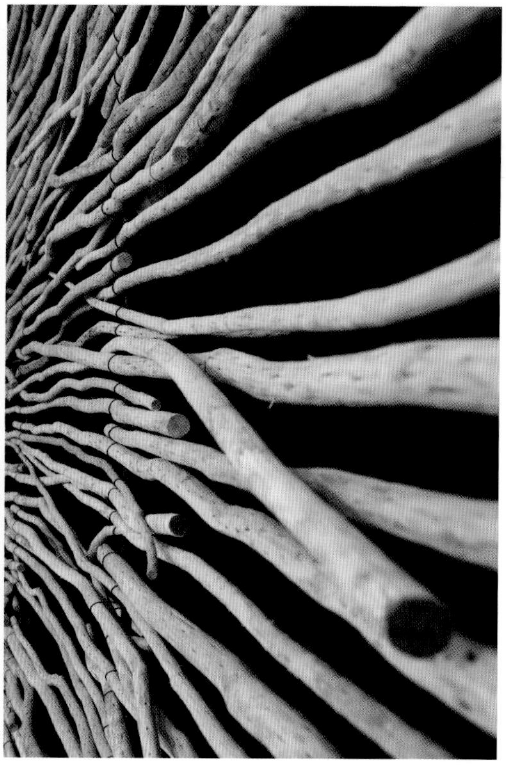

Above, examples of the wood used to create a harmony of surfaces that appear to be old or new as circumstances require. Below, floor plans and a marble block reception counter that is cantilevered from a wooden wall.

Oben Beispiele für das Holz, mit dem, je nach Raumerfordernis, alt oder neu wirkende harmonische Oberflächen erzielt wurden. Unten Grundrisse und ein Empfangstisch aus Marmor, der aus einer Holzwand ragt.

Ci-dessus, différentes utilisations du bois permettent de créer une harmonie de surfaces d'aspect soit ancien soit neuf selon les circonstances. Ci-dessous, des plans et un comptoir de réception en bloc de marbre qui sort en porte-à-faux d'un mur en bois.

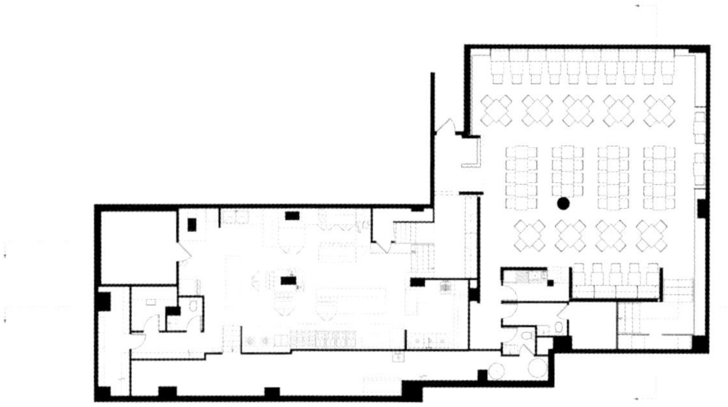
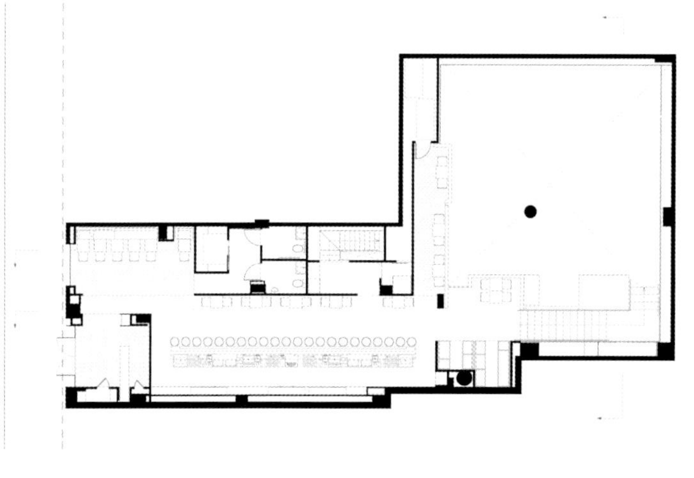

JÜRGEN MAYER H.

J. MAYER H. und Partner, Architekten
Zementhaus
Knesebeckstrasse 30
10623 Berlin
Germany

Tel: +49 30 644 90 77 00
Fax: +49 30 644 90 77 11
E-mail: contact@jmayerh.de
Web: www.jmayerh.de

JÜRGEN MAYER H. was born in Stuttgart, Germany, in 1965. He studied at Stuttgart University (Architecture and Town Planning, 1986–92), the Cooper Union (1990–91), and Princeton University (M.Arch, 1992–94). He created his firm J. Mayer H. Architects in Berlin in 1996. Jürgen Mayer H. has taught at Princeton University, University of the Arts Berlin, Harvard University, Kunsthochschule Berlin, Architectural Association (London), Columbia University (New York), and the University of Toronto. His projects include the Town Hall in Ostfildern; a student center at Karlsruhe University (Karlsruhe, Germany, 2006); the Dupli.Casa (near Ludwigsburg, Germany, 2006–08); and the Metropol Parasol, the redevelopment of the Plaza de la Encarnación (Seville, Spain, 2005–2011, published here). More recently the architect has completed a number of buildings in Georgia—the Sarpi Border Checkpoint (Sarpi, 2010–11); Mestia Police Station (Mestia, 2011–12); and rest stops at Gori (Gori, 2011–12).

JÜRGEN MAYER H. wurde 1965 in Stuttgart geboren. Sein Studium absolvierte er an der Universität Stuttgart (Architektur und Stadtplanung, 1986–92), der Cooper Union (1990–91) und der Universität Princeton (M.Arch., 1992–94). 1996 gründete er sein Büro J. Mayer H. Architects in Berlin. Jürgen Mayer H. lehrt u.a. an der Universität Princeton, der Universität der Künste Berlin, der Universität Harvard, der Kunsthochschule Berlin, der Architectural Association (London), der Columbia University (New York) sowie der Universität Toronto. Zu seinen Projekten gehören das Stadthaus in Ostfildern, die Mensa der Universität Karlsruhe (2006), die Dupli.Casa (bei Ludwigsburg, 2006–08) sowie Metropol Parasol, die Neugestaltung der Plaza de la Encarnación in Sevilla (Spanien, 2005–11, hier vorgestellt). Aktuelle Projekte sind eine Reihe von Gebäuden in Georgien: der Grenzübergang von Sarpi (2010–11), die Polizeistation von Mestia (2011–12) und Raststätten in Gori (2011–12).

JÜRGEN MAYER H. est né à Stuttgart en 1965. Il a fait ses études à l'université de Stuttgart (architecture et urbanisme, 1986–92), Cooper Union (1990–91) et Princeton (M.Arch., 1992–94). Il a créé son entreprise, J. Mayer H. Architects à Berlin en 1996. Il a enseigné à l'université Princeton, l'Université des arts de Berlin, Harvard, la Kunsthochschule de Berlin, l'Architectural Association (Londres), l'université Columbia (New York) et l'université de Toronto. Ses projets récents comprennent l'Hôtel de ville d'Ostfildern (Allemagne) ; un centre étudiant à l'université de Karlsruhe (Allemagne, 2006) ; la Dupli.Casa (près de Ludwigsburg, Allemagne, 2006–08) et Metropol Parasol, le réaménagement de la Plaza de la Encarnación (Séville, 2005–2011, publié ici). Plus récemment, l'architecte a réalisé une série de bâtiments en Géorgie – le poste-frontière de Sarpi (Sarpi, 2010–11), le poste de police de Mestia (Mestia, 2011–12) et plusieurs aires de repos à Gori (Gori, 2011–12).

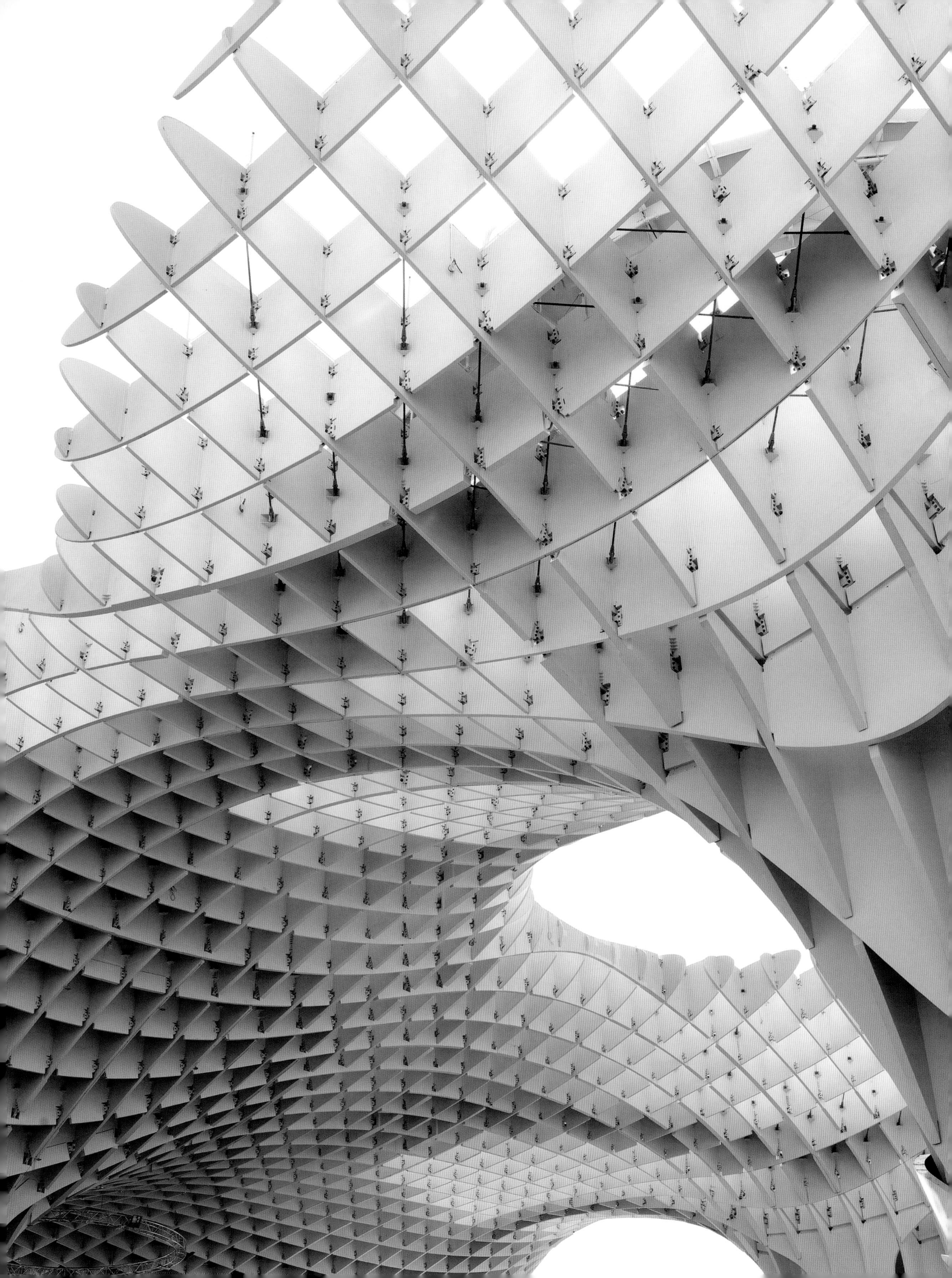

METROPOL PARASOL

Seville, Spain, 2005–2011

Address: Plaza de la Encarnación 18, 41003 Seville, Spain, www.metropolsevilla.com
Area: 12 670 m². Client: Ayuntamiento de Sevilla and SACYR
Cost: €90 million

This project involves the redevelopment of the Plaza de la Encarnación in Seville. The architects were awarded the first prize in a 2004 international competition for the site. Described as a "new icon for Seville," the project involves the creation of a number of polyurethane-coated timber parasols that house or cover bars, restaurants, and public space. The architect states that the "parasols grow out of an archeological excavation site into a contemporary landmark." The columns are, in reality, prominent points of access to the museum below, as well as to the plaza and panorama deck above, defining a new relationship between the historical city and contemporary life. Because of its multiple uses, this can neither be defined as a traditional work of architecture nor as a park installation. It is intended to renew the heritage of Seville even more than the Expo '92 structures that were physically set apart from the historic city.

Bei diesem Projekt ging es um die Sanierung der Plaza de la Encarnación in Sevilla. 2004 gewannen die Architekten den internationalen Wettbewerb für die Platzgestaltung. Die Anlage, ein „neues Wahrzeichen für Sevilla", besteht aus mehreren polyurethanbeschichteten Holzsonnenschirmen, die Platz bieten für Bars, Restaurants und öffentliche Bereiche. Der Architekt erklärt: „Die Sonnenschirme wachsen aus einer archäologischen Grabungsstätte und werden zur zeitgenössischen Landmarke." Die Säulen entpuppen sich als prominente Zugänge zum unterirdisch gelegenen Museum sowie zu einer oberirdischen Plaza und einem Panoramadeck. Es entstehen neue Bezüge zwischen historischer Altstadt und zeitgenössischem Leben. Aufgrund seiner Multifunktionalität lässt sich das Bauwerk weder als Gebäude im üblichen Sinne noch als Parkinstallation verstehen. Vielmehr ging es darum, das historische Erbe Sevillas noch weiter zu erneuern, als das die Bauten für die Expo '92 konnten, die räumlich von der Altstadt getrennt sind.

Le projet est centré sur le réaménagement de la Plaza de la Encarnación à Séville. Les architectes ont remporté le premier prix d'un concours international en 2004 pour le site. Présenté comme un « nouvel emblème pour Séville », le projet comprend la création de nombreux parasols en bois revêtu de polyuréthane qui abritent ou accueillent des bars, restaurants et lieux publics. L'architecte constate que les « parasols sont passés de site archéologique au statut d'icône contemporaine ». Les piliers sont en réalité les principaux points d'accès au musée en dessous, ainsi qu'à la plaza et à la terrasse panoramique, l'ensemble définissant un nouveau lien entre la cité historique et la vie moderne. Du fait de sa polyvalence, il ne peut être décrit comme une œuvre architecturale traditionnelle, ni comme une installation dans un parc, il vise à renouveler l'héritage de Séville davantage encore que les constructions de l'Expo '92 qui étaient physiquement à l'écart du centre historique.

An aerial view on the left page shows how the new structure fits into the old city, crossing boundaries and creating sheltered space, seen above and in the drawing below.

Die Luftaufnahme auf der linken Seite zeigt, wie sich das Bauwerk in die Altstadt integriert, Grenzen überschreitet und geschützte Zonen schafft (oben und Zeichnung unten).

La vue aérienne sur la page de gauche montre l'intégration de la nouvelle structure dans la vieille ville, dont elle transgresse les limites pour créer un espace abrité qu'on voit ci-dessus et sur le schéma ci-dessous.

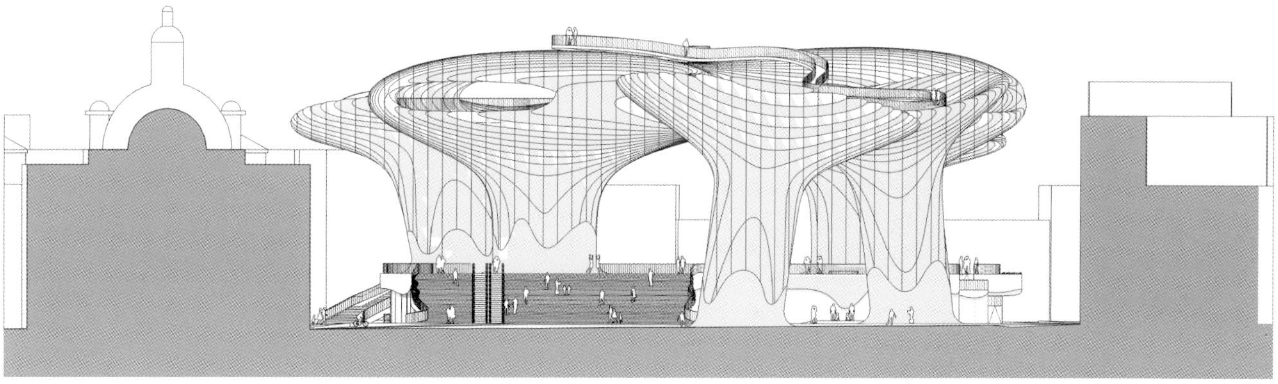

The design is unexpected to say the least, obviously influenced by natural forms and yet taking into account the real possibilities of modern, light architecture offered by wood.

Der Entwurf ist mehr als überraschend und offensichtlich von organischen Formen inspiriert. Zugleich profitiert er von dem Potenzial, das Holz für moderne Leichtbaukonstruktionen bietet.

Le design est pour le moins inattendu, visiblement influencé par les formes naturelles, tout en prenant en compte les possibilités réelles d'architecture moderne et légère qu'offre le bois.

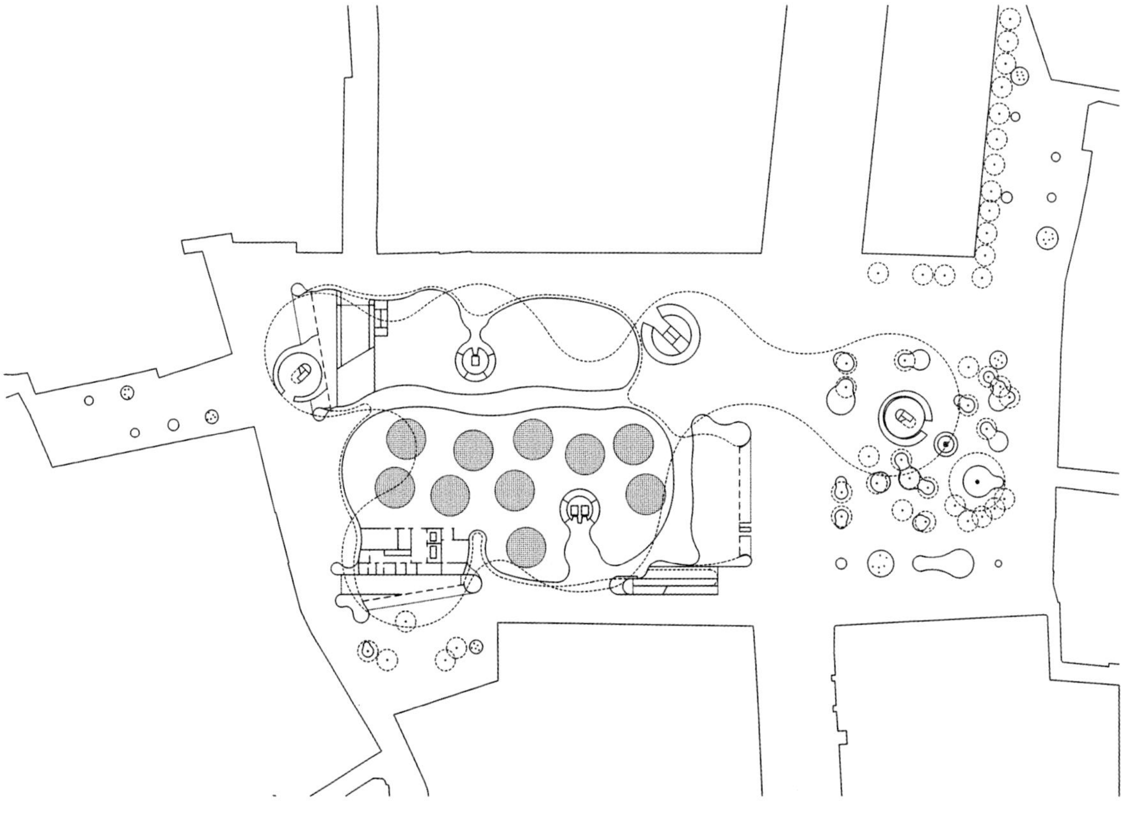

Seen from its upper surfaces the structure confirms the honeycomb design seen from below, with a walkway permitting visits to this higher level.

Von oben gesehen zeigt sich dieselbe Wabenstruktur der Konstruktion wie aus der Untersicht. Ein Fußgängersteg erlaubt Besuchern, die obere Ebene zu erkunden.

Vue depuis les niveaux supérieurs, la structure conserve le motif en nid d'abeilles vu d'en bas. Une passerelle permet de visiter le niveau supérieur.

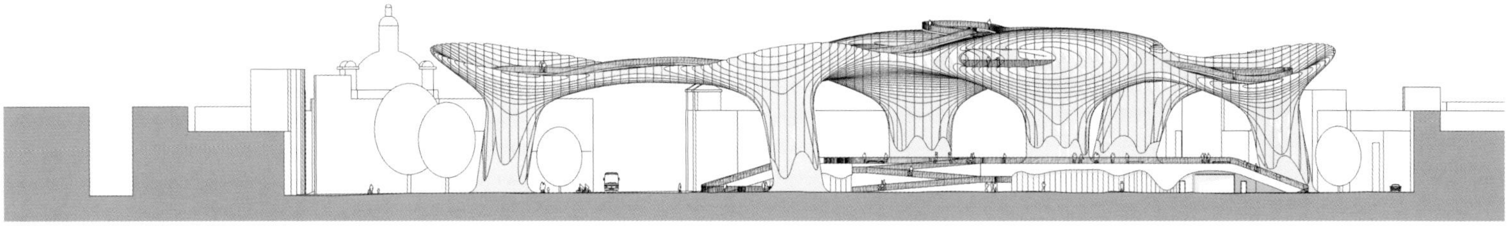

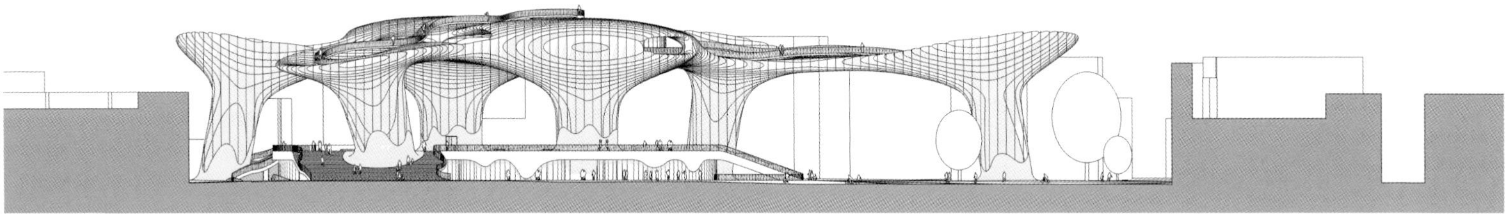

At night the space is convivial and protective. Elevation drawings on the left page show the large scale of the project. Above, a staircase leads up to the ground level from below the structure.

Nachts ist das Bauwerk belebt und geschützt. Aufrisse (links) zeigen die enorme Größe des Projekts. Oben eine Treppe, die Untergeschoss und Straßenebene verbindet.

La nuit, l'espace créé est convivial et protecteur. Les élévations de la page de gauche témoignent de l'ampleur du projet. Ci-dessus, un escalier mène au niveau inférieur sous la structure.

MCBRIDE CHARLES RYAN

McBride Charles Ryan
4/21 Wynnstay Road
Prahran, Victoria 3181
Australia

Tel: +61 3 9510 1006
Fax: +61 3 9510 0205
E-mail: mail@mcbridecharlesryan.com.au
Web: www.mcbridecharlesryan.com.au

ROBERT MCBRIDE was born in Tarnworth, NSW, Australia, in 1960. He received his B.Arch degree from RMIT (Melbourne) in 1985 and his M.Arch degree from the same institution in 1994. McBride Charles Ryan was founded in 1988. **DEBBIE RYAN** studied interior design at RMIT, arts at Monash University, and interior decoration at the Melbourne College of Decoration. Robert McBride's and Debbie Ryan's significant works include Kent Court Residence (Toorak, Victoria, 2005); Narveno Court Residence (Hawthorn, Victoria, 2005); Pine Street Residence (Camberwell, Victoria, 2007); Klein Bottle House (Rye, Victoria, 2007); Mondaco House (Melbourne, Victoria, 2007); and Letterbox House (Blairgowrie, Victoria, 2006–08, published here), all in Australia. The Klein Bottle House won the 2008 Robyn Boyd Award for New Residential Architecture (AIA National Annual Award) and the 2009 World Architecture Award for house design.

ROBERT MCBRIDE wurde 1960 in Tarnworth, NSW, Australien, geboren. Am RMIT in Melbourne erwarb er 1985 zunächst seinen B. Arch., 1994 dann seinen M. Arch. Die Gründung von McBride Charles Ryan erfolgte 1988. **DEBBIE RYAN** studierte Design am RMIT, Kunst an der Monash University sowie Innenausstattung am Melbourne College of Decoration. Zu Robert McBrides und Debbie Ryans bedeutendsten Arbeiten zählen die Kent Court Residence (Toorak, Victoria, 2005), die Narveno Court Residence (Hawthorn, Victoria, 2005), die Pine Street Residence (Camberwell, Victoria, 2007), das Klein Bottle House (Rye, Victoria, 2007), das Mondaco House (Melbourne, Victoria, 2007) sowie das Letterbox House (Blairgowrie, Victoria, 2006–08, hier vorgestellt), alle in Australien. Das Klein Bottle House wurde 2008 mit dem Robyn Boyd Award für neue Wohnarchitektur ausgezeichnet (Nationaler Jahrespreis der AIA) sowie 2009 mit dem World Architecture Award für Wohnbauten.

ROBERT MCBRIDE est né à Tarnworth (NGS), en Australie, en 1960. Il a obtenu son B.Arch. du RMIT (Melbourne, 1985) et son M.Arch. de la même institution en 1994. L'agence McBride Charles Ryan a été fondée en 1988. **DEBBIE RYAN** a étudié l'architecture intérieure au RMIT, les arts à l'université Monash, et la décoration intérieure au Melbourne College of Decoration. Parmi leurs réalisations notables : la Kent Court Residence (Toorak, Victoria, 2005) ; la Narveno Court Residence (Hawthorn, Victoria, 2005) ; la Pine Street Residence (Camberwell, Victoria, 2007) ; la Klein Bottle House (Rye, Victoria, 2007) ; la Mondaco House (Melbourne, Victoria, 2007) et la Letterbox House (Letterbox House, Blairgowrie, Victoria, 2006–08, publiée ici), le tout en Australie. La Klein Bottle House a remporté le prix Robyn Boyd 2008 pour une nouvelle architecture résidentielle (prix annuel national de l'AIA) et le 2009 World Architecture Award pour les maisons individuelles.

LETTERBOX HOUSE

Blairgowrie, Victoria, Australia, 2006–08

Address: not disclosed. Area: 290 m². Client: Heather Ryan. Cost: $836 000
Collaboration: Adam Pustola, Meredith Dufour, Angela Woda

"We like the buildings that make you smile (not laugh)," say the architects. "It makes people smile, a building with the smallest façade on the peninsula—the building begins as a letterbox and unfurls to become this healthy scaled verandah; to some it is an upturned boat, to others it is a wave or a cliff." This house won the Australian Institute of Architects (AIA)—Victorian Chapter—Harold Desbrowe-Annear Award for Residential Architecture. It is indeed the copper letterbox of this house situated at its very tip that appears to be the point from which the entire design develops. The ground floor contains the garage, three bedrooms, a hall and lounge, courtyard, living and dining areas, a children's room, and a laundry area, with an ample exterior terrace. On the top level, just the master bedroom and a smaller deck complete the design.

„Wir mögen Häuser, die Menschen zum Lächeln (nicht etwa zum Lachen) bringen", meinen die Architekten. „Ein Haus mit der kleinsten Fassade auf der gesamten Halbinsel bringt die Leute zum Lächeln – das Gebäude beginnt als Briefkasten und entwickelt sich hin zu einer recht großzügig dimensionierten Veranda. Für manche ist es ein umgedrehtes Boot, für andere eine Welle oder ein Kliff." Ausgezeichnet wurde das Haus mit dem Harold Desbrowe-Annear Award für Wohnarchitektur, einem Preis des Australian Institute of Architects (AIA – Regionalverband Victoria). Tatsächlich scheint sich der gesamte Entwurf aus dem kupfernen Briefkasten an der äußersten Spitze des Hauses zu entwickeln. Im Erdgeschoss befinden sich die Garage, drei Schlafzimmer, eine Diele und eine Lounge, ein Hof, Wohn- und Essbereich, ein Kinderzimmer und eine Waschküche sowie eine großzügige Terrasse. Im Obergeschoss wird der Entwurf mit einem Elternschlafzimmer und einer kleineren Terrasse abgerundet.

« Nous aimons les constructions qui font sourire (pas rire) », précisent les architectes. « Elle fait sourire, en effet, cette maison qui possède la plus petite façade de la péninsule. Elle commence par une boîte aux lettres et se déploie en véranda de bonnes dimensions. Pour certains, c'est un bateau à l'envers, pour d'autres, une vague ou une falaise. » Cette maison a remporté le prix Harold Desbrowe-Annear de l'architecture résidentielle décerné par l'Australian Institute of Architectes (AIA, section du Victoria). C'est bien en effet une boîte aux lettres en cuivre posée à son extrémité qui semble être le point à partir duquel le projet tout entier se développe. Le rez-de-chaussée contient le garage, trois chambres, un hall et un salon, une cour, le séjour-salle à manger, une pièce pour les enfants, une lingerie, ainsi qu'une vaste terrasse. L'étage n'est occupé que par la chambre principale et une petite terrasse.

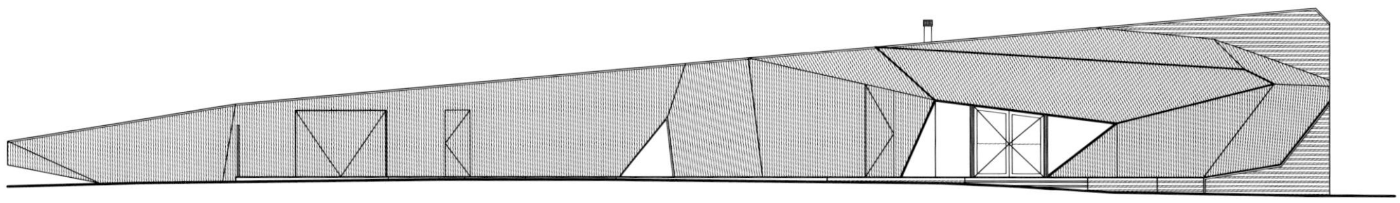

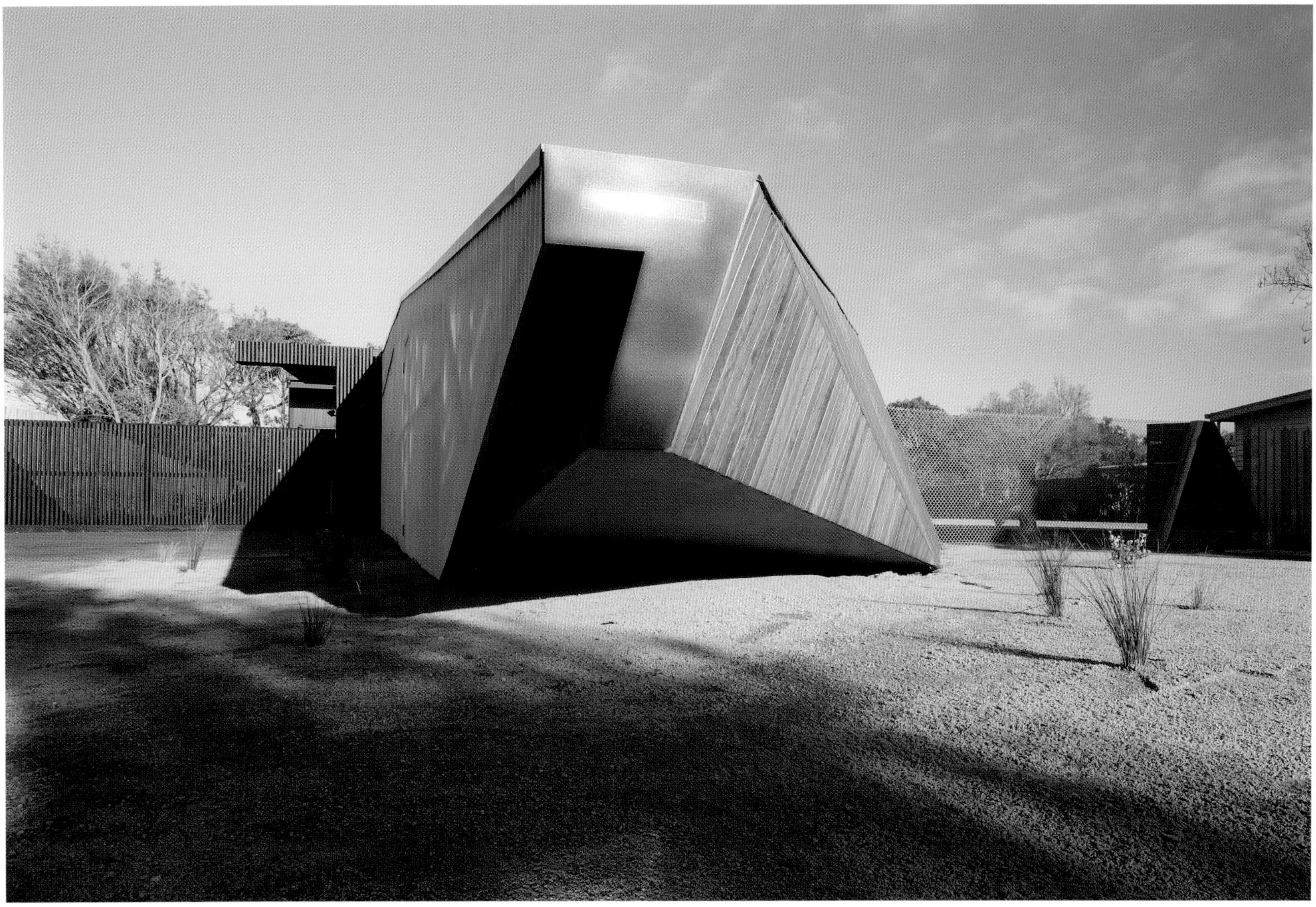

The surprising wedge-like form of the house is articulated in timber with few openings on this side, but an integrated terrace visible in the image below.

Die überraschende Keilform des Hauses zeigt sich in Holz mit wenigen Öffnungen zur Seite. Im Foto unten ist die in den Baukörper integrierte Terrasse zu sehen.

L'étonnante forme de cale de cette maison de bois s'articule dans une sorte de continuité. Elle ne possède que peu d'ouvertures de ce côté mais une terrasse intégrée, visible ci-dessous.

The red structuring elements visible in these images provide a marked contrast with the more continuous lines of the wooden exterior.

Die tragenden roten Bauteile bilden einen markanten Kontrast zu den eher fließenden Linien der holzverkleideten äußeren Hülle.

Les éléments structurants rouges contrastent fortement avec les lignes continues de la façade en bois.

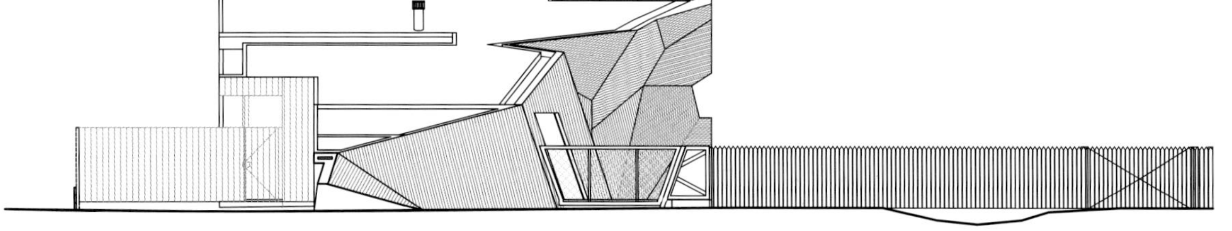

Plans show the long outside terrace visible on the previous double page, as well as the interior spaces of the ground floor.

Die Grundrisse zeigen die lange Terrasse, zu sehen auf der vorhergehenden Seite, sowie die Räume im Erd- und Obergeschoss.

Plans montrant la terrasse allongée vue sur la double page précédente ainsi que les espaces intérieurs du rez-de-chaussée.

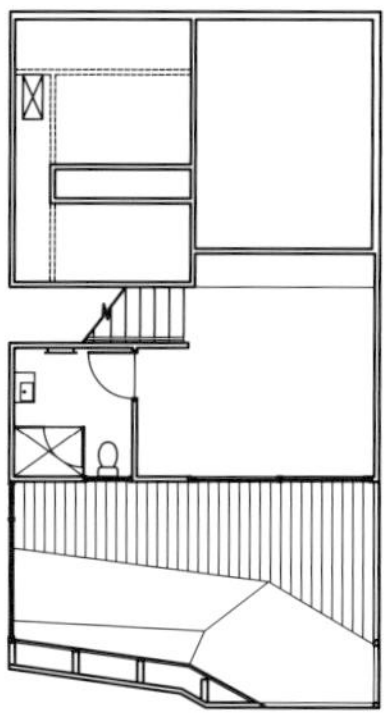

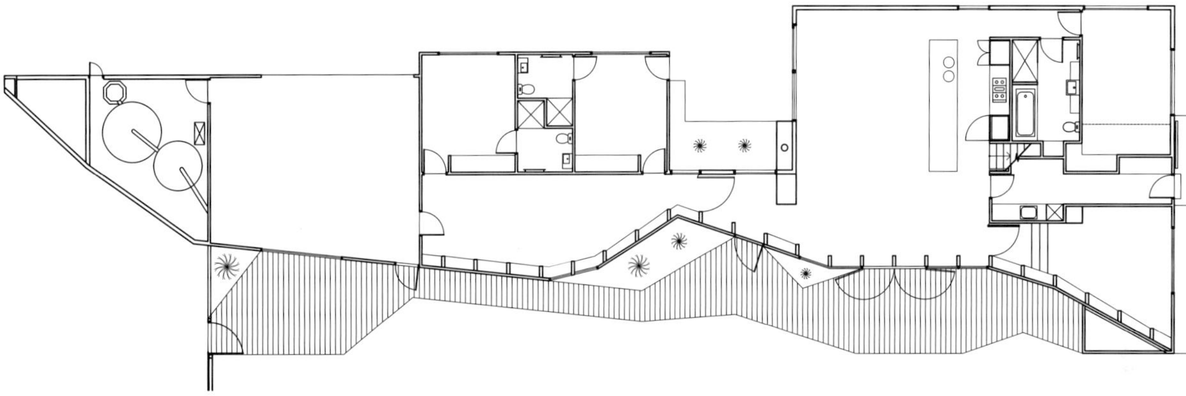

NIALL MCLAUGHLIN

Niall McLaughlin Architects
39–51 Highgate Road
London NW5 1RT
UK

Tel: +44 20 74 85 91 70
Fax: +44 20 74 85 91 71
Email: info@niallmclaughlin.com
Web: www.niallmclaughlin.com

NIALL MCLAUGHLIN was born in Geneva, Switzerland, in 1962. He was educated in Dublin, Ireland, and received his architectural degree from University College Dublin in 1984. He worked for Scott Tallon Walker in Dublin and London between 1984 and 1989, before establishing his own practice in 1991. He won the Young British Architect of the Year award in 1998. He was chair of the RIBA Awards Group from 2007 to 2009. **TIM ALLEN-BOOTH** was born in Sheffield, UK, in 1974 and studied at the University of Nottingham. After graduating in 1996 he moved to London and joined Niall McLaughlin Architects in 2006. **ANNE SCHROELL** was born in Luxembourg in 1977 and studied architecture at the Bartlett, University College London. In her "year out" she worked for Bartenbach Lichtlabor, a lighting designer in Innsbruck, Austria. After graduating from the Bartlett, she joined Tonkin Lui and then worked for De Matos Storey Ryan Architects on several private houses. In 2006 she joined Niall McLaughlin Architects. Their recent work includes Castleford Forum Museum and Library (Wakefield, 2005); a House at Piper's End (Hertfordshire, 2006–08); the Café-Bar on Deal Pier (Deal, Kent, 2008, published here); a House at Anglesea Road (Dublin, Ireland, 2008); TQ2 Bridge (Bristol, 2008); the Alzheimer's Respite Center (Dublin, Ireland, 2009); student accommodation and library buildings, Somerville College, Oxford University (Oxford, 2010); and the Bishop Edward King Chapel (Oxford, 2012), all in the UK unless stated otherwise.

NIALL MCLAUGHLIN wurde 1962 in Genf, Schweiz, geboren. Er wuchs in Dublin auf und machte 1984 seinen Abschluss in Architektur am University College Dublin. Danach arbeitete er von 1984 bis 1989 bei Scott Tallon Walker in Dublin und London; 1991 gründete er sein eigenes Büro. 1998 wurde ihm der Young British Architect of the Year Award verliehen. 2007 bis 2009 war er Vorsitzender der RIBA Awards Group. **TIM ALLEN-BOOTH** wurde 1974 in Sheffield geboren und studierte an der University of Nottingham. Nach seinem Abschluss 1996 zog er nach London und trat 2006 bei Niall McLaughlin Architects ein. **ANNE SCHROELL** wurde 1977 in Luxemburg geboren und studierte Architektur am Bartlett University College, London. In einem Jahr „Auszeit" arbeitete sie bei Bartenbach Lichtlabor, einer Firma für Lichtplanung in Innsbruck. Nach ihrem Abschluss am Bartlett war sie bei Tonkin Liu und dann bei De Matos Storey Ryan Architects an der Planung mehrerer privater Wohnhäuser beteiligt. 2006 trat sie bei Niall McLaughlin Architects ein. Zu den neueren Werken dieses Büros zählen Castleford Forum Museum und Bibliothek (Wakefield, 2005), ein Wohnhaus in Piper's End (Hertfordshire, 2006–08), ein Café mit Bar am Deal Pier (Deal, Kent, 2008, hier veröffentlicht), ein Wohnhaus in der Anglesea Road (Dublin, 2008), die TQ2-Brücke (Bristol, 2008), ein Pflegeheim für Alzheimerpatienten (Dublin, 2009), Studentenwohnungen und Bibliothek des Somerville College, Oxford University (Oxford, 2010) sowie die Bishop Edward King Chapel (Oxford, 2012).

Né à Genève en 1962, **NIALL MCLAUGHLIN** a grandi à Dublin. Il sort diplômé du University College à Dublin en 1984. Il a travaillé pour Scott Tallon Walker à Dublin et Londres de 1984 à 1989, avant de créer son agence en 1991. Il a remporté le prix du Jeune architecte britannique de l'année en 1998. Il a été président du RIBA Awards Group de 2007 à 2009. **TIM ALLEN-BOOTH**, né à Sheffield (Grande-Bretagne) en 1974, a étudié à l'université de Nottingham. Après son diplôme (1996), il s'est installé à Londres et est entré chez Niall McLaughlin Architects en 2006. **ANNE SCHROELL**, née à Luxembourg en 1977, a étudié l'architecture au Bartlett, University College à Londres. Pendant une année hors cursus, elle a travaillé pour Bartenbach Lichtlabor, un designer de luminaires d'Innsbruck en Autriche. Une fois diplômée du Bartlett, elle a rejoint Tonkin Lui puis De Matos Storey Ryan Architects, intervenant sur plusieurs résidences privées. En 2006, elle est entrée chez Niall McLaughlin Architects. Parmi leurs réalisations récentes : le musée et la bibliothèque du Castleford Forum (Wakefield, 2005) ; une maison à Piper's End (Hertfordshire, 2006–08) ; le café-bar sur Deal Pier (Deal, Kent, 2008, publié ici) ; une maison à Anglesea Road (Dublin, 2008) ; le pont TQ2 (Bristol, 2008) ; le Centre pour le traitement de la maladie d'Alzheimer (Dublin, 2009) ; des logements pour étudiants et une bibliothèque pour le Somerville College (Oxford University, 2010) et la Bishop Edward King Chapel (Oxford, 2012).

CAFÉ-BAR ON DEAL PIER

Deal, Kent, UK, 2008

Address: Beach Street, Deal, Kent CT14 6HZ, UK, +44 13 04 61 62 63, jasinsrestaurant.co.uk
Area: 180 m². Client: Dover District Council. Cost: €1.1 million

Deal developed as a seaport, where sailboats would wait for fair wind. When the town later became a resort, several piers were created. The most recent is a concrete pile structure built in 1957. The end of this pier was designed with three levels for viewing, boating, and fishing. The café-bar for this pier was commissioned in a RIBA competition. The architects state: "We wanted to make the building from a single material that would weather and improve with age. We hoped that it would eventually fade into the battered concrete on the pier." They created a laminated iroko structure with large glazed surfaces inspired to some extent by 19th-century industrial timber buildings. The structure is divided into two parts, an opaque section containing toilets, kitchens, and an entrance area. The other, glazed section contains a café "which is conceived as a single simple space open to the outside."

Deal war ursprünglich ein Seehafen, in dem Segler auf günstigeren Wind warteten. Als die Stadt sich später zu einem Seebad entwickelte, wurden mehrere Landungsbrücken errichtet. Die letzte von ihnen wurde 1957 als Pfahlkonstruktion aus Beton erbaut. An ihrem Ende gibt es drei Ebenen: eine zur Aussicht, eine als Anlände und eine zum Angeln. Das Café auf diesem Pier wurde vom Royal Institute of British Architects (RIBA) als Wettbewerb ausgeschrieben. Die Architekten erklären: „Wir wollten das Gebäude aus einem Material errichten, das mit der Zeit verwittert und dabei anschaulicher wird. Wir hoffen, dass es schließlich in den abgenutzten Beton des Piers aufgehen wird." Sie wählten eine verleimte Konstruktion aus Iroko-Holz mit großen, verglasten Flächen, die in gewisser Weise von den hölzernen Industriebauten des 19. Jahrhunderts beeinflusst wurde. Das Gebäude besteht aus zwei Teilen: einem undurchsichtigen Bereich, der Toiletten, Küchen und eine Eingangshalle enthält, und einem verglasten für das Café, „das als ein einziger, schlichter, nach außen geöffneter Raum konzipiert wurde".

Deal était à l'origine un port de mer dans lequel les bateaux attendaient les vents favorables. Lorsque la ville devint un lieu de vacances, plusieurs jetées furent créées. La plus récente est une construction en béton édifiée en 1957. L'extrémité de la jetée comportait trois niveaux : un pour l'observation, les deux autres pour l'accostage des bateaux et la pêche. Le café-bar est une commande obtenue à l'issue d'un concours organisé par le RIBA. « Nous voulions réaliser cette construction dans un matériau unique qui puisse se patiner et s'améliorer avec le temps, expliquent les architectes ; nous souhaitions qu'ils se confondent même avec le béton délabré de la jetée. » L'agence a dessiné une structure en lamellé d'Iroko à grandes baies vitrées inspirées dans une certaine mesure des bâtiments en bois du XIXe siècle. L'ensemble est divisé en deux parties, une section fermée contenant les toilettes, les cuisines et une entrée, l'autre, vitrée, réservée au café « conçu comme un vaste et simple espace, ouvert sur l'extérieur ».

The café-bar is set on the end of the existing wood-columned pier, aligned perpendicular to its elongated form.

Das Café befindet sich am Ende einer Landungsbrücke auf Holzpfeilern und folgt deren langgestreckter Form.

Le café-bar a été implanté à l'extrémité de la jetée à piliers de bois, perpendiculaire à sa forme allongée.

The plan shows the long pier and the café-bar at its end. Above, the new structure sitting on concrete pilings.

Der Lageplan zeigt die lange Landungsbrücke und das Café an ihrem Ende. Oben: Der Neubau steht auf Betonpfeilern.

Le plan montre la longue jetée et le café-bar à sa pointe. Ci-dessus, la nouvelle construction qui s'appuie sur des piliers de béton.

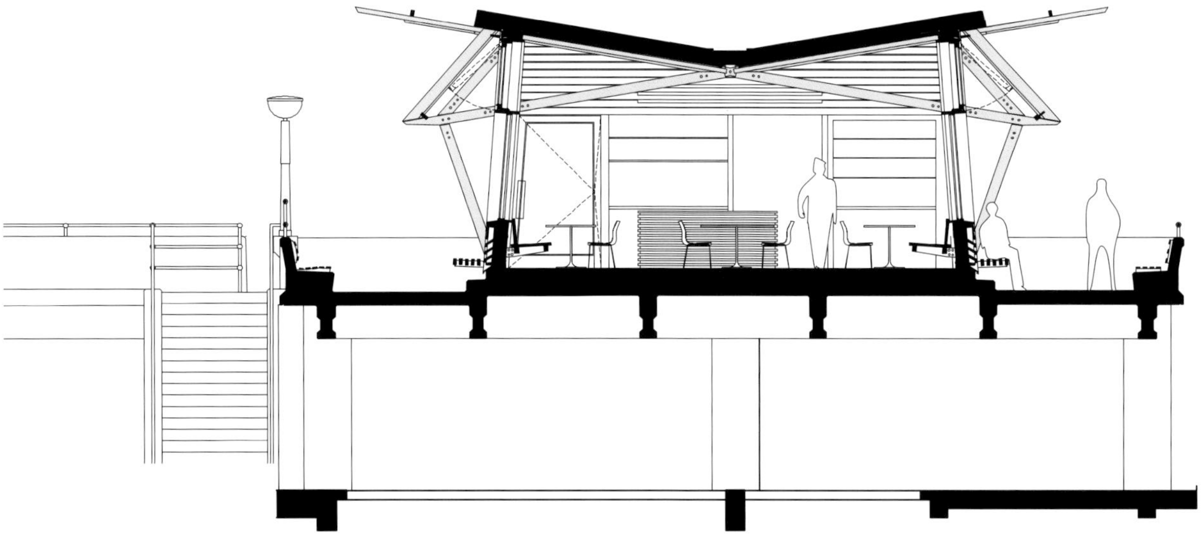

The sides of the café are fully glazed, giving patrons the impression of hovering above the sea. Above, a section drawing shows the X-shaped form and the placement of the facility on the pier.

Die Seitenwände des Cafés sind voll verglast und vermitteln den Besuchern den Eindruck, als schwebten sie über dem Meer. Oben: Eine Schnittzeichnung zeigt die x-förmige Gestalt und die Lage des Gebäudes auf dem Pier.

Les façades latérales du café sont entièrement vitrées, ce qui donne l'impression aux clients de se trouver en suspension au-dessus de la mer. Ci-dessus, une coupe montre l'ossature, la charpente en X et le positionnement de la construction sur la jetée.

With its wooden slat roof, the building is as open to its environment as the weather permits. Above, the concrete pilings and platform on which the café-bar is built.

Mit seinem hölzernen Lattendach ist das Gebäude so offen zu seinem Umfeld, wie es das Wetter gestattet. Oben: die Betonpfeiler und die Plattform, auf der das Café errichtet wurde.

Doté d'une toiture en poutrelles de bois, le café est aussi ouvert sur son environnement que le temps le permet. Ci-dessus les piliers de béton et la plate-forme sur laquelle il a été construit.

BEATRIZ MEYER

Beatriz Meyer
Rua Senador César Lacerda Vergueiro 87
05435–060 São Paulo, SP
Brazil

Tel: +55 11 98476 2000
E-mail: beatrizmeyer05@gmail.com
Web: www.beatrizmeyer.com.br

BEATRIZ MEYER was born in São Paulo, Brazil, in 1977. She attended Mackenzie Presbyterian University in São Paulo (1996–2000) and worked the following four years on scenography for the theater. From 2004 until 2009 she had her own office. Since 2009 she has been working in the office of Marcio Kogan (studio mk27). In 2005 she participated in the International Biennial of São Paulo with the Open School project. She received a prize from IAB (Brazilian Architects Institute), the 8th Young Architect Award for her Chapel (Tatuí, São Paulo, 2006, published here). In 2008 she participated in the VI BIAU (Ibero-American Biennial of Architecture and Urbanism) in Lisbon with the Chapel project.

BEATRIZ MEYER wurde 1977 in São Paulo, Brasilien, geboren und studierte an der Universidade Presbiteriana Mackenzie in São Paulo (1996–2000). In den darauffolgenden vier Jahren arbeitete sie als Bühnenbildnerin am Theater. Von 2004 bis 2009 hatte sie ein eigenes Büro; seit 2009 arbeitet sie in der Firma von Marcio Kogan (studio mk27). 2005 nahm sie mit dem Projekt einer „offenen Schule" an der Internationalen Biennale von São Paulo teil. Für ihre Kapelle (Tatuí, São Paulo, 2006, hier veröffentlicht) erhielt sie einen Preis vom brasilianischen Architektenverband IAB, den 8th Young Architect Award. 2008 beteiligte sie sich mit dem Entwurf für diese Kapelle an der VI. BIAU (Bienal Iberoamerican de Arquitectura y Urbanismo) in Lissabon.

BEATRIZ MEYER, née à São Paulo en 1977, a étudié à la Universidade Presbiteriana Mackenzie à São Paulo (1996–2000) et travaillé ensuite pendant quatre ans sur des projets de scénographies pour le théâtre. De 2004 à 2009, elle a dirigé sa propre agence et, depuis 2009, est entrée chez Marcio Kogan (studio mk27). En 2005, elle a participé à la Biennale internationale de São Paulo avec le projet de l'École ouverte. Elle est titulaire du 8e prix du jeune architecte décerné par l'IAB (Institut des architectes brésiliens) pour une chapelle (Tatuí, São Paulo, 2006, publiée ici). En 2008, elle a participé à la VIe BIAU (Biennale ibéro-américaine d'architecture et d'urbanisme) à Lisbonne avec ce projet de chapelle.

CHAPEL

Tatuí, São Paulo, Brazil, 2006

Address: not disclosed. Area: 60 m²
Client: not disclosed. Cost: $100 000

The **CHAPEL** was commissioned by the owners of a ranch in the countryside of the state of São Paulo. It is set between two lines of pine trees and is surrounded by lush vegetation. "Their ultimate purpose," says the architect, "was to have a place where it would be possible to enjoy peace and be close to nature." The construction material was chosen because other structures on the ranch were in wood. Large glazed areas allow a closer communion with the natural setting. An Alwitra membrane roof was used to permit a low angle. A stone wall with a cruciform cutout stands behind the altar. Recuperated wood is used inside, and dry-sealed bricks are used for the exterior floor. The architect designed benches and the altar for the project. Inlaid floor lighting marks the pillars and the path leading to the altar.

Die **KAPELLE** wurde von den Besitzern einer Ranch im Staat São Paulo in Auftrag gegeben. Sie steht zwischen zwei Reihen von Kiefern und ist von üppiger Vegetation umgeben. „Eigentlich war sie als ein Ort gedacht", sagt die Architektin, „an dem man den Frieden genießen und der Natur nahe sein kann." Das Baumaterial entspricht dem der anderen Holzbauten auf der Ranch. Durch große, verglaste Bereiche wurde eine engere Verbindung zur natürlichen Umgebung erreicht. Das Dach ist mit einer Alwitra-Membrane versehen, die eine leichte Neigung gestattete. Eine Steinmauer mit ausgeschnittenem Kreuz steht hinter dem Altar. Das Innere ist mit wiederverwendetem Holz ausgestattet, der Boden außen mit wasserabweisenden Ziegeln gepflastert. Die Architektin entwarf auch die Bänke und den Altar dieser Kapelle. In den Boden eingelassene Strahler beleuchten die Stützen und den Weg zum Altar.

Cette **CHAPELLE** est une commande des propriétaires d'un ranch de l'État de São Paulo. Implantée entre deux alignement de pins, elle est entourée d'une végétation luxuriante. « Le but ultime [des clients], explique l'architecte, était de disposer d'un lieu où il soit possible de profiter de la paix au plus près de la nature. » Le matériau de construction a été choisi, entre autres, parce que tous les autres bâtiments de la propriété sont en bois. De vastes murs vitrés assurent une communion étroite avec le cadre naturel. La toiture est recouverte d'une membrane en Alwitra, ce qui a permis de lui conserver une faible inclinaison. Un mur de pierre dans lequel est découpée une croix se dresse derrière l'autel. L'intérieur est en bois de récupération et les sols extérieurs en briques à joint de mortier sec. L'architecte a également dessiné les bancs et l'autel. Un éclairage intégré dans le sol signale les piliers et l'allée vers l'autel.

The full-height glazing of three sides of the chapel makes it particularly open. Wood is used everywhere aside from the rear stone wall.

Die auf drei Seiten in voller Höhe verglaste Kapelle wirkt besonders offen. Mit Ausnahme der rückwärtigen Natursteinwand wurde überall Holz verwendet.

Les murs de verre toute hauteur des trois côtés de la chapelle lui confèrent un aspect extrêmement ouvert. Le bois est partout présent, à l'exception du mur en pierre de l'autel.

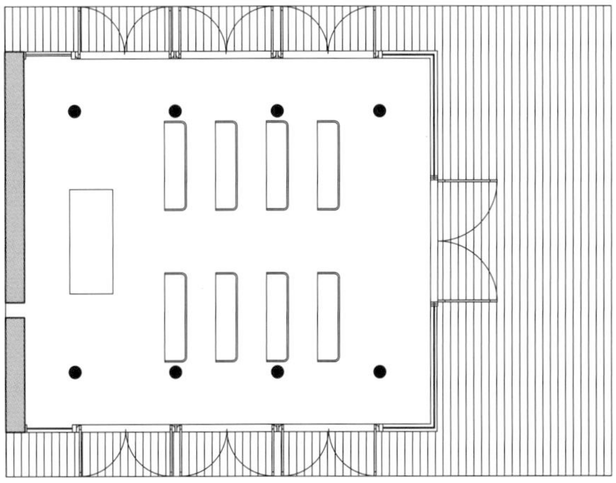

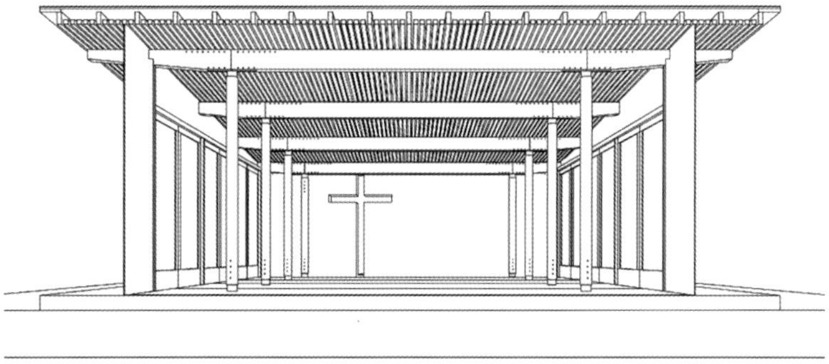

Seen in plan and elevation, the structure is simple, basically a square with carefully aligned pews and a simple table serving as an altar.

Im Grundriss und in der Ansicht gesehen, ist das Gebäude schlicht konzipiert, im Grunde als ein Quadrat mit überlegt platzierten Bänken und einem einfachen Altartisch.

Vu en plan et en élévation, le petit bâtiment est pratiquement carré. Il contient les bancs soigneusement alignés et une table simple qui fait office d'autel.

Lake Hills Suncheon Country Club

KEN SUNGJIN MIN

SKM Architects
SKM Building
60–15 Samseong-dong, Gangnam-gu
Seoul 135–896
South Korea

Tel: +82 2 543 2027
Fax: +82 2 548 2027
E-mail: skm@skma.com
Web: www.skma.com

KEN SUNGJIN MIN received his B.Arch degree from the University of Southern California, School of Architecture (1989), and his M.Arch in Urban Design (MAUD) from the Harvard GSD (1993). He created SKM Architects in 1996. The recent work of the firm includes the Hilton Namhae Golf and Spa (Nam-myeon, Namhae-gun, 2006); the Kumgang Ananti Golf & Spa Resort (Gangwon-do, North Korea, 2008); Lake Hills Suncheon Country Club (Suncheon, JeollaNam-do, 2008, published here); Asiana Airlines Weihai Point Golf & Resort (Weihai, China, 2009); Asiana Airlines Laolaob Bay Golf & Spa Resort (Saipan, Marianas, USA, 2009); Arumdaun Golf & Spa Resort (Chungcheongnam-do, 2009); Ananti Club Seoul (Gapyeoung-gun, Gyeonggi-do, 2009–10); all in South Korea unless stated otherwise. The Hilton Namhae Golf and Spa Resort was the winner of a World Travel Award in 2013 as South Korea's leading resort.

KEN SUNGJIN MIN absolvierte seinen B. Arch. an der Architekturfakultät der University of Southern California (1989) und seinen M.Arch. in Stadtplanung (MAUD) an der Harvard GSD (1993). 1996 gründete er sein Büro SKM Architects. Jüngere Projekte des Büros sind u. a. das Hilton Namhae Golf & Spa (Nam-myeon, Namhae-gun, 2006), das Kumgang Ananti Golf & Spa Resort (Gangwon-do, Nordkorea, 2008), der Lake Hills Suncheon Country Club (Suncheon, JeollaNam-do, 2008, hier vorgestellt), das Asiana Airlines Weihai Point Golf & Resort (Weihai, China, 2009), das Asiana Airlines Laolaob Bay Golf & Spa Resort (Saipan, Marianas, USA, 2009), der Arumdaun Golf & Spa Resort (Chungcheongnam-do, 2009), der Ananti Club Seoul (Gapyeoung-gun, Gyeonggi-do, 2009–10), alle in Südkorea, sofern nicht anders angegeben. Das Hilton Namhae Golf and Spa Resort gewann als Südkoreas bestes Resort den World Travel Award 2013.

KEN SUNGJIN MIN a obtenu son B.Arch. à l'École d'architecture de l'université de Caroline du Sud (1989) et son M.Arch. en urbanisme (MAUD) à la Harvard GSD (1993). Il a créé SKM Architects en 1996. Les réalisations récentes de l'agence comprennent le golf et spa Hilton Namhae (Nam-myeon, Namhae-gun, 2006) ; la station thermale et golf Kumgang Ananti (Gangwon-do, Corée-du-Nord, 2008) ; le club de loisirs Lake Hills Suncheon (Suncheon, JeollaNam-do, 2008, publié ici) ; la station et golf Asiana Airlines de Weihai Point (Weihai, Chine, 2009) ; la station thermale et golf Asiana Airlines de Laolaob Bay (Saipan, îles Mariannes, États-Unis, 2009) ; la station thermale et golf Arumdaun (Chungcheongnam-do, 2009) ; le club Ananti de Séoul (Gapyeoung-gun, Gyeonggi-do, 2009–10), toutes en Corée-du-Sud sauf mention contraire. En 2013, la station thermale et golf Hilton Namhae ont gagné un prix World Travel Award comme meilleure station de Corée-du-Sud.

LAKE HILLS SUNCHEON COUNTRY CLUB

Suncheon, Jeollanam-do, South Korea, 2008

Address: 54 Haengjeong-ri, Juam-myeon, Suncheon-si, Jeollanam-do, South Korea, www.lakehillssuncheon.com. Area: 16 311 m²
Client: Lake Hills Golf & Resorts Group. Cost: $17 million

The architects explain that this complex is "inspired by the region's rolling hills as well as the history and traditions of the area." A division between the natural landscape and the architecture in the form of an earthen berm marks the perimeter of the design. Concrete elements are buried partially in the earth while prefabricated glulam post-and-beam buildings "reinterpret traditional Korean architecture, providing a light and spacious foil to the earthen structures beneath them." The main public spaces—including the lobby, restaurant, and lounge—are set in the wooden volumes. Skylights and curtain walls make "visual connections with the sky and surrounding hillside topographies."

Die Architekten erklären, dass diese Anlage „von der Topografie der hügeligen Region wie auch von ihrer Geschichte und Tradition inspiriert wurde". Eine Trennung der natürlichen Landschaft von der Architektur in Form eines umlaufenden Erdwalls kennzeichnet diese Planung. Ein Teil der Betonelemente wurde im Erdboden verborgen, während vorgefertigte Ständerkonstruktionen aus Schichtholz „die traditionelle koreanische Architektur neu interpretieren sowie eine leichte und großzügige Erweiterung der darunter im Boden verhafteten Strukturen bilden". Die wichtigen öffentlichen Räume – zu denen die Lobby, das Restaurant und die Lounge gehören – befinden sich in den hölzernen Volumen. Oberlichter und Vorhangfassaden bieten „visuelle Verbindungen zum Himmel und der Topografie des bergigen Umfelds".

Selon les architectes, ce complexe « s'inspire des vallonnements de la région mais aussi de l'histoire et des traditions du lieu ». Une berme de terre suit le périmètre du projet et marque la séparation entre le paysage naturel et l'architecture. Les éléments en béton sont en partie enterrés dans le sol. Les ossatures à poutres et poteaux en lamellé-collé préfabriquées « réinterprètent l'architecture traditionnelle coréenne, tout en offrant des espaces et un éclairage généreux aux parties enterrées ». Les principaux espaces collectifs – dont le hall d'accueil, le restaurant et le salon – sont répartis dans ces volumes en bois. Des verrières et des murs rideaux établissent des « connexions visuelles avec le ciel et la topographie des collines environnantes ».

An aerial view of the complex with its curving roofs visible in the mountain setting.

Luftaufnahme der Anlage mit ihren geschwungenen Dächern inmitten der bergigen Umgebung.

Vue aérienne du complexe et de ses toits incurvés dans son cadre de montagnes.

The curved roofs are seen in both the section drawings (below) and the image above. There is a hint of reference to tradition in this architecture, without any sense of "pastiche," or imitation of the old.

Die geschwungenen Dächer sind in den Schnitten (unten) wie auch auf dem Foto oben zu sehen. In dieser Architektur ist ein Bezug zum traditionellen Bauen erkennbar, ohne dass sie zu einem „Pastiche" oder einer Imitation des Alten geworden ist.

La courbure des toits vue à la fois dans les dessins en coupe ci-dessous et l'image ci-dessus. On note un soupçon de référence à la tradition dans cette architecture sans aucune tentative de « pastiche » ou d'imitation de l'ancien.

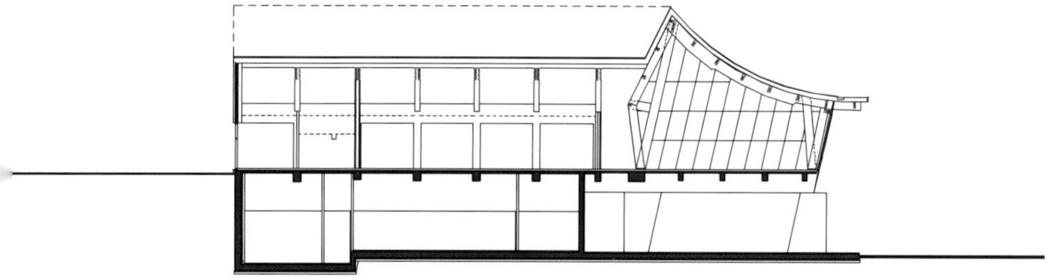

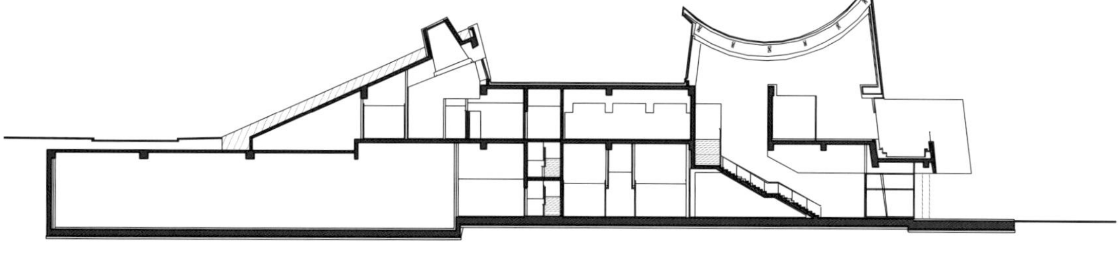

Damiani Holz &
Ko Headquarters

MODUS

MoDus Architects
Fallmerayerstrasse 7
39042 Brixen
Italy

Tel/Fax: +39 04 72 20 15 81
E-mail: info@modusarchitects.com
Web: www.modusarchitects.com

MATTEO SCAGNOL, born in 1968 in Trieste, graduated from the University of Venice, IUAV in 1995. Shortly thereafter he worked two years in Naples before attending the Graduate School of Design at Harvard University where he completed a Master in Architecture in 1999 and was recognized as Best Designer of the graduating class. **SANDY ATTIA** was born in 1974 in Cairo, Egypt. She completed her Bachelor of Arts in Architecture in 1995 at the University of Virginia and her Master in Architecture at the Graduate School of Design at Harvard in 2000. The two architects met in the United States during their studies at Harvard University and began their work together in 2000. Their work includes Villa Terzer (Appiano, 2007–09); the Bressanone-Varna Ring road, (Bressanone, 2006–11); working farmhouse complex (Renon, 2010–12); artist's atelier and private residence (Castelrotto, 2010–12); Damiani Holz & Ko Headquarters (Bressanone, 2010–12, published here); elementary school addition and refurbishment (Ora, 2008–13); Brenner highway pedestrian passage (Brennero, 2011–13); and a mountain refuge (Dolomites, 2012–14), all in Italy.

MATTEO SCAGNOL, 1968 in Triest in Italien geboren, schloss sein Studium 1995 an der IUAV in Venedig ab. Er arbeitete zwei Jahre in Neapel und besuchte im Anschluss die Harvard GSD, wo er 1999 seinen M. Arch. machte und als „Best Designer" seiner Abschlussklasse ausgezeichnet wurde. **SANDY ATTIA** wurde 1974 in Kairo in Ägypten geboren. Sie erlangte ihren B. Arch. 1995 an der University of Virginia und ihren M. Arch. 2000 an der Harvard Graduate School of Design (GSD). Die zwei Architekten lernten sich beim Studium in Harvard kennen und praktizieren seit 2000 gemeinsam. Zu ihren Projekten zählen die Villa Terzer (Eppan, 2007–09), die Umgehungsstraße Brixen-Vahrn (2006–11), ein Hofkomplex (Renon, 2010–12), ein Künstleratelier mit Wohnung (Kastelruth, 2010–12), die Hauptniederlassung Damiani Holz & Ko (Brixen, 2010–12, hier vorgestellt), Sanierung und Erweiterung einer Grundschule (Ora, 2008–13), ein Fußweg an der Brenner-Autobahn (2011–13) sowie eine Berghütte (Dolomiten, 2012–14), alle in der italienischen Provinz Bozen.

Né à Trieste en 1968, **MATTEO SCAGNOL** est diplômé de l'université IUAV de Venise (1995). Il a ensuite travaillé deux ans à Naples, avant de rejoindre la Harvard GSD où il a obtenu un M.Arch. en 1999 et a été couronné « meilleur designer » de sa promotion. **SANDY ATTIA** est née en 1974 au Caire en Égypte. Elle a obtenu son B.Arch. en 1995 à l'université de Virginie et son M.Arch. à la Harvard GSD en 2000. Ils se sont rencontrés aux États-unis pendant leurs études à la Harvard GSD et ont commencé à travailler ensemble en 2000. Leurs réalisations comprennent la villa Terzer (Appiano, Bolzano, 2007–09) ; la rocade Bressanone-Varna (Bressanone, Bolzano, 2006–11) ; un complexe fermier (Renon, Bolzano, 2010–12) ; un atelier d'artiste et résidence privée (Castelrotto, Bolzano, 2010–12) ; le siège de Damiani-Holz & Ko (Bressanone, 2010–12, publié ici) ; l'extension et le réaménagement d'une école élémentaire (Ora, Bolzano, 2008–13) ; le passage piéton de la route nationale du Brenner (Brennero, Bolzano, 2011–13) et un refuge de montagne (Dolomites, Bolzano, 2012–14), toutes en Italie.

GNOALP

DAMIANI HOLZ & KO HEADQUARTERS

Bressanone, Italy, 2010–12

Address: Via Julius Durst 68, 39042 Bressanone, Italy
+39 04 72 97 57 90, www.lignoalp.it
Area: 225 m². Client: Damiani Holz & Ko. Cost: €2.9 million

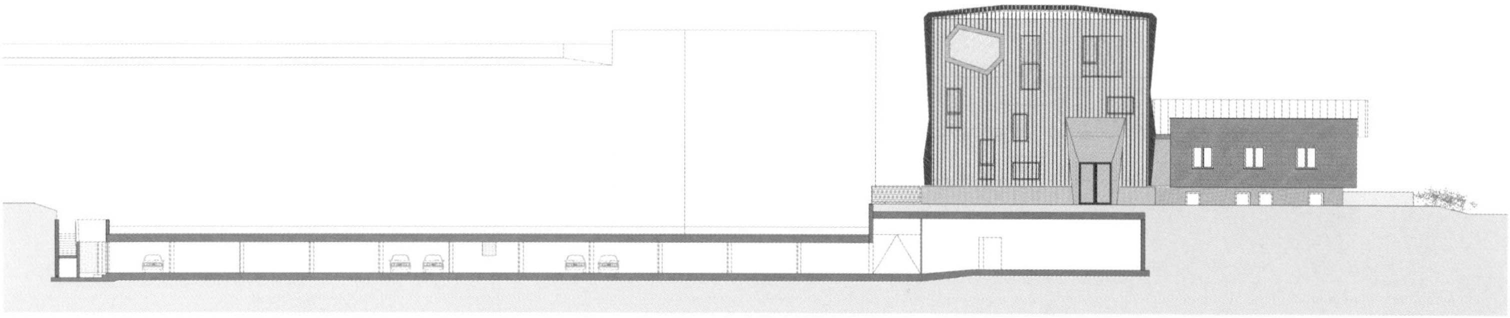

The section drawing shows the long underground parking area near the structure (top left). The sculpted wood form of the main building sits on its concrete base. Its form is neither fully regular nor fully irregular.

Der Querschnitt (oben links) zeigt die lange Tiefgarage neben dem Gebäude. Der skulpturale Holzaufbau ruht auf einem Betonsockel – seine Form ist weder vollkommen regelmäßig noch gänzlich unregelmäßig.

La coupe fait apparaître le long parking souterrain qui jouxte la structure (en haut à gauche). La forme de bois sculptée qui constitue le bâtiment principal est posée sur une base de béton. Elle n'est ni parfaitement régulière, ni parfaitement irrégulière.

Unexpected window and door placement add to the ambiguity of the design, making function and internal structure impossible to guess.

Überraschende Platzierungen von Fenster- und Türöffnungen betonen die Mehrdeutigkeit des Entwurfs und machen es unmöglich, Funktion oder Innenaufteilung des Baus zu erraten.

La disposition surprenante de la fenêtre et de la porte ajoute à l'ambiguïté de l'ensemble et rend la fonction et la structure interne impossibles à deviner.

Winners of a 2008 invited competition, the architects undertook the refurbishment of and addition to the existing headquarters of a wood construction company. Since the company "designs and develops building systems in wood and pursues the use of environmentally conscientious wood building products and techniques," the project had to take these factors into account. The completed structure is something of a "showcase" for the methods and products of the firm. The structure has received a KlimaHaus Gold+ certification, the highest standard in energy efficiency and eco-compatible building materials set by the KlimaHaus council of Bolzano. The building is essentially a wooden monolith on a black concrete base. Wooden slats of varying density form a second skin, although the wood structure has load-bearing wall systems. The office addition is a five-story building with underground parking for 40 cars. Different floor designs in wood participate in the varied use of the company's products. All the furniture was custom designed and built with the exception of the chairs.

Nachdem sich die Architekten 2008 in einem geladenen Wettbewerb durchsetzen konnten, folgte die Sanierung und Erweiterung der Hauptniederlassung eines Holzbauunternehmens. Bei einer Firma, die „Holzbausysteme plant und entwickelt und sich auf umweltgerechte Holzbauprodukte und -techniken spezialisiert hat", galt es, entsprechende Faktoren bei der Planung zu berücksichtigen. Der realisierte Bau dient zugleich als Beispiel für die Techniken und Produkte des Unternehmens. Der Bau erhielt das Zertifikat KlimaHaus Gold+, die höchste Auszeichnung für Energieeffizienz und umweltgerechte Baustoffe, vergeben vom KlimaHaus-Gremium in Bozen. Der Bau ist ein Monolith aus Holz über einem schwarzen Betonsockel. Über die tragenden Wände der Holzkonstruktion zieht sich eine zweite Haut aus Holzleisten unterschiedlicher Stärke. Der Büroanbau, ein fünfstöckiger Komplex, verfügt über eine Tiefgarage mit 40 Stellplätzen. Die individuelle Gestaltung der einzelnen Etagen unterstreicht die vielfältige Nutzbarkeit der Holzprodukte der Firma. Alle Möbel mit Ausnahme der Stühle wurden eigens entworfen und gebaut.

Vainqueurs d'un concours organisé par l'entreprise en 2008, les architectes ont eu à réaliser le réaménagement et l'extension du siège d'une société de construction en bois. L'entreprise « crée et développe des systèmes de construction en bois et encourage l'utilisation de produits et techniques de construction en bois écologiquement responsables » et le projet devait tenir compte de ces facteurs. La structure réalisée est pour ainsi dire une « vitrine » des méthodes et produits de l'entreprise. Elle a reçu la certification « KlimaHaus Gold+ », la plus haute note qui récompense l'efficacité énergétique et l'utilisation de matériaux de construction éco-compatibles, décernée par le conseil « KlimaHaus » de Bolzano. Le bâtiment est essentiellement composé d'un bloc monolithique de bois sur une base de béton noir. Des lattes de bois aux densités variables forment une seconde peau – même si la structure en bois présente des systèmes de murs porteurs. L'extension qui abrite des bureaux est un immeuble de cinq étages doté d'un parking souterrain de 40 places. Différents motifs en bois au sol présentent les usages variés des produits du constructeur. Tout le mobilier a été conçu et construit sur mesure, à l'exception des chaises.

In the image above, the building is seen behind stacks of wood produced by the client. The relation between the product and the new structure is evident.

Oben ein Blick auf den Bau hinter Holzstapeln aus der Produktion des Auftraggebers. Die Beziehung zwischen Produkt und Neubau ist offensichtlich.

On voit ci-dessus le bâtiment derrière des piles de bois fourni par le client : la relation entre le produit et la nouvelle structure est évidente.

A closer view of the skin of the building gives it an even more organ-ic appearance, like a living wooden skin.

Bei näherer Betrachtung wirkt die Gebäudehülle noch organischer, wie eine lebendige, hölzerne Haut.

Une vue rapprochée de l'enveloppe du bâtiment lui donne une apparence encore plus organique, telle une peau de bois vivante.

Below, section drawings show the shedlike design of the building, with its underground area also visible.

Querschnitte (unten) zeigen, dass der Bau wie ein Schuppen entworfen ist. Auch die Ebenen im Untergeschoss sind zu erkennen.

Ci-dessous, les dessins en coupe font apparaître la forme de hangar du bâtiment, la partie souterraine étant elle aussi visible.

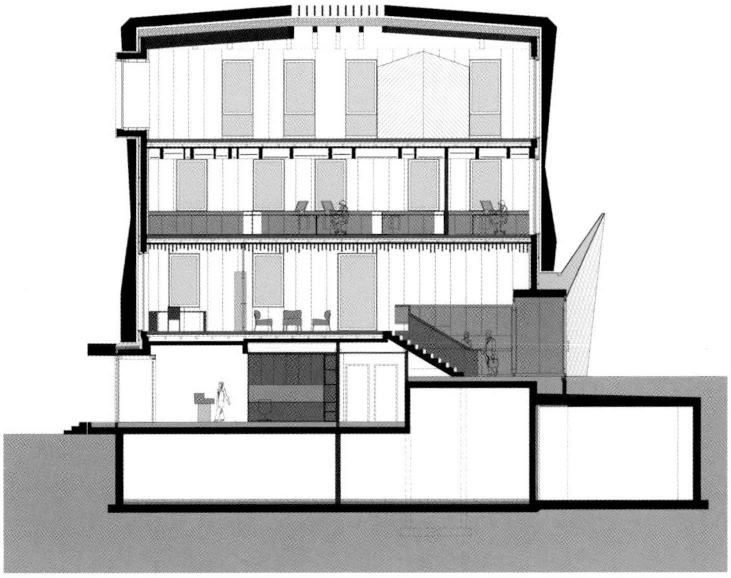

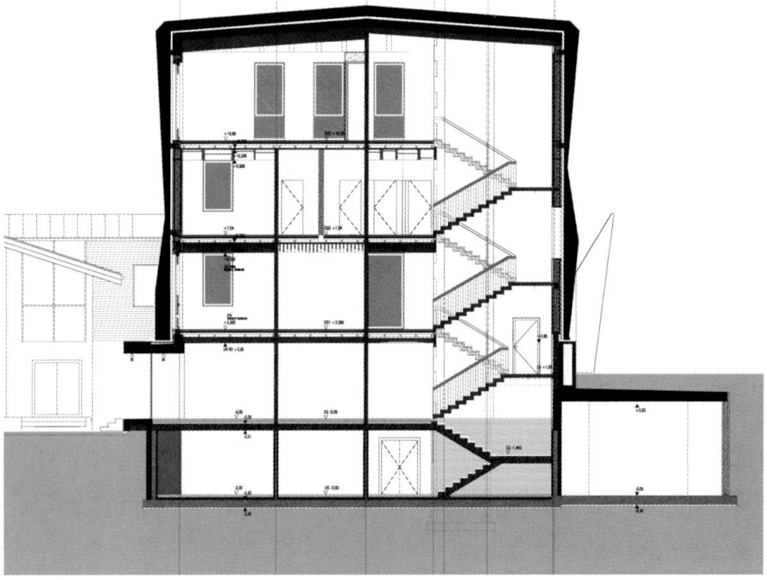

The architects have had the opportunity to give life to the wood design of the building on the interior as well as seen in the play on cutout forms and lighting below.

Die Architekten gestalteten auch das Innere des Gebäudes lebendig mit Holz, wie am Spiel der ausgeschnittenen Formen und der Beleuchtung zu sehen ist (unten).

Les architectes ont eu l'opportunité d'animer le design de bois de l'intérieur comme le montre le jeu de formes découpées et de lumières ci-dessous.

An overall plan shows the new building to the left of the drawing (right). Above, the irregular polyhedron roof responds to the tilted window.

Ein Plan des Gesamtkomplexes (rechts) zeigt links den Neubau. Die unregelmäßige Deckenkassettierung aus Polyedern oben korrespondiert mit dem schiefwinkligen Fenster.

À droite, le plan d'ensemble montre le nouveau bâtiment du côté gauche. Ci-dessus, le toit polyédrique irrégulier répond à l'inclinaison des fenêtres.

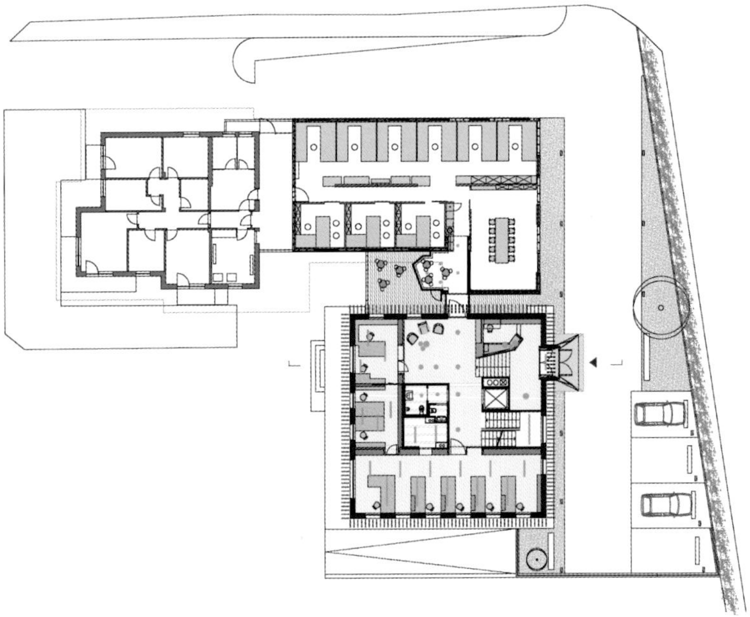

PETE NELSON

Nelson Treehouse and Supply
P.O. Box 1135
Fall City, WA 98024
USA

Tel: +1 425 441 8568
E-mail: info@nelsontreehouseandsupply.com
Web: www.nelsontreehouseandsupply.com

PETE NELSON, the owner of Nelson Treehouse and Supply LLC, is one of the best-known authors on the subject. His firm has built "unique tree houses" all across the United States. They also offer workshops and consulting services for those who prefer to build their own tree house. Pete Nelson was born in Mineola, New York, in 1962. Though he built tree houses as a child with his father, it was the discovery of a book sent to him by a friend on how to build tree houses that convinced Nelson of his vocation. His own 1994 book, *Treehouses: the Art and Craft of Living Out on a Limb*, represents a first publishing effort that met with success. In 1997 he created the Treehouse Workshop with Jake Jacob, before setting up his present firm. Aside from books including *Treehouses of the World* (New York, 2004), Pete Nelson has also worked recently on the Northwest Treehouse School, a teaching facility for design and construction; Treehouse Point, an "environmental tree house retreat center" including the Temple of the Blue Moon (Issaquah, Washington, USA, 2006, published here); and the Tree for All Foundation, "a non-profit corporation inspired by the work of Bill Allen of Forever Young that brings disabled people into nature and tree houses."

PETE NELSON, der Eigentümer von Nelson Treehouse und Supply LLC, ist einer der bekanntesten Autoren auf diesem Gebiet. Seine Firma hat „einzigartige Baumhäuser" in den gesamten USA gebaut. Sie bietet auch Workshops und Beratungen für die diejenigen an, die ihr Baumhaus lieber selbst bauen möchten. Pete Nelson wurde 1962 in Mineola, New York, geboren. Obwohl er schon als Kind mit seinem Vater Baumhäuser gebaut hat, erkannte er seine Berufung erst, als ihm ein Freund ein Buch über das Baumhausbauen schickte. Sein *Treehouses. The Art and Craft of Living Out on a Limb* aus dem Jahr 1994 war sein erster Bucherfolg. Ab 1997 betrieb er gemeinsam mit Jake Jacob den Treehouse Workshop, bevor er seine jetzige Firma gründete. Pete Nelson veröffentlichte weitere Bücher, darunter *Baumhäuser der Welt* (Wien, 2004), und arbeitet seit Kurzem an der Northwest Treehouse School, einem Lehrinstitut für den Entwurf und Bau von Baumhäusern, für das Treehouse Point, ein „umweltbewusstes Baumhaus-Ferien-Center" zu dem der Temple of the Blue Moon gehört (Issaquah, Washington, USA, 2006, hier veröffentlicht), sowie für die Stiftung Tree for All, „ein gemeinnütziges Unternehmen, das von Bill Allen von Forever Young inspiriert wurde, der behinderten Menschen den Zugang zur Natur und zu Baumhäusern ermöglicht".

PETE NELSON, propriétaire de la société Nelson Treehouse and Supply LLC, est l'un des auteurs les plus connus dans le domaine des cabanes dans les arbres. Son entreprise construit des « cabanes dans les arbres à caractère unique » dans tout les États-Unis. Elle propose également des ateliers de formation et des services de conseil pour ceux qui préfèrent les construire eux-mêmes. Pete Nelson est né à Minola (New York) en 1962. Bien qu'il ait déjà construit avec son père des cabanes perchées, c'est la lecture d'un livre sur leur construction offert par un ami qui lui révéla sa vocation. Son propre ouvrage, publié en 1994, *Treehouses. The Art and Craft of Living Out on a Limb*, est le premier de ce genre à avoir connu le succès. En 1997, il a fondé le Treehouse Workshop avec Jake Jacob, avant de créer son entreprise actuelle. En dehors de livres comme *Treehouses of the World* (New York, 2004), Nelson a également travaillé sur le projet récent de la Northwest Treehouse School, un lieu d'enseignement pour la conception et la construction ; Treehouse Point, une « maison dans les arbres environnementale qui est un centre de retraite » comprenant le Temple of the Blue Moon (Issaquah, Washington, États-Unis, 2006), publié ici ; et la Tree For All Foundation, « une association inspirée de l'œuvre de Bill Allen de Forever Young qui veut faciliter l'accès des personnes handicapées à la nature et aux cabanes dans les arbres ».

TEMPLE OF THE BLUE MOON

Issaquah, Washington, USA, 2006

Address: Treehouse Point Overnight Retreat and Event Center, 6922 Preston-Fall City Rd SE, Issaquah, Washington, WA 98027, USA, www.treehousepoint.com, +1 425-441-8087
Area: 23 m². Client: Pete and Judy Nelson. Cost: $115,000

Part of Treehouse Point, a complex intended to promote "a vision of sustainability while providing opportunities for lodging, education, and connection in a unique and natural environment," the **TEMPLE OF THE BLUE MOON** is a 23-square-meter structure built nearly five meters off the ground. Lodged between an ancient Sitka spruce and a western red cedar, the Temple of the Blue Moon was inspired by the form of the Parthenon. Available for rent, the structure has leather reading chairs, a writing desk, bookcase, and armoire, as well as a large bed.

Das 23 m² große Baumhaus **TEMPLE OF THE BLUE MOON** wurde rund 5 m über dem Boden gebaut und gehört zum Treehouse Point, einem Projekt, das sich auf die Fahnen geschrieben hat, eine „Vision von Nachhaltigkeit" zu vermitteln und dabei „Unterkünfte, Bildungsangebote und ein einzigartiges Naturumfeld" anzubieten. Das zwischen einer alten Sitka-Fichte und einer Riesen-Thuja gebaute Baumhaus greift die Giebelform des Parthenon auf. Das Baumhaus, das gemietet werden kann, ist mit Ledersesseln, einem Schreibtisch, Regal, Kleiderschrank und einem großen Bett ausgestattet.

Faisant partie de Treehouse Point, complexe dédié à la promotion d'une « vision de la durabilité tout en offrant des possibilités de logement, d'éducation et de contacts avec un environnement naturel exceptionnel », le **TEMPLE OF THE BLUE MOON** est une construction de 23 m² édifiée à près de 5 m au-dessus du sol. Installé entre un très vieux sapin de Sitka et un cèdre rouge, le temple s'est inspiré du plan du Parthénon. Proposé à la location, il est équipé de sièges de lecture en cuir, d'un bureau, d'une bibliothèque, d'une armoire et d'un grand lit.

Rather luxurious in appearance with evident electric lighting, the interiors offer views into the surrounding trees and the generous ceiling height of a house that might have remained firmly planted on the ground.

Das recht luxuriöse Interieur verfügt über elektrisches Licht, wie hier zu sehen. Von hier aus bietet sich ein Ausblick auf die umstehenden Bäume. Die großzügige Deckenhöhe entspricht einem ebenerdigen Haus.

D'aspect assez luxueux, l'intérieur équipé de l'éclairage électrique offre des vues sur les arbres environnants et la hauteur de plafond d'une résidence terrestre.

SUSANNE NOBIS

Susanne Nobis
Am Fichtenhain 9
82335 Berg
Germany

Tel: +49 81 51 95 91 87
Fax: +49 81 51 95 91 86
E-mail: info@susannenobis.de

SUSANNE NOBIS was born in Munich, Germany, in 1963. She attended the Architecture Polytechnic of Central London (UK, 1991–92) and obtained her Diploma in Architecture from the University of Applied Sciences (Munich, 1987–92). She received a further Diploma in Architecture from the Technical University of Berlin (1996–99). She worked in the Renzo Piano Building Workshop (Genoa, 1992–93), with Herzog+Partner (Munich, 1994–95), and with Ackermann und Partner (Munich, 1995–96), before creating her own office in 2000. Her work includes House D_Residential (Ulm, 2000–05); House RW (Wörthersee, 2006–08); Architektouren Traveling Exhibition (2008); House H, a residence with an exhibition area (Großburgwedel, 2007–09); the design of the Ecological Architecture Exhibition (Starnberg, 2009); and Toward Landscape (Lake Starnberg, Berg, 2006–10, published here), all in Germany.

SUSANNE NOBIS wurde 1963 in München geboren. Sie studierte an der Architecture Polytechnic of Central London (1991–92) und machte ihr Architekturdiplom an der Hochschule für angewandte Wissenschaften in München (1987–92). Außerdem erlangte sie ein Architekturdiplom an der Technischen Universität Berlin (1996 bis 1999). Sie arbeitete für Renzo Piano Building Workshop (Genua, 1992–93), Herzog+Partner (München, 1994–95) und Ackermann und Partner (München, 1995–96), bevor sie 2000 ihr eigenes Büro gründete. Zu ihren Projekten zählen Haus D_Residential (Ulm, 2000–05), Haus RW (Wörthersee, 2006–08), die Wanderausstellung „Architektouren" (2008), Haus H, Wohnhaus mit Galerie (Großburgwedel, 2007–09), die Ausstellungsarchitektur für die „Umwelt 2009 Starnberg" (Starnberg, 2009) sowie Toward Landscape (Starnberger See, Berg, 2006–10, hier vorgestellt).

SUSANNE NOBIS, née à Munich en 1963, a étudié l'architecture à la Polytechnic of Central London (1991–92) puis a obtenu ses diplômes d'architecture à l'Université des sciences appliquées de Munich (1987–92) et à l'Université technique de Berlin (1996–99). Elle a travaillé pour le Renzo Piano Building Workshop (Gênes, 1992–93), Herzog + Partner (Munich, 1994–95) et Ackermann und Partner (Munich, 1995–96) avant de créer son agence en 2000. Parmi ses réalisations, toutes en Allemagne : la Haus D_Residential (Ulm, 2000–05) ; la Haus RW (Wörthersee, 2006–08) ; l'exposition « Architektouren » (2008) ; la Haus H, résidence et galerie d'exposition (Großburgwedel, 2007–09) ; une exposition sur l'architecture écologique « Umwelt 2009 Starnberg » (Starnberg, 2009) et la maison Toward Landscape (lac de Starnberg, Berg, 2006–10, publiée ici).

TOWARD LANDSCAPE

Lake Starnberg, Berg, Germany, 2006–10

Address: not disclosed. Area: 324 m²
Client: not disclosed. Cost: not disclosed

Inspired by the traditional boathouses built along Lake Starnberg near Munich, this project consists in one volume with an open gallery and a two-story "bedroom house." It is the home and place of work of the architect. The two rectangular volumes are slightly lifted off the ground and are connected in the center at ground level. A folded titanium skin is "pulled" over the interior timber structures, with an open, glazed band running through the top of the roofs to provide daylight. Books animate the wall space, but the furnishing of the house remains quite minimal. The two parts of the house have broad glazed façades facing the lake, with terraces raised like the ground level of the structures themselves, allowing the inhabitants to enjoy the beautiful lakeside setting in a house that combines the forms of local tradition with a warm wood interior and modern metal exterior.

Das Haus, inspiriert von den traditionellen Bootshäusern am Starnberger See bei München, umfasst zwei Baukörper, einen mit offener Galerie, einen zweiten als zweistöckiges „Schlafzimmerhaus". Für die Architektin ist es Wohnhaus und Arbeitsplatz zugleich. Die beiden rechteckigen Volumina sind leicht über dem Boden aufgeständert und im Erdgeschoss mittig miteinander verbunden. Eine Titanblechschicht wurde über die innere Holzkonstruktion „gezogen"; ein bandförmiges Oberlicht verläuft durch den Giebel und lässt Tageslicht einfallen. Bücher beleben die Wände, die Möblierung bleibt eher sparsam. Beide Teile des Hauses öffnen sich mit großzügig verglasten Fassaden zum See. Die Terrassen sind wie das Erdgeschoss selbst leicht erhöht und bieten den Bewohnern Gelegenheit, die reizvolle Lage am See zu genießen. In diesem Haus verbinden sich traditionelle Bauformen mit einem warmen Interieur aus Holz und einem modernen Äußeren aus Metall.

Inspiré des hangars à bateaux traditionnels des rives du lac de Starnberg près de Munich, ce projet consiste en un volume longé d'un passage couvert et d'une « maison de chambres » de deux niveaux. C'est la résidence et le lieu de travail de l'architecte. Les deux volumes rectangulaires sont légèrement surélevés par rapport au sol et se connectent en leur centre au rez-de-chaussée. Une peau de titane pliée a été « tendue » sur les ossatures en bois, un bandeau zénithal central fournissant l'éclairage naturel. Si des livres animent les murs, le mobilier reste assez réduit. Les deux parties de la maison tournées vers le lac possèdent des façades entièrement vitrées et des terrasses dans le prolongement de l'intérieur. Les occupants bénéficient ainsi d'un cadre superbe dans une maison qui associe des formes locales traditionnelles à des aménagements intérieurs chaleureux en bois et à la modernité de ses façades métalliques.

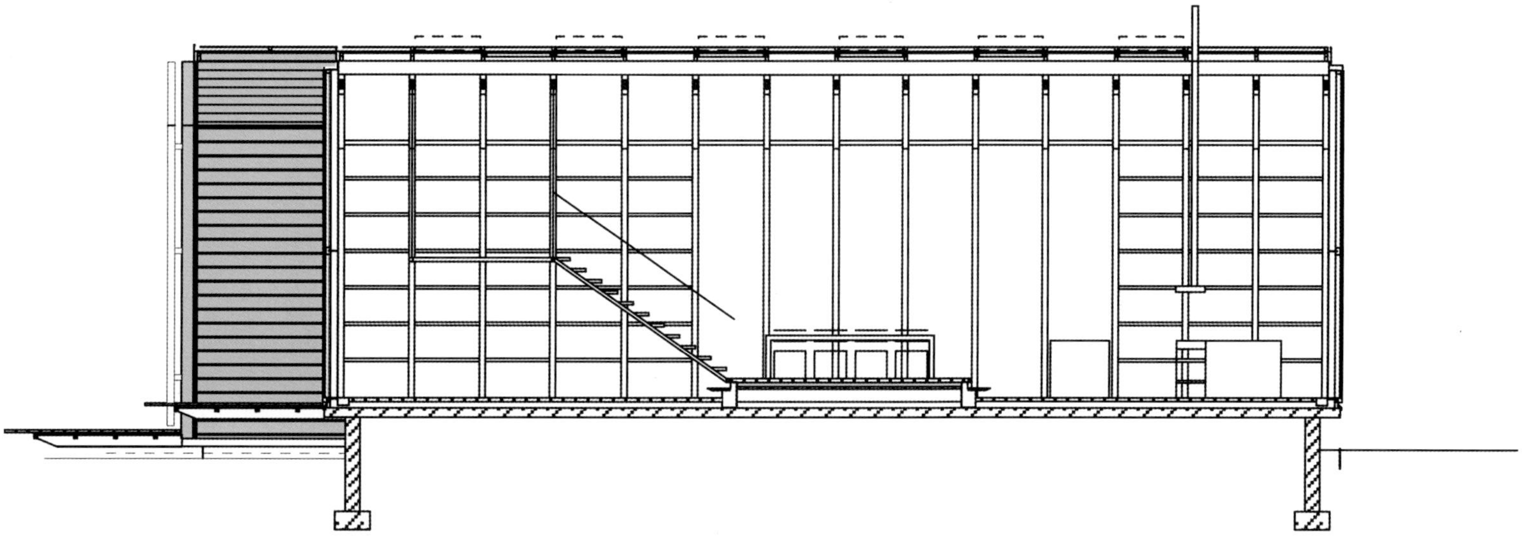

Along the very chic lake edge, near Munich, the architect has created a house and atelier with two shedlike buildings. An elevation shows living space on the mezzanine level reached by a stairway.

In bester Lage am Starnberger See unweit von München baute sich die Architektin Haus und Atelier in zwei scheunenartigen Gebäuden. Ein Aufriss zeigt das Mezzaningeschoss, das über eine Treppe erschlossen wird.

Dans ce quartier élégant en bordure d'un lac près de Munich, l'architecte a créé une maison et un atelier à partir de deux constructions en forme de hangar. L'élévation montre une partie du séjour en mezzanine que l'on atteint par un escalier.

The double-height library space with an elevated platform for the dining room table (left).

Ein Blick in die Bibliothek mit doppelter Raumhöhe. Der Esstisch steht auf einem Podest (links).

L'espace double hauteur de la bibliothèque dans lequel la table des repas a été placée sur une plate-forme (ci-contre).

On the right page, a suspended metal stair and a bridge cross over the library volume and the living space, which opens into the terrace garden.

Auf der rechten Seite eine abgehängte Brücke und Treppe schweben über dem Bibliotheks- und Wohnbereich, der sich zu Terrasse und Garten öffnet.

Page de droite, un escalier métallique suspendu et une passerelle qui traverse le séjour-bibliothèque ouvert sur le jardin.

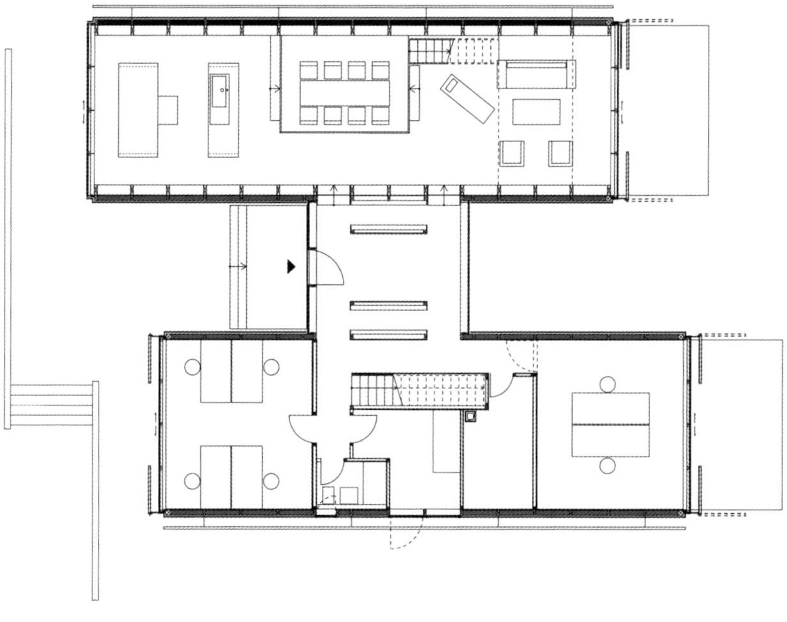

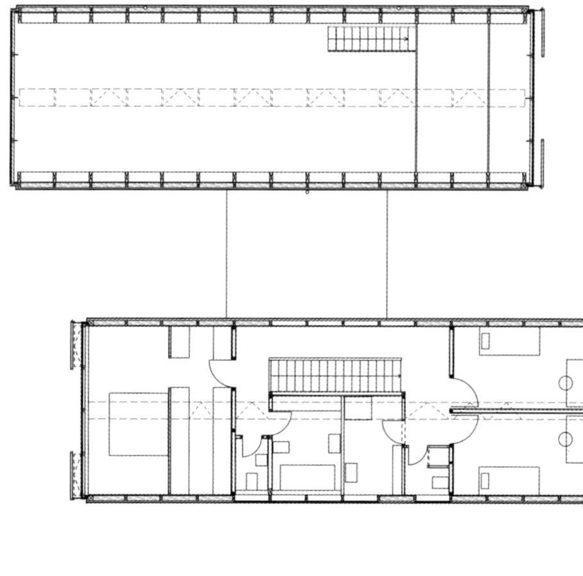

PACIFIC ENVIRONMENTS

Pacific Environments NZ Ltd
L2, 6 Basque Road, Eden Terrace
Auckland 1150
New Zealand

Tel: +64 9 308 0070
Fax: +64 9 308 0071
E-mail: info@penzl.co.nz
Web: www.pacificenvironments.co.nz

Born in 1959 in Wellington, New Zealand, **PETER EISING** obtained his B.Arch degree from the University of Auckland in 1984. From 1977 to 1984 he worked as a draftsman in the Ministry of Works and Development in Wellington. In 1988, he established Architects Patterson Limited with Andrew Patterson. He was a Director of that firm until 2006, when he became the Director of Pacific Environments. **LUCY GAUNTLETT** was born in 1981 in Melbourne, Australia. She graduated from the School of Architecture at Auckland University in 2004. She is also a professional photographer. Their work includes the Crater Lake House (Orakei, Auckland, 2004–06); Laidlaw Commercial Business Park (East Tamaki, Auckland, 2005–06); Tristar Gymnasium (Mount Roskill, Auckland, 2004–07); Saint Stephens Avenue Apartments (Parnell, Auckland, 2006–07); and the Yellow Tree House restaurant (Hokianga Harbour, Northland, 2008, published here). Their ongoing work includes the Navy Training Facilities, Shakespeare's Point (Whangaparaoa Peninsula, Auckland, 2005–); and the Oceanic Artifacts Museum (Bora Bora, Tahiti, 2008–), all in New Zealand unless stated otherwise.

Der 1959 in Wellington, Neuseeland, geborene **PETER EISING** erwarb 1984 seinen B. Arch. an der University of Auckland. Von 1977 bis 1984 arbeitete er als Bauzeichner im Arbeits- und Entwicklungsministerium in Wellington. 1988 gründete er mit Andrew Patterson das Büro Architects Patterson Limited. Er war bis 2006 Leiter dieser Firma und übernahm dann die Leitung von Pacific Environments. **LUCY GAUNTLETT** wurde 1981 in Melbourne, Australien, geboren und beendete 2004 ihr Studium an der Auckland University. Sie ist auch ausgebildete Fototografin. Zu den Werken des Büros gehören das Crater Lake House (Orakei, Auckland, 2004–06), der Gewerbepark Laidlaw (East Tamaki, Auckland, 2005–06), das Tristar Gymnasium (Mount Roskill, Auckland, 2004–07), die Apartments Saint Stephens Avenue (Parnell, Auckland, 2006–07) und das Restaurant Yellow Tree House (Hokianga Harbour, Northland, 2008, hier veröffentlicht). In Arbeit befinden sich die Marine-Ausbildungsanlage Shakespeare's Point (Halbinsel Whangaparaoa, Auckland, seit 2005) und das Oceanic Artifacts Museum (Bora Bora, Tahiti, seit 2008), alle in Neuseeland, sofern nicht anders angegeben.

Né en 1959 à Wellington en Nouvelle-Zélande, **PETER EISING** est titulaire d'un B.Arch. de l'université d'Auckland (1984). De 1977 à 1984, il a également travaillé comme dessinateur pour le ministère des Travaux et du Développement à Wellington. En 1988, il fonde Architects Patterson Limited avec Andrew Patterson. Il dirige l'agence jusqu'en 2006, date à laquelle il devient directeur de Pacific Environments. **LUCY GAUNTLETT**, née en 1981 à Melbourne (Australie), est diplômée de l'École d'architecture de l'université d'Auckland (2004). Elle est également photographe professionnelle. Parmi leurs réalisations figurent : la Crater Lake House (Orakei, Auckland, 2004–06) ; le parc d'affaires Laidlaw (East Tamaki, Auckland, 2005–06) ; le gymnase Tristar (Mount Roskill, Auckland, 2004–07) ; un immeuble d'appartements sur Saint Stephens Avenue (Parnell, Auckland, 2006–07) et le restaurant Yellow Tree House (Hokianga Harbour, Northland, 2008, publié ici). Ils travaillent actuellement à des installations de formation pour la Marine à Shakespeare's Point (Whangaparaoa Peninsula, Auckland, 2005–) et sur le projet du Musée des artefacts d'Océanie (Bora Bora, Tahiti, 2008–), toutes en Nouvelle-Zélande, sauf mention contraire.

YELLOW TREE HOUSE

Hokianga Harbour, Northland, New Zealand, 2008

Address: 168 West Coast Road, RD1 Kohukohu Hokianga Northland, New Zealand, +64 9 405 5855, www.treehouse.co.nz
Floor area: 44 m². Client: Yellow Pages Group. Cost: €320 000

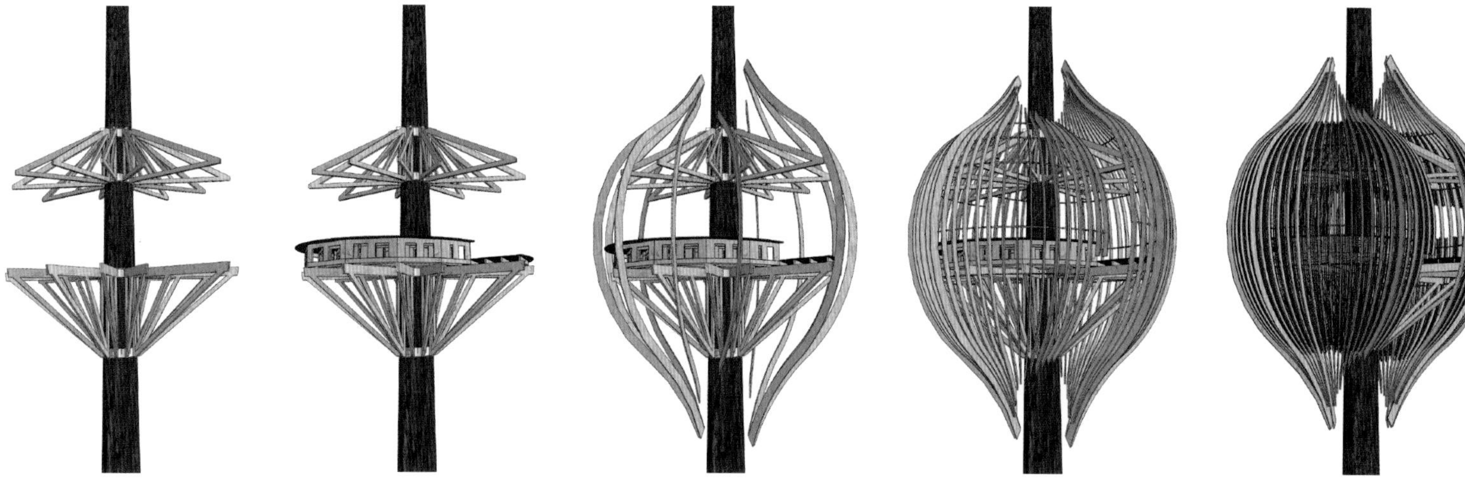

The surprising nautilus-shell design of the restaurant is fully visible in the drawings above, showing how the structure is wrapped around the tree.

Die erstaunliche Gestaltung des Restaurants in Form einer Nautilusschnecke ist in den Zeichnungen oben gut erkennbar; sie zeigen, wie das Gebäude sich um den Baum windet.

Ci-dessus : dessins de la structure de cet étonnant restaurant en forme de nautile et de son enveloppement autour du tronc d'un arbre.

The architects explain: "It's not often that a commission to design a tree house is offered, so when Colenso BBDO—on behalf of Yellow Pages—briefed Pacific Environments Architects for a 'reality' TV advert for an off-the-wall functioning restaurant, Pacific Environments jumped at the opportunity." The concept of this structure was to find all of the products and services required through Yellow Pages listings. A 40-meter-high redwood tree, 1.7 meters in diameter at its base, located north of Auckland, was selected for the project. The architects describe the site, in an open meadow near a stream at the edge of the woods, as "enchanted." Their design "has loose similarities to a seashell with the open ends spiraling to the center. It's the tree house we all dreamed of as children but could only do as an adult fantasy." The access to the restaurant is through a 60-meter-long tree-top walkway. Despite its unexpected location, the restaurant seats 18 people and staff, and includes a bar. The architects also had to take into account camera angles for the advertisements to be filmed there. Kitchen and toilet facilities are located at ground level. The split-level floor of the restaurant is set no less than 10 meters above the ground. The structure was completed in December 2008.

Die Architekten erklären: „Es passiert nicht oft, dass einem der Entwurf für ein Baumhaus angeboten wird. Pacific Environments Architects ergriffen daher sofort die Gelegenheit, als Colenso BBDO ihnen – im Namen von Yellow Pages – den Auftrag für ein schräges, für einen ‚Reality-TV'-Spot vorgesehenes Restaurant erteilten." Das Konzept für dieses Gebäude bestand darin, alle erforderlichen Produkte und Dienstleistungen durch die Yellow Pages, die Gelben Seiten, zu finden. Für das Projekt wurde ein nördlich von Auckland stehender, 40 m hoher Redwoodbaum mit einem Basisdurchmesser von 1,7 m ausgewählt. Die Architekten schildern das an einem Fluss gelegene, offene Wiesengelände am Waldrand als „bezaubernd". Ihr Entwurf hat „entfernte Ähnlichkeit mit einer Meeresmuschel, deren Enden sich zum Mittelpunkt drehen. Es ist das Baumhaus, von dem wir alle als Kinder träumten, das wir aber erst als Erwachsenenfantasie verwirklichen konnten." Der Zugang zum Restaurant erfolgt über einen 60 m langen Fußweg auf die Höhe des Baumes. Trotz seiner ungewöhnlichen Lage bietet das Lokal Platz für 18 Gäste plus Bedienung und umfasst eine Bar. Die Architekten mussten auch die Position der Kamera für die Werbeaufnahmen berücksichtigen. Küche und Toiletten befinden sich auf Geländehöhe. Das Split-Level-Geschoss des Restaurants liegt 10 m über dem Boden. Im Dezember 2008 wurde das Gebäude fertiggestellt.

Dans leur présentation de ce projet, les architectes expliquent : « Il est rare de se voir proposer la commande d'une maison dans les arbres et lorsque l'agence Colins BBDO – pour leur client les Yellow Pages – nous a briefés pour une publicité pour la télévision autour d'une idée de restaurant suspendu, nous avons sauté sur cette opportunité. » Le concept de départ était de trouver dans les « Pages jaunes » tous les produits et services requis par la construction. Un arbre (redwood) de 40 m de haut et de 1,7 m de diamètre à sa base, a été repéré au nord d'Auckland et sélectionné pour l'opération. Les architectes présentent le site – une prairie ouverte au bord d'un ruisseau à la lisière des bois – comme un « lieu enchanté ». Leurs plans « présentent certaines similarités avec un coquillage en forme de spirale ouverte. C'est la maison dans les arbres dont nous avons tous rêvé quand nous étions enfants mais que nous ne pouvons réaliser que comme une fantaisie d'adulte ». L'accès au restaurant se fait par une passerelle de 60 m de long suspendue dans le haut des arbres. Malgré cette situation surprenante, le restaurant peut recevoir dix-huit personnes (clients et personnel) et comprend également un bar. Les architectes ont également dû prendre en compte les angles de prise de vue des caméras pour le tournage du film publicitaire prévu. La cuisine et les toilettes se trouvent au rez-de-chaussée. Le plancher à deux niveaux du restaurant se trouve à 10 m au-dessus du sol. L'ensemble a été achevé en décembre 2008.

Daylight views of the Yellow Tree House and its dining space show its open, airy design.

Die Tageslichtaufnahmen des Yellow Tree House und der Speiseraum zeigen die offene, luftige Gestaltung.

Vue de jour de la Yellow Tree House et de l'espace des repas montrant son aspect ouvert et aérien.

Lighting is by ECC Lighting (Auckland), and acrylic floor lighting by PSP (Auckland). In these night views, the restaurant takes on an almost magical presence. Right, the architects' sketches of the structure.

Die Beleuchtung wurde von ECC Lighting (Auckland) ausgeführt, die Bodenbeleuchtung aus Acryl von PSP (Auckland). Auf diesen Nachtaufnahmen zeigt das Restaurant eine fast magische Präsenz. Rechts: Skizzen der Architekten vom Gebäude.

L'éclairage est de ECC Lighting (Auckland) et les spots de sol en acrylique de PSP (Auckland). Dans ces vues nocturnes, le restaurant projette une présence presque magique. À droite, des croquis structurels des architectes.

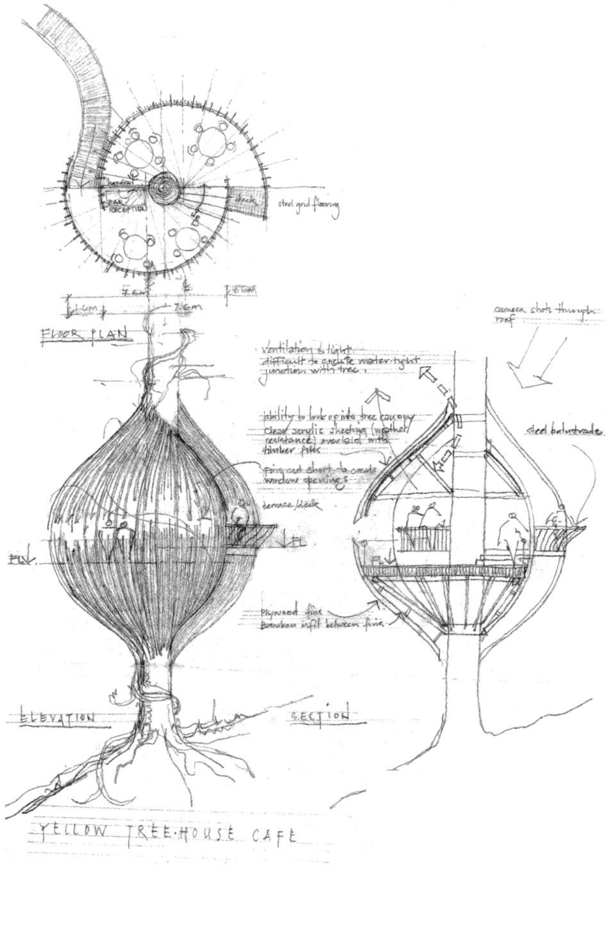

RENZO PIANO

Renzo Piano Building Workshop
34 Rue des Archives, 75004 Paris, France

Tel: + 33 1 44 61 49 00
Fax: +33 1 42 78 01 98
E-mail: france@rpbw.com
Web: www.rpbw.com

Renzo Piano Building Workshop
Via Rubens 29, 16158 Genoa, Italy

Tel: +39 01 06 17 11
Fax: +39 01 06 17 11 350
E-mail: italy@rpbw.com
Web: www.rpbw.com

RENZO PIANO was born in 1937 in Genoa, Italy. He studied at the University of Florence and at Milan's Polytechnic Institute (1964). He formed his own practice (Studio Piano) in 1965, associated with Richard Rogers (Piano & Rogers, 1971–78)—completing the Pompidou Center in Paris in 1977—and then worked with Peter Rice (Piano & Rice Associates, 1978–80), before creating the Renzo Piano Building Workshop in 1981 in Genoa and Paris. Piano received the RIBA Gold Medal in 1989. His built work includes Jean-Marie Tjibaou Cultural Center (New Caledonia, 1992–98, published here); Maison Hermès (Tokyo, Japan, 1998–2001); Rome Auditorium (Italy, 1994–2002); conversion of the Lingotto Factory Complex (Turin, Italy, 1983–2003); the Padre Pio Pilgrimage Church (San Giovanni Rotondo, Foggia, Italy, 1991–2004); the Woodruff Arts Center Expansion (Atlanta, Georgia, USA, 1999–2005); renovation and expansion of the Morgan Library (New York, New York, USA, 2000–06); and the New York Times Building (New York, New York, USA, 2005–07). More recently completed work includes the Broad Contemporary Art Museum (Phase I of the LACMA expansion, Los Angeles, California, USA, 2003–08); California Academy of Sciences (San Francisco, California, USA, 2008); the Modern Wing of the Art Institute of Chicago (Chicago, Illinois, USA, 2005–09); St. Giles Court mixed-use development (London, UK, 2002–10); the Resnick Pavilion (Phase II of the LACMA expansion, Los Angeles, USA, 2006–10); the Ronchamp Gatehouse and Monastery (France, 2006–11); the London Bridge Tower (London, UK, 2009–12); and the Tjuvholmen Icon Complex (Oslo, Norway, 2009–12).

RENZO PIANO wurde 1937 in Genua geboren. Er studierte an der Universität von Florenz und am Polytechnischen Institut von Mailand (1964). 1965 gründete er Studio Piano, später schloss er sich mit Richard Rogers zusammen (Piano & Rogers, 1971–78), mit dem er 1977 das Centre Pompidou in Paris realisierte. Im Anschluss arbeitete er mit Peter Rice (Piano & Rice Associates, 1978–80), bevor er 1981 sein Büro Renzo Piano Building Workshop, mit Sitz in Genua und Paris, gründete. Piano erhielt 1989 die RIBA-Goldmedaille. Zu seinen Arbeiten zählen u. a. das Kulturzentrum Jean-Marie Tjibaou (Neukaledonien, 1992–98, hier vorgestellt), die Maison Hermès (Tokio, 1998–2001), das Auditorium Parco della Musica in Rom (1994–2002), ein Umbau der Fiat-Werke in Lingotto (Turin, 1983–2003), die Pilgerkirche Padre Pio (San Giovanni Rotondo, Foggia, 1991–2004), eine Erweiterung des Woodruff Arts Center (Atlanta, Georgia, 1999–2005), die Sanierung und Erweiterung der Morgan Library (New York, 2000–06) sowie das New York Times Building (New York, 2005–07). Jüngere Arbeiten sind u. a. das Broad Contemporary Art Museum (1. Bauabschnitt der Erweiterung des LACMA, Los Angeles, Kalifornien, 2003–08), die California Academy of Sciences (San Francisco, Kalifornien, 2008), ein Flügel für moderne Kunst am Art Institute of Chicago (Chicago, Illinois, 2005–09), der St. Giles Court mit Mischnutzung (London, 2002–10), der Resnick Pavilion (2. Bauabschnitt der Erweiterung des LACMA, Los Angeles, 2006–10), Torhaus und Kloster von Ronchamp (Frankreich, 2006–11), der London Bridge Tower (London, 2009–12) und der Icon Complex im Quartier Tjuvholmen (Oslo, 2009–12).

Né en 1937 à Gênes, en Italie, **RENZO PIANO** fait ses études à l'université de Florence et à l'École polytechnique de Milan (1964). Il s'établit (Studio Piano) en 1965, s'associe avec Richard Rogers (Piano & Rogers, 1971–78) – terminant le Centre Pompidou à Paris in 1977 – puis travaille avec Peter Rice (Piano & Rice Associates, 1978–80) avant de créer Renzo Piano Building Workshop en 1981, à Gênes et Paris. Piano reçoit la médaille d'or du RIBA en 1989. Parmi ses réalisations, on trouve le Centre culturel Jean-Marie Tjibaou (Nouvelle-Calédonie, 1992–98, publié ici), la Maison Hermès (Tokyo, 1998–2001) ; l'auditorium Parco della Musica (Rome, 1994–2002) ; la reconversion de l'usine Lingotto (Turin, 1983–2003) ; l'église de pèlerinage Padre Pio (San Giovanni Rotondo, Foggia, Italie, 1991–2004) ; l'extension du Woodruff Arts Center (Atlanta, Georgie, 1999–2005) ; la rénovation et l'extension de la bibliothèque Morgan (New York, 2000–06) et la tour du New York Times (New York, 2005–07). Parmi les projets terminés plus récemment, on trouve le Broad Contemporary Art Museum (Phase I de l'extension du LACMA, Los Angeles, 2003–08) ; la California Academy of Sciences (San Francisco, 2008) ; l'aile moderne de l'Art Institute of Chicago (Chicago, 2005–09) ; le projet d'aménagement polyvalent St. Giles Court (Londres, 2002–10) ; le Resnick Pavilion (Phase II de l'extension du LACMA, Los Angeles, 2006–10) ; La Porterie de Notre-Dame-du-Haut et le couvent des Clarisses de Ronchamp (France, 2006–11) ; la London Bridge Tower (Londres, 2009–12) et le complexe Tjuvholmen Icon (Oslo, 2009–12).

JEAN-MARIE TJIBAOU CULTURAL CENTER

Nouméa, New Caledonia, 1992–98

Address: Rue des accords de Matignon, Tina, Nouméa, New Caledonia, +687 41 45 45, www.adck.nc. Floor area: 7650 m²
Client: Agency for the Development of Kanak Culture, Marie-Claude Tjibaou (President). Cost: €30.5 million

From the outset, Renzo Piano included the question of the identity of the Kanak people in his concept for a cultural center named after a local proponent of independence from France. Specifically non-European in its concept, this alignment of ten conical wooden "houses" connected by a glass and wood corridor drawn out over some 250 meters is surrounded by a garden of carefully chosen local plants. The ten structures are aligned in three groups according to their function: entrance, exhibition space and cafeteria; multimedia and temporary exhibitions; video rooms, and classrooms for courses in local culture. The naturally ventilated "houses" turn their curved backs to the ocean, which is to say against the prevailing winds that can attain a hurricane force of over 240 km/h. There was no question of the architect copying any local architecture—rather he has given a sensitive and unexpected contemporary interpretation to the design of this center, which is located on a small peninsula 10 km northwest of the capital, Nouméa.

Von Anfang an bezog Renzo Piano die Frage nach der Identität der Südseeinsulaner in seinen Entwurf für ein Kulturzentrum ein, das nach einem Kämpfer für die Unabhängigkeit Neukaledoniens von Frankreich benannt ist. Die Folge von zehn kegelförmigen hölzernen „Häusern", die durch einen etwa 250 m langen Korridor aus Glas und Holz miteinander verbunden sind, ist von einem Garten mit sorgfältig ausgewählten einheimischen Pflanzen umgeben. Die zehn Bauten sind entsprechend ihrer Funktion in drei Gruppen aufgeteilt: Eingang, Ausstellungsbereich und Cafeteria; Multimedia und Wechselausstellungen; Video- und Unterrichtsräume für das Studium der einheimischen Kultur. Die natürlich belüfteten „Häuser" wenden ihre gekrümmten Rückseiten dem Meer zu und trotzen dem Wind, der hier eine Geschwindigkeit von mehr als 240 km/h erreichen kann. Piano hat die regionale Architektur mit dieser Anlage auf einer kleinen Halbinsel 10 km nordwestlich der Hauptstadt Nouméa ebenso einfühlsam wie überraschend interpretiert.

Dès le départ, Renzo Piano a intégré dans son projet qui porte le nom d'un leader indépendantiste assassiné, le problème de l'identité du peuple kanak. De concept non-européen, cet alignement de dix «maisons» coniques en bois réunies par un corridor en bois et en verre, se développe sur environ 250 m de long, entouré d'un jardin de plantes locales choisies avec soin. Les deux structures sont disposées en trois groupes selon leur fonction : entrée, espace d'exposition et cafétéria ; expositions temporaires et multimédia ; salles vidéo et salles de cours sur la culture locale. Les « maisons » qui bénéficient d'une ventilation naturelle tournent leurs dos arrondi à l'océan, et donc aux vents dominants qui peuvent atteindre jusqu'à 240 km/h. Plutôt que de copier l'architecture locale, Piano a préféré en donner une interprétation sensible et inattendue. Le Centre se dresse sur une péninsule à 10 km au nord-ouest de la capitale, Nouméa.

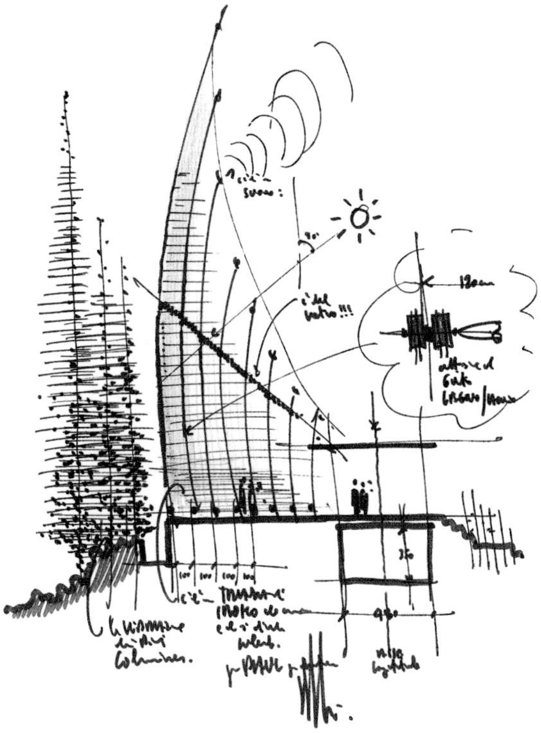

Inspired by local architecture, the complex is meant to resemble a village of wooden huts. Left, a sketch by Piano shows his attention to matters of scale and the position of the sun.

Die von der lokalen Architektur inspirierte Anlage ist einem Dorf mit Holzhütten nachempfunden. Pianos Skizze (links) zeigt, wie er die Größenverhältnisse und den Stand der Sonne berücksichtigt.

Inspiré de l'architecture locale, ce complexe culturel ressemble à un village de huttes modernes. À gauche, une esquisse de Piano montre l'attention portée aux proportions et à la position du soleil.

Despite its surprising wooden shell construction, the center makes use of the most modern technology available.

Trotz der überraschenden Außenhülle aus Holz verfügt das Zentrum über modernste Technologie.

La construction en bois n'empêche pas le centre de faire appel aux technologies les plus récentes.

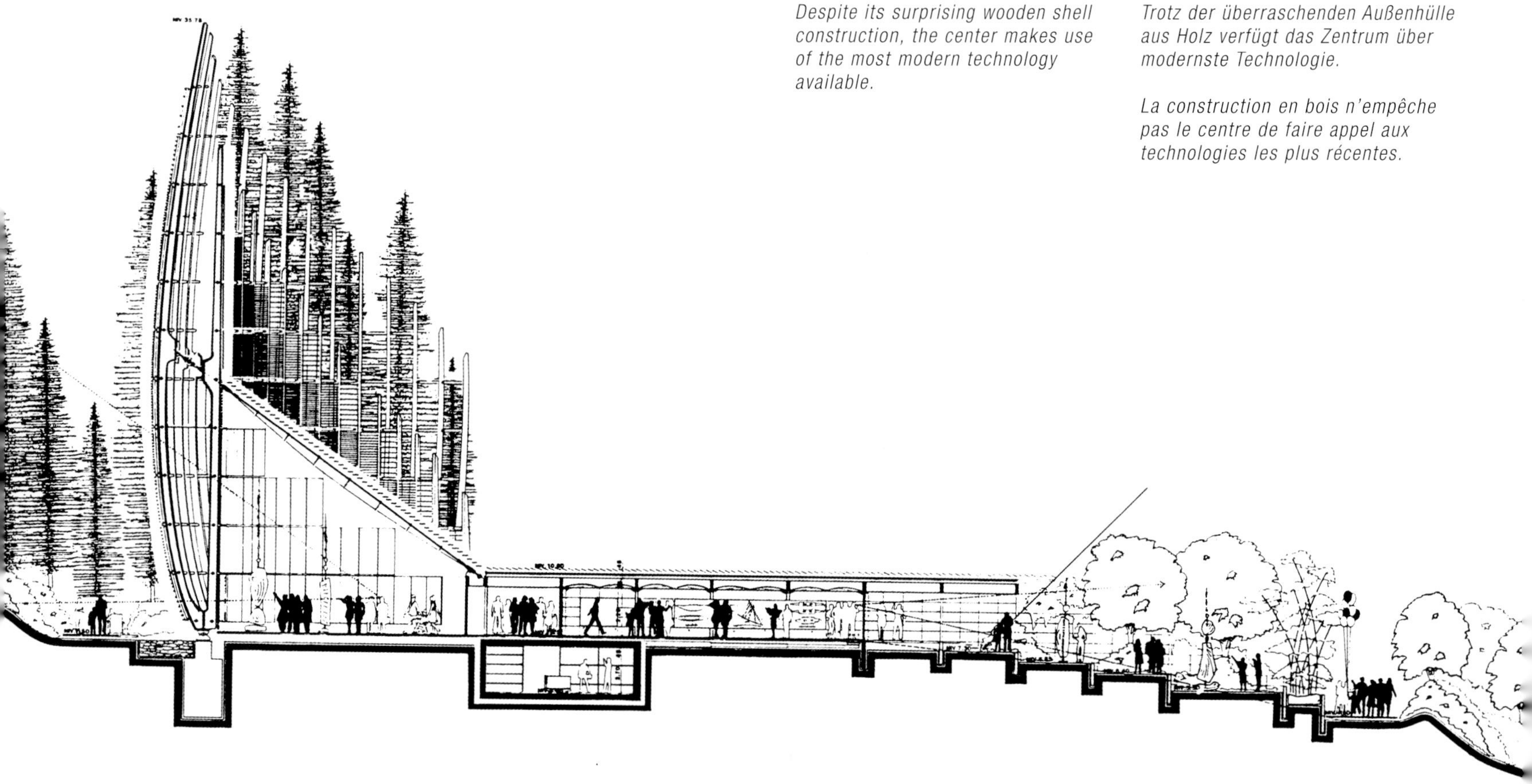

A gallery view (above) and a basic plan of the complex show how the architect combines rectilinear and circular forms in a convincing sequence. Wood is present everywhere.

Ein Blick in die Galerie (oben) und der Grundriss des Komplexes zeigen, wie der Architekt rechtwinklige und runde Formen überzeugend kombiniert. Holz ist dabei überall zu finden.

Une vue de la galerie (ci-dessus) et un plan du complexe montrent la manière dont l'architecte combine les formes rectilignes et circulaires en un ensemble pertinent. Le bois est omniprésent.

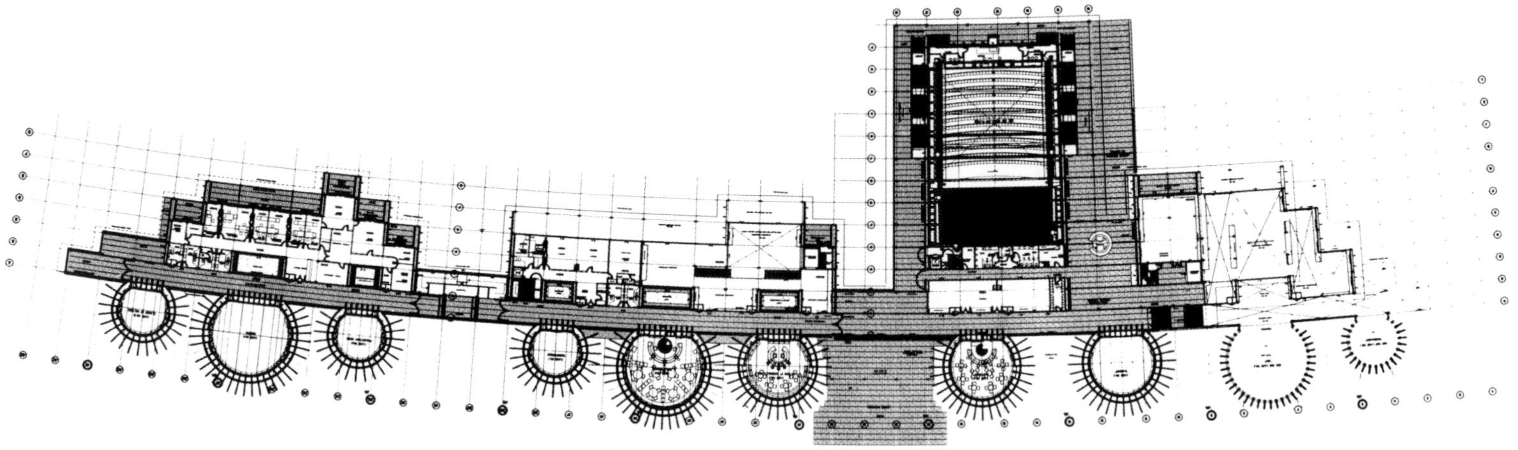

Orchideorama of the Botanical Garden of Medellín

PLAN:B + JPR/CR

Plan:b Arquitectos
Carrera 33 # 5G – 13 Ap. 301
Edificio El Atajo
Medellín, Colombia

Tel: +57 43 11 91 51
E-mail: planb.arq@gmail.com
Web: www.planbarquitectura.com

JPR/CR
J. Paul Restrepo S. Arquitectos
Calle 5G 32–103 Interior 9903
Medellín, Colombia

Tel: +57 42 68 19 51
E-mail: jpaulrpo@gmail.com
Web: www.jpaulrestrepo.net

JUAN FELIPE MESA RICO was born in 1975 in Medellín, Colombia. He studied Architecture at the Universidad Pontificia Bolivariana (Medellín, 1993–98) and received his M.Arch degree from the Universidad Politécnica de Cataluña (UPC Barcelona, 1999–2000). He founded Plan:b Arquitectos in 2000, and took Alejandro Bernal Camargo as an Associate in 2005. **ALEJANDRO BERNAL CAMARGO** was born in Medellín in 1973. He also studied at the Universidad Pontificia Bolivariana (1991–95). Their work includes a new building for the Colegio Hontanares (Medellín, Antioquia, 2006); Gráficas Diamante (Envigado, Antioquia, 2006); the Orchideorama of the Botanical Garden of Medellín (Medellín, Antioquia, 2006–07, published here); and the Time Out Bar (Medellín, Antioquia, 2008), all in Colombia. **CAMILO RESTREPO OCHOA** was born in Medellín in 1974 and graduated from the Universidad Pontificia Bolivariana in 1998. Like Juan Felipe Mesa, he received a Master's degree from the UPC in Barcelona (2005). **J. PAUL RESTREPO** was born in Medellín in 1944, graduating from the Universidad Pontificia Bolivariana in 1970. He worked with Camilo Restrepo from 2002 to 2007 at JPR/CR Arquitectos. Recent projects of JPR/CR include a hotel in Medellín.

JUAN FELIPE MESA RICO wurde 1975 in Medellín, Kolumbien, geboren. Er studierte Architektur an der Universidad Pontificia Bolivariana (Medellín, 1993–98) und machte seinen M. Arch. an der Universidad Politécnica de Cataluña (UPC Barcelona, 1999–2000). 2000 gründete er sein Büro Plan:b Arquitectos, 2005 wurde Alejandro Bernal Camargo sein Partner. **ALEJANDRO BERNAL CAMARGO** wurde 1973 ebenfalls in Medellín geboren und studierte 1991 bis 1995 an der dortigen Universidad Pontificia Bolivariana. Zu den Arbeiten des Büros zählen ein neues Gebäude für das Colegio Hontanares (Medellín, Antioquia, 2006) und für Gráficas Diamante (Envigado, Antioquia, 2006), das Orchideorama im Botanischen Garten Medellín (Medellín, Antioquia, 2006–07, hier vorgestellt) sowie die Time Out Bar (Medellín, Antioquia, 2008). **CAMILO RESTREPO OCHOA** wurde 1974 in Medellín geboren und erhielt seinen Abschluss 1998 an der Universidad Pontificia Bolivariana. Wie Juan Felipe Mesa schloss auch er einen Master an der UPC in Barcelona (2005) an. **J. PAUL RESTREPO** (geboren 1944 in Medellín) beendete sein Studium 1970 an der Universidad Pontificia Bolivariana. Von 2002 bis 2007 arbeitete er mit Camilo Restrepo bei JPR/CR Arquitectos. Zu den jüngeren Projekten von JPR/CR gehört u. a. ein Hotel in Medellín.

JUAN FELIPE MESA RICO est né en 1975 à Medellín, en Colombie. Il étudie l'architecture à l'université Pontificia Bolivariana (Medellín, 1993–98) et obtient son diplôme à l'Université polytechnique de Catalogne (UPC Barcelone, 1999–2000). Il fonde Plan:b Arquitectos en 2000, et prend Alejandro Bernal Camargo comme associé en 2005. **ALEJANDRO BERNAL CAMARGO** est né à Medellín en 1973. Il étudie également à l'université Pontificia Bolivariana (1991–95). Leurs réalisations incluent un nouveau bâtiment pour le Colegio Hontanares de Medellín (Antioquia, 2006), un autre pour Gráficas Diamante (Envigado Antioquia, 2006), l'Orchidéorama du jardin botanique de Medellín (Antioquia, 2006–07, publié ici), et le bar Time Out à Medellín (Antioquia, 2008), toutes situées en Colombie. **CAMILO RESTREPO OCHOA**, né à Medellín en 1974, obtient son diplôme de l'université Pontificia Bolivariana en 1998. Comme Juan Felipe Mesa, il obtient un master de l'UPC de Barcelone (2005). **J. PAUL RESTREPO** est né à Medellín en 1944. Il est diplômé de l'université Pontificia Bolivariana en 1970 et a travaillé avec Camilo Restrepo de 2002 à 2007 chez JPR/CR Arquitectos. Les réalisations récentes de JPR/CR incluent un hôtel à Medellín.

ORCHIDEORAMA OF THE BOTANICAL GARDEN OF MEDELLÍN

Medellín, Antioquia, Colombia, 2006–07

Address: Carrera 52, Sevilla, Medellín, Antioquia, Colombia. Area: 4200 m²
Client: Medellín Botanical Garden. Cost: $2.2 million

The orchid exhibition facilities of the Botanical Garden of Medellín are located at 1540 meters above sea level with an average temperature between 18°C and 28°C. The architects sought "not to make any distinction between natural and artificial" in their project. Their honeycomb or flower design with the size and properties of a tree permits the creations of shade or a forest garden. Water facilities are located in the hollow trunks of the supports. The Orchideorama is composed of ten "flower-tree" structures, which can be built individually, allowing the system to grow or respond to uncertainties, such as budgetary constraints, construction problems, or political decisions. Different areas are intended for small temporary gardens, orchids, exotic and tropical flowers, and for birds or butterflies.

Die Orchideenhäuser im Botanischen Garten von Medellín liegen 1540 m über N.N. und sind durchschnittlich mit 18 °C bis 28 °C temperiert. Den Architekten ging es darum, bei ihrem Projekt „nicht zwischen ‚natürlich' und ‚künstlich' zu unterscheiden". Die bienenwaben- bzw. blütenförmigen Konstruktionen sind in Größe und Eigenschaften mit Bäumen zu vergleichen, spenden Schatten und bilden so etwas wie einen Wald. Die Wasserversorgung ist in den hohlen Stämmen untergebracht. Das Orchideorama besteht aus zehn „Blüten-Baum"-Strukturen, die auch einzeln errichtet werden können, sodass das Gesamtsystem flexibel auf Unwägbarkeiten wie Budgetbeschränkungen, technische Probleme oder politische Entscheidungen reagieren kann. Geplant sind verschiedene Bereiche für kleine temporäre Gärten, Orchideen, exotische und tropische Gewächse sowie Vögel und Schmetterlinge.

Les installations d'exposition des orchidées du jardin botanique de Medellín sont situées à 1540 m d'altitude et sont soumises à une température moyenne comprise entre 18°C et 28°C. Les architectes ont cherché à « ne faire aucune distinction entre naturel et artificiel » dans leur projet. Leur projet d'éléments arborescents, en forme de nid d'abeille ou de fleurs, permet de créer un jardin d'ombre ou un jardin forestier. Les équipements d'arrosage sont logés dans les troncs creux des supports. L'Orchidéorama est composé de dix « arbres-fleurs » pouvant être construits individuellement, ce qui permet au système de croître ou de s'adapter aux incertitudes des contraintes budgétaires, des problèmes de construction ou des décisions politiques. Des zones différentes sont affectées à des petits jardins temporaires d'orchidées, de fleurs exotiques ou tropicales, ou à des espaces pour les oiseaux et les papillons.

Left, a site plan shows the Orchideorama right of center. Right, an aerial photo of the site, and above, a ground-level view of the structures.

Der Lageplan links zeigt das Orchideorama auf der rechten Seite. Rechts eine Luftaufnahme des Areals, oben ein Blick auf die Bauten aus der Froschperspektive.

À gauche, un plan de situation montre l'Orchidéorama juste au centre. À droite, une photo aérienne du site, et ci-dessus, une vue des structures prise du niveau du sol.

Clearly inspired by the vegetal forms that surround them, the Orchideorama structures fit well into the environment and shelter plants and visitors.

Eindeutig formal inspiriert von der Vegetation, fügen sich die Bauten des Orchideorama ideal in ihre Umgebung und bieten Pflanzen und Besuchern Schutz.

Nettement inspirées des formes végétales qui l'entourent, les structures de l'Orchidéorama s'intègrent bien dans l'environnement et abritent plantes et visiteurs.

ANTOINE PREDOCK

Antoine Predock Architect PC
300 12th Street NW
Albuquerque, NM 87102, USA

Tel: +1 505 843 7390 / Fax: +1 505 243 6254
E-mail: studio@apredock.com / Web: www.predock.com

Born in 1936 in Lebanon, Missouri, **ANTOINE PREDOCK** studied at the University of New Mexico and received his B.Arch from Columbia University in 1962. He has been the Principal of Antoine Predock Architect PC since 1967. He was a Visiting Lecturer at SCI-Arc from 1995 to 2000 and has held teaching positions at Harvard, Clemson, and UCLA. In 2006 Antoine Predock received the AIA Gold Medal. His notable buildings include the Zuber House (Phoenix, Arizona, 1989); the Nelson Fine Arts Center, Arizona State University (Tempe, Arizona, 1990); the Hotel Santa Fe, Euro Disney, (Marne-la-Vallée, France, 1992); the Classroom, Laboratory & Administration Building, California Polytechnic State University (Pomona, California 1993); the American Heritage Center and Art Museum (University of Wyoming, Laramie, Wyoming, 1993); the Civic Arts Plaza, Thousand Oaks Performing Arts Center and City Hall (Thousand Oaks, California, 1994); the Ventana Vista Elementary School (Tucson, Arizona, 1994); the Arizona Science Center (Phoenix, Arizona, 1996); the Gateway Center, University of Minnesota (Minneapolis, Minnesota, 2000). More recent work includes the Tacoma Art Museum (Tacoma, Washington, 2003); the Flint RiverQuarium (Albany, Georgia, 2004); the Austin City Hall and Public Plaza (Austin, Texas, 2004); the Student Activity and Recreation Center, Ohio State University (Columbus, Ohio, 2006). Current work includes the Logjam House (Rio Blanco, Colorado, 2007, published here); the Doudna Fine Arts Center, Eastern Illinois University (Charleston, Illinois, 2007); the Science Canyon, Academy School (Colorado Springs, Colorado, 2008); the Canadian Museum for Human Rights (Winnipeg, Manitoba, Canada, 2010); and the National Palace Museum (Chiayi County, Taiwan, 2011), all in the USA unless stated otherwise.

ANTOINE PREDOCK wurde 1936 in Lebanon, Missouri, geboren und studierte an der University of New Mexico. 1962 erhielt er seinen B. Arch. an der Columbia University. Seit 1967 ist er leitender Partner bei Antoine Predock Architect PC. Zwischen 1995 und 2000 war er Gastdozent an der SCI-Arc und bekleidete verschiedene weitere Positionen als Lehrender in Harvard, Clemson und an der UCLA. 2006 erhielt Antoine Predock die Goldmedaille der AIA. Zu seinen wichtigsten Bauten zählen das Zuber House (Phoenix, Arizona, 1989), das Nelson Fine Arts Center an der Arizona State University (Tempe, Arizona, 1990), das Hotel Santa Fe in Euro Disney (Marne-la-Vallée, Frankreich, 1992), ein Lehrsaal-, Labor- und Verwaltungsgebäude für die California Polytechnic State University (Pomona, Kalifornien, 1993), das American Heritage Center and Art Museum (University of Wyoming, Laramie, Wyoming, 1993), die Civic Arts Plaza am Performing Arts Center und das Rathaus von Thousand Oaks (Thousand Oaks, Kalifornien, 1994), die Ventana Vista Elementary School (Tucson, Arizona, 1994), das Arizona Science Center (Phoenix, Arizona, 1996) und das Gateway Center an der University of Minnesota (Minneapolis, Minnesota, 2000). Jüngere Projekte sind u. a. das Tacoma Art Museum (Tacoma, Washington, 2003), das Flint RiverQuarium (Albany, Georgia, 2004), die Austin City Hall und Public Plaza (Austin, Texas, 2004), das Student Activity and Recreation Center an der Ohio State University (Columbus, Ohio, 2006). Zu den aktuellen Projekten zählen das Logjam House (Rio Blanco, Colorado, 2007, hier vorgestellt), das Doudna Fine Arts Center an der Eastern Illinois University (Charleston, Illinois, 2007), der Science Canyon für die Academy School (Colorado Springs, Colorado, 2008), das Canadian Museum for Human Rights (Winnipeg, Manitoba, Kanada, 2010) sowie das Nationale Palastmuseum (Chiayi, Taiwan, 2011).

Né en 1936 à Lebanon, Missouri, **ANTOINE PREDOCK** étudie à l'université du Nouveau-Mexique et obtient son B.Arch. à l'université Columbia (1962). Il dirige Antoine Predock Architect PC depuis 1967. Il a été professeur invité au SCI-Arc de 1995 à 2000 et a également enseigné ponctuellement à Harvard, Clemson et l'UCLA. En 2006, il reçoit la médaille d'or de l'AIA. Parmi ses réalisations les plus connues : la Zuber House (Phoenix, Arizona, 1989) ; le Nelson Fine Arts Center, Arizona State University (Tempe, Arizona, 1990) ; l'hôtel Santa Fe, Euro Disney, (Marne-la-Vallée, 1992) ; des salles de cours, des laboratoires et l'immeuble de l'administration de la California Polytechnic State University (Pomona, Californie, 1993) ; l'American Heritage Center and Art Museum (université du Wyoming, Laramie, Wyoming, 1993) ; le Civic Arts Plaza, Thousand Oaks Performing Arts Center and City Hall (Thousand Oaks, Californie, 1994) ; l'école élémentaire Ventana Vista (Tucson, Arizona, 1994) ; l'Arizona Science Center (Phoenix, Arizona, 1996) ; le Gateway Center, université du Minnesota (Minneapolis, Minnesota, 2000). Récemment, il a réalisé le Tacoma Art Museum (Tacoma, Washington, 2003) ; le Flint RiverQuarium (Albany, Géorgie, 2004) ; l'hôtel de ville d'Austin et une place publique (Austin, Texas, 2004) ; le Centre pour les activités et loisirs des étudiants, Ohio State University (Columbus, Ohio, 2006). Ses projets actuels sont : la Logjam House (Rio Blanco, Colorado, 2007, publiée ici) ; le Doudna Fine Arts Center, Eastern Illinois University (Charleston, Illinois, 2007) ; le Science Canyon, Academy School (Colorado Springs, Colorado, 2008) ; le Musée canadien des droits de l'homme (Winnipeg, Manitoba, 2010) et le Musée national du palais (comté de Chiayi, Taiwan, 2011), tous aux États-Unis, sauf mention contraire.

LOGJAM HOUSE

Rio Blanco, Colorado, USA, 2007

Address: not disclosed. Floor area: 269 m². Client: not disclosed
Cost: not disclosed

The house stands in solitary splendor in the forest, echoing the trees with its main volume, lifted up off the ground on trunk-sized pilotis.

In einsamer Pracht steht das Haus im Wald. Aufgeständert auf baumstammähnlichen Stützen erinnert der Hauptbau formal an die Bäume.

La maison se dresse, isolée, au milieu d'une forêt ; les pilotis aux proportions de troncs du volume principal rappellent les arbres.

The connection between the house and the forest is affirmed by an unusual use of logs that actually enter the structure.

Unterstrichen wird die Verbindung von Haus und Wald durch den ungewöhnlichen Einsatz von Holzstämmen, die den Bau regelrecht durchstoßen.

La connexion entre la maison et la forêt se renforce par la présence des grumes qui vont jusqu'à pénétrer dans la structure.

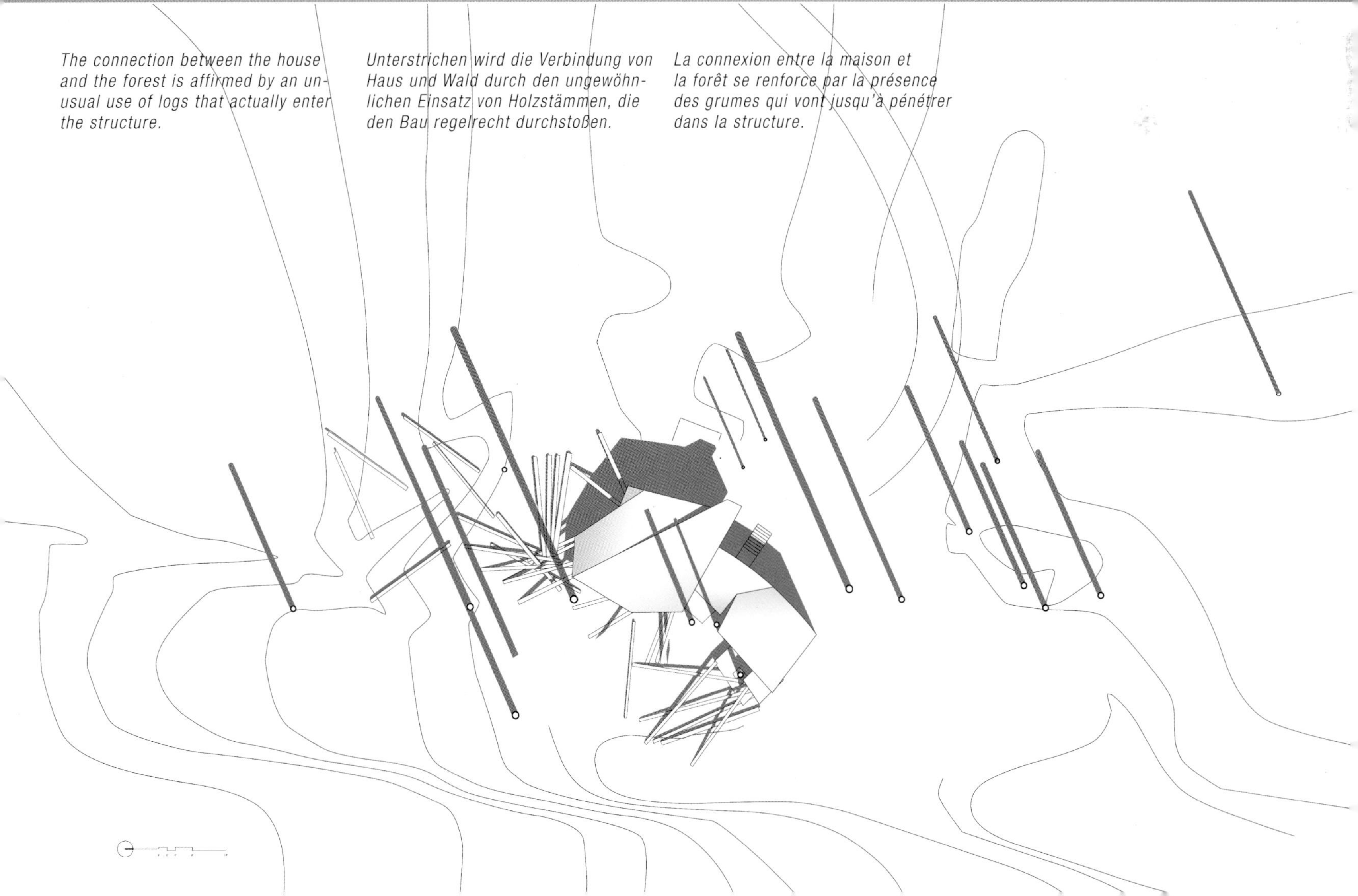

This house is located at the northeastern end of the Rio Blanco River Basin in a mountainous area occupied mostly by farms or ranches. The site includes a number of Ponderosa Pine trees. The architect imagined that at some future point these pines might be felled, "a symbolic warping of time in which the decomposed grove produces new life" in the form of this house. Large glazed surfaces allow for constant views of the trees, as do large "floating" decks on the southern and eastern sides of the house. Rather than a "formal entry," circulation into the house is through an equipment room where bicycles, skis, and other gear are displayed. The living spaces are conceived as a continuous high volume with a guest bedroom and workroom looking down into them. A glazed catwalk leads to the private areas, with the master bedroom perched high "as though it were a tree house." Predock's work often has a direct relation to the earth, and in this instance, the **LOGJAM HOUSE** rises from the trees that surround it.

Das Haus liegt am nordöstlichen Ende des Rio-Blanco-Flussbeckens in einer überwiegend mit Farmen und Ranches besiedelten Berggegend. Auf dem Grundstück stehen einige Gelbkiefern. Der Architekt malte sich aus, dass die Kiefern irgendwann in der Zukunft gefällt werden könnten, „eine symbolische Zeitschleife, in der aus dem verfallenen Wäldchen" in Gestalt des Hauses „neues Leben entsteht". Großzügig verglaste Flächen ebenso wie die „schwebenden" Terrassen an der Süd- und Ostseite des Hauses erlauben den ungehinderten Ausblick in die Bäume. Statt durch einen „offiziellen Eingangsbereich" wird der Besucher durch einen Geräteraum, in dem Fahrräder, Skier usw. untergebracht sind, ins Haus geleitet. Die Wohnbereiche wurden als kontinuierliches hohes Raumvolumen definiert, in die Gästezimmer und Arbeitsraum hinabblicken. Ein verglaster Gang führt zu den Privatbereichen hinauf, wo sich das Hauptschlafzimmer „wie ein Baumhaus" an den Bau zu klammern scheint. Predocks Projekte haben oft einen unmittelbaren Bezug zur Natur – hier erhebt sich das **LOGJAM HOUSE** aus den Bäumen seiner Umgebung.

Cette maison se trouve à l'extrémité nord-est du bassin du Rio Blanco, dans une zone montagneuse principalement occupée par des fermes ou des ranchs. Le terrain est planté d'un certain nombre de pins de Ponderosa. L'architecte a pensé que, dans un certain laps de temps, ces arbres pourraient être coupés, comme « un glissement symbolique du temps dans lequel la futaie décomposée produit une vie nouvelle », sous la forme de cette maison. Les vastes surfaces vitrées offrent des vues sur les arbres, de même que les grandes terrasses « flottantes » des côtés sud et est. L'entrée ne se fait pas par une pièce formelle, mais par une sorte de vestiaire où sont rangés les vélos, les skis et autres accessoires de sports. Un atelier et une chambre d'amis à l'étage donnent sur les espaces de vie formant un volume continu de grande hauteur. Une coursive vitrée conduit à la partie plus privative. La chambre principale est perchée tout en haut « comme une maison dans les arbres ». Le travail de Predock entretient souvent une relation directe avec la terre. Ici, la **LOGJAM HOUSE** semble s'élever naturellement parmi les arbres qui l'entourent.

The logs that are seen to enter the house from the outside penetrate the house and give it a more "rustic" appearance than the clean white walls and sophisticated materials employed elsewhere.

Die Stämme, die das Haus von außen durchstoßen, verleihen dem Gebäude eine rustikalere Atmosphäre als die schlichten weißen Wände und eleganteren Materialien, die sonst zum Einsatz kommen.

Les grumes que l'on voit pénétrer la maison lui donnent un aspect « rustique » qui ponctue les murs blancs et les matériaux sophistiqués utilisés par ailleurs.

A drawing below shows the pattern akin to felled trees that represents the penetration of the architecture by tree trunks. From some angles (right) the house appears less intentionally forest-bound.

Die Zeichnung unten visualisiert die Durchstoßpunkte der Stämme durch den Bau, ein Muster, das an gefällte Bäume erinnert. Aus bestimmten Blickwinkeln (rechts) scheint das Haus weitaus weniger an die waldige Umgebung gebunden.

Le plan de composition ci-dessous évoque des arbres tombés qui expliquent la pénétration de la maison par les grumes. Sous certains angles (à droite), la maison est moins liée à son environnement.

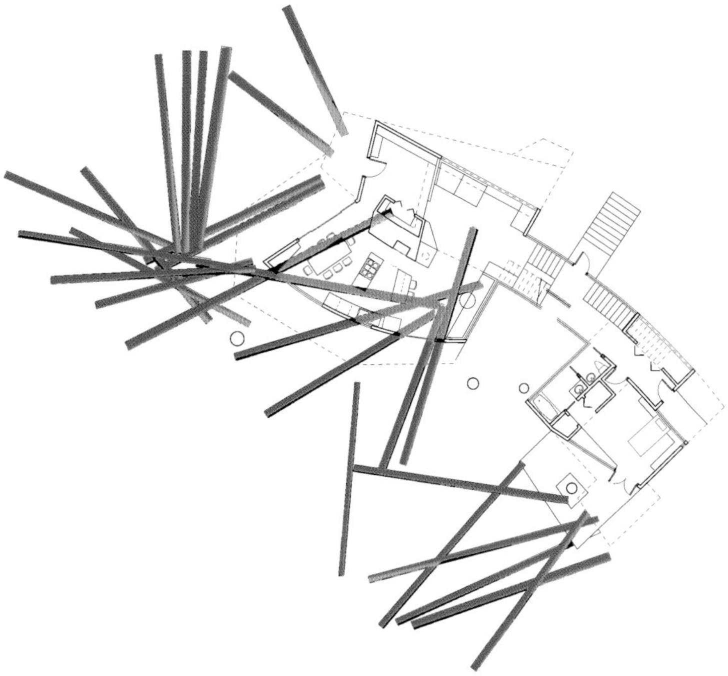

ARNE QUINZE

Arne Quinze
Hooglatemweg 18b
9830 Sint-Martens-Latem
Belgium

Tel: +32 486 29 51 21
E-mail: info@arnequinze.com
Web: www.arnequinze.com

ARNE QUINZE was born in 1971 in Belgium and lives and works in Sint-Martens-Latem, Belgium, and Shanghai, China. While most biographies of architects or designers tend to emphasize their university degrees, Quinze's CV on his Web site reads in part: "Lacking a sterling education and shaped by the street life of his youth, Arne Quinze hung out with a motorcycle gang." In the 1980s, he began working as a graffiti artist but never finished an official art education. Perhaps because he is self-taught, Arne Quinze seems to see no reason why design, architecture, and art cannot coexist and be created by the same person. This fact is borne out in his numerous pieces of installation art, often executed on a very large scale in wood. His work includes the installation "Uchronia: Message out of the Future" at the Burning Man Festival (Black Rock City, Black Rock Desert, Nevada, 2006); the interior design of L'Eclaireur, a women's boutique (Paris, France, 2009, published here); "The Visitor" (Beirut, Lebanon, 2009); "Red Beacon" (Jing'An Sculpture Park, Shanghai, China, 2010); "Camille" (Rouen, France, 2010, also published here); "My Home My House My Stilthouse" (Louisiana Museum, Humlebaek, Denmark, 2011); "Chaos Wind," a 2013 installation in Shanghai; and a "Tribute to Alexander Calder" (Mamac, Nice, France, 2013). His exhibition "Chaos in Motion" was also held at the Mamac in 2013.

ARNE QUINZE wurde 1971 in Belgien geboren. Er lebt und arbeitet im belgischen Sint-Martens-Latem und in Schanghai. Während die meisten Architekten und Designer ihre Universitätsabschlüsse in den Vordergrund stellen, liest sich der Lebenslauf von Quinze im Internet auszugsweise folgendermaßen: „Arne Quinze hat keine solide Ausbildung absolviert, geprägt hat ihn dafür seine Jugend, in der er mit einer Motorradgang rumhing." In den 1980er-Jahren arbeitete er als Graffitikünstler, schloss jedoch nie eine formale Kunstausbildung ab. Vielleicht weil er Autodidakt ist, sieht Quinze keinen Grund, warum Design, Architektur und Kunst nicht miteinander verbunden und von einer einzigen Person geschaffen werden können. Sinnfällig wird dies angesichts zahlreicher, oft großformatiger Kunstinstallationen aus Holz. Zu seinen Arbeiten gehören die Installationen „Uchronia: Message out of the Future" im Rahmen des Burning Man Festival (Black Rock City, Black Rock Desert, Nevada, 2006), die Innenarchitektur der Boutique L'Eclaireur (Paris, 2009, hier vorgestellt), „The Visitor" (Beirut, Libanon, 2009), „Red Beacon" (Skulpturenpark Jing'An, Schanghai, 2010), „Camille" (Rouen, Frankreich, 2010, ebenfalls hier vorgestellt), „My Home My House My Stilthouse" (Louisiana Museum, Humlebaek, Dänemark, 2011) sowie die Installation „Chaos Wind" (Schanghai, 2013) und „Tribute to Alexander Calder" (Mamac, Nizza, 2013). Im Mamac fand 2013 zudem die Ausstellung „Chaos in Motion" statt.

ARNE QUINZE est né en Belgique en 1971 ; il vit et travaille à Laethem-Saint-Martin, Belgique, et à Shanghai, Chine. Alors que la plupart des biographies d'architecte ou de designer ont tendance à privilégier leur diplôme universitaire, on peut lire sur le curriculum vitae de Quinze présenté sur son site Internet les informations suivantes : « N'ayant pas bénéficié d'une excellente formation et façonné pendant sa jeunesse par la vie de la rue, Arne Quinze fréquentait une bande de motards. » Dans les années 1980, il a commencé à travailler comme artiste graffiteur, mais n'a jamais achevé de formation artistique officielle. Peut-être parce qu'il est autodidacte, Arne Quinze ne voit pas pourquoi le design, l'architecture et l'art ne pourraient pas coexister et être créés par la même personne. Cela se manifeste dans ses nombreuses installations artistiques, souvent réalisées en bois et à très grande échelle. On peut citer parmi ses œuvres l'installation *Uchronia: Message out of the Future* au festival Burning Man (Black Rock City, Black Rock Desert, Nevada, 2006) ; le design intérieur de la boutique pour femmes L'Éclaireur (Paris, France, 2009, publiée ici) ; *The Visitor* (Beyrouth, Liban, 2009) ; *Red Beacon* (parc de sculptures de Jing'An, Shanghai, Chine, 2010) ; *Camille* (Rouen, France, 2010, également publiée ici) ; *My Home My House My Stilthouse* (Musée d'art moderne Louisiana, Humlebaek, Danemark, 2011) et une installation présentée en 2013 à Shanghai, *Chaos Wind*, mais aussi *Tribute to Alexander Calder* (Mamac, Nice, France, 2013). Son exposition « Chaos in Motion » a aussi eu lieu au Mamac en 2013.

L'ECLAIREUR

Paris, France, 2009

Address: 40 Rue de Sévigné, 75003 Paris, France, +33 1 48 87 10 22, www.leclaireur.com
Area: 435 m². Client: L'Eclaireur. Cost: not disclosed

The designers have inserted images of eyes into the irregular, sculptural walls seen in the image below.

Der Designer integrierte Bilder von Augen in die unregelmäßigen, skulpturalen Wandflächen (unten).

Le designer a inséré des images d'yeux dans les murs sculpturaux aux formes irrégulières (ci-dessous).

Arne Quinze is known for his impromptu structures usually made from scrap wood (above). Below, a drawing of the floor plan with its irregular display spaces.

Arne Quinze ist bekannt für seine spontan wirkenden Konstruktionen aus Altholz (oben). Unten eine Zeichnung des Grundrisses mit der unregelmäßigen Verkaufsfläche.

Arne Quinze est connu pour ses structures temporaires généralement en bois de récupération (ci-dessus). Ci-dessous, plan au sol et implantation des espaces de présentation de formes irrégulières.

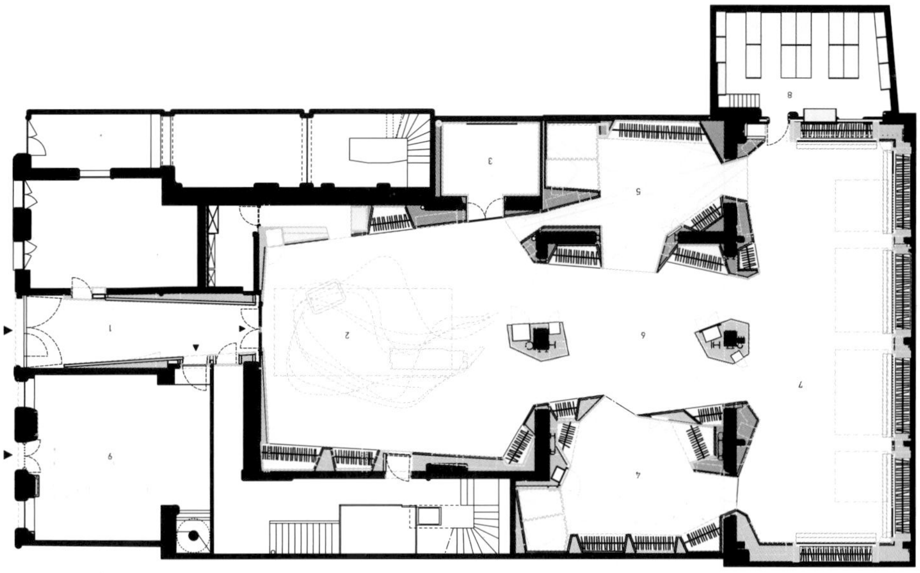

Located on Rue de Sévigné in the fourth arrondissement of Paris, **L'ECLAIREUR** is a haute-couture women's boutique. The designer used more than two tons of recycled wood planks, cardboard, and used aluminum print-plates to create the décor of the store. He states: "The interior is conceived by the perimeter the sculptured walls follow to envelop the space. Though composed of recycled material, the walls have a luxurious finish. The effect is not only visual but also tactile and puts the first-time visitor off guard." As though in an intimate dressing room, the visitor plays a privileged role in the art of discovering and "unveiling" the exposed goods, as though they might well be works of art. This scenography reaches its height in the back area of the store, lit only by sky domes and a video installation.

L'ECLAIREUR, gelegen an der Rue de Sévigné im 4. Arrondissement von Paris, ist eine Boutique für Haute-Couture-Damenmode. Der Designer verarbeitete über zwei Tonnen recycelte Baubretter, Pappe und ausgemusterte Druckplatten aus Aluminium für die Gestaltung des Innenraums. Er erklärt: „Das Interieur wird durch die Kontur der skulptural gestalteten Wände definiert, die den Raum umgeben. Trotz der recycelten Materialien wirkt die Oberfläche der Wände edel. Dieser Effekt ist nicht ausschließlich visuell, sondern ebensosehr taktil und trifft den Besucher beim ersten Mal völlig unvorbereitet." Wie in einem intimen Ankleidezimmer spielt der Besucher die Hauptrolle als Entdecker und „Enthüller" der ausgestellten Mode – gerade so, als handle es sich um Kunstwerke. Ihren Höhepunkt erreicht die Szenografie im hinteren Bereich des Ladens, der nur durch kuppelartige Dachöffnungen und eine Videoinstallation erhellt wird.

Rue de Sévigné dans le 4ᵉ arrondissement de Paris, **L'ÉCLAIREUR** est une boutique de prêt-à-porter féminin de créateurs. Le designer a utilisé plus de deux tonnes de planches de bois de récupération, de carton et de plaques d'impression en aluminium pour en créer le décor : « L'intérieur a été conçu à partir de son périmètre, les murs sculptés suivant l'enveloppe de l'espace. Bien qu'en matériaux recyclés, ils donnent une impression d'une finition luxueuse. L'effet n'est pas seulement visuel mais également tactile et surprend le client venu pour la première fois », explique Arne Quinze. Comme dans un dressing-room personnel qui lui serait ouvert, le visiteur détient un rôle privilégié : il peut découvrir et « dévoiler » les articles exposés, comme s'il s'agissait d'œuvres d'art. Cette scénographie atteint son sommet dans le fond de la boutique, uniquement éclairé par des verrières en coupole et une installation vidéo.

Occasional touches of color enliven spaces that are based on richly articulated surfaces and contrasted lighting.

Farbakzente hier und da beleben den Raum, der von den ausdrucksstark artikulierten Flächen und kontrastreicher Beleuchtung lebt.

Quelques touches de couleur animent les espaces construits à partir de plans richement articulés et d'éclairages contrastés.

Curious objects or books alternate with images of eyes or the actual merchandise of the store.

Es entsteht ein Wechselspiel zwischen ungewöhnliche Objekten, Büchern, Bildern von Augen und dem eigentlichen Warenangebot des Geschäfts.

Des objets curieux ou des livres alternent avec des images de regards et les articles en vente.

Shoes or bags are placed in the completely irregular series of wall niches seen in the image to the left.

In den konsequent unregelmäßigen Wandnischen (links) werden Schuhe und Taschen präsentiert.

Les chaussures et les sacs sont disposés dans des niches murales de forme complètement irrégulière (à gauche).

"CAMILLE"

Rouen, France, 2010

Area: 137 m (length) x 27 m (width)
Client: City of Rouen. Cost: not disclosed

"CAMILLE" was built on the Boieldieu Bridge in Rouen as part of a 2010 festival commemorating the emergence of the Impressionist art school in the region. Arne Quinze chose the location, which required the closing of the bridge for the duration of the festival, even though 40% of the vehicular traffic of the city normally crosses the Seine River at this point. Pedestrian crossing was of course permitted, and it is estimated that two million people saw the work during the two months that it was in place. Arne Quinze emphasizes that in this way, his work brought together the residents of Rouen, who are otherwise accustomed to having their city divided by the river. Although residents did launch a petition to remove the work, the city subsequently looked into the possibility of placing art installations nearby on the riverbank. The designer lists the materials required for the project: 45 000 meters of Douglas pine wood, screws, paint, and Flame Safe© fireproof treatment.

„CAMILLE" wurde 2010 im Rahmen eines Festivals errichtet, das an die Anfänge des Impressionismus in der Region erinnern sollte. Arne Quinze wählte die Boieldieu-Brücke als Standort, obwohl während des Festivals damit ein Verkehrsweg gesperrt werden musste, auf dem 40 % des städtischen Verkehrs die Seine überquerten. Fußgänger konnten die Brücke weiterhin nutzen. Schätzungsweise zwei Millionen Menschen sahen die Arbeit während ihrer zweimonatigen Ausstellung. Arne Quinze betont, sie habe die Bewohner Rouens, die ansonsten daran gewöhnt seien, in einer durch den Fluss getrennten Stadt zu leben, zusammengebracht. Zwar lancierten Bewohner eine Petition zur Entfernung der Arbeit. Dennoch prüfte die Stadt nach Ablauf der zwei Monate, ob „Camille" unweit am Flussufer platziert werden könne. Dem Architekten zufolge kamen 45 000 m Douglasienholz, Schrauben, Farbe und ein Flame-Safe©-Anstrich zum Einsatz.

« CAMILLE » a été construit sur le pont Boieldieu à Rouen dans le cadre d'un festival organisé en 2010 pour commémorer l'émergence du mouvement impressionniste dans la région. Arne Quinze a choisi le site – ce qui a nécessité la fermeture du pont pendant toute la durée du festival – même si 40 % du trafic automobile de la ville traverse en temps normal la Seine à ce niveau. La traversée piétonne a évidemment été autorisée ; on estime que deux millions de personnes ont vu l'œuvre au cours des deux mois d'installation. Arne Quinze insiste sur le fait que son œuvre a réuni les habitants de Rouen, si habitués à voir leur ville divisée par le fleuve. Bien que des résidents aient lancé une pétition pour déplacer l'œuvre, la ville a par la suite cherché la possibilité de mettre en place des installations artistiques à proximité de la rive. Le designer dresse la liste des matériaux nécessaires pour le projet : 45 000 m de pin Douglas, des vis, de la peinture et un traitement ignifugeant Flame Safe©.

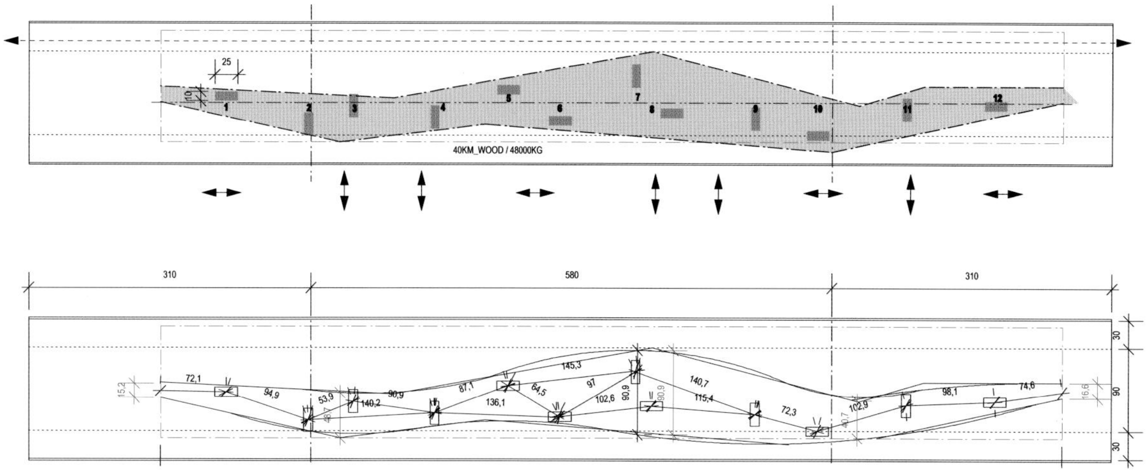

The complex wood installations of Arne Quinze have graced a number of cities around the world, from Brussels to Beirut. Here, the work appears to float above the river and the bridge.

Die aufwendigen Holzkonstruktionen von Arne Quinze waren von Brüssel bis Beirut weltweit in einer Vielzahl von Städten zu sehen. Hier scheint seine Arbeit über Fluss und Brücke zu schweben.

Les complexes installations en bois d'Arne Quinze ont embelli de nombreuses villes dans le monde, de Bruxelles à Beyrouth. Ici, l'œuvre semble flotter au-dessus de la rivière et du pont.

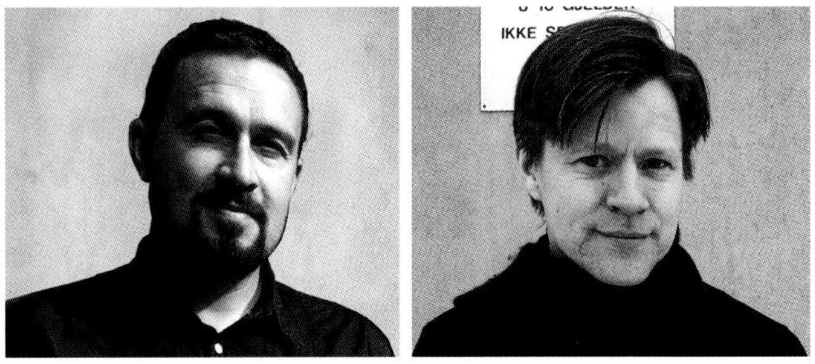

RINTALA EGGERTSSON

Rintala Eggertsson Architects
Bentsebrugata 13f
0476 Oslo
Norway

Tel: +47 22 22 03 22
E-mail: post@ri-eg.com
Web: www.rintalaeggertsson.com

Rintala Eggertsson Architects was established in 2007 by the Finnish architect **SAMI RINTALA** and the Icelandic architect **DAGUR EGGERTSSON**. Today the office also includes the architects Vibeke Jenssen, Kaori Watanabe, and Masae Asada. Sami Rintala was born in 1969 in Helsinki. He obtained his degree in architecture from the Helsinki University of Technology (1990–99). Dagur Eggertsson was born in 1965 in Reykjavik. He obtained his M.Arch from the Helsinki University of Technology (1995–97), having previously studied at the Oslo School of Architecture and Design (1986–92). Seeking to "occupy the space between architecture and public art," their work has been seen in the Victoria and Albert Museum in London, the MAXXI Museum in Rome, and in the Venice Biennale. Their work includes the "Ark Booktower" (Victoria and Albert Museum, London, UK, 2010); "Into the Landscape" (Seljord, Telemark, Norway, 2010, published here); an arboretum (Gjövik, Norway, 2011); Seljord Watchtower (Seljord, Telemark, Norway, 2011); Suidal Bridge (Suidal, Norway, 2013); and the Zhoushan Art Gallery (Zhoushan, Zhejiang, China, currently in development).

Rintala Eggertsson Architects wurde 2007 von dem finnischen Architekten **SAMI RINTALA** und dem isländischen Architekten **DAGUR EGGERTSSON** gegründet. Inzwischen sind Vibeke Jenssen, Kaori Watanabe und Masae Asada dazugestoßen. Sami Rintala wurde 1969 in Helsinki geboren und absolvierte ein Architekturstudium an der Technischen Universität Helsinki (1990–99). Dagur Eggertsson wurde 1965 in Reykjavik geboren und schloss sein Studium an der Technischen Universität Helsinki (1995–97) mit einem M. Arch. ab, nachdem er bereits an der Hochschule für Architektur und Design in Oslo studiert hatte (1986–92). Die Arbeiten der Architekten, deren Ziel es ist, „den Raum zwischen Architektur und öffentlicher Kunst zu besetzen", waren im Victoria and Albert Museum in London zu sehen, im Museum MAXXI in Rom und auf der Biennale in Venedig. Zu ihren Projekten gehören u. a. der „Ark Booktower" (Victoria and Albert Museum, London, 2010), „Into the Landscape" (Seljord, Telemark, Norwegen, 2010, hier vorgestellt), ein Arboretum (Gjövik, Norwegen, 2011), der Seljord-Aussichtsturm (Seljord, Telemark, Norwegen, 2011), die Suidal-Brücke (Suidal, Norwegen, 2013) und die Zhoushan Art Gallery (Zhoushan, Zhejiang, China; derzeit in Arbeit).

Rintala Eggertsson Architects a été fondé en 2007 par l'architecte finlandais **SAMI RINTALA** et l'architecte islandais **DAGUR EGGERTSSON**. L'agence comprend aujourd'hui également les architectes Vibeke Jenssen, Kaori Watanabe et Masae Asada. Sami Rintala est né en 1969 à Helsinki. Il a obtenu son diplôme d'architecte à l'Université technologique de Helsinki (1990–99). Dagur Eggertsson est né en 1965 à Reykjavik. Il a obtenu son M.Arch. à l'Université technologique de Helsinki (1995–97) après des études à l'École d'architecture et de design d'Oslo (1986–92). Visant à « occuper l'espace entre architecture et art public », leur œuvre a été exposée au Victoria and Albert Museum de Londres, au musée MAXXI à Rome et à la Biennale de Venise. Parmi leurs réalisations figurent l'*Ark Booktower* (Victoria & Albert Museum, Londres, 2010) ; *Into the Landscape* (Seljord, Telemark, Norvège, 2010, publié ici) ; un arboretum (Gjövik, Norvège, 2011) ; la tour d'observation à Seljord (Seljord, Telemark, Norvège, 2011) ; le pont Suidal (Suidal, Norvège, 2013) et la galerie d'art Zhoushan (Zhoushan, Zhejiang, Chine, en cours de réalisation).

"INTO THE LANDSCAPE"

Seljord, Telemark, Norway, 2010

Area: 39 m². Client: Seljord Municipality
Cost: €25 000

The town of Seljord is located next to a lake where a serpent is said to dwell. With tourism in mind, the municipality decided in 2008 to use this myth as a point of departure for a development program that Rintala Eggertsson and curators Springer kulturstudio were asked to manage. The project was divided into two parts: three small installations in the middle and southeast section of the lake, and a main viewpoint at the southwest end of the lake close to the small town. All of the structures were made essentially with wood. The first part of the program was organized as a design-build workshop with art and architecture students and teachers from the Nuova Accademia di Belle Arte and Politecnico in Milan and students from the Norwegian Theater Academy under the leadership of Rintala Eggertsson. The architects explain: "The workshop was thematically focused on the issue of anchoring man-made installations to characteristic features in the landscape without dominating them. The three installations are presented under the title **'INTO THE LANDSCAPE'** on our Web site."

Die Gemeinde Seljord liegt an einem See, in dem, wie es heißt, ein Schlangenungeheuer haust. 2008 beschloss man, die Sage zum Ausgangspunkt für ein Tourismusprogramm zu machen und beauftragte Rintala Eggertsson und die Agentur Springer kulturstudio mit dessen Entwicklung. Das Projekt sollte aus zwei Teilen bestehen: drei kleineren Installationen im südöstlichen und mittleren Uferbereich des Sees und einem zentralen Aussichtspunkt am südwestlichen Ende, unweit der kleinen Stadt. Alle Bauten bestehen vor allem aus Holz. Die erste Planungsetappe fand als Bauworkshop mit Kunst- und Architekturstudenten, Lehrkräften der Nuova Accademia di Belle Arte und des Politecnico in Mailand sowie Studenten der norwegischen Theaterakademie unter der Leitung von Rintala Eggertsson statt. Die Architekten erklären: „Im Workshop setzten wir uns vor allem damit auseinander, wie menschengemachte Installationen mit charakteristischen Merkmalen der Landschaft verankert werden können, ohne sie zu dominieren. Die drei Installationen sind auf unserer Website unter dem Titel **‚INTO THE LANDSCAPE'** zu sehen."

La ville de Seljord est située près d'un lac censé abriter un serpent. Motivée par des arrière-pensées touristiques, la ville de Seljord a décidé en 2008 d'utiliser ce mythe comme point de départ pour un programme de développement confié à Rintala Eggertsson et aux commissaires d'exposition de Springer kulturstudio. Le projet est divisé en deux parties : d'une part, trois petites installations au centre et dans la partie sud-est du lac et, d'autre part, un point de vue principal à l'extrémité sud-ouest du lac, près de la petite ville. Toutes ces structures ont été principalement réalisées en bois. La première partie du programme a été organisée sous forme d'ateliers de construction avec des étudiants en art et en architecture de la Nouvelle Académie des beaux-arts (NABA) et de l'École polytechnique de Milan, ainsi qu'avec des étudiants de l'Académie norvégienne de théâtre sous la direction de Rintala Eggertsson. Les architectes donnent l'explication suivante : « L'atelier se focalisait thématiquement sur l'ancrage d'installations faites par l'homme sur des éléments caractéristiques du paysage sans volonté de domination. Les trois installations sont présentées sur notre site Internet sous le titre **"INTO THE LANDSCAPE"**. »

Imagined essentially as a viewpoint on a lake, this wooden structure contrasts with the natural environment and yet seems to be very much anchored to its specific location.

Die als Aussichtspunkt für einen See konzipierte Holzkonstruktion steht in Kontrast zu ihrem natürlichen Umfeld, wirkt aber trotzdem in die Umgebung eingebunden.

Conçue avant tout comme un point de vue sur un lac, la structure en bois contraste certes avec l'environnement naturel, mais semble toutefois parfaitement ancrée dans son site spécifique.

The impression of belonging to the natural setting is heightened by such gestures as decks that have openings for existing trees. Above, and right page, views of the lake are the main attraction of the design.

Der Eindruck, Teil der Landschaft zu sein, wird z. B. durch Baumöffnungen in den Terrassen noch verstärkt. Der Ausblick auf den See ist die eigentliche Attraktion (oben und rechte Seite).

L'impression d'appartenir au cadre naturel est renforcée par des gestes comme ces terrasses traversées par des arbres. En haut et page de droite, les vues sur le lac constituent le principal attrait de la conception.

In these images, black wood plank bridges allow tourists to see the coastline and to walk along its rock formations.

Diese Bilder zeigen schwarze Holzstege, die es den Touristen ermöglichen, das Ufer zu sehen und es mit seinen Felsformationen zu erkunden.

Ces images montrent les ponts formés de planches de bois noir qui permettent aux touristes d'admirer le rivage et de se promener le long de ses formations rocheuses.

ROTOR

Rotor vzw-asbl
99 Rue de Laeken
1000 Brussels
Belgium

Tel: +32 485 87 57 63
Fax: +32 22 19 20 11
E-mail: rotorasbl@gmail.com
Web: www.rotordb.org

The principals of the non-profit organization **ROTOR** call it "a platform for the endorsement of industrial waste reuse. Rotor wants, among other things, to encourage contacts between producers of 'interesting' waste and potential reusers from the field of industry, design, or architecture." Maarten Gielen was born in Aalst, Belgium, in 1984. He is a founding member of Rotor, created in 2005. Tristan Boniver was born in Brussels in 1976 and studied architecture there at the Saint-Luc Institute, the Sint-Lucas School of Architecture, and La Cambre School of Architecture (ISACF). He is another founding member of the team. Lionel Devlieger was born in Rwamagana, Rwanda, in 1972. He obtained his Master in Architecture and Urbanism degree from Ghent University (1996) and a Ph.D. in Engineering Sciences/Architecture from the same university in 2005. He joined Rotor in 2006. Benjamin Lasserre was born in Lille in 1985 and studied stage design at the Saint Luc Institute in Brussels. He became a member of Rotor after taking part in the KFDA09 project published here. Melanie Tamm was born in West Berlin in 1974 and joined Rotor in 2008. Their projects include RDF181, temporary offices (Brussels, Belgium, 2006–07); "Deutschland im Herbst" exhibition at the Ursula Blickle Stiftung (Kraichtal, Germany, 2008); the Festival Center for Kunstenfestivaldesarts 2009 – KFDA09 (Brussels, Belgium, 2009); and Usus/Usures, 12th International Architecture Biennale (Venice, Italy, 2010).

Die Partner der gemeinnützigen Organisation **ROTOR** definieren sich als „Plattform für die Wiederverwertung von Industriemüll. Rotor will, u. a., Kontakte zwischen den Produzenten ‚interessanter' Abfälle und potenziellen Wiederverwendern in Industrie, Design und Architektur fördern". Maarten Gielen wurde 1984 in Aalst, Belgien, geboren. Er ist eines der Gründungsmitglieder des 2005 ins Leben gerufenen Rotor-Teams. Tristan Boniver wurde 1976 in Brüssel geboren und studierte dort Architektur am Institut Saint-Luc, der Hogeschool Sint Lukas und an der Architekturhochschule La Cambre (ISACF). Auch er zählt zu den Gründungsmitgliedern des Teams. Lionel Devlieger wurde 1972 in Rwamagana, Ruanda, geboren. Er absolvierte seinen Master in Architektur und Stadtplanung an der Universität Gent (1996) und promovierte 2005 in Ingenieurwissenschaften/Architektur an derselben Universität. Seit 2006 ist er Mitglied von Rotor. Benjamin Lasserre wurde 1985 in Lille geboren und studierte Bühnenbild am Institut Saint-Luc in Brüssel. Er wurde nach seiner Mitarbeit am hier vorgestellten Projekt KFDA09 Mitglied bei Rotor. Melanie Tamm wurde 1974 in Berlin geboren und kam 2008 zu Rotor. Die Projekte des Teams sind u. a. RDF181, temporäre Büros (Brüssel, 2006–07), „Deutschland im Herbst", Ausstellung der Ursula Blickle Stiftung (Kraichtal, Deutschland, 2008), das Festivalcenter für das Kunstenfestivaldesarts 2009 – KFDA09 (Brüssel, 2009) sowie „Usus/Usures", XII. Internationale Architekturbiennale (Venedig, 2010).

Les dirigeants de **ROTOR** présentent cette association à but non lucratif, créée en 2005, comme une « plate-forme pour la promotion de la réutilisation des déchets industriels. Rotor souhaite, entre autres, encourager les contacts entre les producteurs de déchets "intéressants" et leurs réutilisateurs potentiels dans les domaines de l'industrie, du design et de l'architecture ». Maarten Gielen, né à Alost (Belgique) en 1984, est membre fondateur de Rotor, créé en 2005. Tristan Boniver, né à Bruxelles en 1976, a étudié l'architecture à l'Institut Saint-Luc Institute, à l'école Sint-Lucas et à l'Institut d'architecture de La Cambre à Bruxelles et a également participé à la fondation de Rotor. Lionel Devlieger, né à Rwamagana (Rwanda) en 1972, a obtenu son master en architecture et urbanisme à l'université de Gand (1996) et son Ph.D. en sciences de l'ingénierie-architecture à la même université en 2005. Il a rejoint Rotor en 2006. Benjamin Lasserre est né à Lille en 1985 et a étudié la scénographie à l'Institut Saint-Luc de Bruxelles. Il est devenu membre de Rotor après avoir participé au projet KFDA09, publié ici. Melanie Tamm est née à Berlin-Ouest en 1974, et a rejoint Rotor en 2008. Leurs projets comprennent : RDF181, des bureaux temporaires (Bruxelles, 2006–07) ; « Deutschland im Herbst », exposition à la Fondation Ursula Blickle (Kraichtal, Allemagne, 2008) ; le Centre pour le festival Kunstenfestivaldesarts 2009 – KFDA09 (Bruxelles, 2009) et Usus/Usures pour la XIIe Biennale internationale d'architecture de Venise (2010).

FESTIVAL CENTER FOR KFDA09

Brussels, Belgium, 2009

Area: 36 m² (mezzanine); Terrace: 180 m² (terrace); 212 m² (converted interior)
Client: KFDA09. Cost: not disclosed

Rotor was asked to revamp the interior of the Brigittines Arts Center for a three-week period with a modest budget. They added a mezzanine to the hall of the building. The architects state: "We opted for a design that took into account the future destination of the materials used in its creation. We worked with rented prefab elements used as formwork in the building industry and different kinds of wood waste for finishings. Melaminated chipboard from unmarketable furniture was used as flooring. In this way, the large structures erected for the festival left hardly any supplementary waste after their purposes were fulfilled." The use of scaffolding or manifestly temporary elements in this installation served to reinforce the lively, dynamic nature of the activities in the space.

Der Auftrag von Rotor lautete, die Innenräume des Kunstzentrums Les Brigittines für einen Zeitraum von drei Wochen im Rahmen eines bescheidenen Budgets umzugestalten. Sie realisierten daraufhin ein Mezzaningeschoss im Foyer des Gebäudes. Die Architekten führen aus: „Wir entschieden uns für ein Design, das die zukünftige Verwendung der eingesetzten Materialien von vornherein mit berücksichtigte. Wir arbeiteten mit gemieteten Fertigbauelementen, die in der Industrie als Schalungsmaterial zum Einsatz kommen sowie mit verschiedenen Arten von Holzabfällen für die Verkleidung. Melaminharzbeschichtete Spanplatten von unverkäuflichen Möbeln diente als Bodenbelag. Auf diese Weise hinterließen die für das Festival aufgebauten Großkonstruktionen kaum zusätzliche Abfälle, nachdem sie ihren Zweck erfüllt hatten." Der Einsatz von Gerüsten und augenscheinlich temporären Elementen für diese Installation trugen dazu bei, die Lebendigkeit und Dynamik der in den Räumen stattfindenden Aktivitäten hervorzustreichen.

On avait demandé à Rotor de redonner un style au Centre d'art contemporain des Brigittines, qui devait être utilisé pendant trois semaines par le festival. Le budget était modeste. L'équipe a créé une mezzanine dans le hall du bâtiment. « Nous avons opté pour un projet prenant en compte la future destination des matériaux utilisés dans sa création. Nous avons travaillé à partir d'éléments préfabriqués loués comme des coffrages de chantier de bâtiment et divers types de matériaux de récupération pour les finitions. Des planches d'aggloméré mélaminé, récupérées sur des meubles invendables, ont servi à faire les sols. Ainsi, les constructions de grandes dimensions érigées pour la durée du festival n'ont généré pratiquement aucun déchet supplémentaire une fois leur fonction remplie. » L'utilisation d'échafaudages ou d'éléments manifestement temporaires renforçait par ailleurs la dynamique et le caractère vivant des activités qui se déroulaient dans cet espace.

The architects specialize in attaching new temporary spaces to existing structures, using rough, available materials.

Die Architekten haben sich darauf spezialisiert, temporäre Anbauten an bestehenden Gebäuden zu realisieren und nutzen dafür verfügbare, oftmals grobe Materialien.

Ces architectes se sont spécialisés dans la création d'espaces temporaires rattachés à des constructions existantes, réalisés à partir de matériaux bruts, souvent de récupération.

Below, extending from the exterior like a temporary wooden platform set up on pipe scaffolding, the structure embraces and expands on the older building.

Die Konstruktion unten, eine temporäre Plattform aus Holz und Gerüststangen, ragt aus der Fassade heraus, knüpft an das ältere Gebäude an und erweitert es zugleich.

Ci-dessous, la plate-forme en bois temporaire posée sur des tubes d'échafaudage enveloppe et agrandit le bâtiment ancien.

tickets

The use of pipe scaffolding emphasizes the temporary nature of the space, which is seen in the drawings on the right as the darker added terrace space in the plan.

Die Verwendung von Gerüststangen unterstreicht die temporäre Natur des Anbaus, der auf den Zeichnungen rechts als dunklerer Terrassenbereich zu erkennen ist.

L'utilisation d'éléments d'échafaudage tubulaire matérialise la nature temporaire de l'espace créé, présent dans les plans à droite, au-dessus de la zone ombrée délimitant la terrasse.

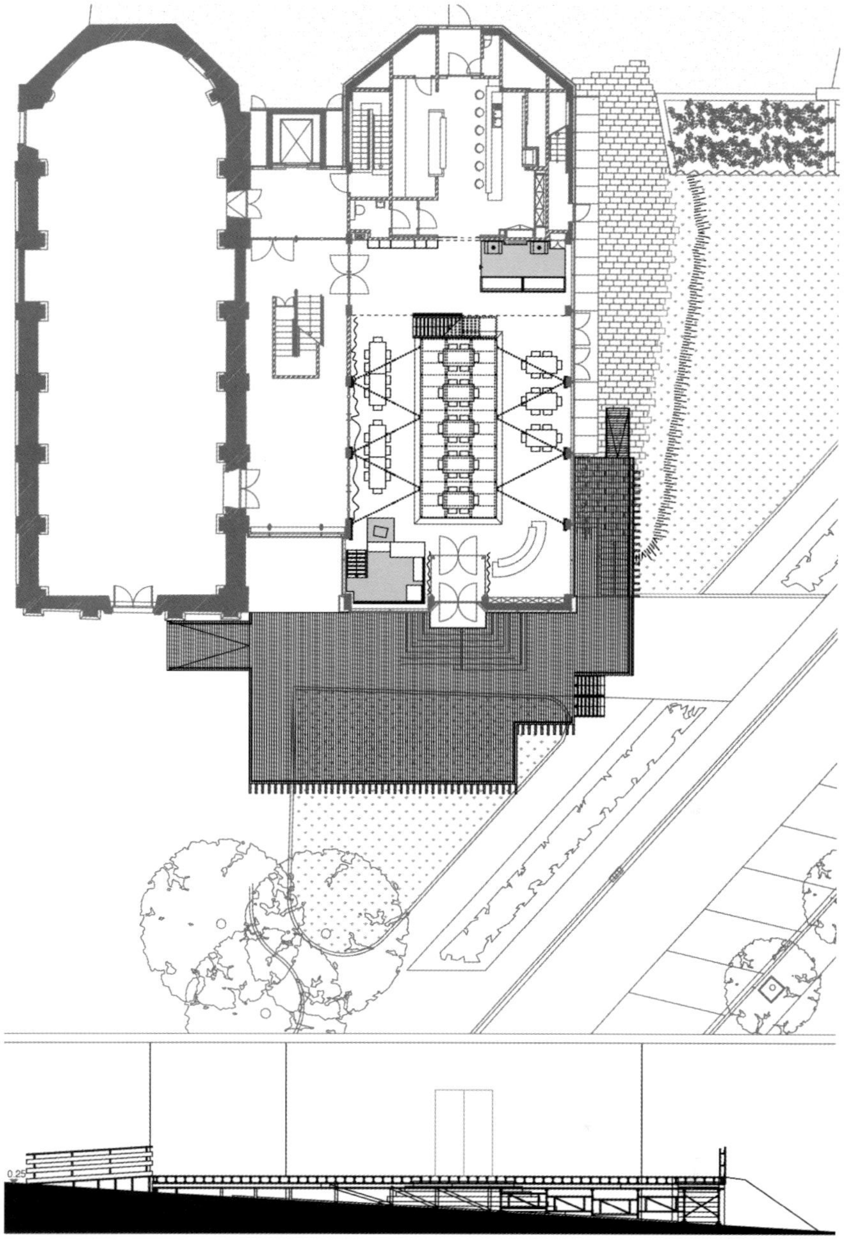

HANS-JÖRG RUCH

Ruch & Partner Architekten AG
Via Brattas 2
7500 Saint Moritz
Switzerland

Tel: +41 81 837 32 40 / Fax: +41 81 837 32 50
E-mail: info@ruch-arch.ch
Web: www.ruch-arch.ch

HANS-JÖRG RUCH was born in 1946 and received his diploma in architecture from the ETH in Zurich in 1971. He received his master's degree from the Rensselaer Polytechnic Institute (Troy, New York, 1973) with a thesis entitled "Towards an Architecture of Tourism." From 1974 to 1977 he worked in the office of Obrist und Partner, Saint Moritz, and then created a partnership with Urs Hüsler (Ruch + Hüsler, Architekten, Saint Moritz, 1977–88). He created his own firm in 1989, and a new entity, Ruch & Partner with Peter Lacher, Stefan Lauener, Heinz Inhelder, and Thorsten Arzet in 2010. Widely traveled, Ruch has nonetheless made his career largely in the Engadine region of Switzerland, specializing in the renovation of the area's rich patrimony of old stone and wood houses. His delicate and knowing touch on these buildings provides an interesting answer to the question of how to modernize structures that may date, in some cases, from medieval times. Since completing the Hotel Saratz in Pontresina (1995); the Electrical Substation "Albanatscha" at the Julier Passroad (1996); and the Chesa Madalena in Zuoz (2001–02), he has realized numerous projects including the Palace Gallery in front of Badrutt's Palace Hotel (Saint Moritz, 2002); Hotel Castell (Zuoz, 2004, renovation project, undertaken with UNStudio); Not Vital House (Tschlin, 2004); Badrutt's Palace Hotel (Saint Moritz, south façade renovation, 2005); Chesa Albertini (Zuoz, 2006); a Vacation House (Sent, 2006, published here); and the reconstruction and extension of the Chamanna da Tschierva Hut for the Swiss Alpine Club (Saint Moritz, 2007), all in Switzerland.

HANS-JÖRG RUCH wurde 1946 geboren und machte sein Architekturdiplom 1971 an der Eidgenössischen Technischen Hochschule Zürich und den Master am Rensselaer Polytechnic Institute (Troy, New York, 1973) mit der Abschlussarbeit „Towards an Architecture of Tourism". Von 1974 bis 1977 arbeitete er im Büro Obrist und Partner, Sankt Moritz, und ging dann eine Partnerschaft mit Urs Hüsler ein (Ruch + Hüsler, Architekten, Sankt Moritz, 1977–88). 1989 gründete er eine eigene Firma und 2010 mit Peter Lacher, Stefan Lauener, Heinz Inhelder und Thorsten Arzet das neue Büro Ruch & Partner. Trotz seiner weiten Reisen setzt Ruch den Schwerpunkt seiner Arbeit weitgehend auf das Schweizer Engadin und hat sich auf die Erneuerung des in dieser Region reichen Bestands an alten Naturstein- und Holzhäusern spezialisiert. Sein einfühlsamer und kenntnisreicher Umgang mit diesem Baubestand ist eine interessante Antwort auf die Frage, wie man Bauten modernisiert, die in einigen Fällen sogar aus dem Mittelalter stammen. Nachdem er das Hotel Saratz in Pontresina (1995), das Umspannwerk Albanatscha auf dem Julierpass (1996) und die Chesa Madalena in Zuoz (2001–02) fertiggestellt hatte, sind zahlreiche weitere Projekte realisiert worden: die Palace Gallery vor dem Hotel Badrutt's Palace (Sankt Moritz, 2002), das Hotel Castell (Zuoz, 2004, Modernisierung zusammen mit UNStudio), das Haus Not Vital (Tschlin, 2004), das Hotel Badrutt's Palace (Sankt Moritz, Erneuerung der Südfassade, 2005), Chesa Albertini (Zuoz, 2006), ein Ferienhaus (Sent, 2006, hier veröffentlicht) sowie der Umbau und die Erweiterung der Berghütte Chamanna da Tschierva für den Schweizer Alpen-Club (Sankt Moritz, 2007), alle in der Schweiz.

HANS-JÖRG RUCH, né en 1946, est diplômé en architecture de l'ETH à Zurich (1971). Il passe son master au Rensselaer Polytechnic Institute (Troy, New York, 1973) en soutenant un mémoire intitulé : *Vers une architecture du tourisme*. De 1974 à 1977, il travaille pour l'agence Obrist und Partner à Saint-Moritz, puis s'associe avec Urs Hüsler (Ruch + Hüsler, Architekten, Saint-Moritz, 1977–88). Il a créé sa propre agence en 1989 et une nouvelle entité, Ruch & Partner avec Peter Lacher, Stefan Lauener, Heinz Inhelder et Thorsten Arzet, en 2010. S'il voyage beaucoup, il a néanmoins mène une grande partie de sa carrière en Engadine (Suisse), où il s'est spécialisé dans la rénovation du riche patrimoine local de maisons de pierre et de bois anciennes. Son approche délicate et savante de ces constructions est une intéressante réponse à la question de la modernisation d'un bâti datant, dans certains cas, de l'époque médiévale. Suite à la réalisation de l'Hôtel Saratz à Pontresina (1995) ; de la sous-station électrique Albanatscha sur la route du col de Julier (1996) et de la Chesa Madalena à Zuoz (2001–02), il a mené à bien de nombreux projets dont la Palace Gallery devant le Badrutt's Palace Hotel (Saint-Moritz, 2002) ; l'hôtel Castell (Zuoz, 2004, rénovation, avec UNStudio) ; la maison Not Vital (Tschlin, 2004) ; le Badrutt's Palace Hotel (Saint-Moritz, rénovation de la façade sud, 2005) ; la Chesa Albertini (Zuoz, 2006) ; une maison de vacances (Sent, 2006, publiée ici) et l'extension du refuge Chamanna da Tschierva pour le Club alpin suisse (Saint-Moritz, 2007), tous en Suisse.

VACATION HOUSE

Sent, Switzerland, 2006

Address: Via Sura, 7554 Sent, Switzerland
Area: 165 m². Client: not disclosed. Cost: €550 000
Collaboration: Heinz Inhelder, Thorsten Arzet

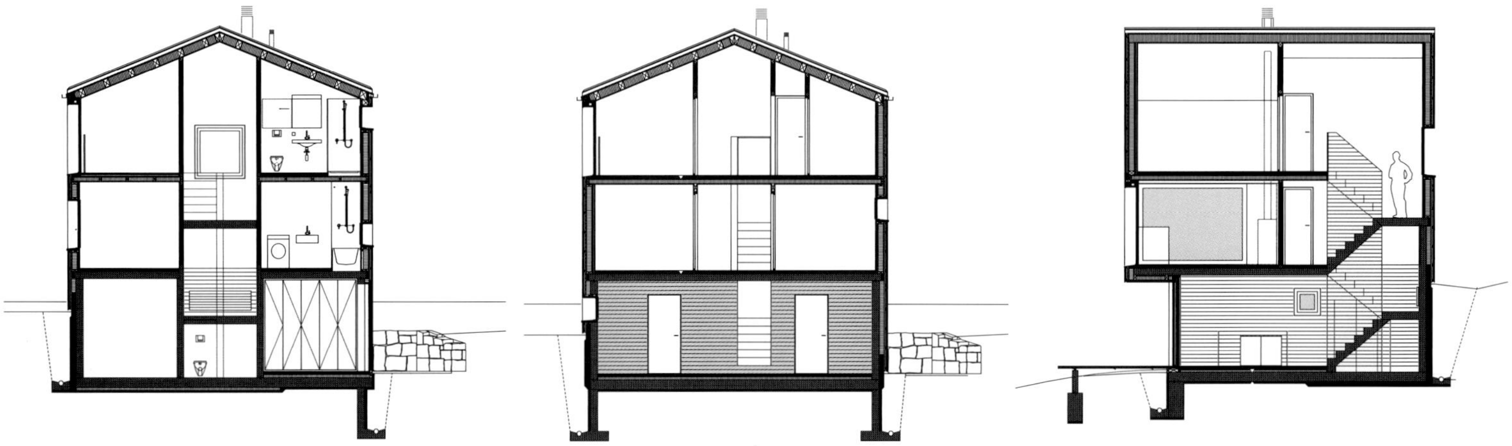

Specialized in the restoration of old structures in the Engadine area of Switzerland, Hans-Jörg Ruch also creates modern buildings like this house, where wood cladding and a metal roof recall local structures.

Hans-Jörg Ruch hat sich auf die Restaurierung alter Bauten im Schweizer Kanton Engadin spezialisiert, plant aber auch moderne Gebäude wie dieses Haus, bei dem die Holzverkleidung und ein Metalldach auf die örtliche Bebauung Bezug nehmen.

Spécialisé dans la restauration de constructions anciennes en Engadine (Suisse), Hans-Jörg Ruch crée également des maisons modernes comme celle-ci, dans laquelle l'habillage de bois et le toit en tôle de métal rappellent les constructions locales.

This **VACATION HOUSE** is located to the east of the village of Sent on a sloping, south-facing site with a view toward local mountains such as the Piz Lischana. To profit from this view, and to maintain the terraced nature of the location, the architect set the house on the upper part of the site, making the three-story building as compact as possible. Sitting on a concrete base, the house is covered in locally harvested larch boards. An irregular arrangement of small and large windows accentuates the unexpected appearance of the house. An anthracite cement floor is contrasted with an interior cladding of larch in most areas, including bathrooms. The architect concludes: "Maintaining the continuity of the characteristic landscape of terraces in Sent was as important in this project as making a contemporary use of wood as a building material."

Dieses **FERIENHAUS** liegt östlich des Dorfs Sent auf einem nach Süden orientierten Hanggrundstück mit Blick auf die umgebenden Berge wie den Piz Lischana. Wegen dieser Aussicht und unter Berücksichtigung des terrassierten Geländes setzte der Architekt das Haus auf den oberen Teil des Grundstücks und plante das dreigeschossige Gebäude so kompakt wie möglich. Es steht auf einem Betonfundament und ist mit vor Ort gewonnen Lärchenbrettern verkleidet. Die unregelmäßig angeordneten, kleinen und großen Fenster setzen Akzente im ungewöhnlichen Erscheinungsbild dieses Hauses. Im Innern bildet der anthrazitfarbige Zementfußboden einen Kontrast zur Lärchenholzverkleidung fast aller Räume, einschließlich der Badezimmer. Der Architekt erklärt abschließend: „Die Kontinuität der charakteristischen terrassierten Landschaft von Sent zu bewahren, war bei diesem Projekt ebenso wichtig wie eine zeitgemäße Verwendung von Holz als Baumaterial."

Cette **MAISON DE VACANCES** est située à l'est du village de Sent sur une pente orientée au sud donnant dans le lointain sur les montagnes de la région dont le Piz Laschana. Pour profiter de cette vue et maintenir le caractère de l'aménagement en terrasses du site, l'architecte a implanté la maison en partie supérieure de la parcelle et a réussi à rendre cette construction de trois niveaux aussi compacte que possible. Reposant sur une base en béton, elle est habillée de planches de mélèze d'exploitation locale. Le positionnement irrégulier des fenêtres grandes et petites accentue l'aspect assez surprenant de l'ensemble. À l'intérieur, le sol en ciment anthracite contraste avec un habillage en mélèze présent dans la plupart des pièces, y compris les salles de bains. « Maintenir la continuité du paysage étagé caractéristique de Sent a joué un rôle important dans ce projet, de même que l'utilisation du bois comme matériau de construction contemporain », conclut l'architecte.

HIROSHI SAMBUICHI

Hiroshi Sambuichi Architects
8–3–302 Nakajima naka-ku
Hiroshima 730–0811
Japan

Tel: +81 82 544 1417
Fax: +81 82 544 1418
E-mail: samb@d2.dion.ne.jp

HIROSHI SAMBUICHI was born in 1968. He graduated from the Department of Architecture in the Faculty of Science and Technology at Tokyo University of Science. After working for Shinichi Ogawa and Associates, he established Hiroshi Sambuichi Architects and began design work in Hiroshima. His work includes the Running Green Project (Yamaguchi, 2001); Air House (Yamaguchi, 2001); Miwa-gama (Yamaguchi, 2002); Sloping North House (Yamaguchi, 2003); Stone House (Shimane, 2005); and the Inujima Art Project Seirensho (Okayama, 2006–08), a museum located on a small island in the Inland Sea of Japan, carried out for the client responsible for Tadao Ando's work on the nearby island of Naoshima. In 2008, Hiroshi Sambuichi completed the Hiroshima Project offices, Miyajima Office (Hatsukaichi, Hiroshima, published here); and, in 2013, the Rokko Observation Platform (Kobe, Hyogo), all in Japan.

HIROSHI SAMBUICHI wurde 1968 geboren. Sein Architekturstudium schloss er an der Fakultät für Naturwissenschaften und Technik an der Universität Tokio ab. Nachdem er zunächst für Shinichi Ogawa & Associates gearbeitet hatte, gründete er sein Büro Hiroshi Sambuichi Architects und begann in Hiroshima zu praktizieren. Zu seinen Projekten zählen u. a.: Running Green Project (Yamaguchi, 2001), Air House (Yamaguchi, 2001), Miwa-gama (Yamaguchi, 2002), Sloping North House (Yamaguchi, 2003), Stone House (Shimane, 2005) und das Kunstprojekt von Inujima Seirensho (Okayama, 2006–08), ein Museum auf einer kleinen Insel in der Seto-Inlandsee, für denselben Bauherrn, für den Tadao Ando auf der nahe gelegenen Insel Naoshima Projekte realisiert hatte. 2008 konnte Hiroshi Sambuichi das Hiroshima-Projektbüro, das Miyajima-Büro, fertigstellen (Hatsukaichi, Hiroshima, hier vorgestellt) und 2013 die Rokko-Aussichtsplattform (Kobe, Hyogo), alle in Japan.

Né en 1968, **HIROSHI SAMBUICHI** est diplômé du département d'architecture de la faculté des sciences et technologies de l'Université des sciences de Tokyo. Après avoir travaillé pour Shinichi Ogawa and Associates, il a fondé l'agence Hiroshi Sambuichi Architects et commencé à travailler à Hiroshima. Parmi ses réalisations, toutes au Japon : le Running Green Project (Yamaguchi, 2001) ; la Air House (Yamaguchi, 2001) ; Miwa-gama (Yamaguchi, 2002) ; la Sloping North House (Yamaguchi, 2003) ; la Stone House (Shimane, 2005–) et le projet artistique d'Inujima Seirensho (Okayama, 2006–08), musée situé sur une petite île de la mer Intérieure du Japon, réalisé à la demande du client à l'origine des interventions de Tadao Ando sur l'île voisine de Naoshima. En 2008, Hiroshi Sambuichi a achevé le projet des bureaux Miyajima (Hatsukaichi, Hiroshima, publié ici) et, en 2013, la plate-forme d'observation de Rokko (Kobe, Hyogo).

MIYAJIMA OFFICE

Hatsukaichi, Hiroshima, Japan, 2007–08

Address: Miyajima-cho, Hatsukaichi, Hiroshima 739–0500, Japan
Area: 78 m². Client: Funakura Accountants Office. Cost: not disclosed

For this project, the architect sought to make maximum use of the topography and the "latent energy" of the site to reduce carbon emissions to a strict minimum. Located 500 meters from a Unesco World Heritage Site (Itsukushima-jinja Shrine), the office is powered in good part by solar and convection energy. The most visible feature of the building is a "chimney of glass" that brings to mind the wind towers seen in Middle Eastern countries such as Iran, although the architect does not make reference to these traditions. Continuing along the same lines, Sambuichi found a stock of wood that had been left unused for 40 years in a local warehouse, employing the wood to give character to the new building. "I gave idle materials new life and created a rich space while drawing out the charm of the materials," he states. With his characteristic modesty and humor, the architect concludes: "I think that a new endemic species suitable for this area was born."

Bei diesem Projekt ging es dem Architekten darum, die Topografie und „latente Energie" des Geländes maximal zu nutzen, um die CO_2-Emissionen auf ein absolutes Minimum zu reduzieren. Das nur 500 m von einer UNESCO-Weltkulturerbestätte (dem Itsukushima-Schrein) entfernte Büro wird zum Großteil mit Sonnen- und Konvektionsenergie versorgt. Auffälligstes Merkmal des Gebäudes ist sein „gläserner Kamin", der an Windfänger erinnert, wie sie in Ländern des Mittleren Ostens wie dem Iran verbreitet sind, obwohl der Architekt sich nicht explizit auf solche Traditionen bezieht. Mit derselben Haltung entdeckte Sambuichi einen Holzbestand, der seit 40 Jahren ungenutzt in einem örtlichen Lagerhaus gelegen hatte, und setzte das Holz ein, um dem Neubau einen besonderen Charakter zu geben. „Ich habe ungenutzten Materialien neues Leben gegeben, einen facettenreichen Raum geschaffen und zugleich den Charme der Materialien zur Geltung gebracht", erklärt er. Mit der für ihn typischen Bescheidenheit und Ironie folgert der Architekt: „Ich glaube, hier wurde eine neuartige einheimische Spezies geboren, die dieser Gegend entspricht."

Pour ce projet, l'architecte a cherché à utiliser au maximum la topographie et « l'énergie latente du site » pour réduire au strict minimum les émissions de carbone. Situé à 500 m d'un site répertorié au Patrimoine de l'humanité de l'Unesco (le mausolée Itsukushima-jinja), ce petit immeuble de bureaux est en grande partie alimenté par l'énergie solaire et par convection. L'élément le plus caractéristique du projet est une « cheminée de verre » qui rappelle les tours de vent de certains pays du Moyen-Orient comme l'Iran, bien que l'architecte ne se réfère pas à ces traditions. Selon la même approche, Sambuichi a trouvé un stock de bois abandonné pendant quarante ans dans un entrepôt local et l'a utilisé pour renforcer le caractère qu'il voulait donner à son projet. « J'ai offert une nouvelle vie à des matériaux inutilisés, et créé un espace plus riche en m'appuyant sur leur charme », explique l'architecte. Avec l'humour et la modestie qui le caractérisent, il conclut : « Je pense qu'une nouvelle espèce endémique adaptée à cette région vient de naître. »

The surprisingly tall, tapered wood-clad tower of the office is its most visible exterior feature.

Der erstaunlich hohe, leicht konische, holzverkleidete Turm des Büros ist von außen das auffälligste Merkmal.

Étonnement élevée et effilée, la tour habillée de bois est la caractéristique extérieure la plus visible du projet.

The wooden interior of the tower creates a light well of sorts, an unoccupied, high space that redefines the interior.

Das Innere des Holzturms wirkt wie eine Art Lichtschacht, ein ungenutzter hoher Raum, der den Innenraum neu definiert.

L'intérieur vide de la tour doublé de bois fait office de puits de lumière et personnalise l'intérieur.

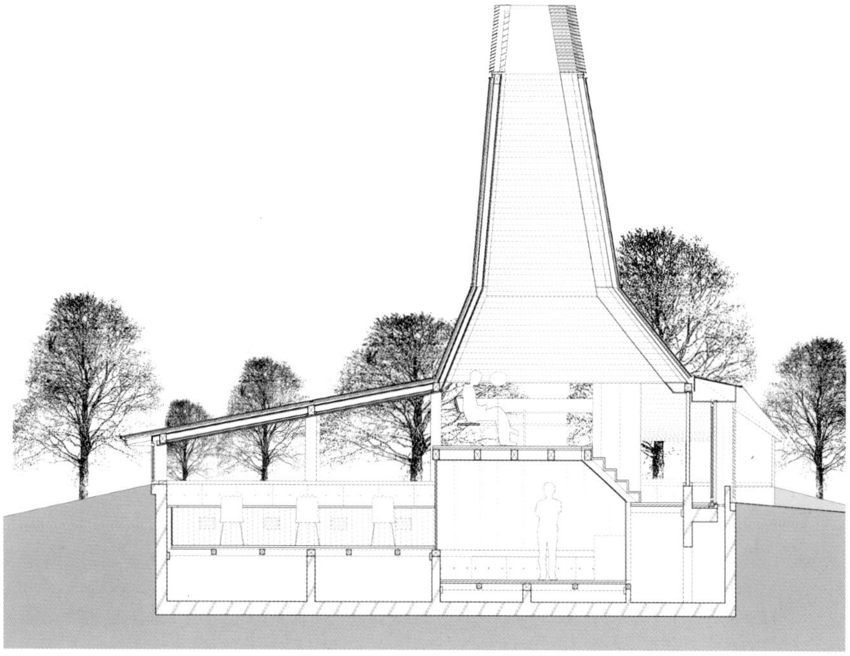

Metla, Finnish Forest Research Institute

SARC ARCHITECTS

SARC Architects
Tammasaarenlaituri 3
00180 Helsinki
Finland

Tel: +358 9 62 26 18 0
Fax: +358 9 62 26 18 40
E-mail: sarc@sarc.fi
Web: www.sarc.fi

ANTTI-MATTI SIIKALA was born in 1964 in Turku, Finland, and obtained an MS degree in architecture from the Helsinki University of Technology in 1993. He is a Partner of SARC and a Professor of building technology, Department of Architecture, Helsinki University of Technology / Aalto University (2002–). **SARLOTTA NARJUS** was born in 1966 in Turku. She obtained her MS degree in architecture from the Helsinki University of Technology in 1996. She worked with Heikkinen-Komonen Architects (1989–98) before becoming a Partner of SARC in 1998. Their work includes Expo 2000 Finnish Pavilion (Hanover, Germany, 2000); University of Oulu, Faculty of Medicine, Main Building (Oulu, 2003); Metla, the Finnish Forest Research Institute (Joensuu, 2004, published here); Oulu City Hall (Oulu, 2008); and the Tapiola Headquarters (Espoo, 2010), all in Finland unless stated otherwise.

ANTTI-MATTI SIIKALA wurde 1964 in Turku, Finnland, geboren und machte 1993 seinen Master in Architektur an der Technischen Universität Helsinki. Er ist Partner von SARC und Professor für Bautechnik an der Architekturabteilung der Technischen Universität Helsinki/Aalto-Universität (seit 2002). **SARLOTTA NARJUS** wurde 1966 in Turku geboren und machte ihren Master 1996 an derselben Universität. Sie arbeitete bei Heikkinen-Komonen Architects (1989–98) und wurde 1998 Partnerin bei SARC. Zu den Werken dieses Büros zählen der Finnische Pavillon auf der Expo 2000 (Hannover, 2000), das Hauptgebäude der medizinischen Fakultät an der Universität Oulu (Oulu, 2003), Metla, das finnische Institut für Waldforschung (Joensuu, 2004, hier veröffentlicht), das Rathaus Oulu (Oulu, 2008) und die Hauptverwaltung von Tapiola (Espoo, 2010), alle in Finnland, sofern nicht anders angegeben.

ANTTI-MATTI SIIKALA, né en 1964 à Turku, en Finlande, est titulaire d'un M.Sc. en architecture de l'Université de technologie d'Helsinki (1993). Il est partenaire de l'agence SARC et professeur de technologie de la construction du département d'architecture de l'Université de technologie d'Helsinki/université Aalto (2002–). **SARLOTTA NARJUS**, née en 1966 à Turku, est titulaire d'un M.Sc. en architecture de l'Université de technologie d'Helsinki (1996). Elle a travaillé chez Heikkinen-Komonen Architects (1989–98) avant de devenir partenaire de SARC en 1998. Parmi leurs réalisations, presque toutes en Finlande : le pavillon finlandais pour Expo 2000 (Hanovre, Allemagne, 2000) ; le bâtiment principal de la faculté de médecine de l'université d'Oulu (Oulu, 2003) ; Metla, Institut finlandais de recherche forestière (Joensuu, 2004, publié ici) ; l'hôtel de ville d'Oulu (Oulu, 2008) et le siège de Tapiola (Espoo, 2010).

METLA
METSÄNTUTKIMUSLAITOS

METLA, FINNISH FOREST RESEARCH INSTITUTE

Joensuu, Finland, 2004

Address: Joensuu Research Unit, Yliopistokatu 6, Box 68, FI-80101 Joensuu, Tel. +358 10 2111, www.metla.fi
Area: 7400 m². Client: Finnish Forest Research Institute. Cost: not disclosed

This building, an expansion of the existing Institute, intended for a staff of 150–170 employees, is located on the Joensuu University campus, near the city center. The Institute does applied forestry research and research on wooden materials. The architects explain: "The primary goal of the project was to use Finnish wood in innovative ways. Hence, wood is the main material used throughout the building, from the post-beam-slab system in the structural frame to the exterior cladding." The work areas are arrayed around a central courtyard and lobby. The walls of the entrance to the courtyard are made up of 100-year-old timber. Tall pines grow through the terrace in the courtyard. A conference space "resembles an overturned boat and fish-chest-inspired tilted wooden columns."

Dieses Gebäude, eine Erweiterung des bestehenden Instituts, bietet 150 bis 170 Arbeitsplätze und steht auf dem Campus der Universität Joensuu in der Nähe des Stadtzentrums. Das Institut führt angewandte Forschungen über Waldwirtschaft und über Materialien aus Holz durch. Die Architekten erklären: „Oberstes Ziel dieses Projekts war die Nutzung finnischen Holzes auf innovative Weise. Daher wurde Holz als Hauptbaumaterial für das gesamte Gebäude verwendet, von der Ständerkonstruktion des Tragwerks bis zur Außenverkleidung." Die Arbeitsbereiche sind um einen zentralen Innenhof und eine Lobby angeordnet. Die Wände des Eingangsbereichs zu diesem Innenhof bestehen aus 100 Jahre altem Holz. In diesem Hof wachsen hohe Kiefern durch die Terrasse. Die Form des Konferenzraums „ähnelt einem umgedrehten Boot und einer Fischkiste und wurde von den gebogenen Holzstützen bestimmt".

Ce bâtiment, qui est une extension de l'Institut installé sur le campus de l'université de Joensuu, près du centre-ville, a été conçu pour un personnel de 150 à 170 chercheurs et employés. L'Institut mène des recherches sur la forêt et les matériaux en bois. Selon les architectes : « L'objectif premier du projet est d'utiliser le bois finlandais selon des techniques novatrices. C'est pourquoi le bois est le principal matériau utilisé dans l'intégralité du bâtiment, du système d'ossature à poutres et poteaux sur dalle au parement extérieur. » Les zones de travail se répartissent autour d'une cour centrale et d'un hall d'accueil. Les murs de l'entrée qui donne sur la cour sont en bois de cent ans d'âge. De grands pins poussent dans la cour. On note un espace de conférences « ressemblant à une coque de bateau renversée et des colonnes en bois en forme de navettes inclinées ».

The Metla building demonstrates that wood can, indeed, be used to create an elegant, modern structure on a large scale.

Der Metla-Bau beweist, dass Holz in der Tat auch für elegante, moderne und großmaßstäbliche Bauten verwendet werden kann.

Le bâtiment du Metla montre que le bois peut servir à créer des constructions modernes et élégantes de grandes dimensions.

The basic plan of the building (see below) is square with a notched, interior courtyard. Splayed columns made of wood connect the wood ceiling to the tiled floor.

Die Grundform des Gebäudes (unten) ist quadratisch mit einem eingeschnittenen Innenhof. Schräg gestellte Stützen aus Holz verbinden die Holzdecke mit dem Fliesenboden.

Le plan du bâtiment décrit un carré (ci-dessous) dans lequel a été découpée une cour intérieure. Des colonnes inclinées en bois font le lien entre le plafond de bois et le sol carrelé.

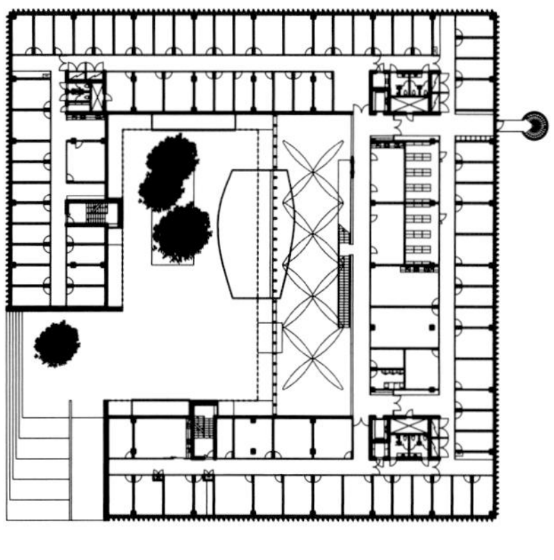

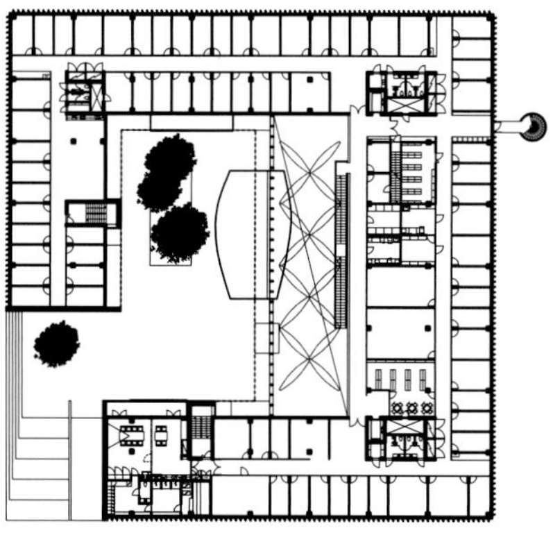

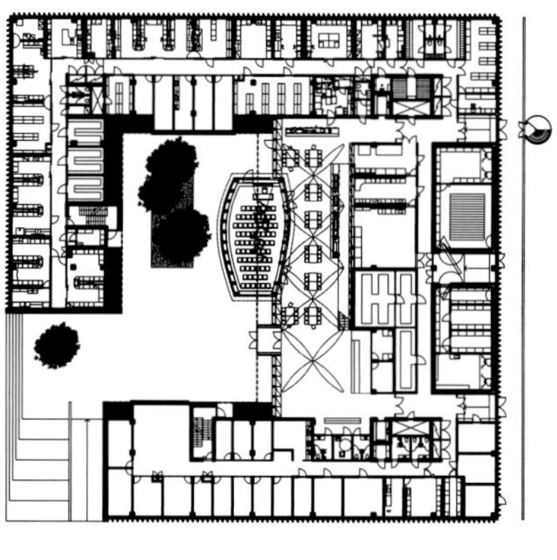

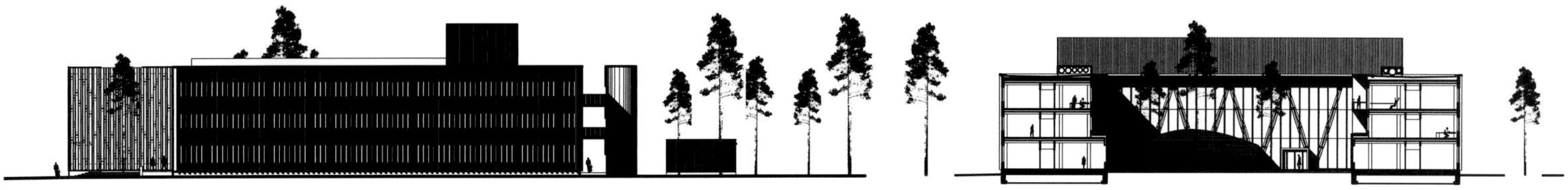

Glazed façades alternate with the more closed surfaces seen in the elevations above. In the image above is the space seen on the left page from a different angle.

Verglaste Flächen wechseln mit geschlossenen, wie die Ansichten oben zeigen. Unten: der auf der linken Seite dargestellte Innenraum aus einem anderen Blickwinkel.

Des façades vitrées alternent avec des plans plus fermés comme le montrent les élévations ci-dessus. Ci-dessus, l'espace de la page de gauche vu sous un angle différent.

TODD SAUNDERS

Saunders Architecture
Vestre Torggaten 22
5015 Bergen
Norway

Tel: +47 97 52 57 61
E-mail: post@saunders.no
Web: www.saunders.no

TODD SAUNDERS was born in 1969 in Gander, Newfoundland, Canada. He obtained his M.Arch from McGill University (Montreal, Canada, 1993–95) and a Bachelor of Environmental Planning from the Nova Scotia College of Art and Design (1988–92). He has worked in Austria, Germany, Russia, Latvia, and Norway (since 1997). He teaches part-time at the Bergen School of Architecture. His work includes the Aurland Lookout (with Tommie Wilhelmsen, Aurland, 2006); Villa Storingavika (Bergen, 2004–07); Villa G (Hjellestad, Bergen, 2007–09); and Solberg Tower and Park (Sarpsborg, Østfold, 2010), all in Norway. He is currently realizing the Fogo Island Studios, with four out of a total of six having already been completed, including Squish Studio (Fogo Island, Newfoundland, Canada, 2011, published here); he is also completing the Fogo Island Inn (2012) in the same location.

TODD SAUNDERS wurde 1969 in Gander, Neufundland, Kanada, geboren. Er absolvierte seinen M. Arch. an der McGill University (Montreal, Kanada, 1993–95) sowie einen Bachelor in Umweltplanung am Nova Scotia College of Art and Design (1988–92). Er war in Österreich, Deutschland, Russland, Lettland und Norwegen (seit 1996) tätig. Er lehrt in Teilzeit an der Architekturschule von Bergen. Zu seinen Projekten zählen der Aurland-Aussichtspunkt (mit Tommie Wilhelmsen, Aurland, 2006), die Villa Storingavika (Bergen, 2004–07), die Villa G (Hjellestad, Bergen, 2007–09) und der Solberg-Turm und -Park (Sarpsborg, Østfold, 2010), alle in Norwegen. Aktuell arbeitet er an den Fogo Island Studios, von denen vier der insgesamt sechs Studios bereits fertiggestellt sind, darunter das Squish Studio (Fogo Island, Neufundland, Kanada, 2011, hier vorgestellt). Außerdem beteiligt sich Saunders an einem Wettbewerb für das Fogo Island Inn (2012) am selben Standort.

Né en 1969 à Gander (Terre-Neuve, Canada), **TODD SAUNDERS** a obtenu son M.Arch. à l'université McGill (Montréal, 1993–95) et un bachelor en planification environnementale au Collège d'art et de design de la Nouvelle-Écosse (1988–92). Il a travaillé en Autriche, Allemagne, Russie, Lituanie et Norvège (depuis 1996). Il enseigne à temps partiel à l'École d'architecture de Bergen. Parmi ses réalisations, toutes en Norvège : le belvédère d'Aurland (avec Tommie Wilhelmsen, Aurland, 2006) ; la villa Storingavika (Bergen, 2004–07) ; la villa G (Hjellestad, Bergen, 2007–09) et la tour et le parc Solberg (Sarpsborg, Østfold, 2010). Il travaille en ce moment aux ateliers sur l'île de Fogo, où quatre sur six sont déjà achevés, dont le Squish Studio (île de Fogo, Terre-Neuve, Canada, 2011, publié ici) et termine l'hôtel Fogo Island Inn (2012) au même endroit.

SQUISH STUDIO

Fogo Island, Newfoundland, Canada, 2011

Address: not disclosed. Area: 28 m²
Client: Shorefast Foundation and Fogo Island Arts Corporation
Cost: not disclosed

The **SQUISH STUDIO** is located near the small town of Tilting on the eastern end of Fogo Island. First settled in the mid-18th century, Tilting was recently designated as a National Cultural Landscape District of Canada. The angled white form of the studio obviously contrasts with local architecture, and sits directly on the rocky shore. The southern end of the studio rises to a height of six meters, while the opposite side does not surpass three meters. The architect explains: "The compact, trapezium-shaped plan of the studio is augmented by the extension of the east and west exterior walls to create a sheltered, triangulated south entry deck and a north terrace that overlooks the ocean. From a distant view, the streamlined form of the Squish Studio becomes apparent with its high back and low (squished) front designed, in part, to deflect the winds from the stormy North Atlantic." Power is supplied by solar panels located on an adjacent hill. The interior and exterior are clad in white-painted spruce planks.

Das **SQUISH STUDIO** liegt unweit der kleinen Stadt Tilting am östlichen Ende von Fogo Island. Tilting, erstmals Mitte des 18. Jahrhunderts besiedelt, wurde erst kürzlich zum nationalen Landschaftskulturgebiet Kanadas erklärt. Die spitzwinklige weiße Form des Baus kontrastiert unverkennbar mit der lokalen Architektursprache und liegt direkt an der felsigen Küste. Während das Studio an der Südseite bis zu 6 m hoch ist, misst die gegenüberliegende Seite gerade einmal 3 m. Der Architekt erklärt: „Der kompakte, trapezförmige Grundriss des Studios gewinnt zusätzlich an Dramatik durch die vorgezogenen Ost- und Westfassaden, wodurch ein geschützter Eingangsbereich nach Süden und eine Nordterrasse mit Blick aufs Meer entsteht." Aus der Ferne wird deutlich, dass die windschnittige Form des Squish Studio mit der hochgezogenen Rückwand und der niedrigen („squished", dt. gestauchten) Front z.T. auch als Schutz vor den stürmischen Winden des Nordatlantiks geplant wurde. Die Energieversorgung erfolgt über eine Solaranlage auf einem nahe gelegenen Hügel. Innen und außen wurde der Bau mit weiß lackierter Fichte verschalt.

Le **SQUISH STUDIO** est situé à proximité de la petite ville de Tilting, à l'extrémité orientale de l'île de Fogo. Colonisée pour la première fois au milieu du XVIIIe siècle, le district canadien de Tilting a été désigné récemment paysage culturel national. La forme anguleuse et la couleur blanche de l'atelier contrastent délibérément avec l'architecture locale, d'autant plus qu'il est placé directement sur la côte rocheuse. L'extrémité sud se dresse à une hauteur de 6 m, tandis que le côté opposé ne dépasse pas 3 m. L'architecte explique que « le plan compact en forme de trapèze du bâtiment est agrandi par les prolongations des murs extérieurs est et ouest, qui créent un porche d'entrée triangulaire abrité au sud et une terrasse au nord au-dessus de l'océan ». Vue de loin, la forme profilée du Squish Studio apparaît avec sa haute façade arrière et sa façade avant basse (écrasée) conçues notamment pour dévier les vents violents de l'Atlantique Nord. L'électricité est fournie par des panneaux solaires placés sur une colline voisine. L'intérieur et l'extérieur du bâtiment sont recouverts de planches d'épicéa peintes en blanc.

With its curious, angled forms and the way it sits lightly on the site, the Squish Studio seems to hover between two dimensions and three.

Das Squish Studio mit seiner ungewöhnlichen, schiefwinkligen Form tangiert den Baugrund kaum und changiert geradezu zwischen Zwei- und Dreidimensionalität.

Avec ses étranges formes anguleuses et la légèreté avec laquelle il est posé, le Squish Studio semble flotter entre deux et trois dimensions.

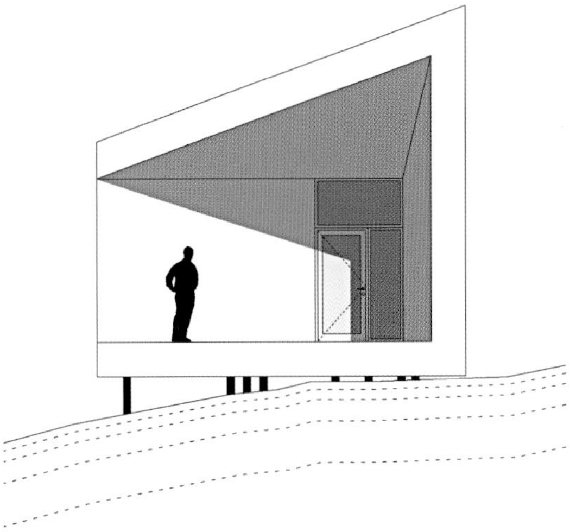

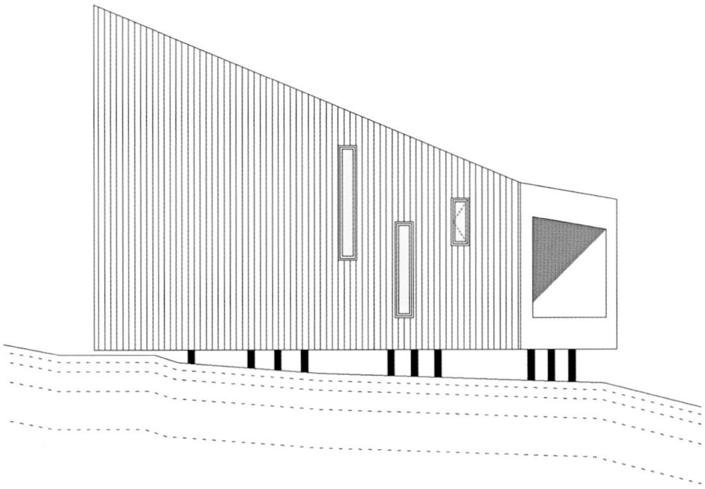

Though there is not a great deal of floor space, ceiling height and the generous glazing give the structure a very open feeling, surely propitious to the creation of works of art.

Trotz begrenzter Nutzfläche gewinnt der Bau durch seine Deckenhöhe und großzügige Verglasung besondere Offenheit, was dem künstlerischen Schaffensprozess sicher zuträglich ist.

Malgré une surface au sol réduite, la hauteur du plafond et le généreux vitrage confèrent à l'ensemble un sentiment de grande ouverture certainement propice à la création d'œuvres d'art.

The interiors are as simple and "clean" as might be expected from the exterior of the structure—the empty space allows artists to create as they will.

Wie schon der Außenbau vermuten lässt, ist das Interieur schlicht und klar gehalten – der leere Raum lässt den Künstlern freie Hand bei seiner Nutzung.

L'intérieur est aussi simple et « pur » que l'extérieur du bâtiment le laisse présager – l'espace vide permet aux artistes de laisser libre cours à leur créativité.

RODRIGO SHEWARD

Rodrigo Sheward
Blanca Estela 1055, departament 411
Bosques de montemar, ConCon
Región de Valparaíso
Chile

Tel: +56 997 767 4057
E-mail: rodrigosheward@gmail.com
Web: www.grupotalca.cl

RODRIGO SHEWARD was born in Chile in 1979 and attended the University of Talca (2000–07). Before obtaining his diploma in 2007, he worked on the Cudico House (Villarrica, 2003) and collaborated with the architect Fernando Montoya on the Sushi Home Restaurant (Viña del Mar, 2004). Recent projects include the Pinohuacho Observation Deck (Pinohuacho, Villarrica, 2006, published here); the Quincho Gorro Capucha, tourism facilities (Pinohuacho, 2009); and the Santa Fe Port service facilities (Las Ventanas, Valparaiso, 2009), all in Chile.

RODRIGO SHEWARD wurde 1979 in Chile geboren und studierte an der Universidad de Talca (2000–07). Schon vor seinem Diplom 2007 arbeitete er am Haus Cudico (Villarrica, 2003) und mit dem Architekten Fernando Montoya am Sushi Home Restaurant (Viña del Mar, 2004). Seine neueren Projekte sind eine Aussichtsterrasse in Pinohuacho (Villarrica, 2006, hier veröffentlicht), die Tourismusanlagen Quincho Gorro Capucha (Pinohuacho, 2009) und Dienstleistungseinrichtungen im Hafen von Santa Fe (Las Ventanas, Valparaiso, 2009), alle in Chile.

RODRIGO SHEWARD, né au Chili en 1979, a étudié à l'université de Talca (2000–07). Avant d'obtenir son diplôme d'architecte en 2007, il a dessiné les plans de la maison Cudico (Villarrica, 2003) et collaboré avec l'architecte Fernando Montoya sur le projet du restaurant Sushi Home (Viña del Mar, 2004). Parmi ses projets récents figurent la plate-forme d'observation de Pinohuacho (Villarrica, 2006, publiée ici) ; les installations touristiques de Quincho Gorro Capucha (Pinohuacho, 2009) et des installations de service pour le port de Santa Fe (Las Ventanas, Valparaiso 2009), tous au Chili.

PINOHUACHO OBSERVATION DECK

Pinohuacho, Villarrica, Araucanía, Chile, 2006

Address: Pinohuacho, Villarrica, Araucanía,
Chile, +56 9 9041 5230, www.pinohuacho.blogspot.com
Area: 78 m². Client: Pedro Vazquez, Miguel Vazquez. Cost: $3000

Access to this project requires an hour's walk along a winding path near forests and an old logging area. The logged area is being used for subsistence farming. Rodrigo Sheward's goal was to "bring architecture where there is none… creating a space to talk, and in order to do that manage, design, and build. An unpaved road for an architect who planned his *opera prima.*" There are actually two volumes located 80 meters apart with a view toward the Villarrica volcano. Each piece of wood was found and sawed on site: "gleaned at the scene, invented on the spot," as the architect says. He takes some pride in the fact that those cutting the wood worked with the same determination they once used to devastate the site. Sheward also points to his will to discuss the use of their own land with the local population.

Dieses Projekt ist nur nach einer einstündigen Wanderung auf einem gewundenen Pfad durch Wälder und einen alten Holzeinschlag erreichbar. Letzterer wird heute landwirtschaftlich genutzt. Rodrigo Shewards Ziel war es, „Architektur dorthin zu bringen, wo es keine gibt …, einen Ort zum Gespräch zu gestalten, ihn zu organisieren, zu entwerfen und zu bauen. Ein hindernisreicher Weg für einen Architekten, um seine opera prima zu planen." Es handelt sich eigentlich um zwei 80 m voneinander entfernte Bauten mit Blick auf den Vulkan Villarrica. Jedes Stück Holz wurde vor Ort gefunden und bearbeitet – „am Standort aufgelesen und dort verwendet", wie der Architekt es ausdrückt. Er ist stolz darauf, dass diejenigen, die einst das Gelände zerstörten, jetzt mit der gleichen Entschlossenheit das Holz bearbeiteten. Sheward verweist auch auf seine Bereitschaft, mit der örtlichen Bevölkerung über die Nutzung ihres eigenen Landes zu diskutieren.

Il ne faut pas moins d'une heure de marche sur un chemin qui serpente entre des forêts et une ancienne zone d'exploitation forestière aujourd'hui cultivée pour accéder à cette plate-forme. L'objectif de Rodrigo Sheward a été « d'apporter l'architecture là où il n'en existait pas … de créer un espace pour parler, et pour cela de gérer, de concevoir et de construire. Une voie difficile pour un architecte qui réalise sa première œuvre ». Le projet consiste en fait en deux volumes éloignés de 80 m l'un de l'autre qui donnent sur le volcan de Villarica. Chaque morceau de bois utilisé a été trouvé et scié sur place : « Glané sur les lieux, inventé sur place », comme aime à le dire l'architecte. Il fait remarquer que ceux qui ont découpé ce bois avaient participé avec la même détermination à la dévastation du site. Sheward insiste également sur sa volonté de discuter de l'usage du sol avec la population locale.

The roughness and simplicity of this structure is, of course, fully intentional. Looking like a closed wooden box from the side (left page), the building is, in fact, entirely open.

Die Rauheit und Schlichtheit dieses Bauwerks ist natürlich absolut gewollt. Von der Seite gesehen, wirkt es zwar wie eine geschlossene Kiste (linke Seite), tatsächlich ist es aber vollständig offen.

La simplicité rustique de cette construction est bien évidemment intentionnelle. Présentant un aspect de boîte fermée d'un côté (page de gauche), elle est en fait entièrement ouverte.

The edges of the viewing platform are irregular, and the wood is left rough, a product of this place assembled to allow visitors to appreciate the views.

Les bords de la plate-forme d'observation sont irréguliers et le bois laissé brut, comme un produit issu du lieu que le touriste vient admirer.

Die Ränder der Aussichtsplattform sind ungleichmäßig und das Holz unbehandelt, ein Produkt dieses Standorts, der errichtet wurde, damit Besucher die Aussicht genießen können.

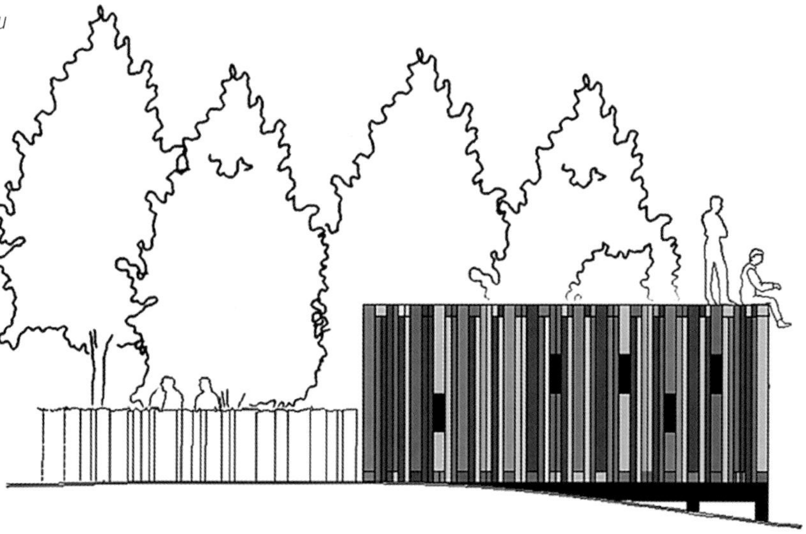

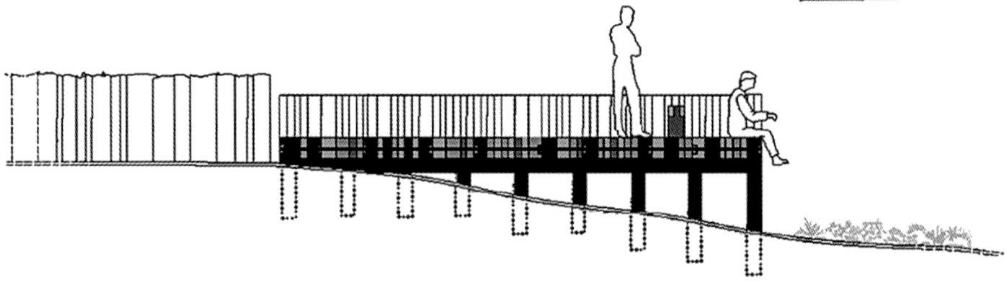

The deck seen on the left page is approximately 80 meters away from the shed, visible below and in the elevation drawing.

Die auf der linken Seite gezeigte Terrasse ist etwa 80 m von dem Unterstand entfernt, der in der Ansichtszeichnung und unten zu sehen ist.

La terrasse (page de gauche) est située à 80 m environ de l'abri visible ci-dessous et sur l'élévation.

SHIM-SUTCLIFFE

Shim-Sutcliffe Architects Inc.
441 Queen Street East
Toronto
Ontario M5A 1T5
Canada

Tel: +1 416 368 3892
Fax: +1 416 368 9468
E-mail: info@shimsut.com
Web: www.shimsut.com

BRIGITTE SHIM was born in Kingston, Jamaica, in 1958. She received her B.Arch and her B.E.S. degrees from the University of Waterloo in Ontario, Canada. She worked in the office of Arthur Erickson (1981), and Baird/Sampson in Toronto, before creating her own firm, Brigitte Shim Architect (1988–94). She is a Principal and cofounder of Shim-Sutcliffe, created in Toronto in 1994. **HOWARD SUTCLIFFE** was born in Yorkshire, England, in 1958. He also received his B.Arch and his B.E.S. degrees from the University of Waterloo in Ontario. He worked in the offices of Barton Myers (1984–86) and Merrick Architecture until 1993, creating Shim-Sutcliffe with Brigitte Shim the following year. Their recent work includes the Frum African Gallery in the Art Gallery of Ontario (Toronto, Ontario, 2006–08); Integral House (Toronto, Ontario, 2005–09); House on Henry's Meadow (Vale Perkins, Quebec, 2007–09, published here); Fung Loy Kok Institute of Taoism Place of Worship (Markham, Ontario, 2009–); the Harrison Island Cabin (Georgian Bay, Ontario, 2010); master plan and bridge for The Narrows for the Mnjikaning Fish Fence Circle (Orillia, Ontario, 2010–); and the New Polyot Retreat Conference Center, Skolkovo Innovation Center (Russian Federation, 2011–), all in Canada unless stated otherwise.

BRIGITTE SHIM wurde 1958 in Kingston, Jamaica, geboren. Sie machte ihren B. Arch. sowie ihren Bachelor of Environmental Studies an der University of Waterloo in Ontario. Sie arbeitete für Arthur Erickson (1981) und Baird/Sampson in Toronto, bevor sie ihr Büro Brigitte Shim Architect (1988–94) gründete. Sie ist Seniorpartnerin und Mitbegründerin von Shim-Sutcliffe, gegründet 1994 in Toronto. **HOWARD SUTCLIFFE** wurde 1958 in Yorkshire geboren. Auch er machte seinen B. Arch. und einen Bachelor of Environmental Studies an der University of Waterloo in Ontario. Er arbeitete für Barton Myers (1984–86) und bis 1993 Merrick Architecture und gründete mit Brigitte Shim im darauffolgenden Jahr Shim-Sutcliffe. Zu ihren jüngeren Projekten zählen die Frum Gallery für Afrikanische Kunst in der Art Gallery of Ontario (Toronto, 2006–08), das Integral-Haus (Toronto, 2005–09), das Haus auf Henrys Wiese (Vale Perkins, Quebec, 2007–09, hier vorgestellt), der Andachtsraum am Fung Loy Kok Institute of Taoism (Markham, seit 2009), eine Hütte auf Harrison Island (Georgian Bay, Ontario, 2010), ein Masterplan und eine Brücke über die Narrows für den Mnjikaning Fish Fence Circle (Orillia, seit 2010) sowie das Neue Polyot-Retreat- und Konferenzzentrum am Innovationszentrum Skolkowo (Russische Föderation, seit 2011), alle in Kanada, sofern nicht anders angegeben.

BRIGITTE SHIM, née à Kingston en Jamaïque en 1958 a obtenu son B.Arch. et son B.E.S. de l'université de Waterloo (Ontario, Canada). Elle a travaillé chez Arthur Erikson (1981) et Baird/Sampson à Toronto, avant de créer sa propre agence, Brigitte Shim Architect (1988–94). Elle est cofondatrice et dirigeante de l'agence Shim-Sutcliffe fondée à Toronto en 1994. **HOWARD SUTCLIFFE**, né dans le Yorkshire (GB) en 1958, a obtenu ses diplômes de B.Arch. et de B.E.S. de la même université. Il a travaillé chez Barton Myers (1984–86) et Merrick Architecture jusqu'en 1993, avant de créer Shim-Sutcliffe l'année suivante. Parmi leurs réalisations récentes, la plupart au Canada : la galerie d'art africain de la collection Frum au Musée des beaux-arts de l'Ontario (Toronto, 2006–08) ; l'Integral House (Toronto, 2005–09) ; la Maison sur la prairie d'Henry (Vale Perkins, Québec, 2007–09, publiée ici) ; l'Institut du taoïsme et sanctuaire Fung Loy Kok (Markham, 2009–) ; la Harrison Island Cabin (baie Georgienne, Ontario, 2010) ; le plan directeur du pont des Détroits pour le Mnjikaning Fish Fence Circle (Orillia, 2010–) et le nouveau Centre de retraite et de conférence de Polyot, Centre d'innovation de Skolkovo (Russie, 2011–).

HOUSE ON HENRY'S MEADOW

Vale Perkins, Quebec, Canada, 2008–09

Address: not disclosed. Area: 266 m². Client: Glenn and Susan Lowry
Cost: not disclosed. Collaboration: Olga Pushkar

This residence, built for the Director of New York's Museum of Modern Art, is located on the western shore of Lake Memphremagog, near the border between Quebec and Vermont. The house is built on a property with several existing buildings, including a 1920s log cabin that served as a family meeting place for decades. The local tradition of surrounding farms with walls of stacked firewood served as a starting point for the house. Visitors to the house first see a stacked-log wall, and then "a vertical sky-lit slot above wooden light coffers [that] provides deep views through the house and of the stair to the lower level. A clerestory window bringing light to the lower level also allows the seemingly heavy stacked-wood wall to float above the reflecting pool," according to the architects. The north and south elevations are clad in painted wood siding. The main living space is clad with local white pine boards and provides glimpses of Henry's Meadow through the stacked-wood walls on one side and panoramic views of the lake on the other.

Das am Westufer des Lake Memphremagog gelegene Haus unweit der Grenze von Quebec und Vermont entstand für den Direktor des New Yorker Museum of Modern Art. Auf dem Grundstück stehen bereits mehrere ältere Bauten, darunter ein Blockhaus aus den 1920er-Jahren, das der Familie jahrzehntelang als Treffpunkt diente. Ausgangspunkt für den Entwurf war die ländliche Tradition, Kaminholz an den Hauswänden zu stapeln. Besuchern fällt zunächst eine Wand aus gestapeltem Holz ins Auge, erst später „die Treppe zur unteren Ebene und Durchblicke durch das Haus, ermöglicht durch ein vertikales Lichtband über kassettierten Oberlichtern aus Holz. Das Oberlichtfenster, das die untere Ebene mit Tageslicht versorgt, lässt den Eindruck entstehen, die scheinbar massive Kaminholzwand schwebe über dem Spiegelbecken", so die Architekten. Nord- und Südseite haben eine Außenwandverschalung aus gestrichenem Holz. Der Hauptwohnraum wurde mit Brettern aus regionaler Kiefer verkleidet und bietet durch die Kaminholzstapel einen Blick auf Henrys Wiese sowie auf der anderen Seite einen Panoramablick auf den See.

Cette maison, construite pour le directeur du Musée d'art moderne de New York, est située sur la côte ouest du lac Memphremagog, près de la frontière entre le Québec et le Vermont. Elle a été édifiée sur un terrain occupé par plusieurs constructions dont une cabane en rondins des années 1920 utilisée par la famille depuis des décennies. Le projet a pris pour point de départ la tradition locale d'empiler le bois de chauffage contre les murs. Les visiteurs se trouvent tout d'abord confrontés à un mur de bûches de bois. « Une ouverture verticale étroite offre une perspective à travers la maison et sur l'escalier au niveau inférieur. Un lanterneau filant qui éclaire le niveau inférieur donne l'impression que le mur de bûches flotte au-dessus d'un bassin », expliquent les architectes. Les façades nord et sud sont parées de bardeaux de bois peint. Le séjour, habillé de planches de pin clair, offre une vue sur la prairie d'Henry à travers le mur en bûches et des vues panoramiques vers le lac.

The dark coloring of the house allows it to blend into the forest environment, which has been left largely untouched.

Mit seiner eher dunklen Palette fügt sich der Bau harmonisch in die Waldlandschaft, die weitgehend unberührt blieb.

La teinte foncée du bois laisse la maison se fondre encore mieux dans son cadre boisé, laissé en grande partie intact.

A site plan shows the proximity of the house to the lake. Above, an alternation of low stone walls, gravel surfaces, and a pond eases the transition to the forest, which is just beyond.

Ein Lageplan veranschaulicht die Nähe des Hauses zum See. Oben ein Wechselspiel von niedrigen Natursteinmauern, Kies und einem Teich – so entsteht ein fließender Übergang zum Wald direkt hinter dem Haus.

Le plan du site montre la proximité de la maison et du lac. Ci-dessus, l'alternance de murets de pierre, de surfaces en gravier et d'un bassin rend plus fluide la transition vers la forêt, juste derrière.

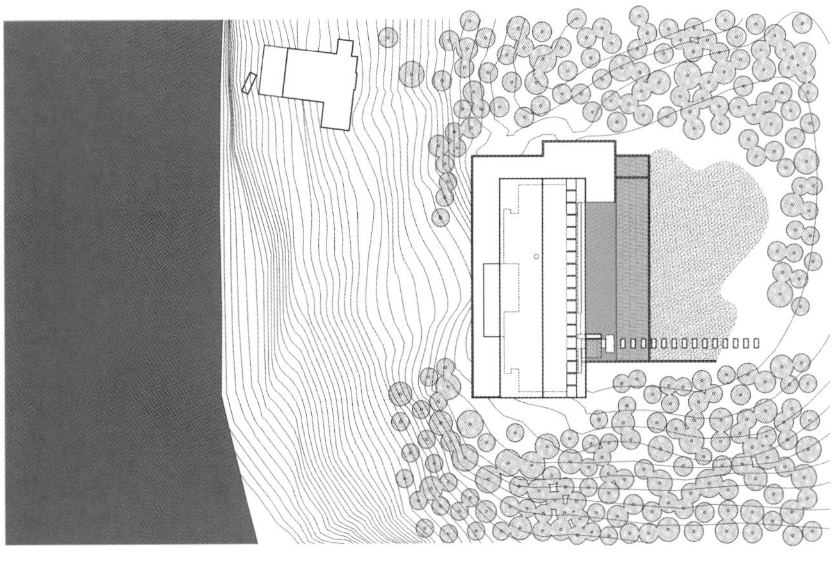

Using the local practice of stacking wood, the architects have made an entire façade of logs, giving the house a decidedly rural appearance from this angle.

Die Architekten griffen die lokale Tradition auf, Kaminholz vor dem Haus zu stapeln, und gestalteten eine entsprechende Fassade, die dem Bau deutlich rustikalen Charme verleiht.

S'inspirant d'une coutume locale d'entreposage du bois, les architectes ont entièrement habillé de rondins une façade, conférant à ce projet un aspect résolument rural, vu sous cet angle.

ÁLVARO SIZA

Álvaro Siza Arquitecto SA
Rua do Aleixo 53–2
4150–043 Porto / Portugal
Tel: +351 22 616 72 70 / Fax: +351 22 616 72 79
E-mail: geral@sizavieira.pt / Web: www.sizavieira.pt

Born in Matosinhos, Portugal, in 1933, **ÁLVARO SIZA** studied at the University of Porto School of Architecture (1949–55). He created his own practice in 1954, and worked with Fernando Tavora from 1955 to 1958. He received the European Community's Mies van der Rohe Prize in 1988 and the Pritzker Prize in 1992. He built a large number of small-scale projects in Portugal, and worked on the restructuring of the Chiado in Lisbon (Portugal, 1989–); the Meteorology Center in Barcelona (Spain, 1989–92); the Vitra Furniture Factory (Weil am Rhein, Germany, 1991–94); the Porto School of Architecture, Porto University (Portugal, 1986–95); the University of Aveiro Library (Aveiro, Portugal, 1988–95); the Portuguese Pavilion for the 1998 Lisbon World's Fair (with Eduardo Souto de Moura); and the Serralves Foundation (Porto, Portugal, 1996–99); and House in Oudenburg (Belgium, 1995–2001, published here). More recent projects include the Aldega Mayor Winery (Campo Maior, Portugal, 2005–06); and the Iberê Camargo Foundation (Porto Alegre, Rio Grande do Sul, Brazil, 2008).

ÁLVARO SIZA wurde 1933 in Matosinhos, Portugal, geboren und studierte an der Architekturfakultät der Universität Porto (1949–55). Er eröffnete 1954 sein eigenes Büro und arbeitete von 1955 bis 1958 mit Fernando Tavora zusammen. 1988 erhielt er den Mies-van-der-Rohe-Preis der Europäischen Gemeinschaft, 1992 den Pritzker-Preis. In Portugal hat er eine Vielzahl kleinerer Projekte realisiert und war bei der Restaurierung des Chiado-Viertels in Lissabon tätig (seit 1989). Zu seinen weiteren Projekten gehören das Zentrum für Meteorologie in Barcelona (1989–92), die Vitra-Fabrikhalle (Weil am Rhein, 1991–94), die Architekturfakultät der Universität Porto (Portugal, 1986–95), die Universitätsbibliothek von Aveiro (Aveiro, Portugal, 1988–95), der Portugiesische Pavillon der Weltausstellung 1998 in Lissabon (gemeinsam mit Eduardo Souto de Moura), die Serralves-Stiftung (Porto, 1996–99) und das Haus in Oudenburg (Belgien, 1995–2001, hier veröffentlicht). Zu den jüngeren Projekten zählen u. a. die Weinkellerei Aldega Mayor (Campo Maior, Portugal, 2005–06) und die Stiftung Iberê Camargo (Porto Alegre, Brasilien, 2008).

Né à Matosinhos, Portugal, en 1933, **ÁLVARO SIZA** a fait ses études à l'École d'architecture de l'université de Porto (1949–55). Il a ouvert son agence en 1954 et a travaillé avec Fernando Tavora de 1955 à 1958. Il a reçu le prix Mies van der Rohe de la Communauté européenne en 1988 et le prix Pritzker en 1992. Au Portugal, il a réalisé beaucoup de petits projets et a travaillé à la restructuration du quartier du Chiado à Lisbonne (1989–) ; ainsi qu'au Centre météorologique de Barcelone (Espagne, 1989–92) ; à l'usine de meubles Vitra (Weil am Rhein, Allemagne, 1991–94) ; à l'École d'architecture de l'université de Porto (Portugal, 1986–95) ; à la bibliothèque de l'université d'Aveiro (Portugal, 1988–95) ; au pavillon du Portugal de l'Exposition universelle de Lisbonne 1998 (avec Eduardo Souto de Moura) ; à la fondation Serralves (Porto, 1996–99) et à la maison à Oudenburg (Belgique, 1995–2001, publiée ici). Ses projets plus récents comprennent le vignoble Aldega Mayor (Campo Maior, Portugal, 2005–06) et la fondation Iberê Camargo (Porto Alegre, Brésil, 2008).

HOUSE IN OUDENBURG

Oudenburg, Belgium, 1995–2001

Address: not disclosed. Area: not disclosed
Client: not disclosed. Cost: not disclosed

The architect clearly inspires himself with local farm architecture, taking the occasion to limit window surfaces to create the kind of relatively closed façades he favors.

Der Architekt ließ sich von lokalen ländlichen Bauweisen inspirieren; willkommener Anlass, um Fensteröffnungen sparsam einzusetzen und die von ihm bevorzugten, eher geschlossenen Fassaden zu gestalten.

L'architecte s'est à l'évidence inspiré de l'architecture agricole locale, saisissant l'occasion pour limiter la surface des ouvertures afin d'obtenir le type de façade fermée qu'il affectionne.

Part of a farm complex, this project involves the renovation and extension of existing buildings to create a house and an art gallery. Álvaro Siza employed forms inspired by the farm structures to create simple, "unpretentious" volumes. In one unusual aspect of the design, Siza used vertical boards of western red cedar for cladding the new building, with a lead roof. Limited glazing, which is frequent in his work, but also corresponds to the older buildings on the site, is used in a way that carefully studies the light conditions in Belgium, obviously quite different from those in Portugal. Contemporary art is displayed in a renovated building with a skylight and a single column. Despite insisting on the simplicity of the whole, in this instance the architect takes an existing U-shaped complex and turns it into a carefully orchestrated group of related forms, with interiors that do show some of the angular complexity that characterizes many of his buildings. Outside, the older brick buildings are either stripped bare or painted in white, which also enriches the visual palette employed.

Das in eine Hofanlage integrierte Projekt umfasste auch die Sanierung und Erweiterung verschiedener Altbauten, um ein Wohnhaus und eine Galerie zu schaffen. Álvaro Siza griff die Formensprache der ländlichen Architektur auf und entwarf schlichte, „unprätentiöse" Gebäude. Ungewöhnlich ist u.a. seine Entscheidung, den Neubau mit einer vertikalen Verblendung aus Zedernholz und einer Dachhaut aus Blei zu versehen. Die geringe Durchfensterung ist ein häufiges Merkmal bei Sizas Entwürfen, korrespondiert hier jedoch auch mit älteren Gebäuden auf dem Areal. Die Fenster wurden auf belgische Lichtverhältnisse zugeschnitten, die sich grundlegend von denen in Portugal unterscheiden. In einem sanierten Gebäude mit Oberlicht und einer einzelnen freistehenden Stütze wird zeitgenössische Kunst präsentiert. Trotz des bewussten Beharrens auf Schlichtheit schafft der Architekt mit der bestehenden hufeisenförmigen Hofanlage eine einfühlsam gestaltete Gruppe aufeinander bezogener Baukörper. Die Interieurs lassen etwas von jener verwinkelten Komplexität ahnen, die viele seiner Bauten kennzeichnet. Die vorhandenen Backsteinfassaden wurden entweder freigelegt oder geweißt, eine weitere Bereicherung der hier angewandten Palette.

Ce projet portait sur l'extension et la rénovation de bâtiments d'une exploitation agricole existante pour créer une résidence et une galerie d'art. Alvaro Siza a conçu des volumes simples, « sans prétention », en s'inspirant du vocabulaire formel de l'architecture agricole. Une des caractéristiques inhabituelles du projet est le parement de cette nouvelle construction à toiture en plomb avec des bardeaux verticaux en cèdre rouge. Le nombre limité d'ouvertures – fréquent dans son œuvre – évoque également les anciens bâtiments présents sur le site, mais est en fait soigneusement adapté aux conditions et à l'éclairage naturels, évidemment différentes en Belgique et au Portugal. Les œuvres d'art contemporain sont présentées dans un bâtiment rénové doté d'une verrière zénithale. Tout en optant pour une grande simplicité de l'ensemble, l'architecte a fait de ce complexe en forme de U une composition de formes soigneusement orchestrées. Les intérieurs présentent à l'occasion cette complexité anguleuse que l'on observe dans beaucoup de ses réalisations. À l'extérieur, les bâtiments anciens en brique ont été soit nettoyés, soit peints en blanc, enrichissant du coup la palette chromatique du projet.

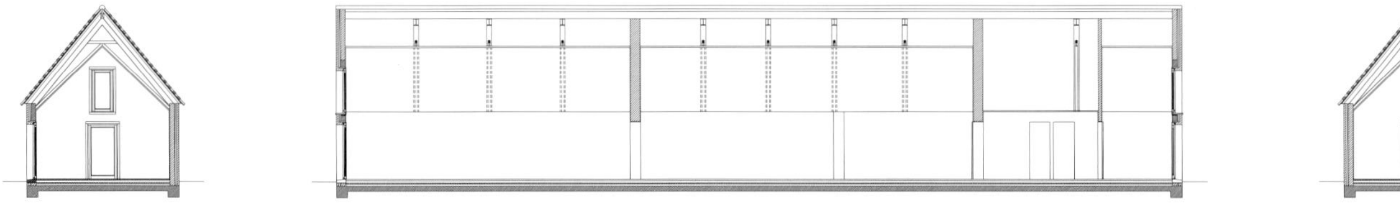

The unexpected projecting rectangular window—seen in the image to the right, and from inside, below—offers an intriguing, truncated view of the landscape.

Das überraschend auskragende rechteckige Fenster – siehe rechts und in einer Innenansicht unten – rahmt einen faszinierenden Blick auf die Landschaft.

L'étonnante fenêtre rectangulaire en projection – vue sur la photo à droite et de l'intérieur ci-dessous – offre une étonnante vue tronquée du paysage.

Left page, an older brick building neighbors the house designed by Siza. Strict simplicity and off-axis openings identify his work even when he blends in a willful manner with local style. Sections (below) show the strict adherence to a rectilinear vocabulary.

Linke Seite: Ein älterer Backsteinbau ist dem von Siza entworfenen Haus benachbart. Strenge Schlichtheit und asymmetrisch platzierte Öffnungen lassen seine Handschrift erkennen, selbst wo er sich auf lokale Bauweisen einlässt. Querschnitte (unten) bestätigen die konsequent geradlinige Formensprache.

La maison de Siza est voisine d'une ferme ancienne en brique. Sa simplicité rigoureuse et le rythme irrégulier des ouvertures signent cette intervention, même lorsqu'il joue avec le style local. Des coupes (ci-dessous) illustrent la rigueur géométrique du vocabulaire utilisé.

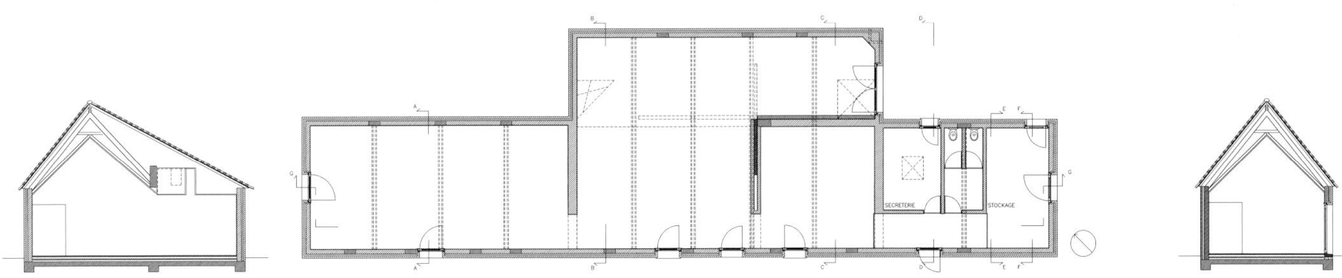

In the living room, the large rectangular window seems to confront the black corner fireplace. The ceiling design allows for recessed lighting and spatial variety.

Das große rechteckige Fenster im Wohnzimmer wirkt wie ein Pendant zum schwarzen Eckkamin. Die Konzeption der Decke ermöglicht indirekte Beleuchtung und sorgt für räumliche Vielfalt.

Dans le séjour, la vaste fenêtre rectangulaire semble répondre à la cheminée noire positionnée à l'angle d'un mur. Le plafond crée une certaine variété et permet de dissimuler un système d'éclairage.

A wood-plank floor, a double-slope ceiling corresponding to the roof, a window, and a door make up this space where simplicity and modernity are in harmony even with a rural setting (top and right page).

Ein Dielenboden, ein offener Spitzgiebel, der die Konturen des Dachs nachvollzieht, ein Fenster und eine Tür definieren den Raum, dessen Einfachheit und Modernität auch mit der ländlichen Umgebung harmonieren (ganz oben und rechte Seite).

Un sol en parquet, un plafond à double pente reprenant le profil du toit et une porte surmontée d'une fenêtre composent cet espace dans lequel la simplicité et la modernité s'harmonisent aussi avec un environnement rural (en haut et page de droite).

Termas Geométricas
Hot Springs Complex

GERMÁN DEL SOL

Germán del Sol, Architecto
Camino Las Flores 11 441
Las Condes, Santiago
Chile

Tel: +56 2 214 12 48
Fax: +56 2 214 20 20
E-mail: contacto@germandelsol.cl
Web: www.germandelsol.cl

GERMÁN DEL SOL GUZMÁN was born in Santiago de Chile in 1949. He graduated in 1973 from the ETSAB of Barcelona, Spain. He created his own firm in Barcelona (1973–79), before returning to Santiago, where he worked on his own (1980–83) and then spent two years in the office of R. Elmore in Palo Alto, California (1984–86). He then returned to his own practice in Santiago, where he has been based since 1986. Between 1988 and 1998, he created and directed explora, a company dedicated to promoting new travel destinations in remote places in South America. Between 1995 and 1998, he created and directed "Viña Gracia," a new Chilean vineyard. Germán del Sol then created and directed a new Hot Springs Complex, next to the Villarrica volcano, in Pucón (Chile, 2001–05). He won the National Association of Chilean Architects Award in 2006. His built work includes the Hotel explora en Atacama (San Pedro de Atacama, 1998); horse stables (San Pedro de Atacama, 1999); saunas and pools (Atacama, 2000); Puritama Hot Springs Complex (Atacama, 2000); Hotel Remota (Patagonia, 2005–06); Remota Spot (Patagonia, 2007); and Termas Geométricas Hot Springs Complex, Coñaripe (Villarrica National Park, Chile, Phase 1: 2004, Phase 2: 2008, published here), all in Chile. Also in 2008, he completed an apartment building in Vallecas, Spain.

GERMÁN DEL SOL GUZMÁN wurde 1949 in Santiago de Chile geboren. Sein Studium schloss er 1973 an der Escuela Técnica Superior de Arquitectura de Barcelona in Spanien ab. Nachdem er zunächst in Barcelona ein eigenes Büro betrieb (1973–79), kehrte er nach Santiago zurück, wo er selbstständig arbeitete (1980–83), bevor er zwei Jahre lang für R. Elmore in Palo Alto, Kalifornien, tätig war (1984–86). Schließlich kehrte er zu seinem eigenen Büro in Santiago zurück, von wo aus er seit 1986 praktiziert. Von 1988 bis 1998 leitete er die von ihm gegründete Agentur Explora, die sich auf die Erschließung neuer Reiseziele an abgelegenen Orten Südamerikas spezialisiert hatte. Von 1995 bis 1998 führte er das von ihm gegründete chilenische Weingut Viña Gracia. Schließlich baute und leitete Germán del Sol auch eine Hotelanlage an den Thermalquellen am Vulkan Villarrica in Pucón (Chile, 2001–05). 2006 gewann er den Preis der nationalen Vereinigung der chilenischen Architekten. Zu seinen realisierten Projekten zählen das Hotel Explora en Atacama (San Pedro de Atacama, 1998), Pferdeställe (San Pedro de Atacama, 1999), Saunen und Pools (Atacama, 2000), die Thermalquellen Puritama (Atacama, 2000), das Hotel Remota (Patagonien, 2005–06), Remota Spot (Patagonien, 2007) sowie der Thermalquellenkomplex Geométricas in Coñaripe (Nationalpark Villarrica, 2004: Bauabschnitt 1, 2008: Bauabschnitt 2, hier vorgestellt), alle in Chile. 2008 konnte außerdem ein Apartmentgebäude in Vallecas, Spanien, fertiggestellt werden.

GERMÁN DEL SOL GUZMÁN, né à Santiago du Chili en 1949, est diplômé de l'ETSAB de Barcelone. Il a fondé une agence à Barcelone (1973–79), avant de revenir à Santiago où il a travaillé pour son compte (1980–83) et a passé deux années chez R. Elmore à Palo Alto (Californie, 1984–86). Il est ensuite revenu à Santiago où son agence est basée depuis 1986. Entre 1988 et 1998, il a créé et dirigé « explora », une société de promotion de nouvelles destinations de voyages dans des lieux mal connus d'Amérique du Sud. Entre 1995 et 1998, il a créé et dirigé « Viña Gracia », un nouveau vignoble chilien, puis un nouveau complexe thermal, près du volcan de Villarrica à Pucón (Chili, 2001–05). Il a remporté le prix de l'Association nationale des architectes chiliens en 2006. Parmi ses réalisations, toutes au Chili : l'hôtel Explora à Atacama (San Pedro de Atacama, 1998) ; des écuries (San Pedro de Atacama, 1999) ; des saunas et piscines (Atacama, 2000) ; le complexe thermal de Puritama (Atacama, 2000) ; l'hôtel Remota (Patagonie, 2005–06) ; le Remota Spot (Patagonie, 2007) et le complexe thermal des Termas Geométricas de Coñaripe (Parc national de Villarrica, Chili, 2004, Phase 1, 2008, Phase 2, publié ici). En 2008, il a réalisé un immeuble d'appartements à Vallecas, en Espagne.

TERMAS GEOMÉTRICAS
HOT SPRINGS COMPLEX

Coñaripe, Villarrica National Park, Los Lagos Region, Chile, 2004 (Phase 1), 2008 (Phase 2)

Address: +569 7477 1708, www.termasgeometricas.cl. Area: 10 000 m²
Client: Termas Geométricas. Cost: €1.5 million
Collaboration: José Luis Ibañez (Architect), Carlos Venegas (Architect)

Channels carry both visitors and water amidst the spectacular natural setting.

Kanäle und Stege leiten Wasser bzw. Besucher durch die spektakuläre Landschaft.

Ces « canaux » facilitent la circulation de l'eau et des visiteurs au milieu d'un cadre naturel spectaculaire.

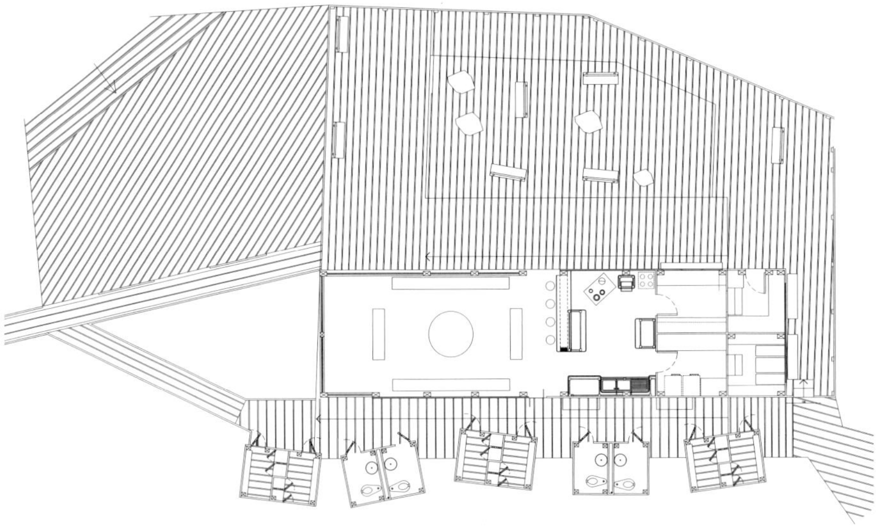

Located 725 kilometers south of Santiago in Chile's southern Lake Country, this bath complex includes 17 slate-covered pools fed by hot spring waters that emerge from the earth as a mountain stream. Native coigüe wood is used for the paths that connect these pools, and the same material is used for the wooden conduits that direct the water into the pools from beneath the walkway. Each pool has a wood pavilion and private bathrooms or locker rooms. A large, covered, and secluded space with an open fire invites guests to relax with a cup of tea or a glass of water. The roof of this structure is planted with wild grass. The architect states: "They are named Termas Geométricas because it is a work of architecture built with strong primitive geometric elements that allow one to be captivated again by natural elements in the midst of wild, brutal nature."

Der 725 km südlich von Santiago de Chile im südlichen Seengebiet gelegene Thermalquellenkomplex umfasst 17 Wasserbecken aus Schiefer, die von Thermalquellen gespeist werden, die als Fluss aus dem Boden treten. Die Stege zwischen den Becken sind aus regionalem Coigüe-Holz gefertigt, dasselbe Material wurde für die hölzernen Wasserrinnen genutzt, die das Wasser unter den Stegen in die einzelnen Becken leiten. Zu jedem Becken gehört ein Holzpavillon mit Toiletten und Umkleiden. Ein großzügiger überdachter und geschützter Bereich mit einem offenen Feuer lädt Besucher zu einer Tasse Tee oder einem Glas Wasser ein. Das Dach ist mit wilden Gräsern begrünt. Der Architekt führt aus: „Die Termas Geométricas verdanken ihren Namen der Architektur aus markanten, allereinfachsten geometrischen Elementen, die es erlauben, sich wieder von den Naturwundern gefangen nehmen zu lassen, und das inmitten einer wilden, ungezähmten Natur."

Situé à 725 km au sud de Santiago dans le pays des lacs, ce complexe thermal compte 17 bassins en ardoise alimentés par des sources chaudes qui débouchent dans un torrent. Un bois local, le coigüe, a servi à construire des coursives qui relient ces bassins, mais aussi à acheminer l'eau dans les bassins. Chacun d'eux est accompagné d'un petit pavillon de bois et de toilettes privées ou de vestiaires. Un vaste espace couvert et isolé, équipé d'une cheminée à feu ouvert, permet aux hôtes de se détendre autour d'un thé ou d'un verre d'eau. Le toit de cette construction est recouvert d'herbes sauvages. « Nous avons appelé ces installations "Thermes géométriques", parce qu'elles sont vraiment une œuvre d'architecture réalisée à l'aide de composants géométriques puissants, voire primitifs, qui permettent de se laisser captiver par les éléments naturels au milieu d'une nature sauvage et brutale », explique l'architecte.

Bathhouses are also made of red wood, like the meandering paths that lead visitors to their destinations. Left page, a site plan (top) and a plan of the main building area (below).

Auch die Badehäuser wurden aus rotem Holz gebaut, ebenso wie die mäandernden Stege, auf denen die Besucher ihr Ziel erreichen. Links oben ein Lageplan, darunter ein Plan des Hauptbaugeländes.

Les maisons de bains sont également en bois teinté en rouge, comme les coursives qui les desservent. Page de gauche, en dessus, un plan de situation ; un plan du site du bâtiment principal en dessous.

Ferraz Gourmet

SOTERO ARCHITECTS

Sotero Arquitetos
Avenida Contorno 1010
40015–160 Bahia Marina Salvador, BA
Brazil

Tel/Fax: +55 71 3321 0987
E-mail: contato@soteroarquitetos.com.br
Web: www.soteroarquitetos.com.br

ADRIANO MASCARENHAS was born in 1974. He graduated from the Universidade Federal da Bahia (UFBA) in 1999. After graduation, he worked in Brazil for the French firm Citélum as a lighting designer for two years. In 2003 he joined DB Arquitetos (David Bastos) as a Partner and over a period of six years developed private projects in Brazil and other countries, such as the United Arab Emirates (Dubai) and Portugal. He founded Sotero Arquitetos in 2007 in Salvador, Bahia. Sotero's recent projects include the Soho Paseo Restaurant (Salvador, Bahia, 2008); Gurilândia School (Salvador, Bahia, 2010); AABB Concert Hall (Salvador, Bahia, 2011); the Soho Restaurant at Lago Sul (Brasília, 2011); Ferraz Gourmet (Salvador, Bahia, 2011, published here); Monorail Stations for public transport (Salvador, Bahia, 2011); Tecnocentro, a building for the seat of government of the State of Bahia in the technology park TecnoBahia (Salvador, Bahia, 2008–12); and Bahia Marina Design Hotel (Salvador, Bahia, 2011–), all in Brazil.

ADRIANO MASCARENHAS, geboren 1974, schloss sein Studium 1999 an der Universidade Federal da Bahia (UFBA) ab. Nach seinem Abschluss arbeitete er zunächst zwei Jahre in Brasilien als Leuchtendesigner für die französische Firma Citélum. 2003 schloss er sich DB Arquitetos (David Bastos) als Partner an und entwickelte in den folgenden sechs Jahren private Projekte in Brasilien und weiteren Ländern, darunter den Vereinigten Arabischen Emiraten (Dubai) und Portugal. 2007 gründete er Sotero Arquitetos in Salvador, Bahia. Zu Soteros jüngeren Projekten zählen das Restaurant Soho Paseo (Salvador, 2008), die Gurilândia-Schule (Salvador, 2010), das Konzerthaus AABB (Salvador, 2011), das Restaurant Soho in Lago Sul (Brasilia, 2011), Ferraz Gourmet (Salvador, 2011, hier vorgestellt), Monorail-Stationen für den Nahverkehr (Salvador, 2011), Tecnocentro, ein Gebäude für den Regierungssitz des Staates Bahia im Technologiepark TecnoBahia (Salvador, 2008–12) sowie das Designhotel Bahia Marina (Salvador, seit 2011), alle in Brasilien.

ADRIANO MASCARENHAS est né en 1974. Il est diplômé (1999) de l'Université fédérale de Bahia (UFBA). Il a ensuite travaillé au Brésil pour l'entreprise française Citélum comme créateur de luminaires pendant deux ans. En 2003, il a rejoint DB Arquitetos (David Bastos) dont il est devenu partenaire et a réalisé des projets privés pendant six ans au Brésil et dans d'autres pays comme les Émirats arabes unis (Dubaï) et le Portugal. Il a fondé Sotero Arquitetos en 2007 à Salvador, Bahia. Ses projets récents comprennent : le restaurant Soho Paseo (Salvador, 2008) ; l'école Gurilândia (Salvador, 2010) ; la salle de concerts AABB (Salvador, 2011) ; le restaurant Soho de Lago Sul (Brasilia, 2011) ; Ferraz Gourmet (Salvador, 2011, publié ici) ; des stations de monorail pour les transports publics (Salvador, 2011) ; Tecnocentro, un bâtiment pour le siège du gouvernement de l'État de Bahia dans le parc technologique TecnoBahia (Salvador, 2008–12) et l'hôtel design Bahia Marina (Salvador, 2011–), tous au Brésil.

FERRAZ GOURMET

Salvador, Bahia, Brazil, 2011

Address: Rua Ceará 339, Pituba, Salvador, 41830–450 Bahia, BA, Brazil, www.ferrazrestaurante.com.br, +55 71 3355 0027. Area: 320 m². Client: Sergio and Ricardo Ferraz. Cost: not disclosed

FERRAZ GOURMET was created on the occasion of the return of chef Ricardo Ferraz to Brazil after seven years working in acclaimed Italian restaurants (La Bastiglia, Il Rigoletto). The architects sought out the "cozy tone of tropical Sucupira wood" to define the atmosphere of the space. The restaurant remains open to the busy urban environment thanks to broad glazed surfaces but, within, the use of wood for the walls, linings, and furniture, together with gray limestone for the floor, counter, and lower walls, defines a space that is set apart from the city. As a counterpoint to the largely monochromatic décor, a specially commissioned work by the Bahian artist Bel Borba evokes themes related to gastronomy. The wood and leather furniture used in this project were entirely designed by Sotero. The restaurant occupies four levels, with toilets and employees' area in the basement, the main dining area, bar, and balcony on the ground floor, and the upper levels reserved for the kitchen and storage spaces.

FERRAZ GOURMET wurde von Ricardo Ferraz gegründet, nachdem er sieben Jahre in berühmten italienischen Restaurants gearbeitet hatte (La Bastiglia, Il Rigoletto) und schließlich nach Brasilien zurückgekehrt war. Die Architekten entschieden sich bewusst für den „warmen Farbton des tropischen Sucupira-Holzes", um Atmosphäre zu schaffen. Dank großzügiger Verglasung bleibt das Restaurant seinem belebten urbanen Umfeld verbunden, doch innen sorgt der Einsatz von Holz für die Wände, Verkleidungen und das Mobiliar im Zusammenspiel mit grauem Kalkstein für Böden, Tresen und Sockelzone für eine Stimmung, die sich von der Stadt abzusetzen versteht. Als Kontrapunkt zum überwiegend monochromatischen Dekor greift ein Auftragswerk von Bel Borba, einem Künstler aus Bahia, Motive aus der Welt der Gastronomie auf. Das gesamte Mobiliar aus Holz und Leder wurde von Sotero entworfen. Das Restaurant verteilt sich über vier Ebenen: Mitarbeiterräume und Toiletten liegen im Untergeschoss, Hauptgastraum, Bar und Balkon im Parterre sowie Küche und Lagerräume in zwei Obergeschossen.

FERRAZ GOURMET a été créé pour le retour au Brésil du chef Ricardo Ferraz après sept ans passés à travailler dans des restaurants italiens remarqués (*La Bastiglia, Il Rigoletto*). Les architectes ont eu recours au « ton chaleureux du bois tropical de sucupira » pour créer l'atmosphère de l'espace. Le restaurant est ouvert sur l'environnement urbain animé par de larges surfaces vitrées, mais à l'intérieur le choix du bois pour les murs, les revêtements et le mobilier, associé au calcaire gris du sol, du comptoir et du bas des murs, permet de définir un espace qui se distingue de la ville. En contrepoint du décor majoritairement monochrome, une œuvre spécialement commandée à l'artiste de Bahia Bel Borba évoque des thèmes liés à la gastronomie. Le mobilier de bois et de cuir a été entièrement créé par Sotero. Le restaurant occupe quatre niveaux : les toilettes et l'espace réservé aux employés au sous-sol, la salle principale, le bar et le balcon au rez-de-chaussée, les étages supérieurs étant réservés à la cuisine et à des espaces de rangement.

The warm, wood-clad atmosphere of the restaurant is complemented by purpose-designed furniture, a bar that displays bottles individually, and the green and red artwork seen at the back of the images.

Das warme, holzvertäfelte Ambiente des Restaurants wird ergänzt durch speziell entworfenes Mobiliar, eine Bar, die Flaschen als Solitäre präsentiert, und das grüne und rote Kunstwerk im Hintergrund.

L'atmosphère chaleureuse du restaurant lambrissé de bois est parachevée par le mobilier spécialement créé, le bar aux présentoirs de bouteilles individuels et l'œuvre d'art rouge et verte vue à l'arrière-plan des photos.

The enveloping texture of the wood creates a convivial space that is interrupted only by artworks or pottery.

Holz prägt den einladenden Raum als großes Thema. Kontraste sind allein die Kunstwerke und einzelne Keramikobjekte.

La texture enveloppante du bois crée un espace convivial uniquement entrecoupé par des œuvres d'art ou des poteries.

Spotlights highlight the artworks but also the tables and other furnishings, making them stand out from the wood background.

Punktbeleuchtung hebt die Kunstwerke hervor, ebenso die Tische und andere Einbauten, die sich so vor dem Hintergrund aus Holz behaupten.

Des spots éclairent les œuvres d'art, mais aussi les tables et d'autres meubles, les faisant ressortir sur le fond de bois.

STUDIO OF CINEMATIC ARCHITECTURE

Studio Of Cinematic Architecture (SOCA)
Hackney Picturehouse
270 Mare Street
London E8 1HE
UK

Tel: +44 77 46 39 57 27
E-mail: gabby@socalondon.com
Web: www.socalondon.com

GABBY SHAWCROSS was born in 1976 in Edinburgh, Scotland. He received his architectural education at the Bartlett School of Architecture (UCL, 1998–2005). He worked as an architectural assistant at Hopkins Architects (London, 1999–2003), and was a Senior Designer in the Jason Bruges Studio (London (2004–11) before becoming Director of the Studio Of Cinematic Architecture (SOCA). Cofounder of SOCA, **TUGHELA GINO** was born in 1975 in San Juan, Puerto Rico. She also studied architecture at the Bartlett (1999–2008). She worked in the offices of Terry Farrell (1997–98), Nicholas Grimshaw (2003), and Arup Associates (2003–05), before creating her own office (Tughela Gino Architecture, 2007–11). Their recent work includes Lucy in Disguise (London, UK, 2010); East-West House (London, UK, 2011); "London Dresser" (London, UK, 2012, published here); and the Bloomberg Visitor Experience (New York, USA, 2012).

GABBY SHAWCROSS wurde 1976 in Edinburgh, Schottland, geboren. Sein Studium absolvierte er an der Bartlett School of Architecture (UCL, 1998–2005). Er war Assistent bei Hopkins Architects (London, 1999–2003) und Senior Designer im Jason Bruges Studio (London, 2004–11), bevor er Direktor des Studio Of Cinematic Architecture (SOCA) wurde. Mitbegründerin von SOCA war die 1975 in San Juan, Puerto Rico, geborene **TUGHELA GINO**. Auch Gino studierte an der Bartlett School (1999–2008). Sie arbeitete in den Büros von Terry Farrell (1997–98), Nicholas Grimshaw (2003) und Arup Associates (2003–05), bevor sie ihr eigenes Büro gründete (Tughela Gino Architecture, 2007–11). Jüngere Arbeiten sind u. a. Lucy in Disguise (London, 2010), East-West House (London, 2011), „London Dresser" (London, 2012, hier vorgestellt) und das Bloomberg Visitor Experience (New York, 2012).

GABBY SHAWCROSS est né à Édimbourg, Écosse. Il a suivi ses études d'architecture à l'École d'architecture Bartlett (UCL, 1998–2005). Il a travaillé comme architecte assistant pour Hopkins Architects (Londres, 1999–2003) et comme concepteur senior pour Jason Bruges Studio (Londres (2004–11), avant de devenir directeur du Studio Of Cinematic Architecture (SOCA). Cofondatrice du SOCA, **TUGHELA GINO** est née en 1975 à San Juan, Porto Rico. Elle a également étudié l'architecture à l'École d'architecture Bartlett (1999–2008). Elle a travaillé pour les agences de Terry Farrell (1997–98), Nicholas Grimshaw (2003) et Arup Associates (2003–05) avant de créer la sienne (Tughela Gino Architecture, 2007–11). Parmi ses réalisations récentes figurent Lucy in Disguise (Londres, 2010) ; la East-West House (Londres, 2011) ; *London Dresser* (Londres, 2012, publiée ici) et la Bloomberg Visitor Experience (New York, 2012).

"LONDON DRESSER"

London, UK, 2012

Area: 33 m². Client: Mayor of London. Cost: €108 000
Collaboration: University of Westminster and Millimetre Ltd.

The architects describe the **"LONDON DRESSER"** as a "public space in a box." It was designed to display small-scale models of buildings from London's skyline. These are arranged for viewing at night, and open to create a "playful social gathering space" during the day. Commissioned to function during the 2012 Olympic Games in London, the work was designed in collaboration with students from the University of Westminster and with the Brighton firm Millimetre, which was responsible for the cabinet and seats. The steel-frame structure was clad in blackened English larch board and spruce ply panels. The seats were made from both laser-cut stacked plywood and hand-carved solid timber, and were relocated to a state primary school in Hackney after the installation's presence on Belvedere Road in London.

Die Architekten beschreiben **„LONDON DRESSER"** als „öffentlichen Raum in einer Schachtel", der zur Ausstellung von Modellen von Bauten der Londoner Skyline konzipiert war. Diese wurden abends zum Betrachten in der Box arrangiert, während sie tagsüber zur Schaffung eines „verspielten sozialen Treffpunkts" dienten. Das für die Olympischen Spiele 2012 in London vorgesehene Objekt wurde von Studenten der University of Westminster und der Firma Millimetre in Brighton entwickelt, die für die Ausführung der Ausstellungsbox und der Sitzgelegenheiten verantwortlich war. Die Stahlrahmenkonstruktion wurde mit schwarzen Brettern aus englischem Lärchenholz und Platten aus Fichtensperrholz verkleidet. Die Sitzgelegenheiten wurden aus Sperrholz, das im Laserverfahren zugeschnitten wurde, und handgearbeitetem Massivholz gefertigt. Nach dem Ende der Installation auf der Belvedere Road fanden sie in einer staatlichen Grundschule in Hackney Verwendung.

L'architecte décrit le **"LONDON DRESSER"** comme un « espace public dans une boîte ». Il a été conçu pour exposer des maquettes à échelle réduite de bâtiments de la ligne des toits londonienne. La nuit, ces dernières sont offertes aux regards. Le jour, il s'ouvre pour se transformer en « espace ludique de rencontre sociale ». Prévue pour les Jeux olympiques d'été de Londres 2012, l'œuvre a été mise au point en collaboration avec des étudiants de l'université de Westminster et avec l'agence de Brighton Millimetre chargée de la vitrine et des sièges. L'ossature métallique a été recouverte de planches de mélèze anglais noirci et de panneaux de contreplaqué en épicéa. Les sièges ont été réalisés à partir de plaques de contreplaqué empilées et de bois massif sculpté à la main, tous deux découpés au laser. Après Belvedere Road à Londres, il était prévu de remonter l'installation dans une école primaire à Hackney.

This temporary structure makes use of wood cladding and red wooden architectural models that are brought outside during the day to allow passersby to sit or play. At night, it is like a display case for the models.

Dieses temporäre Projekt zeichnet sich durch seine Holzverkleidung und die roten Architekturmodelle aus Holz aus, die am Tag als Sitzmöbel oder zum Spielen dienen. Nachts wird die Konstruktion zum Modellschaukasten.

Cette structure temporaire présente un revêtement de bois et des maquettes en bois rouge qui sont sorties en journée pour permettre aux passants de s'asseoir ou de jouer. La nuit, elle se transforme en une sorte de vitrine pour les maquettes.

PETER STUTCHBURY

Peter Stutchbury Architecture
5/364 Barrenjoey Road, Newport Beach
NSW 2106, Australia

Tel: +61 2 9979 5030 / Fax: +61 2 9979 5367
E-mail: info@peterstutchbury.com.au / Web: www.peterstutchbury.com.au

A graduate of the University of Newcastle, Australia, in 1978, as a child **PETER STUTCHBURY** lived "on the land" and with aborigines on the banks of the Darling River, and with tribes in the highlands of New Guinea. He works on houses "that nurture their occupants and celebrate a palpable spirit of place." The firm has been given 26 awards by the Royal Australian Institute of Architects (RAIA) since 1999. In 2003, Peter Stutchbury was the first architect ever to win both the top National Architecture Awards from the RAIA for residential and non-residential projects with the Robin Boyd Award for houses for the Bay House at Watson's Bay, Sydney, and the Sir Zelman Cowan Award for Public Buildings for Birabahn, the Aboriginal Cultural Center at the University of Newcastle. Architect of the Sydney 2000 Olympics Archery Pavilion, he has also built several structures on the University of Newcastle campus, including the Design Building and the Nursing Building (with EJE Architecture); the Aboriginal Center (with Richard Leplastrier and Sue Harper); and the Life Sciences Building (with Suters Architects). His built work includes the Treetop House (Clareville, NSW, 1991); the Israel House (Paradise Beach, NSW, 1982–92); the McMaster Residence (Hawk's Nest, NSW, 1995–98); the Kangaroo Valleys Pavilion (Kangaroo Valley, NSW, 1996–98); the Reeves House (Clareville Beach, NSW, 1997–99); and the Wedge House (Whale Beach, NSW, 2001). More recent works are the Beach House (Newport Beach, NSW, 2002–06); the Outcrop House (Northern Beaches, Sydney, NSW, 2006–07, published here); the Avalon House (Avalon, NSW, 2007); and the Flying Museum (Cessnock, NSW, 2004–08), all in Australia.

PETER STUTCHBURY schloss sein Studium an der University of Newcastle, Australien, 1978 ab. Als Kind lebte er „auf dem Land", mit den Aborigines am Ufer des Darling River und mit verschiedenen Stämmen im Hochland von Neuguinea. Er realisiert Häuser, die „ihre Bewohner hegen und nähren und den spürbaren Geist des Ortes würdigen". Seit 1999 hat das Büro 26 Preise des Royal Australian Institute of Architects (RAIA) erhalten. 2003 war Peter Stutchbury der erste Architekt, der jemals die beiden höchsten nationalen Architekturpreise des RAIA für Wohn- bzw. öffentliche Bauten erhielt: Ausgezeichnet wurden das Bay House in der Watson's Bay, Sydney, mit dem Robin Boyd Award für Wohnbauten sowie das Birabahn Aboriginal Cultural Center an der Universität Newcastle mit dem Sir Zelman Cowan Award für öffentliche Bauten. Stutchbury war der Architekt des Bogenschützenpavillons für die Olympischen Spiele in Sydney (2000) und entwarf außerdem verschiedene Bauten auf dem Campus der Universität Newcastle, darunter die Schulen für Design und für Krankenpflege (mit EJE Architecture), das Aboriginal Center (mit Richard Leplastrier und Sue Harper) sowie das Institut für Biowissenschaften (mit Suters Architects). Zu seinen realisierten Bauten zählen das Treetop House (Clareville, NSW, 1991), das Israel House (Paradise Beach, NSW, 1982–92), die McMaster Residence (Hawk's Nest, NSW, 1995–98), der Kangaroo Valleys Pavilion (Kangaroo Valley, NSW, 1996–98), das Reeves House (Clareville Beach, NSW, 1997–99) sowie das Wedge House (Whale Beach, NSW, 2001). Jüngere Projekte sind u. a. das Beach House (Newport Beach, NSW, 2002–06), das Outcrop House (Northern Beaches, Sydney, NSW, 2006–07, hier vorgestellt), das Avalon House (Avalon, NSW, 2007) sowie das Flying Museum (Cessnock, NSW, 2004–08), alle in Australien.

Diplômé de l'université de Newcastle, Australie, en 1978, **PETER STUTCHBURY** avait vécu enfant « à l'intérieur des terres » avec des Aborigènes sur les rives de la Darling River et dans les tribus des plateaux de Nouvelle-Guinée. Il travaille sur des projets de maisons « qui enrichissent leurs occupants et célèbrent un esprit palpable du lieu ». L'agence a reçu pas moins de 26 prix du Royal Australian Institute of Architects (RAIA) depuis 1999. En 2003, Peter Stutchbury a été le premier architecte à remporter à la fois les National Architecture Awards du RAIA pour des projets résidentiels et non résidentiels ; le Robin Boyd Award pour les maisons (Bay House à Watson's Bay, Sydney) ; et le Sir Zelman Cowan Award pour les bâtiments publics pour le Birabahn, le centre culturel aborigène de l'université de Newcastle. Architecte du pavillon de tir à l'arc pour les jeux Olympiques de Sydney en 2000, il également construit plusieurs bâtiments sur le campus de l'université de Newcastle, dont celui des études de design et d'infirmerie (avec EJE Architecture) ; l'Aboriginal Center (avec Richard Leplastrier et Sue Harper) et le bâtiment des sciences de la vie (avec Suters Architects). Il a également réalisé : la Treetop House (Clareville, NSW, 1991) ; la Israel House (Paradise Beach, NSW, 1982–92) ; la McMaster Residence (Hawk's Nest, NSW, 1995–98) ; le pavillon Kangaroo Valleys (Kangaroo Valley, NSW, 1996–98) ; la Reeves House (Clareville Beach, NSW, 1997–99) et la Wedge House (Whale Beach, NSW, 2001). Plus récemment, il a construit la Beach House (Newport Beach, NSW, 2002–06) ; la Outcrop House (Northern Beaches, Sydney, NSW, 2006–07, publiée ici) ; la Avalon House (Avalon, NSW, 2007) et le Flying Museum (Cessnock, NSW, 2004–08), tous en Australie.

OUTCROP HOUSE

Northern Beaches, Sydney, New South Wales, Australia, 2006–07

Address: not disclosed. Floor area: 285 m². Client: not disclosed. Cost: not disclosed
Collaboration: Richard Smith, Sacha Zehnder

The **OUTCROP HOUSE** is located on a typical exposed sandstone escarpment edge above Whale Beach, and yet landward it is in a suburban environment. Indeed, seen from its entrance façade, the house seems to resemble typical suburban residences. Facing south and subject to the ocean winds, the house has a northern courtyard "designed for winter comfort," and has "a single powerful aperture to the view" on the southern side. A balcony and pool extend toward the beach. Despite its exposure to the ocean, the house is considered "one of restraint—an enclave that offers the users comfort, ease, place, and dreaming." The roof is designed to allow "controlled vertical light" into the house, and especially into its primary space.

Das **OUTCROP HOUSE** liegt auf einer typischen Sandsteinsteilwand über Whale Beach, zur Landseite hin ist es jedoch in ein vorstädtisches Umfeld eingebunden. Tatsächlich wirkt das Haus auf der Eingangsseite wie ein typisches Vororthaus. Das nach Süden orientierte, den Winden des Meeres ausgesetzte Haus hat einen Nordhof „für angenehmen Aufenthalt im Winter" sowie auf der Südseite eine „beeindruckende Öffnung zum Panorama". Ein Balkon und ein Pool erstrecken sich in Richtung Strand. Trotz seiner Öffnung zum Meer wird das Haus als „zurückhaltend" empfunden – „eine Enklave, die ihren Bewohnern Komfort, Ungezwungenheit, Raum und Platz zum Träumen lässt". Das Dach ist so gestaltet, dass es „regulierten vertikalen Lichteinfall" in das Haus ermöglicht, insbesondere in den Hauptwohnbereich.

La **OUTCROP HOUSE** (maison saillie) se dresse sur un escarpement de grès caractéristique au-dessus de la plage de la Baleine, tout en appartenant à un environnement de banlieue côté terre. Vue de la façade de l'entrée, la maison ressemble d'ailleurs aux résidences habituelles de cette banlieue. Mais face au Sud et aux vents de l'océan, elle possède une cour « conçue pour assurer le confort en hiver » et « une ouverture unique, mais de forte présence vers le paysage » côté sud. Un balcon et la piscine se projettent vers la plage. Malgré son exposition à l'influence de l'océan, la maison est considérée comme « retenue – une enclave qui offre à ses occupants le confort, l'aisance, un lieu et des rêves ». Le toit a été dessiné pour faciliter « l'éclairage vertical contrôlé » de l'intérieur de la maison, et en particulier de ses volumes principaux.

A cantilevered balcony juts out toward the beach, connecting the interior and exterior of the house to its site.

Ein auskragender Balkon in Richtung Strand schafft eine Verbindung von Innen- und Außenräumen des Hauses mit der Umgebung.

Un balcon en porte-à-faux se projette vers la plage et connecte au site l'intérieur et l'extérieur de la maison

Subtle natural light comes into the living spaces from overhead, where a contrast of materials giving emphasis to wood creates a warm atmosphere.

Von oben fällt auf subtile Weise natürliches Licht in die Wohnräume. Dort sorgen Materialkontraste und das dominierende Holz für eine warme Atmosphäre.

La lumière naturelle pénètre dans le séjour de manière subtile. Le contraste des matériaux met l'accent sur le bois pour créer une atmosphère chaleureuse.

Interior forms show a carefully orchestrated play on degrees of transparency or opacity that allow natural light to penetrate the house in a controlled way.

Die Gestaltung des Interieurs zeugt von einem orchestrierten Spiel mit Transparenz und Opazität, was zugleich kontrollierten Lichteinfall in das Haus ermöglicht.

L'intérieur est un jeu soigneusement orchestré sur divers degrés de transparence et d'opacité qui laisse pénétrer la lumière naturelle de façon contrôlée.

SUPERSUDAKA

Juan Pablo Corvalán Hochberger
c/o Escuela de Arquitectura, Universidad de Talca
2 Norte 685
Talca
Chile

E-mail: info@supersudaca.org
Web: www.supersudaca.org

SUPERSUDAKA was founded by Juan Pablo Corvalán Hochberger and Gabriel Vergara. Juan Pablo Corvalán Hochberger received his architecture degree from the École d'Ingénieurs de Genève (1996), and Master's degree from the Berlage Institute, Rotterdam (2002). Gabriel Vergara graduated as an architect from the Universidad de Talca (2006). Supersudaka has a sister organization called Supersudaca, which bills itself as a "think tank for architecture and urban investigation." The website of Supersudaka starts with the phrase: "We don't want to change the world with architecture, we want to change architecture with the world." Other members of Supersudaka are Pablo Abdala, Natalia Gajardo, José Miguel Mardones, and Ingrid Sepúlveda. Their project list includes Bonachón (Puente Alto, 2003); MAAM (Linares, 2004); Lumineda (Linares, 2005); Hot Spot (Talca, 2005); Moto House (Talca, 2006); Canoe Club (Talca, 2006); Mirage House (Santiago, 2007); Multihouse (Talca, 2007); Patio Vicinity (La Serena, 2007); Kiltro House (Talca, 2006–08, published here); and Church(ita) (Talca, 2006–09), all in Chile.

SUPERSUDAKA wurde von Juan Pablo Corvalán Hochberger und Gabriel Vergara gegründet. Juan Pablo Corvalán Hochberger schloss sein Architekturstudium an der École d'Ingénieurs de Genève (1996) ab und erwarb einen Masterabschluss am Berlage Instituut in Rotterdam (2002). Gabriel Vergara absolvierte sein Architekturstudium an der Universidad de Talca (2006). Supersudaka hat eine Schwesterorganisation, Supersudaca, die sich als „Thinktank für Architektur und Stadterforschung" versteht. Die Website von Supersudaka ist mit dem Satz überschrieben: „Wir wollen die Welt nicht durch Architektur verändern, wir wollen die Architektur durch die Welt verändern." Weitere Mitarbeiter von Supersudaka sind Pablo Abdala, Natalia Gajardo, José Miguel Mardones und Ingrid Sepúlveda. Zu ihren Projekten zählen Bonachón (Puente Alto, 2003), MAAM (Linares, 2004), Lumineda (Linares, 2005), Hot Spot (Talca, 2005), Casa Moto (Talca, 2006), Canoe Club (Talca, 2006), Casa Mirage (Santiago, 2007), Multihouse (Talca, 2007), Patio Vicinity (La Serena, 2007), Casa Kiltro (Talca, 2006–08, hier vorgestellt) sowie Church(ita) (Talca, 2006–09), alle in Chile.

L'agence **SUPERSUDAKA** a été fondée par Juan Pablo Corvalán Hochberger et Gabriel Vergara. Juan Pablo Corvalán Hochberger est diplômé en architecture de l'École d'Ingénieurs de Genève (1996), et titulaire d'un M.Arch. de l'Institut Berlage à Rotterdam (2002). Gabriel Vergara est diplômé en architecture de l'Universidad de Talca (2006). Supersudaka possède une société-sœur appelée Supersudaca, qui se présente comme un «groupe de réflexion pour l'architecture et l'investigation urbaines». Le site web de Supersudaka explique : «Nous ne voulons pas changer le monde par l'architecture, nous voulons changer l'architecture par le monde.» Les autres membres de Supersudaka sont Pablo Abdala, Natalia Gajardo, José Miguel Mardones et Ingrid Sepúlveda. La liste de leurs projets, tous au Chili, comprend : Bonachón (Puente Alto, 2003) ; MAAM (Linares, 2004) ; Lumineda (Linares, 2005) ; Hot Spot (Talca, 2005) ; la maison Moto (Talca, 2006) ; le Canoe Club (Talca, 2006) ; la maison Mirage (Santiago, 2007) ; la Multihouse (Talca, 2007) ; le Patio Vicinity (La Serena, 2007) ; la maison Kiltro (Talca, 2006–08, publiée ici) et Church(ita) (Talca, 2006–09).

KILTRO HOUSE

Talca, Chile, 2006–08

Address: not disclosed
Area: 103 m². Client: Oscar Corvalán. Cost: €65 000

This house was built on a fairly wild natural site in Talca, a city of about 250 000 people located 250 kilometers south of Santiago. According to the architects: "This project is almost a statement of how to accomplish architecture in Latin America. The process was so unsteady that all possible architectural design resources available were exercised to cope with the challenge of this house in the Chilean Central Valley. Everything was in constant change: the program, the surface, building permits, the contractors, even the view… The result: a mix, a bastardized design, a fusion, like a crossbreed dog, in Chilean: a *kiltro*." Lifted up off the ground, and folded in form and plan, the structure has ample terrace space and generous glazing that allow residents to take in the scenery. With its nearly empty ground level and fuller, slatted wood cladding above, the house, especially seen with its roof line, seems to be in a state of symbiosis with the neighboring mountains.

Das Haus wurde auf einem vergleichsweise wilden Naturgrundstück bei Talca erbaut, einer Stadt mit 250 000 Einwohnern 250 km südlich von Santiago. Die Architekten erklären: „Dieses Projekt ist fast so etwas wie ein Paradebeispiel für die Realisierung von Architektur in Lateinamerika. Der gesamte Prozess war so unsicher, dass alle nur möglichen architektonischen Gestaltungsressourcen aktiviert werden mussten, um die Herausforderung, dieses Haus im chilenischen Valle Central zu bauen, zu bewältigen. Alles änderte sich ständig: das Programm, die Geländeoberfläche, die Baugenehmigungen, die Baufirmen, sogar der Ausblick … Das Ergebnis: eine Mischung, ein Zwitterentwurf, eine Fusion – wie ein Mischlingshund oder, auf chilenisch, ein *kiltro*." Der über dem Boden aufgeständerte Bau wurde formal „gefaltet", dasselbe trifft auf den Grundriss zu. Die großzügig bemessenen Terrassen und Fensterflächen ermöglichen den Bewohnern die Aussicht auf die Umgebung. Mit seinem baulich fast ungenutzten Erdgeschoss und dem prominenteren, mit Holzlatten verblendeten Obergeschoss wirkt das Haus – besonders wenn die Dachlinie sichtbar ist – als wolle es sich symbiotisch in die angrenzende Berglandschaft fügen.

Cette maison a été construite dans un cadre naturel presque sauvage près de Talca, ville de 250 000 habitants à 250 km au sud de Santiago. Selon les architectes : « Ce projet est presque un manifeste sur l'architecture en Amérique latine. Le processus était si délicat que toutes les ressources de conception architecturale disponibles ont dû être utilisées pour répondre au défi de cette maison implantée dans la vallée centrale du Chili. Tout changeait en permanence : le programme, la surface, les permis de construire, les enreprises et même la vue … Le résultat : un projet mixte, bâtard, une fusion, comme un chien croisé, en chilien un *kiltro.* » Suspendue au-dessus du sol, de forme et de plan pliés, la maison offre de vastes terrasses et de généreuses baies vitrées qui permettent à ses résidents de profiter pleinement du spectacle de la nature. Par sa surélévation sur pilotis et son habillage en lattes de bois, elle semble en symbiose avec le paysage des montagnes environnantes, en particulier quand on peut percevoir la ligne de sa toiture.

The house is lifted off the ground on pilotis and has a faceted roof form, as seen in the drawing on this page.

Das Haus ist auf dünnen Stützen über dem Boden aufgeständert und hat ein facettiertes Dach, wie auch die Zeichnung auf dieser Seite belegt.

La maison repose sur des pilotis et possède une toiture à facettes, comme le montrent les plans de cette page.

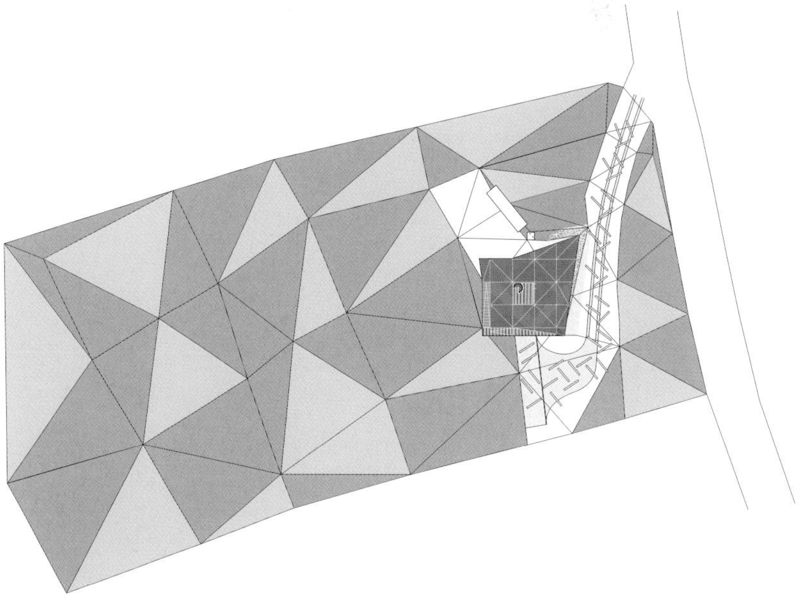

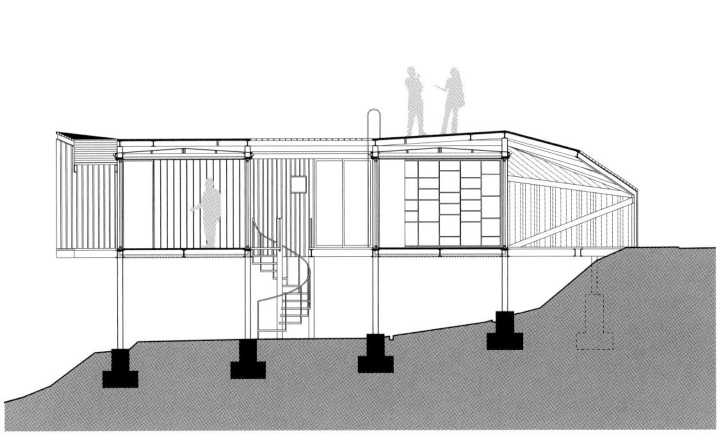

The house with its large windows, unusual openings, and surprising forms is nothing short of spectacular in this natural setting.

Das Haus mit seinen großen Fensterflächen, ungewöhnlichen Öffnungen und überraschenden Formen ist ein spektakuläres Ereignis in der natürlichen Umgebung.

La maison aux vastes fenêtres, aux ouvertures inhabituelles et aux formes surprenantes prend un aspect spectaculaire dans ce cadre naturel.

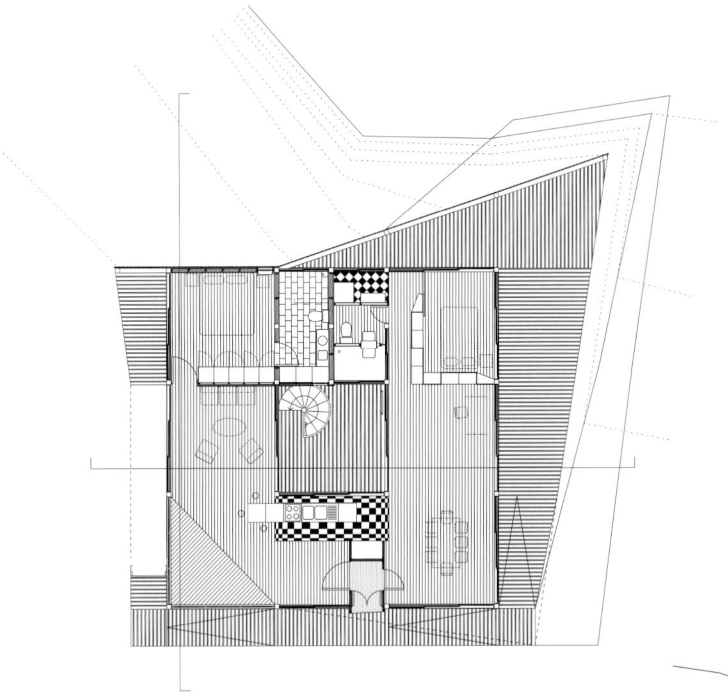

Sitting above the ground, the Kiltro House seems like an ephemeral point of observation in an ever-changing landscape.

Die über dem Boden schwebende Casa Kiltro wirkt wie ein flüchtiger Aussichtspunkt in der sich ständig wandelnden Landschaft.

Surplombant le sol, la maison Kiltro est comme une plate-forme d'observation suspendue au-dessus d'un paysage en perpétuel changement.

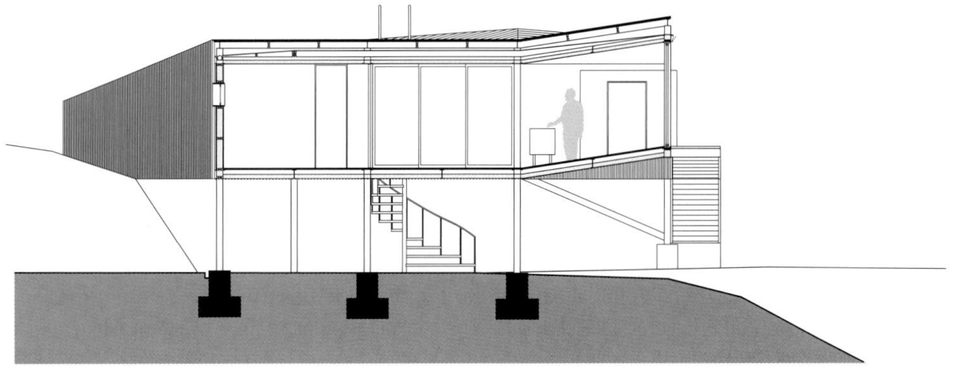

TACKLEBOX

Tacklebox Architecture
55 nassau avenue, Suite 2A1
Brooklyn, NY 11222
USA

Tel: +1 917 553 1723
E-mail: office@tacklebox-ny.com
Web: www.tacklebox-ny.com

JEREMY BARBOUR was born in Roanoke, Virginia, in 1976. He obtained his B.Arch degree from Virginia Tech (Blacksburg, Virginia, 2001) and his M.Arch degree from Columbia University GSAPP (New York, 2006). He is an Adjunct Professor at Parsons The New School of Design and an Adjunct Assistant Professor in the Columbia GSAPP Summer Studio program. He is the owner and Principal of Tacklebox, which he founded in 2006. Prior to that date, he worked with Daniel Rowen Architects (New York, 2001–02), and with Andrew Bartle (ABA Studio, New York, 2002–06). His work includes the 3.1 Phillip Lim Boutique (New York, New York, 2007); and Saipua (Brooklyn, New York, 2009, published here), both in the USA.

JEREMY BARBOUR wurde 1976 in Roanoke, Virginia, geboren. Er absolvierte seinen B. Arch. an der Virginia Tech (Blacksburg, Virginia, 2001) und seinen M. Arch. an der Columbia University GSAPP (New York, 2006). Er ist Lehrbeauftragter am Parsons, The New School of Design, and Lehrbeauftragter am Summer-Studio-Programm der Columbia GSAPP. Barbour ist Inhaber und Direktor des Büros Tacklebox, das er 2006 gründete. Zuvor hatte er für Daniel Rowen Architects (New York, 2001 bis 2002) und Andrew Bartle (ABA Studio, New York, 2002–06) gearbeitet. Zu seinen Projekten zählen die 3.1 Phillip Lim Boutique (New York, 2007) und Saipua (Brooklyn, New York, 2009, hier vorgestellt), beide in den USA.

JEREMY BARBOUR, né à Roanoke (Virginie) en 1976 a obtenu son B.Arch. de la Virginia Tech (Blacksburg, Virginie, 2001) et son M.Arch. de l'université de Columbia GSAPP (New York, 2006). Il est professeur adjoint à Parsons The New School of Design et professeur assistant adjoint pour le programme d'ateliers d'été de la Columbia GSAPP. Il a créé Tacklebox en 2006, qu'il dirige. Auparavant, il avait travaillé chez Daniel Rowen Architects (New York, 2001–02) et Andrew Bartle (ABA Studio, New York, 2002–06). Il a réalisé, entre autres, le magasin 3.1 Phillip Lim (New York, 2007) et la boutique Saipua (Brooklyn, 2009, publiée ici), tous deux aux États-Unis.

SAIPUA

Brooklyn, New York, USA, 2009

Address: 147 Van Dyke Street, Brooklyn, NY 11231, USA,
+1 718 624 2929, www.saipua.com
Area: 65 m². Client: Saipua. Cost: not disclosed

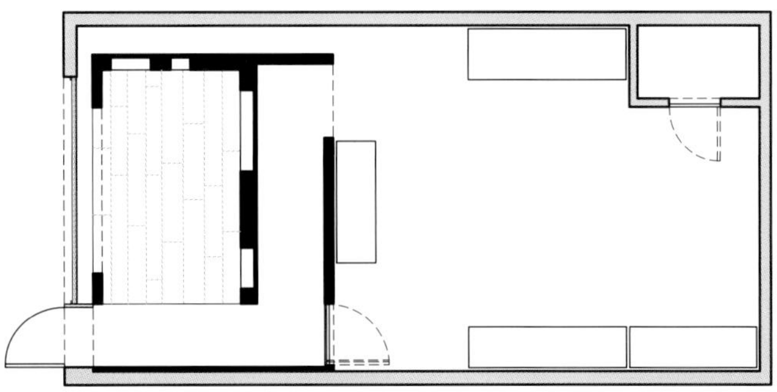

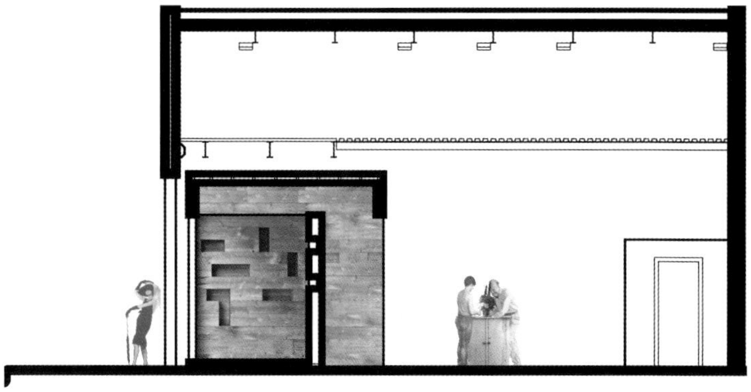

The designers made Saipua look as rugged and rural as possible. In such items as the alcoves destined to contain merchandise, the sophistication of their efforts becomes apparent.

Die Architekten gestalteten die Räume von Saipua so rustikal und ländlich wie möglich. Dennoch zeigt sich an Elementen wie den Wandnischen für die Waren, wie durchdacht das Konzept ist.

Les designers ont donné à la boutique Saipua un style aussi rustique que possible, même si dans les niches destinées à certains articles, la sophistication du projet s'exprime clairement.

The main material used in this project was 167 square meters of reclaimed barn siding from a Shaker barn built in the 1890s in Michigan. **SAIPUA** is a family-run business that sells handmade soaps and floral arrangements. The shop is located in the industrial Red Hook area of Brooklyn. The architect states that the goal was to "create a new timeless space that simultaneously serves as a quiet backdrop and as an active participant in the ongoing act of making that defines Saipua." Located in an existing warehouse, Saipua was imagined as a "freestanding inhabitable box" made with the weathered wood brought from Michigan. The interior is made up of two small rooms, one nested within the other. The outer space dialogues with the street much like the front porch of a house, "serving as a place of gathering and performance: a stage where visitors take on the interchanging roles of performer and audience set against an ever-changing backdrop provided by both the interior life of the shop and the life of the street."

Bei diesem Projekt wurden als Material in erster Linie 167 m² altes Bauholz verwendet, die von der Seitenverkleidung einer alten Shaker-Scheune stammten, die in den 1890er-Jahren in Michigan erbaut worden war. **SAIPUA** ist ein Familienunternehmen, das handgemachte Seife und Blumen verkauft. Das Ladenlokal liegt im industriell geprägten Stadtviertel Red Hook in Brooklyn. Der Architekt betont, Ziel sei gewesen, „einen neuen, zeitlosen Raum zu schaffen, der stille Kulisse und zugleich aktiver Darsteller in der Entstehungsgeschichte von Saipua ist". Der in einem alten Lagerhaus gelegene Laden wurde als „freistehende, bewohnbare Box" konzipiert und aus dem verwittertem Holz aus Michigan gebaut. Das Interieur besteht aus zwei ineinandergeschachtelten Räumen. Der äußere Raum kommuniziert mit der Straße wie die Veranda eines Hauses und „dient als Treffpunkt und Bühne: eine Bühne, auf der die Besucher wechselseitig die Rollen von Darsteller und Publikum übernehmen, vor einer sich ständig wandelnden Kulisse – einerseits dem Interieur des Ladens, andererseits dem Treiben auf der Straße."

Le principal matériau utilisé dans ce projet est un bardage de bois de 167 m², récupéré d'une grange Shaker du Michigan datant des années 1890. **SAIPUA** est une entreprise familiale qui vend des savons artisanaux et des compositions florales. La boutique se trouve dans la zone industrielle de Red Hook à Brooklyn. Pour l'architecte, l'objectif était de « créer un nouvel espace intemporel qui soit en même temps un cadre tranquille et un participant actif à ce qui fait la spécificité de Saipua ». Installé dans un entrepôt existant, le magasin a été pensé comme « une boîte habitable autonome » faite du bois patiné rapporté du Michigan. L'intérieur se compose de deux petites pièces nichées l'une dans l'autre. L'espace extérieur dialogue avec la rue un peu comme le porche d'une maison « servant de lieu de rencontre et de performance à la manière d'une scène sur laquelle les visiteurs peuvent emprunter le rôle à la fois de l'acteur et du public devant le décor en changement permanent de l'activité intérieure de la boutique et du spectacle de la rue ».

Weathered wood, and objects casually placed, as though in an inhabited environment, give Saipua a distinctive flavor that is not obviously modern.

Durch verwittertes Holz und die scheinbar spontan, wie in einem Wohnumfeld platzierten Objekte, gewinnt Saipua ein ganz eigenes Flair, das auf den ersten Blick alles andere als modern wirkt.

Le bois patiné et des objets disposés de manière très libre, un peu comme dans une pièce inhabitée, confèrent à Saipua une personnalité très spécifique qui, à l'évidence, ne se veut pas moderne.

TAO

TAO (Trace Architecture Office)
241–15 Caochangdi
Chaoyang, Beijing 100015
China

Tel: +86 10 5127 3258
Fax: +86-10 5127 3258 1018
E-mail: office@t-a-o.cn
Web: www.t-a-o.cn

The founder and design Principal of TAO (Trace Architecture Office) **HUA LI** was born in 1972 in Lanzhou, China. He received his B.Arch degree from Tsinghua University in 1994 and an M.Arch degree from Yale University in 1999. He worked at Westfourth Architecture and Herbert Beckhard Frank Richlan & Associates in New York, before returning to China in 2003 to start his own practice in Beijing. He established TAO in 2009. Hua Li has also taught at the Central Academy of Fine Arts in Beijing as a Visiting Professor and been a visiting critic at the School of Architecture at Tsinghua University since 2005. Hua Li's completed projects include TAO Architect's Office, a refurbishment of a warehouse in Beijing (2009); Gaoligong Museum of Handcraft Paper (Tengchong, Yunnan, 2009–10, published here); Riverside Clubhouse (Yancheng, 2010); XiaoQuan Elementary School (Sichuan, 2011); and the sports center for Northeast Normal University (ChangChun, 2004–11), all in China.

HUA LI, Gründer und Direktor für Entwerfen bei TAO (Trace Architecture Office), wurde 1972 in Lanzhou, China, geboren. Er absolvierte seinen B. Arch. 1994 an der Universität Tsinghua sowie 1999 einen M. Arch. in Yale. Er arbeitete für Westfourth Architecture und Herbert Beckhard Frank Richlan & Associates in New York, bevor er 2003 nach China zurückkehrte und ein Büro in Peking gründete. 2009 folgte die Gründung von TAO. Hua Li war außerdem Gastdozent an der Zentralakademie für bildende Künste in Peking und ist seit 2005 Gastkritiker an der Architekturfakultät der Universität Tsinghua. Zu seinen realisierten Projekten zählen das Büro von TAO in einem sanierten Speicher in Peking (2009), das Gaoligong Museum für Papierhandwerk (Tengchong, Yunnan, 2009–10, hier vorgestellt), das Riverside Clubhaus (Yancheng, 2010), die Grundschule in XiaoQuan (Sichuan, 2011) und die Sportanlagen für die Nordostchinesische Pädagogische Hochschule (ChangChun, 2004–11), alle in China.

Le fondateur et directeur du design de TAO (Trace Architecture Office), **HUA LI**, est né en 1972 à Lanzhou, en Chine Il est titulaire d'un B.Arch. de l'université Tsinghua (1994) et d'un M.Arch. de Yale (1999). Il a travaillé chez Westfourth Architecture et Herbert Beckhard Frank Richlan & Associates à New York avant de revenir en Chine en 2003 et d'ouvrir son cabinet à Pékin. Il a créé TAO en 2009. Il a également enseigné à l'Académie centrale des beaux-arts de Pékin en tant que professeur associé et il est critique invité à l'école d'architecture de l'université Tsinghua depuis 2005. Les projets déjà réalisés de Hua Li comprennent le cabinet d'architectes TAO, le réaménagement d'un entrepôt à Pékin (2009) ; le musée du Papier artisanal de Gaoligong (Tengchong, Yunnan, 2009–10, publié ici) ; le club Riverside (Yancheng, 2010) ; l'école élémentaire XiaoQuan (Sichuan, 2011) et le centre sportif de l'Université normale du Nord-Est (ChangChun, 2004–11), tous en Chine.

GAOLIGONG MUSEUM OF HANDCRAFT PAPER

Tengchong, Yunnan, China, 2009–10

Area: 361 m². Client: Committee of the Gaoligong Museum of Handcraft Paper
Cost: not disclosed

This museum is situated in a field next to the village of Xinzhuang, near Gaoligong Mountain in Yunnan, a world ecological preserve. The village has a long tradition of handcrafted papermaking. The museum includes a gallery, bookstore, work space, and guest rooms. The complex is conceived as a micro-village, or a cluster of several small buildings. The architect states: "The spatial concept is to create a visiting experience alternating between the interior of galleries and the landscape outside when visitors walk through the museum, so as to provoke an awareness of the inseparable relationship between papermaking and the environment." An emphasis has been placed on environmentally sustainable design, through the use of local craftsmanship (including farmers) and materials such as bamboo and handcrafted paper. Local volcanic stone is used for the exterior, roof, interior cladding, and floors. A traditional timber structural system that uses no nails called SunMao was employed.

Das Museum liegt in einem Feld in der Nähe des Dorfs Xinzhuang, nicht weit vom Gaoligongshan-Gebirge in Yunnan, einem internationalen Naturschutzgebiet. Das Dorf blickt auf eine lange Tradition des Papierhandwerks zurück. Zum Museum gehören eine Galerie, eine Buchhandlung, ein Werkstattbereich sowie Gästezimmer. Der Komplex wurde als Dorf im Kleinen, als Cluster mehrerer kleinerer Bauten konzipiert. Der Architekt führt aus: „Ziel des Raumkonzepts ist es, ein Besuchserlebnis zu ermöglichen, das im Wechsel zwischen Ausstellungsräumen und Landschaft durch das Museum führt und so ein Bewusstsein für die unauflösliche Wechselbeziehung von Papierhandwerk und Umwelt schafft." Besonderer Wert wurde auf nachhaltiges Design gelegt, etwa durch die Zusammenarbeit mit ortsansässigen Handwerkern (und Bauern) oder Baustoffen wie Bambus und handgeschöpftem Papier. Am Außenbau sowie für Dach, Innenverschalung und Böden kam lokaler Vulkanstein zum Einsatz. Gearbeitet wurde außerdem mit SunMao, einem traditionellen Holztragwerk.

Le musée se trouve dans un champ à proximité du village de Xinzhuang – qui possède une longue tradition papetière artisanale – et du mont Gaoligong, dans le Yunnan, une réserve écologique mondiale. Le musée comporte une galerie d'exposition, une librairie, un espace de travail et des chambres d'hôtes. Le complexe est conçu comme un micro-village, ou un groupe de petits bâtiments. Pour l'architecte : « Le concept spatial vise à faire vivre une véritable expérience aux visiteurs, entre l'intérieur des salles d'exposition et le paysage extérieur qu'on voit en parcourant le musée, afin de susciter une prise de conscience du lien indissociable entre la fabrication du papier et l'environnement. » L'accent a été mis sur le design écologiquement durable par le recours au savoir artisanal local (y compris agricole) et l'emploi de matériaux comme le bambou et le papier artisanal. De la pierre volcanique locale a été utilisée pour l'extérieur, le toit, le revêtement intérieur et les sols. Un système traditionnel de structure en bois sans clous, appelé SunMao, a également été utilisé.

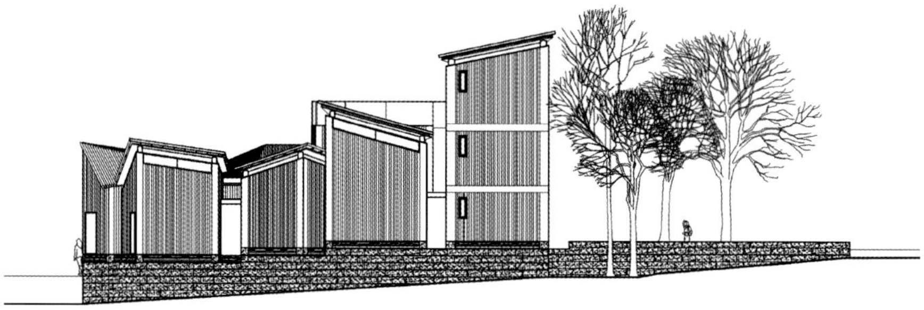

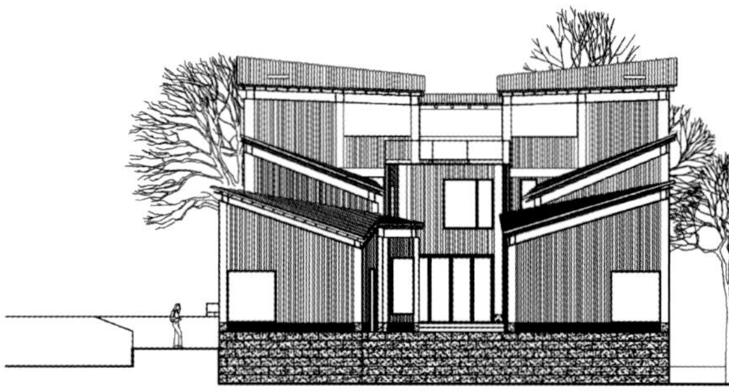

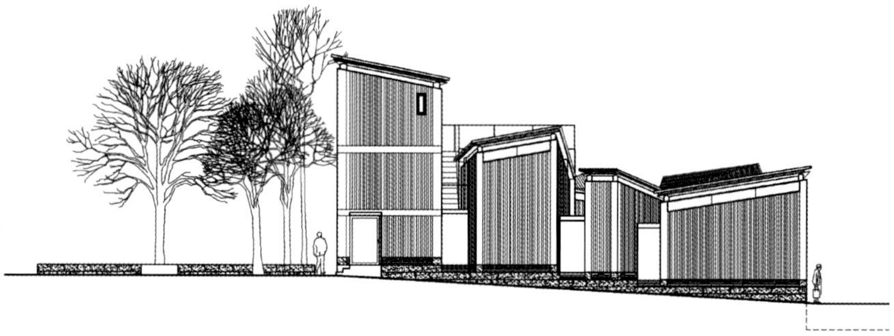

The architect has designed a series of elements that recall traditional village architecture while nonetheless remaining modern. The "village" aspect of the design can be seen in the drawings above—while the modernity is present in the large windows, for example.

Der Entwurf des Architekten zeigt Elemente, die an traditionelle Dorfarchitektur erinnern, aber dennoch modern sind. Der „dörfliche" Charakter wird in den Zeichnungen oben deutlich, während die großen Fenster moderne Akzente setzen.

L'architecte a imaginé des éléments qui rappellent l'architecture villageoise traditionnelle, mais restent néanmoins modernes. On voit cet aspect « villageois » sur les schémas ci-dessus – tandis que la modernité est exprimée, par exemple, par les grandes fenêtres.

Wooden walls and ceilings are contrasted with gray tile floors. The large windows assure ample natural light inside.

Wände und Decken aus Holz kontrastieren mit den grauen Bodenfliesen. Die großen Fenster lassen reichlich Tageslicht einfallen.

Le bois des murs et des plafonds contraste avec les carreaux gris du sol. Les grandes fenêtres laissent largement pénétrer la lumière du jour à l'intérieur.

A drawing shows the pavilion structure with the scale of visitors vis-à-vis the architecture indicated. Above, another interior view with the rather complex angles and large openings of the design visible.

Die Zeichnung zeigt die Pavillonstruktur der Anlage im maßstäblichen Verhältnis. Auf einer weiteren Innenansicht (oben) sind die komplexen Winkel der Architektur und die großen Fensteröffnungen zu sehen.

Le schéma montre la structure pavillonnaire avec les visiteurs à l'échelle par rapport à l'architecture. Ci-dessus, une autre vue intérieure où l'on voit la structure anguleuse plutôt complexe et les larges ouvertures.

THREEFOLD ARCHITECTS

Threefold Architects
Great Western Studios / Studio 203 / 65 Alfred Road
London W2 5EU / UK

Tel: +44 20 89 69 23 23 / Fax: +44 20 75 04 87 04
E-mail: info@threefoldarchitects.com
Web: www.threefoldarchitects.com

JACK HOSEA was born in 1975 in Norwich, UK. He received his RIBA Part 1 B.Sc. in Architecture from the Bartlett School of Architecture, University College London (1995–98), and his Part 2 (2000–01) and Part 3 (2004) diplomas from the same school. He worked in the office of Michael Hopkins (London, 1999–2001), DMWR Architects (London, 2001–02), Big Brown Dog Architects (London, 2002–04), and was a founding Partner of Threefold Architects (2004). **MATTHEW DRISCOLL** was born in 1976 in London. He also received the RIBA Part 1, Part 2, and Part 3 qualifications from the Bartlett School of Architecture (1994–2004). He worked for Michael Hopkins and Partners (London, 1997–99), Sanei Hopkins Architects (London, 2000–01), and Niall McLaughlin Architects (London, 2001–04), before creating Threefold Architects with Jack Hosea. **RENÉE SEARLE** was born in 1976 in Kuala Lumpur. Having studied at the Cooper Union (New York, 1999–2000) and the Bartlett (1995–2004), she joined Threefold as a Director, designer, and project leader in 2009. Their recent work includes Pure Groove (London, 2008); the Ladderstile House, a sustainable family home (Richmond, London, 2006–09, published here); the Apprentice Store, the conversion of Grade II listed structures into a family home (Bath, 2009); a mixed-use (office and residential) project on Turner Street in Whitechapel (London, 2010); the Hurst Avenue House (London, 2009–12); the Long Studio (Norfolk, 2011–12, also published here); and an ongoing commercial art gallery on Roman Road in Bethnal Green (London, 2012–), all in the UK.

JACK HOSEA wurde 1975 in Norwich, Großbritannien, geboren. Sein Studium an der Bartlett School of Architecture des University College London (1995–98) schloss er mit einem RIBA Part 1 B. Sc. ab. RIBA Part 2 (2000–01) und RIBA Part 3 (2004) absolvierte Hosea an derselben Schule. Er arbeitete im Büro von Michael Hopkins (London, 1999–2001), bei DMWR Architects (London, 2001–02), Big Brown Dog Architects (London, 2002–04) und war Gründungspartner von Threefold Architects (2004). **MATTHEW DRISCOLL** wurde 1976 in London geboren. Auch er absolvierte seine Architekturstudien mit den Abschlüssen RIBA Part 1, Part 2 und Part 3 an der Bartlett School of Architecture (1994–2004). Er arbeitete für Michael Hopkins and Partners (London, 1997–99), Sanei Hopkins Architects (London, 2000–01) und Niall McLaughlin Architects (London, 2001–04), bevor er mit Jack Hosea Threefold Architects gründete. **RENÉE SEARLE** wurde 1976 in Kuala Lumpur geboren. Nach Studien an der Cooper Union (New York, 1999–2000) und der Bartlett School (1995–2004) trat sie 2009 als Geschäftsführerin, Designerin und Projektleiterin bei. Jüngere Arbeiten sind u. a. Pure Groove (London, 2008), das Ladderstile House, ein ökologisches Einfamilienhaus (Richmond, London, 2006–09, hier vorgestellt), der Apprentice Store, der Umbau eines denkmalgeschützten Gebäudes in ein Einfamilienhaus (Bath, 2009), ein Büro- und Wohnkomplex in der Turner Street in Whitechapel (London, 2010), das Hurst Avenue House (London, 2009–12), das Long Studio (Norfolk, 2011–12, ebenfalls hier vorgestellt) und eine Galerie auf der Roman Road in Bethnal Green (London, seit 2012).

JACK HOSEA est né à 1975 à Norwich, Royaume-Uni. Il a obtenu son diplôme professionnel du RIBA, partie 1, à l'École d'architecture Bartlett, University College London (1995–98), la partie 2 (2000–01) et la partie 3 (2004) à la même école. Il a travaillé dans l'agence de Michael Hopkins (Londres, 1999–2001), pour DMWR Architects (Londres, 2001–02), Big Brown Dog Architects (Londres, 2002–04) et a été partenaire fondateur chez Threefold Architects (2004). **MATTHEW DRISCOLL** est né en 1976 à Londres. Il a également obtenu son diplôme professionnel du RIBA, parties 1, 2 et 3 à l'École d'architecture Bartlett (1994–2004). Il a travaillé pour Michael Hopkins and Partners (Londres, 1997–99), Sanei Hopkins Architects (Londres, 2000–01) et Niall McLaughlin Architects (Londres, 2001–04), avant de créer Threefold Architects avec Jack Hosea. **RENÉE SEARLE** est née en 1976 à Kuala Lumpur. Après des études à la Cooper Union (New York, 1999–2000) et à la Bartlett (1995–2004), elle a rejoint Threefold en 2009 comme directrice, designer et chef de projet. Parmi leurs œuvres récentes figurent Pure Groove (Londres, 2008) ; la Ladderstile House, une maison familiale durable (Richmond, Londres, 2006–09, publiée ici) ; l'Apprentice Store, la reconversion en maison familiale de structures classées niveau II (Bath, 2009) ; un projet à usage mixte (bureau et habitation) à Turner Street, Whitechapel (Londres, 2010) ; la Hurst Avenue House (Londres, 2009–12) ; le Long Studio (Norfolk, 2011–12, également publié ici) et une galerie d'art en cours de réalisation à Roman Road, Bethnal Green (Londres, 2012–), toutes au Royaume-Uni.

LADDERSTILE HOUSE

Richmond, London, UK, 2006–09

Address: not disclosed. Area: 444 m²
Client: Mr. and Mrs. Devoy. Cost: not disclosed

The architects clearly master the layering of materials and effects, as can be seen in this image of the swimming pool with its entirely open façade.

Wie meisterhaft die Architekten die Schichtung verschiedener Materialien und Effekte beherrschen, belegt u. a. die Ansicht des Schwimmbads mit vollständig zu öffnender Glasfront.

Les architectes ont parfaitement maîtrisé la superposition de matériaux et d'effets, on le voit sur cette photo de la piscine et de sa façade complètement ouverte.

Wood is present in ample quantities, but there are also contrasts with metal and stone, brick and trees in this enclosed outdoor space.

Holz ist deutlich omnipräsent, kontrastiert in diesem geschützten Innenhof jedoch mit Metall und Stein, Ziegeln und Begrünung.

Le bois est présent en abondance, mais cet espace extérieur clos présente aussi des contrastes entre le métal et la pierre, les briques et les arbres.

This large, newly built residence, described as a "contemporary courtyard home," borders Richmond Park and is near Ladderstile Gate. Exposed timber beams span the site at the level of the first floor. The main living spaces are on the eastern side of the site beneath these beams, and are glazed along the side facing a 320-square-meter courtyard. The eastern elevation is clad in brick. An indoor swimming pool connects the two main wings of the house. A block facing south over the swimming pool contains two bedroom suites. Reusable materials, mainly bricks and rubble from the old house demolished on the site, were recycled. The building's superstructure is a prefabricated solid panel system; the walls, floors, roofs, and structural beams are made from sustainably sourced cross-laminated solid spruce. The prefabrication system employed allowed the house to be erected on site in under two weeks. Perforated screens and a planted wall system developed for the project also confirm its sustainable credentials. Rainwater is collected and stored in a 10 000-liter tank and is used to irrigate the green walls, sedum roof, and landscaped courtyards. Geothermal heating, heat exchangers, and high levels of insulation throughout underline the desire of the architects and the clients to create a sustainable residence.

Der große Neubau, ein als „zeitgenössisches Hofhaus" gestaltetes Einfamilienhaus, grenzt an Richmond Park und liegt nicht weit von Ladderstile Gate. Freiliegende Holzträger überspannen das Grundstück auf Höhe des ersten Stocks. Die Hauptwohnräume liegen an der Ostseite des Grundstücks unterhalb dieser Träger und bieten dank verglaster Fronten den Blick in einen 320 m² großen Innenhof. Die Ostfassaden wurden verklinkert. Ein Innenpool verbindet die beiden Hauptflügel des Hauses. In einem Trakt über dem Pool, mit Blick nach Süden, liegen zwei Schlafzimmer mit Nebenräumen. Verwertbare Materialien wie Ziegel und Schutt vom abgerissenen Vorgängerbau wurden recycelt. Der Oberbau des Hauses wurde in Plattenbauweise realisiert, Wände, Böden, Decken und Träger aus massivem Fichten-Brettsperrholz aus nachhaltiger Forstwirtschaft gefertigt. Dank des Fertigbausystems konnte das Haus vor Ort in weniger als zwei Wochen errichtet werden. Perforierte Wandschirme und eine begrünte Wand unterstreichen die Nachhaltigkeit des Projekts. Regenwasser wird in einem 10 000-Liter-Tank gesammelt und dient zur Bewässerung der begrünten Wände sowie des mit Sedum begrünten Dachs und der begrünten Innenhöfe. Eine Erdwärmeheizung, Wärmetauscher und eine hohe Dämmung zeugen vom Engagement der Architekten und Bauherren für nachhaltiges Wohnen.

Cette grande résidence nouvellement construite et décrite comme une « maison contemporaine à cour » est située en bordure du Richmond Park, à proximité de Ladderstile Gate. Des poutres apparentes en bois enjambent l'ensemble au niveau du premier étage. Les principaux espaces à vivre sont situés du côté est, sous ces poutres, et sont vitrés sur le côté, face à une cour de 320 m². La façade est présente un revêtement de briques. Les deux ailes principales de la maison sont reliées par une piscine intérieure. Un bloc face au sud surplombe la piscine et abrite deux suites avec chambres. Des matériaux réutilisables ont été recyclés, surtout des briques et des gravats de l'ancienne maison démolie qui occupait auparavant le site. La superstructure est un système de solides panneaux préfabriqués, tandis que les murs, sols, toits et poutres de charpente sont en lamellé croisé d'épicéa massif issu de forêts gérées durablement. La préfabrication a permis à la maison d'être construite en moins de deux semaines. Des écrans perforés et un système de mur végétalisé développé pour le projet confirment également son caractère durable. L'eau de pluie est récupérée et stockée dans un réservoir de 10 000 l pour arroser la végétation des murs, le toit en sedum et les cours paysagères. Un chauffage géothermique, des échangeurs de chaleur et un niveau d'isolation élevé soulignent la volonté des architectes et de leurs clients de construire une maison durable.

The house is articulated around layers and surfaces, wood, glass and screens, as well as a vertical garden seen to the right.

Das Haus artikuliert sich in Schichten und Oberflächen, Holz, Glas und Wandschirmen sowie einem vertikalen Garten rechts im Bild.

La maison s'articule en plusieurs couches et surfaces autour du bois, du verre et d'écrans perforés, sans oublier le jardin vertical qu'on voit à droite.

Privacy is preserved in the bath area in spite of the full-height glazing. Wood is present in almost every space.

Trotz geschosshoher Verglasung wird auch im Bad die Privatsphäre gewahrt. Holz ist in fast allen Räumen präsent.

La salle de bains préserve l'intimité malgré son vitrage sur toute la hauteur. Le bois est présent dans presque toutes les pièces.

Glazed walls open entirely making the border between inside and outside in this dining space ambiguous. Though straight lines dominate, the layering of materials and spaces gives a surprising variety to these spaces.

Glasfronten, die sich vollständig öffnen lassen, lassen die Grenzen von Innen und Außen verschwimmen, wie hier im Essbereich. Trotz ihrer Geradlinigkeit wirkt die Architektur dank der Schichtung verschiedener Materialien und Räume erstaunlich facettenreich.

Les parois vitrées s'ouvrent entièrement et rendent floues les limites entre intérieur et extérieur dans cette salle à manger. Si les lignes droites dominent, les matériaux et espaces superposés confèrent une étonnante diversité aux différentes pièces.

THE LONG STUDIO

Norfolk, UK, 2011–12

Address: not disclosed. Area: 30 m²
Client: not disclosed. Cost: £37 500

This zero-carbon artists' studio "was designed to capture the sky." It is a linear, black-clad timber-frame structure that could be built by the clients themselves. The architects state: "The dramatic features of the site are the far reaching views across the fields to the north contrasted with the beautiful mature cottage garden to the south. The continuous clerestory that runs along the north elevation captures the expansive horizon and the constantly shifting views and colors of the sky and fields, whereas the glazed doors to the south open up the building to the warmth and texture of the garden." Photovoltaic panels generate more than enough electricity for the structure, and it is heated with a wood-burning stove. The timber used was "sustainably sourced" and recycled cellulose fiber was used for cladding.

Dieses CO_2-neutrale Atelierhaus wurde entworfen, um „den Himmel einzufangen". Die geradlinige, schwarz verkleidete Holzrahmenkonstruktion konnte von den Auftraggebern selbst errichtet werden. Die Architekten: „Eindrucksvolle Charakteristika des Standorts sind der weite Ausblick über die Felder im Norden im Kontrast zu dem sehr schönen Bauerngarten im Süden. Das Fensterband an der Nordseite rahmt den weiten Horizont und die sich stets verändernden Panoramen und Farben des Himmels sowie der Felder, während sich die Glastüren nach Süden zur Wärme des Gartens hin öffnen." Fotovoltaikanlagen erzeugen mehr als genug Energie für das Haus, das mit einem Holzofen beheizt wird. Das verwendete Holz stammt aus „nachhaltiger Erzeugung". Für die Verkleidung wurden recycelte Zellulosefasern eingesetzt.

L'atelier d'artiste zéro carbone « a été conçu pour capturer le ciel ». Il s'agit d'une ossature en bois linéaire avec un bardage noir que les clients auraient pu construire eux-mêmes. L'architecte précise : « Le caractère spectaculaire du site est lié au contraste entre les vues lointaines à travers les champs au nord et les magnifiques jardins de maison au sud. La claire-voie continue qui court le long de la façade nord capture l'horizon en expansion et les vues et couleurs sans cesse changeantes du ciel et des champs, tandis que les portes vitrées au sud ouvrent le bâtiment sur la chaleur et le caractère velouté du jardin. » Des panneaux photovoltaïques produisent plus d'énergie que nécessaire tandis que le chauffage est assuré par un poêle à bois. Le bois utilisé provient de « sources durables » et le bardage est constitué de fibres de cellulose recyclées.

As the drawing to the right shows, the structure is extremely simple. Aesthetically, it plays on the use of different wood colors, with the black walls and roof being the dominant elements.

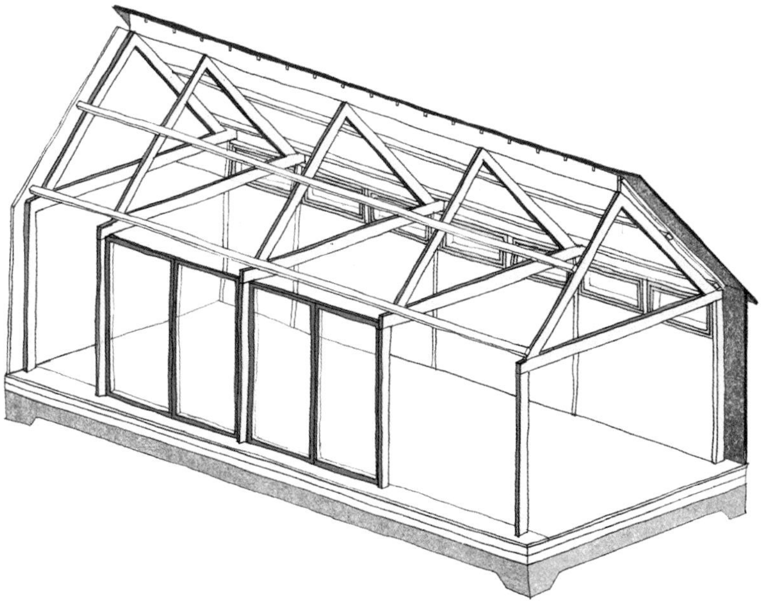

Die Zeichnung rechts zeigt den einfachen Aufbau des Gebäudes. Es spielt ästhetisch mit unterschiedlichen Holzfarben, wobei die schwarzen Wände und das schwarze Dach die dominierenden Elemente sind.

Comme le révèle l'axonométrie à droite, la structure est d'une extrême simplicité. D'un point de vue esthétique, elle joue sur différentes couleurs de bois, les murs noirs et la toiture étant les éléments dominants.

One of the Long Studio's façades has only a high band of windows, as seen on this page; the opposite side is, by contrast, very generously glazed, bringing ample natural light into the space.

Auf dieser Seite ist die Fassade des Long Studio mit dem hoch sitzenden Fensterband zu sehen. Die andere Seite des Gebäudes hingegen ist großzügig verglast und lässt viel natürliches Licht ins Atelier.

Le Long Studio a une façade percée d'une seule bande haute de fenêtres, comme le montre cette page, mais le côté opposé est généreusement vitré afin d'apporter une grande quantité de lumière naturelle à l'intérieur.

Alésia Museum
and Archeological Park

BERNARD TSCHUMI

Bernard Tschumi Architects
227 West 17th Street
New York, NY 10011
USA

Tel: +1 212 807 6340 / Fax: +1 212 242 3693
E-mail: nyc@tschumi.com
Web: www.tschumi.com

BERNARD TSCHUMI was born in Lausanne, Switzerland, in 1944. He studied in Paris and at the ETH, Zurich. He taught at the Architectural Association (AA), London (1970–79), and at Princeton (1976–80). He was Dean of the Graduate School of Architecture, Planning, and Preservation of Columbia University in New York from 1984 to 2003. He opened his own office, Bernard Tschumi Architects (Paris, New York), in 1981. Major projects include Second Prize in the Kansai International Airport Competition (Japan, 1988); the Video Gallery (Groningen, the Netherlands, 1990); Parc de la Villette (Paris, France, 1982–95); Le Fresnoy National Studio for Contemporary Arts (Tourcoing, France, 1991–97); the Lerner Student Center, Columbia University (New York, New York, USA, 1994–98); the School of Architecture (Marne-la-Vallée, France, 1994–98); the Interface Flon Train Station in Lausanne (Switzerland, 2001); the Vacheron Constantin Headquarters (Geneva, Switzerland, 2004); the Linder Athletic Center at the University of Cincinnati (Cincinnati, Ohio, USA, 2006); and the Zénith Concert Hall in Limoges (France, 2007). Among the firm's more recent projects are BLUE, a 17-story residential tower on the Lower East Side of New York (New York, USA, 2007); the New Acropolis Museum in Athens (Greece, 2004–09); a cultural center and concert hall in Bordeaux-Cenon (France, 2010); and the Alésia Museum and Archeological Park (Alésia, France, 2010–12, published here). He is currently working on a renovation of the Zoo de Vincennes in Paris (France, 2009–14); and the ANIMA Cultural Center (Grottammare, Italy, 2012–15).

BERNARD TSCHUMI wurde 1944 in Lausanne, Schweiz, geboren. Er studierte in Paris sowie an der ETH Zürich. Er lehrte an der Architectural Association (AA), London (1970–79) und der Princeton University (1976–80). Von 1984 bis 2003 war er Dekan der Graduiertenfakultät für Architektur, Stadtplanung und Denkmalschutz der Columbia University in New York. 1981 gründete er sein Büro Bernard Tschumi Architects (Paris, New York). Wichtige Projekte sind u. a. der zweite Preis im Wettbewerb für den Internationalen Flughafen Kansai (Japan, 1988), die Video Gallery (Groningen, Niederlande, 1990), der Parc de la Villette (Paris, 1982–95), das Medienzentrum Le Fresnoy (Tourcoing, Frankreich, 1991–97), das Lerner Student Center, Columbia University (New York, 1994–98), die Architekturhochschule Marne-la-Vallée (Frankreich, 1994–98), der Bahnhof Interface Flon in Lausanne (2001), die Zentrale von Vacheron Constantin (Genf, 2004), das Linder-Athletikzentrum der University of Cincinnati (Cincinnati, Ohio, 2006) und die Zénith-Konzerthalle in Limoges (2007). Jüngere Projekte des Büros sind BLUE, ein 17-stöckiges Apartmenthochhaus an der Lower East Side in New York (2007), das neue Akropolis-Museum in Athen (2004–09), ein Kulturzentrum mit Konzerthalle in Bordeaux-Cenon (2010) sowie der Muséo-Parc von Alésia (Frankreich, 2010–12, hier vorgestellt). Zurzeit arbeitet er an der Renovierung des Zoos von Vincennes in Paris (2009–14) und am ANIMA-Kulturzentrum (Grottamare, Italien, 2012–15).

BERNARD TSCHUMI est né à Lausanne en 1944. Il a fait ses études à Paris et à l'ETH de Zurich. Il a enseigné à l'Architectural Association (AA) de Londres (1970–79) et à Princeton (1976–80). Il a été doyen de la Graduate School of Architecture, Planning, and Preservation de l'université Columbia à New York entre 1984 et 2003. Il a ouvert son agence, Bernard Tschumi Architects (Paris, New York), en 1981. Ses projets principaux comprennent le deuxième prix du concours pour l'aéroport international du Kansai (Japon, 1988) ; la Video Gallery (Groningue, Pays-Bas, 1990) ; le parc de la Villette (Paris, 1982–95) ; le Studio national des arts contemporain Le Fresnoy (Tourcoing, France, 1991–97) ; le centre étudiant Lerner de l'université Columbia (New York, 1994–98) ; l'École d'architecture (Marne-la-Vallée, France, 1994–98) ; la gare Interface Flon de Lausanne (2001) ; le siège de Vacheron Constantin (Genève, 2004) ; le centre sportif Linder de l'université de Cincinnati (Cincinnati, Ohio, 2006) et la salle de concerts Zénith de Limoges (2007). Parmi les réalisations plus récentes de la société, on peut citer BLUE, une tour de logements de 17 étages du Lower East Side de New York (2007) ; le nouveau musée de l'Acropole d'Athènes (2004–09) ; un centre culturel et salle de concerts à Bordeaux-Cenon (2010) et le musée et parc archéologique d'Alésia (Alésia, France, 2010–12, publié ici). Bernard Tschumi travaille actuellement à la rénovation du zoo de Vincennes à Paris (France 2009–14) et au centre cultuel ANIMA (Grottammare, Italie, 2012–15).

ALÉSIA MUSEUM AND ARCHEOLOGICAL PARK

Alésia, France, 2010–12

Address: 1 Route des Trois Ormeaux, 21150 Alise-Sainte-Reine, Burgundy, France, +33 3 80 96 96 23, www.alesia.com
Area: 7000 m². Client: Bourgogne Region, France. Cost: not disclosed

Using a basic circular or cylindrical form, Bernard Tschumi succeeds in giving this structure a connection to its site and its history.

Ausgehend von einer schlichten Rundform gelingt es Bernard Tschumi, den Bau in seinen landschaftlichen und historischen Kontext einzubinden.

À l'aide d'une forme de base circulaire, ou cylindrique, Bernard Tschumi est parvenu à ancrer sa structure dans le site et son histoire.

The project marks an archeological site in central France and commemorates the history of the battle between Julius Caesar and the Gauls in 52 B.C. The concept involves the recreation of battlements and earthworks as they might have existed at the time. The partially buried circular stone museum itself is located on a hilltop near a medieval town. A rooftop deck allows visitors to survey the site, which remains much as it was more than 2000 years ago. The separate visitor center, a wooden building, is set nearly a kilometer away close to the position the Romans held below the town. The architects explain: "The roof of the round building is a garden planted with trees and grass, camouflaging the presence of the building when seen from the town above. Visitors may look onto reconstructions of the Roman battlements from the roof garden, or stroll down a path to experience the reconstitutions firsthand." Tschumi concludes: "Giving maximum presence to historical events and respecting the sensitive insertion of buildings into their natural environment responds to the ambition of the project while reflecting the imperative of 'modesty' demanded by archeologists. To be both visible and invisible is the paradox and challenge of the project."

Der MuséoParc-Komplex an einer Grabungsstätte in Zentralfrankreich folgt den Spuren der Schlacht zwischen Julius Caesar und den Galliern 52 v. Chr. Teil des Museumskonzepts ist die historische Rekonstruktion von Befestigungen und Erdbauten der damaligen Zeit. Der teilweise im Boden versenkte Rundbau des Museums liegt auf einem Hügel in der Nähe einer mittelalterlichen Stadt. Von einer Dachterrasse haben die Besucher einen Überblick über das gesamte Gelände, das weitgehend so aussieht wie vor über 2000 Jahren. Das separate Besucherzentrum, ein Holzbau, liegt rund einen Kilometer entfernt, nahe den historischen römischen Stellungen unterhalb der Stadt. Die Architekten führen aus: „Das Dach des Rundbaus ist als Garten mit Rasen und Bäumen gestaltet, was den Bau aus Sicht der höher gelegenen Stadt fast im Umfeld verschwinden lässt. Besucher können vom Dachgarten aus die rekonstruierten römischen Befestigungsanlagen sehen oder auf einem schmalen Weg direkt durch die Rekonstruktion laufen." Tschumi schließt: „Die Entscheidung, den historischen Ereignissen absolute Priorität einzuräumen und die Bauten sensibel in ihr landschaftliches Umfeld einzufügen, entspricht dem ambitionierten Projekt und darüber hinaus der von den Archäologen gewünschten ‚Bescheidenheit'. Sichtbar und zugleich unsichtbar zu sein ist Paradox und Herausforderung dieses Projekts."

Le projet marque un site archéologique dans le Centre de la France et commémore l'histoire de la bataille entre Jules César et les Gaulois en 52 av. J.-C. Le concept comprend la reconstruction de fortifications et d'ouvrages de terrassement tels qu'ils ont pu exister à l'époque. Le musée circulaire construit en pierre, en partie enterré, occupe le sommet d'une colline non loin d'une ville médiévale. Une galerie autour du toit permet aux visiteurs d'observer le site, en grande partie inchangé depuis plus de 2000 ans. Le centre d'accueil des visiteurs, en bois, se trouve à 1 km, près de la position que les Romains tenaient alors en contrebas de la ville. Les architectes expliquent que « le toit du bâtiment rond est un jardin planté d'arbres et de pelouse qui dissimulent sa présence depuis la ville en contrebas. Les visiteurs peuvent observer les fortifications romaines reconstruites depuis le jardin ou descendre un sentier pour vivre les reconstitutions de première main ». Tschumi conclut par ces mots : « L'ambition de ce projet est de donner une présence maximale aux événements historiques et de respecter l'intégration délicate des bâtiments dans la nature environnante tout en tenant compte des impératifs de "modestie" exigés par les archéologues. Être à la fois visible et invisible, c'est le paradoxe et le défi de ce projet. »

Trees on the upper level and terraces below encircle the building, giving it a rapport with the trees on the site and allowing visitors to view the area from any point.

Bäume auf der Dachterrasse und umlaufende Balkone in den Geschossen darunter stellen den Bezug zum Baumbestand auf dem Gelände her und erlauben den Besuchern, die Gegend allseitig zu überblicken.

Les arbres à l'étage supérieur et les terrasses en dessous encerclent le bâtiment et répondent aux arbres du site tout en permettant aux visiteurs de l'admirer de toutes parts.

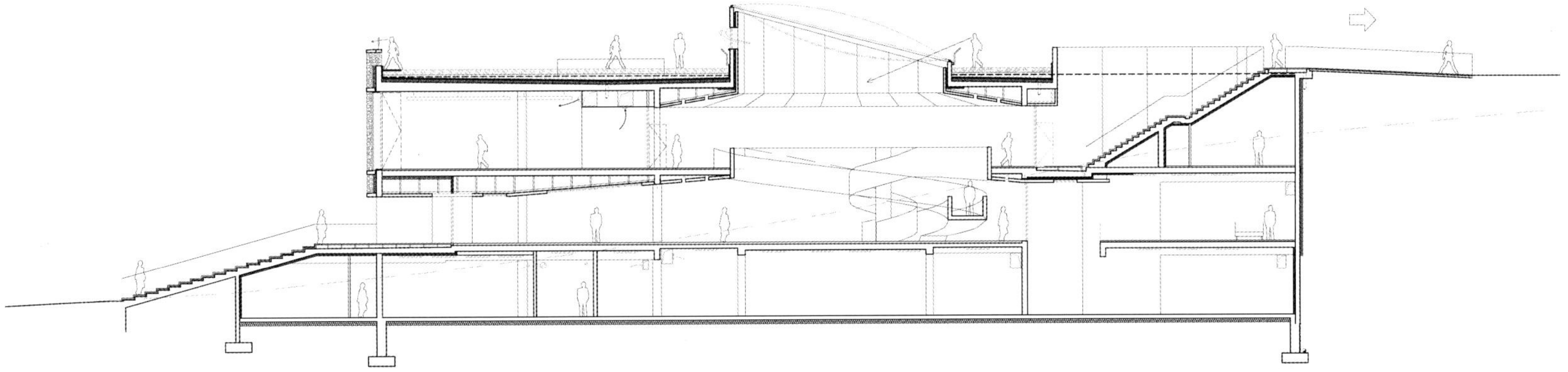

Plans (below) show the perfectly circular plan of the museum. The center of Tschumi's cylinder is the suspended disk and the large open space beneath it.

Grundrisse (unten) zeigen die kompromisslose Rundform des Museums. Herzstück des von Tschumi geplanten „Zylinders" ist eine schwebende Scheibe über einem großzügigen offenen Foyer.

Les plans (ci-dessous) montrent la forme parfaitement circulaire du musée. Au centre du cylindre imaginé par Tschumi se trouve le disque suspendu au-dessus du vaste espace ouvert.

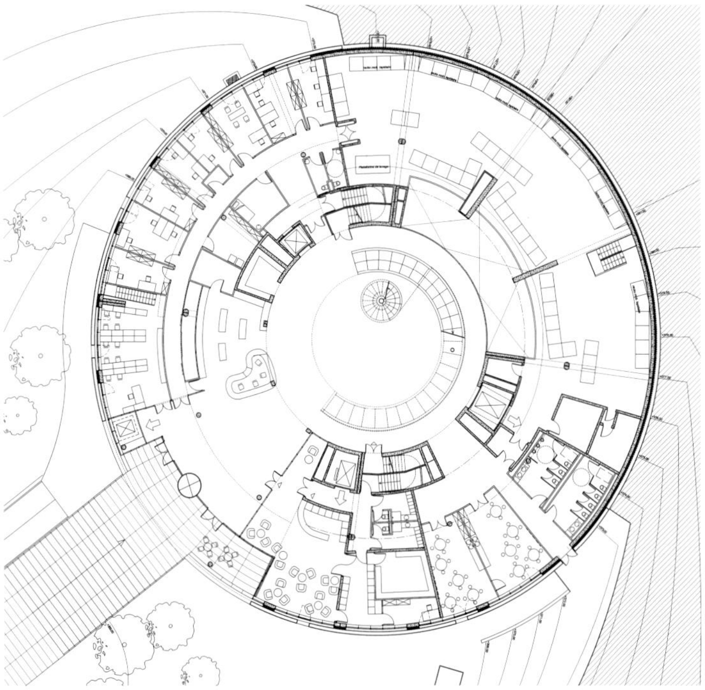

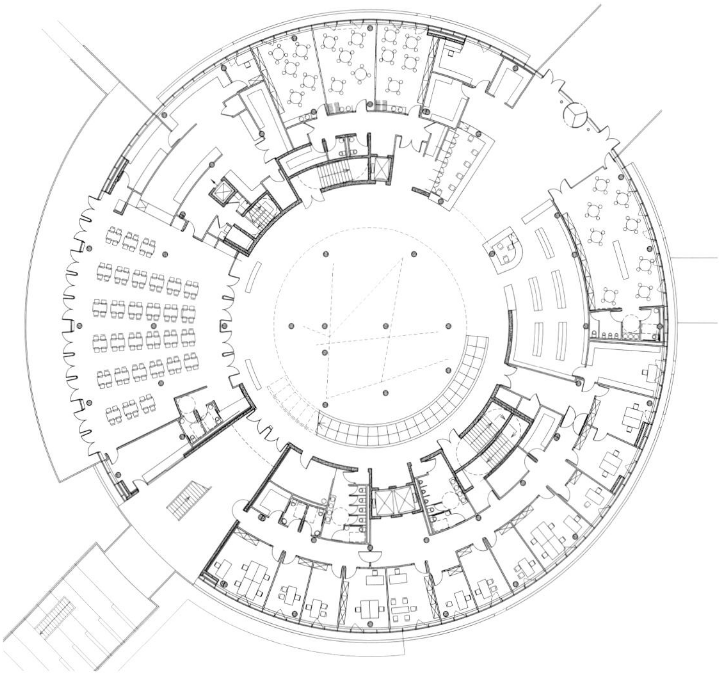

UID ARCHITECTS

Keisuke Maeda / UID architects
MORIxhako 2F
3-10-20 Kinosho-cho
Fukuyama-City
Hiroshima 720-0082
Japan

Tel: +81 8 4927 0136
Fax: +81 8 4927 0146
E-mail: uid@maeda-inc.jp
Web: www.maeda-inc.jp/uid

KEISUKE MAEDA was born in 1974 in Hiroshima, Japan, and graduated from the Department of Architecture of Kokushikan University (1999). UID architects was established by Maeda in Hiroshima in 2003. Aside from architecture, the firm specializes in interior design, furniture, exhibition and product design, urban design, planning, consulting, and research. Keisuke Maeda presently lectures at the Hiroshima Institute of Technology. His work includes the Holocaust Education Center (Hiroshima, 2007); House in Tomonoura (Hiroshima, 2008); Art Flow House (Hiroshima, 2008); Rustic House (Fukuyama, 2009); MORI x Hako (Hiroshima, 2009); Atelier Bisque Doll (Osaka, 2009); Tsumuji+Hako House (Fukuyama, 2010); Nest (Onomichi, Hiroshima, 2010, published here); Machi House (Fukuyama, Hiroshima, 2011); and Peanuts (Hiroshima, 2011–12). Current work includes Dental Clinic O in Matsuyama (2013); and a street renovation in Fukuyama (Hiroshima, 2016), all in Japan.

KEISUKE MAEDA, geboren 1974 in Hiroshima, Japan, machte 1999 seinen Abschluss im Fachbereich Architektur der Universität Kokushikan. 2003 gründete er UID architects in Hiroshima. Neben Architektur ist das Büro auf Interior Design, Möbelgestaltung, Ausstellungs- und Produktdesign, Städteplanung, Beratung und Forschung spezialisiert. Derzeit lehrt Keisuke Maeda am Technologie-Institut Hiroshima. Zu seinen Arbeiten zählen das Holocaust-Bildungszentrum (Hiroshima, 2007), House in Tomonoura (Hiroshima, 2008), Air Flow House (Hiroshima, 2008), Rustic House (Fukuyama, 2009), MORI x Hako (Hiroshima, 2009), das Atelier Bisque Doll (Osaka, 2009), Tsumuji+Hako (Fukuyama, 2010), das Haus Nest (Onomichi, Hiroshima, 2010, hier vorgestellt), machi-House (Fukuyama, 2011) und Peanuts (Hiroshima, 2011–12). Aktuelle Projekte umfassen die Zahnklinik O in Matsuyama (2013) und eine Straßeninstandsetzung (Hiroshima, 2016), alle in Japan.

KEISUKE MAEDA est né en 1974 à Hiroshima, il est diplômé en architecture de l'université Kokushikan (1999). Il a créé UID architects à Hiroshima en 2003. En plus de l'architecture, l'agence est spécialisée en architecture intérieure, mobilier, design d'expositions et de produits, urbanisme, planification, conseil et recherche. Keisuke Maeda enseigne à l'Institut de technologie d'Hiroshima. Ses projets comprennent le Centre d'éducation sur l'Holocauste (Hiroshima, 2007) ; une maison à Tomonoura (Hiroshima, 2008) ; la Art Flow House (Hiroshima, 2008) ; la Rustic House (Fukuyama, 2009) ; MORI x Hako (Hiroshima, 2009) ; l'atelier Bisque Doll (Osaka, 2009) ; la maison Tsumuji+Hako (Fukuyama, 2010) ; la maison Nest (Onomichi, Hiroshima, 2010, publiée ici) ; la Machi House (Fukuyama, Hiroshima, 2011) et Peanuts (Hiroshima, 2011–12). Ses travaux en cours comprennent la clinique dentaire O de Matsuyama (2013) et la rénovation d'une rue à Fukuyama (Hiroshima, 2016), tous au Japon.

NEST

Onomichi, Hiroshima, Japan, 2010

Area: 121 m². Client: not disclosed
Cost: not disclosed

Seen from the exterior at nightfall, the house seems to be completely open inside, as indeed it is.

Von außen betrachtet wirkt das Haus in der Abenddämmerung innen völlig offen – was tatsächlich der Fall ist.

Dans cette vue prise à la tombée de la nuit, la maison semble entièrement ouverte à l'intérieur, ce qu'elle est en réalité.

This house, located in a forest near a mountain, was designed for a mother and her two daughters. Given the relation of the clients, the architect imagined the metaphor of the nest. "It is like a principle that expands from a nest in a forest, to the forest, then to the earth, and ultimately to the universe," says the architect. Spaces inserted into the ground are compared to "a concrete anthill nest," while the areas above are likened to "a floating wooden nest box composed of things like branches and fallen leaves…" The wood surface of the house is punctured by large openings, some glazed and others open. Aside from this repeated metaphor, the house also offers something that Japanese designers (and their clients) often seek—proximity to nature in its many forms, including light, wind, or the feeling of the forest in this instance.

Das in einem Wald bei einem Berg gelegene Haus wurde für eine Mutter und ihre zwei Töchter geplant. Angeregt durch die Familienkonstellation arbeitete der Architekt mit der Metapher des Nests. „Es ist ein Prinzip, das den Bogen schlägt vom Nest zum Wald, zur Erde und hinaus ins Universum", so der Architekt. Die in den Boden versenkten Zonen vergleicht er mit einem „Ameisenhaufen aus Beton", die oberen Bereiche beschreibt er als „schwebenden Nistkasten aus Ästen und Laub …". Die Holzfassade des Hauses ist mit großen Öffnungen durchsetzt, von denen einige verglast, andere offen sind. Abgesehen von der sich wiederholenden Metapher bietet das Haus etwas, das Architekten (und Bauherren) in Japan oft suchen – die Nähe zur Natur in ihrer vielfältigen Gestalt, zum Licht, zum Wind oder, wie hier, zum Wald.

Construite en forêt dans une région montagneuse, cette maison a été conçue pour sa propriétaire et ses deux filles. Afin de répondre à cette configuration familiale particulière, l'architecte a pensé à la métaphore du nid. « C'est un peu comme un principe qui se développerait du nid en forêt vers la forêt, puis vers la terre et enfin vers l'univers », explique-t-il. Les volumes insérés dans le sol sont ainsi comparés à « une vraie fourmilière », et les parties supérieures à « un nid de bois en suspension, composé de choses comme des branches et des feuilles tombées… » La façade en bois de la maison est rythmée de grands percements, certains laissés ouverts, d'autres vitrés. En dehors de cette métaphore, la maison propose également quelque chose que les architectes japonais (et leurs clients) recherchent souvent, la proximité à la nature sous de multiples formes, dont la lumière, le vent ou, comme ici, le sentiment de la présence de la forêt.

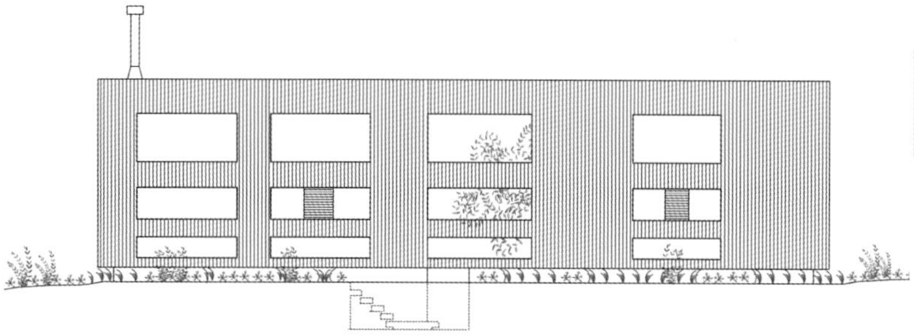

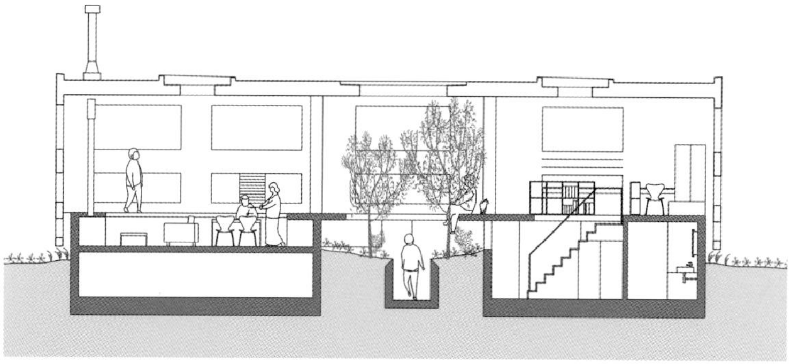

Elevation and section drawings, as well as the interior photo below, show the open interior space with the somewhat surprising tree and rock formation in its midst.

Aufriss und Querschnitte sowie eine Ansicht des Innenraums (unten) zeigen den offenen Innenbereich mit einer überraschenden Baum- und Felsformation in der Mitte.

Les dessins en coupe et d'élévation, ainsi que la photo ci-dessous, montrent le volume intérieur entièrement ouvert avec, au centre, une étonnante rocaille plantée d'un arbre.

As the plan below and the images on this double page demonstrate, the very heart of the house is given over to a nearly natural setting, with trees growing through the open center.

Wie der Grundriss unten und die Aufnahmen auf dieser Doppelseite zeigen, beherrscht eine fast natürliche Szenerie das Herz des Hauses. Bäume wachsen in der offenen Mitte.

Comme le montrent le plan ci-dessous et les deux photographies, le cœur même de la maison est consacré à une reconstitution de décor naturel planté d'arbres.

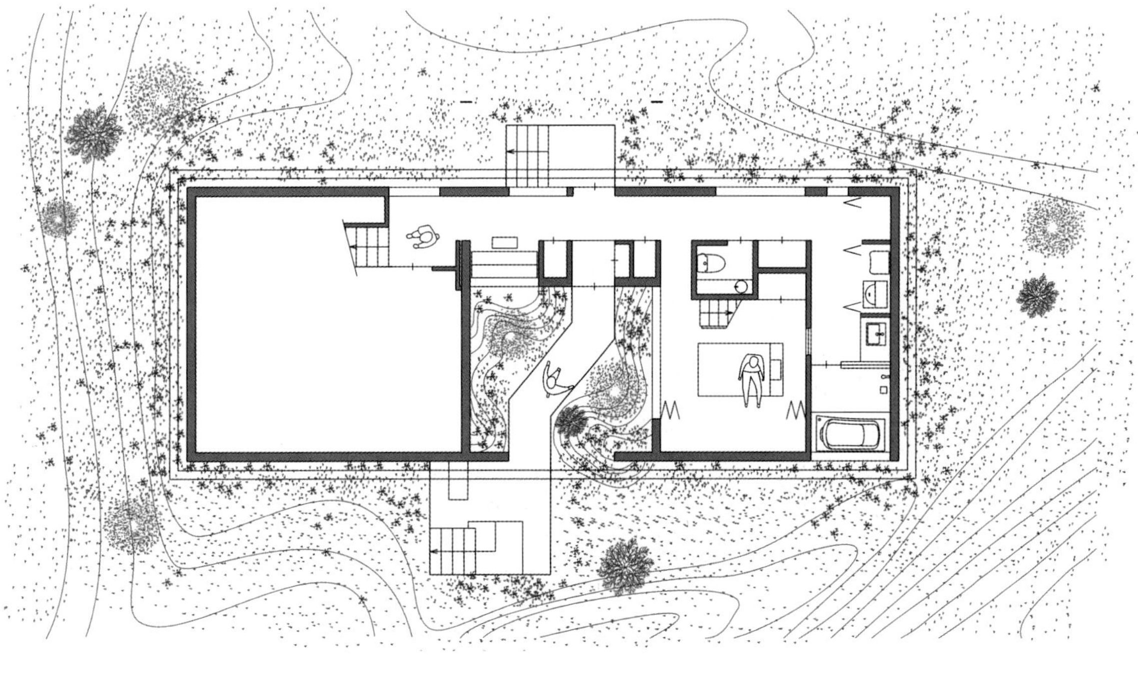

ULLOA + DING

Ulloa + Ding
Rosal 377 C
8320000 Santiago
Chile

Tel: +56 2 632 5244
E-mail: ulloadavet@yahoo.com
Web: www.jud-arq.blogspot.com

DELPHINE DING was born in Switzerland in 1978 and graduated from the École Polytechnique Fédérale de Lausanne (EPFL) in 2005, assisting with teaching in the Geometry Department there (2003–04). She studied Architecture at the Universitat Politécnica de Catalunya (UPC, Barcelona, 2003) before beginning her professional career. **JOSÉ ULLOA DAVET** was born in Chile in 1977. He graduated as an architect from the Universidad Católica de Chile in 2002. Between 1999 and 2000, he studied at the Universitat Politécnica de Catalunya (UPC, Barcelona). Ding and Ulloa Davet have been collaborating on projects in Barcelona and Chile since 2005; Metamorphosis House (Casablanca, Tunquén, Chile, 2008, published here) is an example. Recent work includes the Casa L (Santiago, Chile, 2013).

DELPHINE DING wurde 1978 in der Schweiz geboren und schloss ihr Studium 2005 an der École Polytechnique Fédérale de Lausanne (EPFL) ab, wo sie als Assistentin am Lehrstuhl für Geometrie unterrichtete (2003–04). Sie studierte Architektur an der Universitat Politècnica de Catalunya (UPC, Barcelona, 2003), bevor sie ihre berufliche Laufbahn begann. **JOSÉ ULLOA DAVET** wurde 1977 in Chile geboren. Sein Architekturstudium schloss er im Jahr 2002 an der Universidad Católica de Chile ab. Von 1999 bis 2000 studierte er an der Universitat Politècnica de Catalunya (UPC, Barcelona). Ding und Ulloa Davet arbeiten seit 2005 gemeinsam an Projekten in Barcelona und Chile – ihr Haus Metamorphosis (Casablanca, Tunquén, Chile, 2008, hier vorgestellt) ist ein Beispiel. Zu ihren jüngeren Arbeiten zählt u. a. die Casa L (Santiago, Chile, 2013).

DELPHINE DING, née en Suisse en 1978, est diplômée de l'École polytechnique fédérale de Lausanne (EPFL, 2005), où elle a été assistante au département de géométrie (2003–04). Elle a étudié l'architecture à l'Université polytechnique de Catalogne (UPC, Barcelone, 2003), avant d'entamer sa carrière professionnelle. **JOSÉ ULLOA DAVET**, né au Chili en 1977, est diplômé de l'Université catholique du Chili (2002). De 1999 à 2000, il a également étudié à l'UPC à Barcelone. Ding et Ulloa Davet collaborent, depuis 2005, à des projets à Barcelone et au Chili : la maison Metamorphosis (Casablanca, Tunquén, Chili, 2008, publiée ici) est un exemple de leurs réalisations. La Casa L (Santiago, Chili, 2013) figure parmi leurs réalisations récentes.

METAMORPHOSIS HOUSE

Casablanca, Tunquén, Chile, 2008

Address: not disclosed. Area: 180 m²
Client: not disclosed. Cost: $70 000

Because the architects undertook a reworking of an existing (1990) wooden house in this instance, they called the house "Metamorphosis." The roof of the old house was made into a panoramic deck with an independent access. A new room was cantilevered over the entrance without the use of any visible columns. Although the south façade was enlarged to give a sea view to the new living area, the original layout of the house was otherwise maintained. A "ventilated wooden skin" provides greater thermal stability for the house. With its outside decks and framed views, the house seems nothing if not thoroughly modern and integrated with its site—a substantial achievement for this renovation.

Bei diesem Projekt integrierten die Architekten ein bestehendes Holzhaus (1990), weshalb sie den Bau „Metamorphosis" nannten. Was früher das Dach des älteren Gebäudes war, wurde zu einer Panoramaterrasse mit separatem Zugang. Über dem Eingang wurde ein neuer Raum geschaffen, der in einem Ausleger ohne sichtbare Stützen untergebracht ist. Zwar wurde die Südfassade vergrößert, damit der neue Wohnraum einen Blick aufs Meer hat, ansonsten jedoch wurde der ursprüngliche Grundriss beibehalten. Eine „hinterlüftete Holzhaut" sorgt für einen Temperaturausgleich im Haus. Mit seinen Terrassen und gerahmten Ausblicken wirkt das Haus uneingeschränkt modern und in sein Umfeld integriert – eine beträchtliche Leistung dieser Sanierung.

C'est parce que ce projet consistait à retravailler une maison en bois datant de 1900 que les architectes l'ont appelé « Metamorphosis ». L'ancienne toiture a été transformée en terrasse panoramique à accès indépendant. Une pièce nouvelle a été créée en porte-à-faux au-dessus de l'entrée sans colonnes apparentes. Le plan d'origine de la maison a été maintenu, même si la façade sud a été élargie pour donner une vue sur la mer au nouveau séjour. Une « peau de bois ventilée » apporte une plus grande stabilité thermique à l'ensemble. Par ses terrasses et ses vues cadrées, la maison semble résolument moderne et intégrée à son site, une réussite particulièrement bienvenue pour cette rénovation.

The slope of the wood-clad house follows that of the site, with a rooftop terrace offering unobstructed views of the ocean.

Die Schräge der holzverblendeten Fassade entspricht dem Gefälle des Grundstücks. Eine Dachterrasse erlaubt einen unverstellten Ausblick aufs Meer.

Le plan de la maison, entièrement habillée de bois, suit la pente du terrain. Le toit-terrasse offre une vue illimitée sur l'océan.

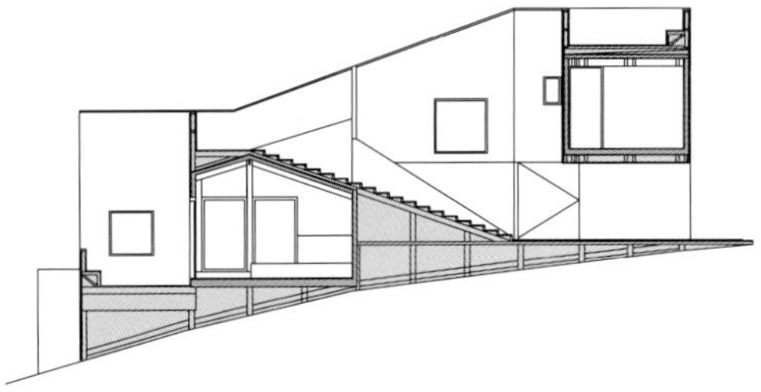

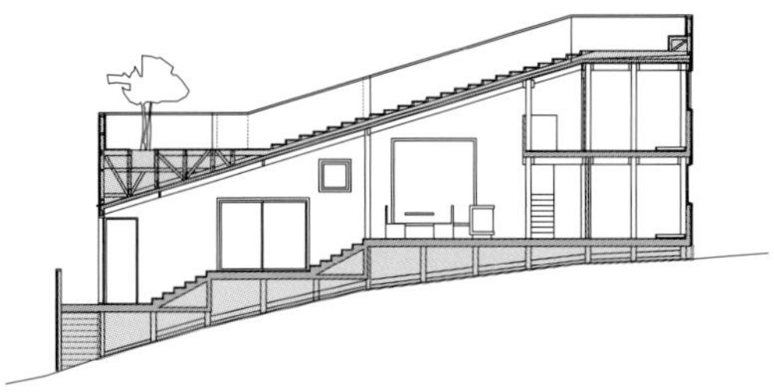

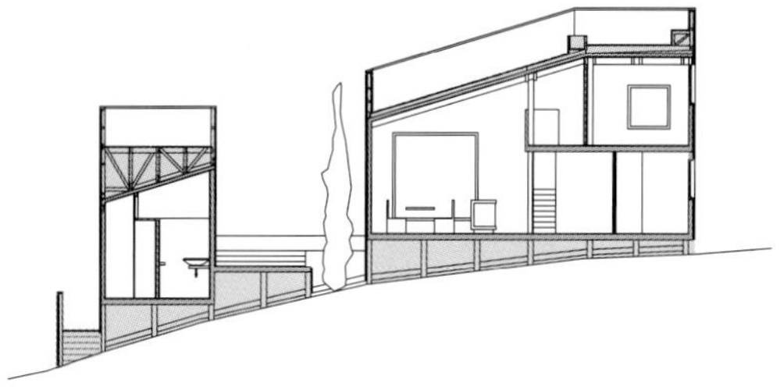

Wood and glass are the most evident materials employed in the interior of the house. Outdoor terraces emphasize the connection between the site and the architecture.

Holz und Glas sind die dominierenden Materialien im Innern des Hauses. Terrassen betonen die Verbindung von Umgebung und Architektur.

Les matériaux utilisés à l'intérieur sont essentiellement le bois et le verre. Les terrasses mettent en évidence le lien entre le site et l'architecture.

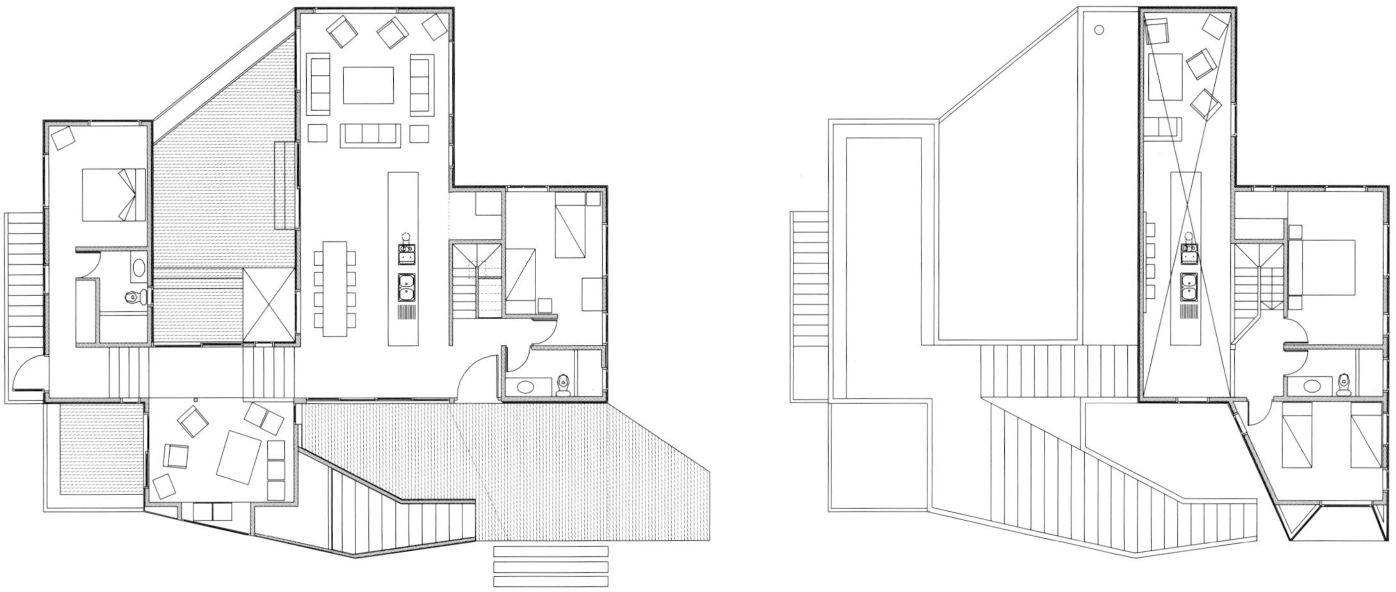

VO TRONG NGHIA

Vo Trong Nghia Architects
8F, 70 Pham Ngoc Thach street
Ward 6, District 3
Ho Chi Minh City
Vietnam

Tel: +84 8 3820 6699
Fax: +84 8 3820 8439
E-mail: hcmc@vtnaa.com
Web: votrongnghia.com

VO TRONG NGHIA was born in Quang Binh Province, Vietnam, in 1976. He attended Ha Noi Architecture University (1994) and received a B.Arch degree from the Nagoya Institute of Technology (Japan, 2002), followed by a Master of Civil Engineering from Tokyo University (2004). His major works are the Ho Chi Minh City University of Architecture (HUA) (with Kazuhiro Kojima and Daisuke Sanuki, Ho Chi Minh City, Mekong Delta, 2006), won by an international design competition in 2006; the wNw Café (Binh Duong, 2006); wNw Bar (Binh Duong, 2008); Trung Nguyen Coffee Culture Center (Hanoi, 2008); Bamboo Wing (Dai Lai, Vinh Phuc Province, 2009, published here); the Vietnam Pavilion for Shanghai Expo (Shanghai, China, 2010); Stacking Green (Ho Chi Minh City, 2011); and Stone Villa (Quangninh, 2011), all in Vietnam unless stated otherwise.

VO TRONG NGHIA wurde 1976 in der Provinz Quang Binh, Vietnam, geboren. Er studierte an der Architekturhochschule von Hanoi (1994) und absolvierte zunächst einen B. Arch. an der Technischen Universität Nagoya (Japan, 2002) sowie anschließend einen Master in Bauingenieurwesen an der Universität von Tokio (2004). Zu seinen wichtigsten Arbeiten zählen die Architekturhochschule in Ho-Chi-Minh-Stadt (HUA) (mit Kazuhiro Kojima und Daisuke Sanuki, Ho-Chi-Minh-Stadt, Mekong-Delta, 2006), Preisträger eines Entwurfswettbewerbs 2006, das wNw Café (Binh Duong, 2006), die wNw Bar (Binh Duong, 2008), das Trung Nguyen Coffee Culture Center (Hanoi, 2008), der Bamboo Wing (Dai Lai, Provinz Vinh Phuc, 2009, hier vorgestellt), der Vietnamesische Pavillon für die Expo Schanghai (Schanghai, China, 2010), Stacking Green (Ho-Chi-Minh-Stadt, 2011) und die Stone Villa (Quangninh, 2011), alle in Vietnam, sofern nicht anders angegeben.

VO TRONG NGHIA, né dans la province de Quang Binh (Viêtnam) en 1976, a étudié à l'Université d'architecture d'Hanoï (1994). Il a obtenu son B.Arch à l'Institut de technologie de Nagoya (Japon, 2002) et un master en ingénierie civile à l'université de Tokyo (2004). Ses réalisations les plus importantes sont l'Université d'architecture d'Hô Chi Minh-Ville (HUA) (avec Kazuhiro Kojima et Daisuke Sanuki, Hô Chi Minh-Ville, delta du Mékong, 2006), projet remporté lors d'un concours international de design en 2006 ; le café wNw (Binh Duong, 2006) ; le bar wNw (Binh Duong, 2008) ; le Centre de la culture du café Trung Nguyen (Hanoï, 2008) ; Bamboo Wing (Dai Lai, province de Vinh Phuc, 2009, publiée ici) ; le pavillon du Viêtnam pour l'Expo de Shanghai (2010) ; la maison Stacking Green (Hô Chi Minh-Ville, 2011) et la Villa de pierre (Quangninh, 2011), toutes au Viêtnam sauf mention contraire.

BAMBOO WING

Dai Lai, Vinh Phuc Province, Vietnam, 2009

Area: 1600 m². Client: Hong Hac Dai Lai Jsc
Cost: not disclosed

The architects sought to use bamboo both as a finishing material and in structural applications. This building is a pure bamboo structure, using "no steel or other man-made structural materials." A 12-meter open space proves the strength and resilience of the material and is used for wedding parties, live music concerts, and ceremonies. Inspired by bird wings, the structure "is good for capturing the wind." The architect writes: "Inspired by nature, **BAMBOO WING** takes the form of bird wings and floats over the natural landscape of its site situated near Hanoi... With its deep eaves and the water in the open spaces, people feel as if they are living in nature."

Dem Architekten ging es darum, Bambus sowohl als Verblendmaterial als auch als Tragwerk zu nutzen. Der Bau ist eine reine Bambuskonstruktion, die gänzlich auf „Stahl oder künstliche Baumaterialien" verzichtet. Ein offener, 12 m tiefer, überbauter Bereich zeugt von der Stärke und Belastbarkeit des Materials: Genutzt wird der Raum für Hochzeiten, Live-Konzerte und andere Feierlichkeiten. Das an die Flügel eines Vogels erinnernde Bauwerk ist darüber hinaus ideal geeignet, „Wind einzufangen". Der Architekt schreibt: „Inspiriert von der Natur, ist der **BAMBOO WING** den Schwingen eines Vogels nachempfunden und schwebt über der Naturlandschaft in der Nähe von Hanoi ... Mit seinem tief vorgezogenen Dach und dem Wasser auf den Freiflächen fühlt man sich hier, als würde man mitten in der Natur wohnen."

Les architectes ont cherché à utiliser le bambou comme matériau de finition ainsi que dans des applications structurelles. Le bâtiment se compose d'une structure entièrement en bambou « sans acier, ni aucun autre matériau de construction artificiel ». Un espace ouvert de 12 m, utilisé pour célébrer des mariages, pour des concerts en direct et des cérémonies, atteste de la solidité et de la résistance du matériau. Inspiré par les ailes des oiseaux, la construction « est bonne pour capter le vent ». L'architecte déclare : « Inspirée par la nature, **BAMBOO WING** prend la forme d'ailes d'oiseaux et flotte au-dessus du paysage naturel de son site, près d'Hanoï. [...] Avec ses profonds avant-toits et l'eau des espaces ouverts, les visiteurs ont l'impression de se trouver en pleine nature. »

The basic forms of the building are visible in the plan above—a semicircular covering arches over spaces for guests of the events organized under the Bamboo Wing.

Die Grundform des Gebäudes ist am Grundriss oben ablesbar – ein Halbrund erhebt sich bogenförmig über einem Gastbereich für Veranstaltungen im Bamboo Wing.

On voit sur le plan ci-dessus les formes de base du bâtiment : des arches couvertes semi-circulaires au-dessus d'espaces pour les spectateurs des manifestations organisées sous la Bamboo Wing.

A basin, whose level is actually higher than that of the seating area, arcs around the bamboo structure. The arcing forms of the building are stunning, as seen in these images.

Ein Wasserbecken, dessen Pegel über Bodenniveau des Gastbereichs liegt, folgt bogenförmig den Konturen des Bambusbaus. Die Bogenkonstruktion ist eindrucksvoll, wie hier zu sehen.

Un bassin, dont le niveau est plus haut que le sol où sont placées les chaises, sinue autour de la structure en bambou. Les formes arquées de la structure que l'on voit ici sont impressionnantes.

The resilience and strength of bamboo are used to their utmost in this structure—which might easily have been imagined in steel or other metals, but the architect has taken pride in avoiding "man-made" materials.

Der Bau lotet die Grenzen der Belastbarkeit und Stabilität von Bambus aus. Der Entwurf wäre leicht in Stahl oder Metall zu realisieren gewesen, doch der Architekt legte besonderen Wert darauf, auf „künstliche" Materialien zu verzichten.

La structure tire un parti optimal de la résistance et de la force du bambou – elle aurait facilement pu être créée en acier ou dans un autre métal, mais les architectes tirent une grande fierté d'avoir évité les matériaux « artificiels ».

WERK A

werk A architektur
Lehrterstr. 57 / Haus 4
10557 Berlin
Germany

Tel: +49 30 89 73 37 63
Fax: +49 30 89 73 37 64
E-mail: kontakt@werk-a-architektur.de
Web: www.werk-a-architektur.de

GUNTRAM JANKOWSKI was born in Gräfelfing near Munich in 1972. He studied architecture at the Technical University of Berlin (1993–2000). From 1994 to 2002 he did freelance work for several firms such as APP Dominique Perrault (Berlin). He founded werk A in 2003, and was also a Partner in Roswag & Jankowski from 2006 to 2009. Since that date he has been the Principal of werk A. His work includes Spindler & Klatt, a club and restaurant (Berlin-Kreuzberg 2006); Westend Green, a rammed-earth house (Berlin-Westend, 2007); the renovation of the Jahili Fort, museum and visitor center (Al-Ain, Abu Dhabi, UAE, 2008); Lake House (Friedrichswalde, 2010, published here); The Grand, restaurant and bar (Berlin-Mitte, 2012); and the Lake House Studio, a studio and workshop building (Friedrichswalde, 2012), all in Germany unless stated otherwise.

GUNTRAM JANKOWSKI wurde 1972 in Gräfelfing bei München geboren. Er studierte Architektur an der Technischen Universität Berlin (1993–2000). Zwischen 1994 und 2002 arbeitete er als freischaffender Architekt u. a. für Büros wie APP Dominique Perrault (Berlin). 2003 folgte die Gründung von werk A, von 2006 bis 2009 war er zudem Partner bei Roswag & Jankowski, seither leitet er eigenverantwortlich werk A. Zu seinen Projekten zählen Spindler & Klatt, Club und Restaurant (Berlin-Kreuzberg 2006), Westend Grün, Einfamilienhaus aus Stampflehm (Berlin-Westend, 2007), Fort Jahili, Sanierung von Museum und Besucherzentrum (Al-Ain, Abu Dhabi, VAE, 2008), Haus am See (Friedrichswalde, 2010, hier vorgestellt), The Grand, Restaurant und Bar (Berlin-Mitte, 2012) sowie ein Atelier- und Werkstattgebäude für das Haus am See (Friedrichswalde, 2012), alle in Deutschland, sofern nicht anders angegeben.

GUNTRAM JANKOWSKI, né à Gräfelding près de Munich en 1972, a étudié l'architecture à l'Université technique de Berlin (1993–2000). De 1994 à 2002, il a travaillé en free-lance pour diverses agences dont APP Dominique Perrault à Berlin. Il a fondé l'agence werk A en 2003, tout en étant partenaire de l'agence Roswag & Jankowski de 2006 à 2009. Parmi ses réalisations, toutes en Allemagne, sauf mention contraire : le club et restaurant Spindler & Klatt (Berlin-Kreuzberg 2006) ; Westend Green, une maison en pisé (Berlin-Westend, 2007) ; la rénovation du fort, musée et centre des visiteurs de Jahili (Al-Ain, Abou Dhabi, EAU, 2008) ; la Maison du lac (Friedrichswalde, 2010, publiée ici) ; le restaurant et bar The Grand (Berlin-Mitte, 2012) et l'atelier de la maison du lac (Friedrichswalde, 2012).

LAKE HOUSE

Friedrichswalde, Germany, 2010

Address: not disclosed. Area: 48 m²
Client: not disclosed. Cost: not disclosed

Although the materials employed, as for this wooden table, are rough, the broad semicircular window is a modern feature.

Obwohl verschiedene Materialien wie bei dem Holztisch eher rustikal sind, ist das halbrunde Fenster ein modernes Detail.

Bien que les matériaux employés restent traditionnels et bruts, comme par exemple le plateau de cette table, la grande baie semi-circulaire est d'esprit très contemporain.

The village of Friedrichswalde is in the UNESCO Schorfheide-Chorin Biosphere Reserve located in the state of Brandenburg near the Polish border. The town was founded in 1748 by a decree of Frederick II, the king of Prussia. The **LAKE HOUSE** is a prefabricated wooden structure set on the field-stone base of an old barn on a property in the main village street. The house has a rough-sawed larch frame filled with clay bricks. Its large oval windows frame the view of Lake Krummen. The interior surfaces are covered in clay plaster and the floor covering is fashioned with recycled panels, tiles, and bricks. A clay-based stove is used for heating.

Die Gemeinde Friedrichswalde liegt in Brandenburg im UNESCO-Biosphärenreservat Schorfheide-Chorin unweit der polnischen Grenze. Die Ortschaft wurde 1748 auf Erlass des Preußenkönigs Friedrich II. gegründet. Das **HAUS AM SEE** ist eine Holzfertigbaukonstruktion und wurde über dem Feldsteinfundament einer alten Scheune auf einem Grundstück an der Dorfstraße errichtet. Das Fachwerk aus sägerauer Lärche wurde mit Tonziegeln ausgemauert. Die ovalen Panoramafenster rahmen den Ausblick auf den Krummensee. Der Innenausbau erfolgte mit Lehmputz, die Böden sind mit alten Fliesen, Paneelen und Ziegeln gestaltet. Geheizt wird mit einem Lehmofen.

Le village de Friedrichswalde, fondé en 1748 par le roi de Prusse Frédéric II, se trouve dans la réserve de la biosphère de Schorfheide-Chorin située dans le land de Brandebourg, près de la frontière polonaise. La **MAISON DU LAC** est une construction préfabriquée en bois posée sur un socle en pierre des champs, qui appartenait à une ancienne grange de la rue principale du village. L'ossature est en bouleau grossièrement débité et le remplissage en briques d'argile. Les grandes fenêtres ovales cadrent des vues sur le lac de Krummen. Les murs intérieurs sont plâtrés et les sol en panneaux de bois recyclé, carrelage et briques. Un poêle en céramique assure le chauffage.

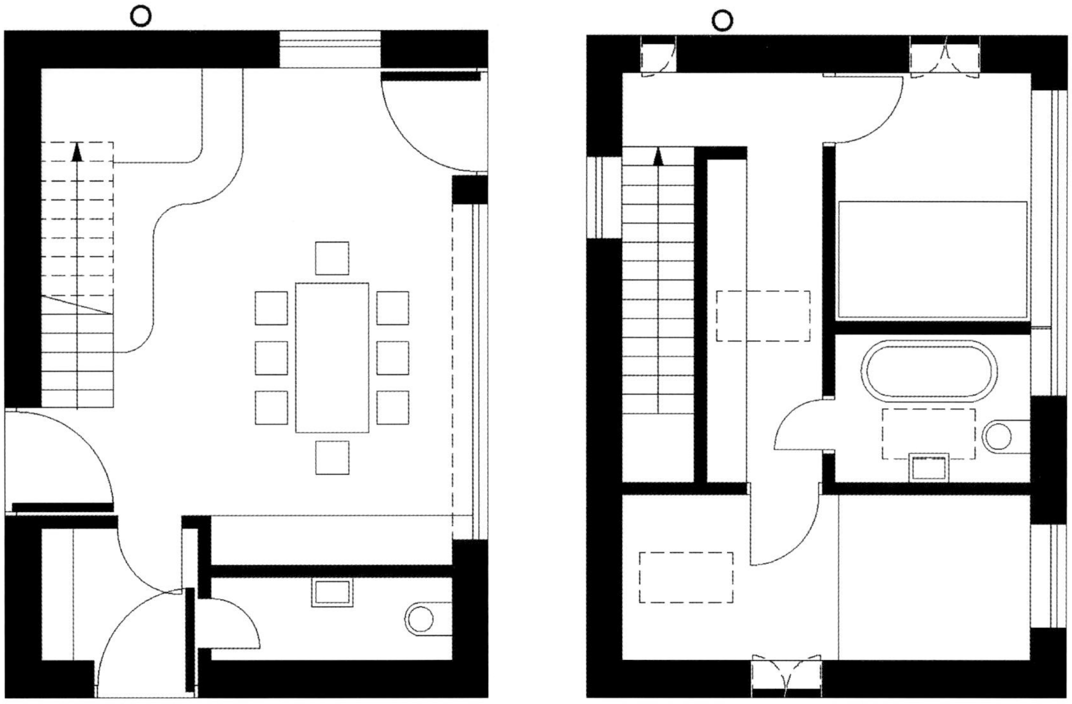

Plans show the strict rectangular configuration of the house. Below, details of the wood cladding and the rounded windows.

Die Grundrisse illustrieren die streng geradlinige Konfiguration des Hauses. Unten Details des Holzverschalung und der Rundfenster.

Le plan montre la configuration strictement orthogonale de la maison. Ci-dessous, détails du bardage extérieur et des fenêtres arrondies.

The round or oval windows make it seem as though interior spaces are entirely open to the exterior. Below, a section drawing with the angled roof visible. Right, the fairly rustic kitchen.

Die runden und ovalen Fenster lassen den Eindruck vollständig offener Räume entstehen. Unten ein Querschnitt, auf dem das Schrägdach zu erkennen ist. Rechts die eher rustikale Küche.

Les fenêtres rondes ou ovales donnent l'impression que les volumes intérieurs sont entièrement ouverts sur l'extérieur. Ci-dessous, une coupe montrant la pente du toit. À droite, la cuisine d'aménagement assez rustique.

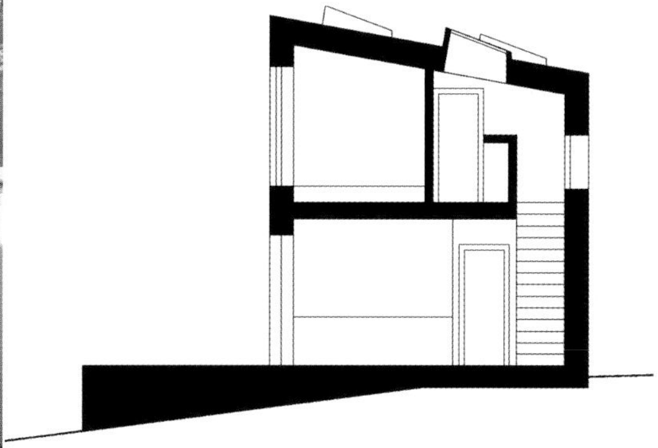

WHITE

White arkitekter AB
P. O. Box 2502
40317 Göteborg
Sweden

Tel: +46 31 60 86 00
Fax: +46 31 60 86 10
E-mail: info@white.se
Web: www.white.se

White is one of Scandinavia's large architectural companies, with 460 employees working at 11 offices in Göteborg, Stockholm, Malmö, Linköping, Halmstadt, Örebro, Uppsala, Umeå, Copenhagen, Ringsted and Naestved. As they say, "We see ourselves as a large, employee-owned ideas factory. Our owner-system acts as an engine, a dynamo, a stabilizer, and a direction indicator, all at the same time. Shared ownership means a shared commitment. Our range of expertise embraces architecture, urban planning, landscaping, interior design, the environmental settings, and project management." **FREDRIK PETTERSSON**, in charge of the Kastrup Sea Bath project (Denmark, 2005, published here), was born in 1972 in Lund, Sweden. He obtained his architectural degrees from Lund University and in Århus. He started at White in Göteborg in 1999, but got a transfer in 2002 to the Copenhagen office. The company's recent work in Sweden includes the Drottningtornet Tower (Linköping, 2006); and the future 16-story Klara Hotel (Stockholm, 2006–10). Their New Psychiatric Clinic in Borås (2013–) was granted the WAN AWARD 2013 for best future Healthcare Project.

White ist mit 460 Angestellten, die in elf Büros in Göteborg, Stockholm, Malmö, Linköping, Halmstadt, Örebro, Uppsala, Umeå, Kopenhagen, Ringsted und Naestved arbeiten, eine der größten Architekturfirmen Skandinaviens. Aus den eigenen Reihen heißt es: „Wir verstehen uns als große Ideenfabrik im Besitz ihrer Angestellten. Unser Eignersystem fungiert gleichzeitig als Motor, Dynamo, Stabilisator und Richtungsweiser. Geteilter Besitz bedeutet geteilte Verantwortung. Die Bandbreite unserer Fachkenntnisse umfasst Architektur, Stadtplanung, Landschaftsgestaltung, Innenarchitektur, umweltgerechte Anlagen sowie Projektleitung." **FREDRIK PETTERSON**, Leiter des hier vorgestellten Projekts Seebad Kastrup (Dänemark, 2005), wurde 1972 in Lund, Schweden, geboren. Er studierte Architektur an der Universität von Lund und in Århus. 1999 eröffnete er das Büro White in Göteborg, wechselte jedoch 2002 in das Kopenhagener Büro. Zu ihren neuesten Bauten in Schweden zählen: Hochhaus Drottningtornet (Linköping, 2006) sowie das 16-geschossige Hotel Klara (Stockholm, 2006–10). Die neue psychiatrische Klinik in Borås (seit 2013) wurde mit dem WAN AWARD 2013 für das beste zukünftige Gesundheitsprojekt ausgezeichnet.

White est l'une des plus importantes agences d'architecture scandinaves, qui emploie 460 collaborateurs travaillant dans ses onze bureaux de Göteborg, Stockholm, Malmö, Linköping, Halmstadt, Örebro, Uppsala, Umeå, Copenhague, Ringsted et Naestved. « Nous nous considérons comme une vaste usine à idées coopératives. Notre système de propriété est tout à la fois un moteur, une dynamo, un stabilisateur et un indicateur de direction. Ce partage de propriété permet l'engagement de tous. Notre champ d'expertise embrasse l'architecture, l'urbanisme, le paysagisme, l'architecture intérieure, le cadre environnemental et la gestion de projets. » **FREDRIK PETTERSSON**, responsable du projet de la jetée de bains de mer de Kastrup (Danemark, 2005, publié ici), est né en 1972, à Lund, Suède. Il est diplômé en architecture des universités de Lund et Århus. Il a fait ses débuts chez White, à Göteborg, en 1999, puis a été transféré en 2002 au bureau de Copenhague. Parmi leurs récentes réalisations érigées en Suède figurent la tour de Drottningtornet, Linköping (2006) et le futur Klara Hotel de quinze étages à Stockholm (2006–10). Leur nouvelle clinique psychiatrique à Borås (2013–) a reçu le WAN AWARD 2013 pour le meilleur projet futur dans le domaine de la santé.

KASTRUP SEA BATH

Kastrup, Denmark, 2005

Address: Amager Strandvej 301, 2770 Kastrup, Denmark. Floor area: 870 m² wooden deck; 70 m² changing area; 90 m² service building on land. Client: City of Kastrup. Cost: €1.2 million. Landscape Design: Fredrik Pettersson (Project Leader), Rasmus Skaarup, Pernille Vermund, Göran Wihl, Henrik Haremst, Johnny Gere

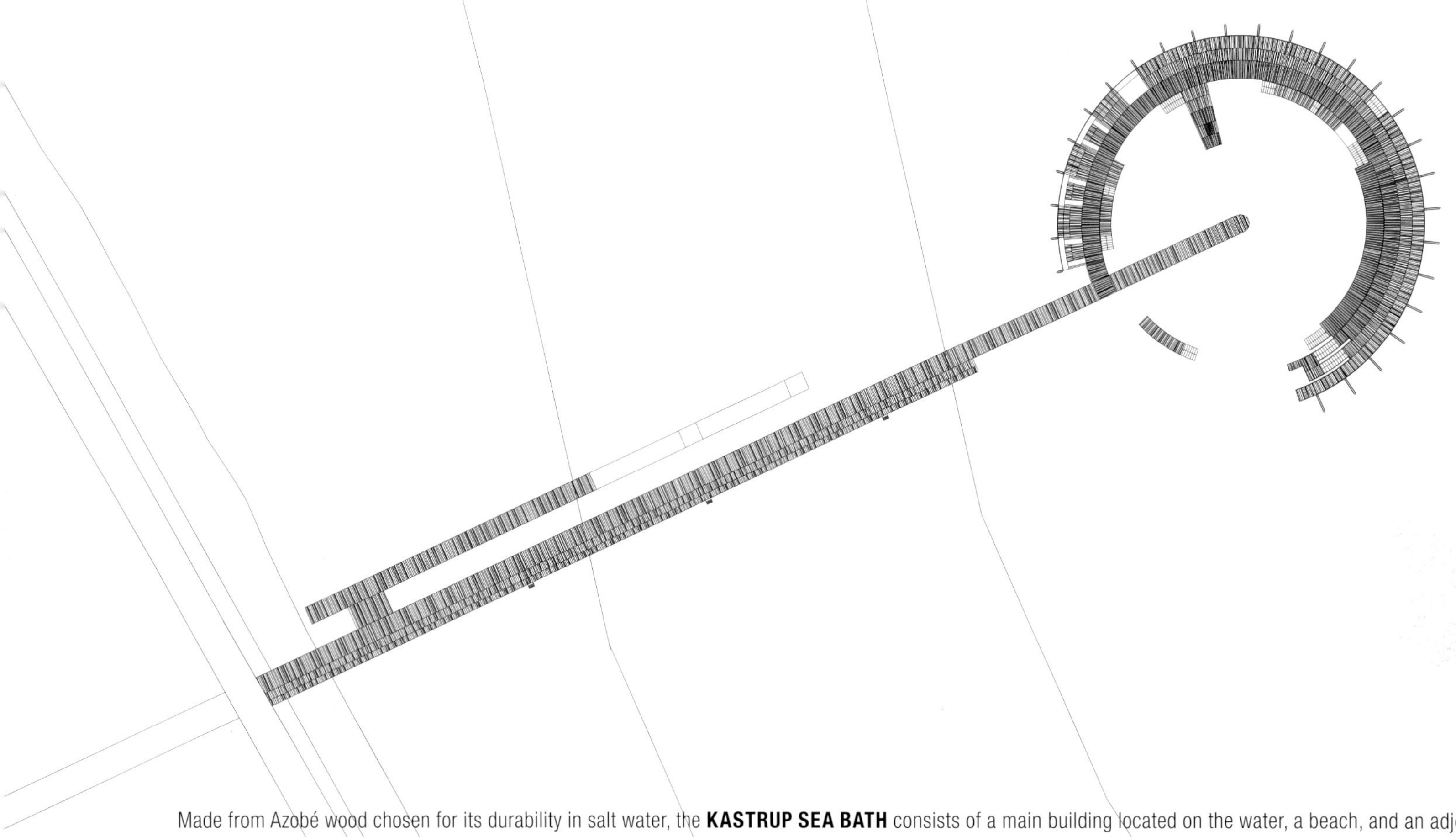

Made from Azobé wood chosen for its durability in salt water, the **KASTRUP SEA BATH** consists of a main building located on the water, a beach, and an adjoining services building with lavatories and a changing room for the handicapped. Visitors move in a circular pattern, gradually rising from the sea's surface and ending up at a five-meter diving platform. Of this feature, the architect Fredrik Pettersson says, "All art is self-expression, and here I've designed a path that inevitably leads to a drop of five meters. I've not dared to jump yet. But the construction is mine, which is a good start." The firm writes, "The Bath is conceived as a sculptural dynamic form, which can be seen from the beach, the sea, and the air. Its silhouette gradually changes as the beholder moves around it. The circular shape creates a concentrated interior, shelter from the winds, and concentrates the sun. The shape opens up toward the landside to connect to the beach and to invite visitors inside. A continuous bench runs along the pier, thus creating an additional rest and leisure area." Careful attention was paid to the night lighting of the facility, making it stand out from its surroundings. Uplights on the interior of the semicircular wall and lines of LED spots running along the pier are the essential elements of the night lighting.

Das wegen seiner Haltbarkeit in Salzwasser aus Azobéholz gefertigte **SEEBAD KASTRUP** besteht aus einem am Meer stehenden Hauptgebäude, einem Strandabschnitt und einem Servicegebäude mit Toiletten und einem behindertengerechten Umkleideraum. Die Anlage wird durch kreisförmig verlaufende Wege erschlossen, über die Besucher sich vom Wasser bis zu einem 5 m hohen Sprungbrett bewegen. Architekt Fredrik Pettersson meint dazu: „Alle Kunst ist Ausdruck der eigenen Persönlichkeit und ich habe hier einen Weg gestaltet, der zwangsläufig zu einem Fall aus 5 m Höhe führt. Ich habe mich bislang nicht zu springen getraut. Aber die Konstruktion stammt von mir und das ist ein guter Anfang." Das Büro schreibt: „Das Bad ist als plastische, dynamische Form konzipiert, die man vom Strand, vom Meer und aus der Luft sehen kann. Während der Betrachter es umrundet, verändert sich seine Silhouette allmählich. Die Kreisform erzeugt einen konzentrierten Innenraum, schirmt den Wind ab und sammelt die Sonne. Die Form öffnet sich zum Land hin, um den Strand anzubinden und Besucher einzuladen. Der Pier ist von einer durchgehenden Bank gesäumt, die einen weiteren Bereich zum Ausruhen und Entspannen schafft." Der nächtlichen Beleuchtung widmete man große Sorgfalt, um die Anlage von ihrer Umgebung abzuheben. Auf die Innenseite der halbkreisförmigen Wand gerichtete Strahler sowie entlang des Piers verlaufende LED-Spots sind die wesentlichen Elemente der Nachtbeleuchtung.

Construite en azobé, bois choisi pour sa résistance à l'eau de mer, cette **JETÉE DE BAINS DE MER DE KASTRUP** consiste en un bâtiment principal sur l'eau, une plage, un bâtiment de services adjacent comprenant des toilettes et un vestiaire pour handicapés. Les visiteurs se déplacent le long d'un parcours circulaire, s'élevant peu à peu du niveau de la mer jusqu'à un plongeoir de 5 m de haut. L'architecte Fredrik Pettersson commente ainsi son projet : « Tout art est une expression de soi et, ici, j'ai conçu un cheminement qui conduit inévitablement à une chute de 5 m. Je n'ai pas encore osé sauter, mais la construction est bien de moi, ce qui est un bon point de départ. » Pour l'agence : « Ce « Bain » est une forme sculpturale dynamique qui peut se voir de la mer, de la plage, et du ciel. Sa silhouette se modifie petit à petit, lorsque le spectateur se déplace autour d'elle. La forme circulaire génère une concentration vers l'intérieur, un abri par rapport au vent et une concentration solaire. Elle s'ouvre vers la terre pour se connecter à la plage et invite le visiteur à la fouler. Un banc continu s'étend le long de la jetée, créant un lieu de détente et de repos supplémentaire. » Un soin particulier a été porté à l'éclairage nocturne, qui met en valeur les installations par rapport à leur environnement. Des projecteurs dirigés vers le haut illuminent la face intérieure semi-circulaire du mur et les lignes de LED, posées le long de la jetée, jouent un rôle essentiel.

With its extremely simple plan and its wooden design lifted up off the water, the Sea Bath allies modernity with a bow to local traditions.

Mit seiner ausgesprochen schlichten Anlage und dem über das Wasser angehobenen Holzbau verbindet das Seebad die Moderne mit lokalen Traditionen.

Sur un plan extrêmement simple et construits en bois sur pilotis au-dessus de l'eau, ces Bains de mer allient modernité et traditions locales.

Although White is a large architectural firm, this structure was largely the work of a talented individual architect, Fredrik Pettersson. It is somewhat quirky and unexpected in ways that a more "corporate" approach would not have allowed.

Obgleich White ein großes Architekturbüro ist, scheint dieser Bau eher das Werk des begabten Individualisten Fredrik Pettersson zu sein. Es ist in einer Weise schrullig und spontan, die eine „unternehmerische" Einstellung nicht zugelassen hätte.

Bien que White soit une grande agence, cette construction semble davantage l'œuvre d'une personnalité de talent, Fredrik Pettersson. Elle est plus bizarre et inattendue que pourrait l'être le produit d'une approche « institutionnelle ».

Gangplanks and stairs leading to the water in the warmer months accompany the sweeping round movement of the main structure.

Laufstege und Treppen, die für das sommerliche Baden zum Wasser führen, begleiten die ausgreifende Rundung des Hauptbaukörpers.

Des appontements et des escaliers pour descendre vers l'eau à la belle saison accompagnent le mouvement en courbe de la structure principale.

The presence of water is a constant factor of the architecture. The architect's unusual idea to lead visitors to a five-meter diving platform appears to have frightened him as much as many users.

Die Präsenz von Wasser ist bei dieser Architektur eine Konstante. Die Idee des Architekten, Besucher zu einem 5 m hohen Sprungturm zu leiten, scheint ihn ebenso erschreckt zu haben wie viele Benutzer.

La présence d'eau est un facteur constant dans cette architecture. L'idée de l'architecte de faire monter les amateurs à un plongeoir à 5 m de haut semble leur faire aussi peur qu'à lui-même.

WILLIAMS AND TSIEN

Tod Williams Billie Tsien Architects
222 Central Park South
New York, NY 10019
USA

Tel: +1 212 582 2385 / Fax: +1 212 245 1984
E-mail: mail@twbta.com
Web: www.twbta.com

TOD WILLIAMS was born in Detroit, Michigan, in 1943. He received his B.A. (1965) and Master of Fine Arts (1967) degrees from Princeton University. After six years as an Associate Architect in the office of Richard Meier in New York, he began his own practice in New York in 1974. **BILLIE TSIEN** was born in Ithaca, New York, in 1949. She received her B.A. at Yale, and her M.Arch from UCLA (1977). She was a painter and graphic designer (1971–75), cofounding Tod Williams Billie Tsien Architects in 1986. Their built work includes the New College, University of Virginia (Charlottesville, Virginia, 1992); the Neurosciences Institute (La Jolla, California, 1995); Rifkind House (Georgica Pond, Long Island, New York, 1997–98, published here); the Cranbrook Natatorium (Bloomfield, Michigan, 1999); the American Folk Art Museum (New York, New York, 2001); and the renovation and extension of the Phoenix Art Museum (Arizona,1996; Phase II, 2006). Recent and future work includes the Asia Society Hong Kong Center (Hong Kong, China, 2011); the Barnes Foundation (Philadelphia, Pennsylvania, 2010–12); the Reva and David Logan Center for Creative and Performing Arts, University of Chicago (Chicago, Illinois, 2012); Orchard Student Residences, Haverford College (Haverford, Pennsylvania, 2012); Tata Consultancy Services Campus (Mumbai, India, Phase I, 2013); Lakeside Center at Prospect Park (Brooklyn, New York, 2014); and the Andlinger Center for Energy and the Environment, Princeton University (Princeton, New Jersey, 2015), all in the USA unless stated otherwise.

TOD WILLIAMS wurde 1943 in Detroit, Michigan, geboren. Er absolvierte einen B. A. (1965) und einen Master of Fine Arts (1967) an der Princeton University. Nach sechs Jahren als Associated Architect im New Yorker Büro von Richard Meier arbeitete er ab 1974 selbstständig. **BILLIE TSIEN** wurde 1949 in Ithaca, New York, geboren. Sie absolvierte einen B. A. in Yale und einen M. Arch. an der UCLA (1977). Sie war als Malerin und Grafikdesignerin tätig (1971–75) und gründete mit Williams 1986 das Büro Tod Williams Billie Tsien Architects. Zu ihren Arbeiten gehören das New College der University of Virginia (Charlottesville, Virginia, 1992), das Neurosciences Institute (La Jolla, Kalifornien, 1995), das Rifkind House (Georgica Pond, Long Island, New York, 1997–98, hier vorgestellt), die Cranbrook Schwimmhalle (Bloomfield, Michigan, 1999), das American Folk Art Museum (New York, 2001) und die Renovierung und Erweiterung des Phoenix Art Museum (Arizona, 1996; 2. Abschnitt 2006). Jüngere und anstehende Projekte sind das Asia Society Hong Kong Center (Hongkong, 2011), die Barnes Foundation (Philadelphia, Pennsylvania, 2010–12), das Reva and David Logan Center for Creative and Performing Arts, University of Chicago (Chicago, Illinois, 2012), das Orchard-Studentenwohnheim, Haverford College (Haverford, Pennsylvania, 2012), der Tata Consultancy Services Campus (Mumbai, Indien, 1. Bauabschnitt, 2013), das Lakeside Center im Prospect Park (Brooklyn, New York, 2014), das Andlinger Center for Energy and the Environment, Princeton University (Princeton, New Jersey, 2015).

Né à Détroit, Michigan, en 1943, **TOD WILLIAMS** obtient son B.A. (1965) et son master des beaux-arts (1967) à l'université de Princeton. Après six ans comme architecte associé dans l'agence de Richard Meier à New York, il ouvre sa propre agence à New York en 1974. Née à Ithaca, New York, en 1949, **BILLIE TSIEN** obtient son B.A. à Yale et son M.Arch. à l'UCLA (1977). Elle est d'abord peintre et graphiste (1971–75) avant de participer à la fondation de Tod Williams Billie Tsien Architects en 1986. Parmi leurs réalisations, l'on peut mentionner le New College, université de Virginie (Charlottesville, Virginie, 1992) ; le Neurosciences Institute (La Jolla, Californie, 1995) ; la Rifkind House (Georgica Pond, Long Island, New York, 1997–98, publiée ici) ; la rénovation et l'extension du Phoenix Art Museum (Arizona, 1996, Phase II, 2006) ; le Cranbrook Natatorium (Bloomfield, Michigan, 1999) et l'American Folk Art Museum (New York, 2001). Parmi leurs projets récents ou futurs, on trouve l'Asia Society Hong Kong Center (Hong Kong, 2011) ; la Fondation Barnes (Philadelphie, 2010–12) ; le Reva and David Logan Center for Creative and Performing Arts de Chicago (Chicago, 2012) ; la résidence pour étudiants Orchard, Haverford College (Haverford, Pennsylvanie, 2012) ; Tata Consultancy Services Campus (Bombay, Phase I, 2013) ; le Lakeside Center à Prospect Park (Brooklyn, New York, 2014) et l'Andlinger Center for Energy and the Environment, de l'université de Princeton (Princeton, New Jersey, 2015), tous aux États-Unis sauf mention contraire.

RIFKIND HOUSE

Georgica Pond, Long Island, New York, USA, 1997–98

Address: not disclosed. Floor area: 465 m²
Client: Robert and Arleen Rifkind. Cost: not disclosed

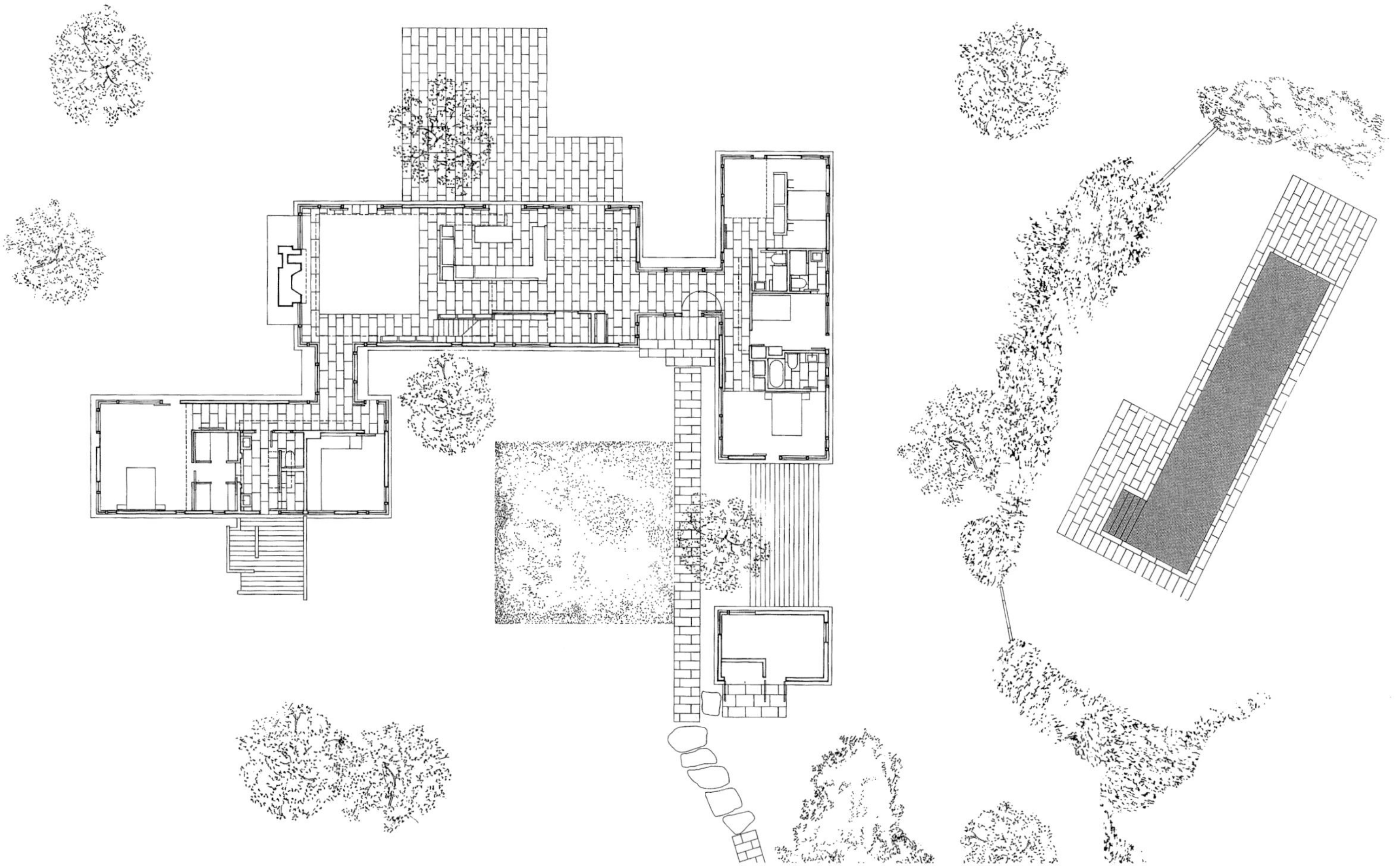

Set on a 1.5-hectare site on the edge of a large pond within view of the ocean, the **RIFKIND HOUSE** was intended to satisfy the client's specifications for "quiet serenity, an openness to the landscape and a sense of spaciousness without monumentality." It is, except for the slightly higher living room area, only about three meters in height. It comprises four units—a planting and storage shed, a three-bedroom guest wing, a master bedroom area, and a "public" section. A wood-frame structure with cedar siding, the house has ample glazing set in mahogany window frames, while inside floors are covered with Douglas fir and New York bluestone. Bookshelves, beds, dressers, and furniture, also designed by the architects, are made of American cherry.

Das **RIFKIND HOUSE** ist auf einem 1,5 ha großen Grundstück mit Blick auf den Atlantik am Rand eines Teichs gelegen. Es sollte auf Wunsch des Bauherrn von „gelassener Heiterkeit, einer Offenheit für die Landschaft und einem Gefühl von Geräumigkeit ohne Monumentalität" geprägt sein. Das gesamte Gebäude ist, mit Ausnahme des leicht erhöhten Wohnraums, nur ca. 3 m hoch und setzt sich aus vier Einheiten zusammen: einer Kombination von Gewächshaus und Lagerschuppen, einem Gästetrakt mit drei Zimmern, einem großen Schlafraum und einem „öffentlichen" Bereich. Die aus einem mit Zedernholz verkleideten Holzgerüst bestehende Außenfassade des Hauses wird von großen Glasflächen mit Mahagoniholzrahmen durchbrochen, während die Böden im Inneren mit Douglasie und blauem Tonsandstein aus dem Hudsongebiet bedeckt sind. Die ebenfalls von den Architekten entworfenen Bücherregale, Betten, Kommoden und auch die anderen Möbel sind aus amerikanischem Kirschbaum gefertigt.

Située au bord d'un étang sur un terrain de 1,5 ha, la **MAISON RIFKIND** répond au souhait du client qui recherchait la « sérénité naturelle, l'ouverture sur le paysage et une impression d'espace sans monumentalité ». A l'exception du séjour, légèrement surélevé, la maison ne dépasse pas 3 m de hauteur. Elle se compose de quatre éléments – un hangar de stockage et de jardinage, une aile pour invités avec trois chambres, une partie réservée à la chambre du maître de maison et une zone « publique ». La structure en bois est bardée de cèdre. Les ouvertures en acajou sont vastes et les sols en pin de Douglas ou pierre bleue de New York. Les rayonnages pour les livres, les lits, les commodes et le mobilier sont en cerisier américain et ont été dessinés par les architectes.

Seen from two different angles, the house appears to be quite closed, with its horizontal cedar siding, or alternatively quite open, with the large vertical glass panels allowing views out toward the wooded site.

Während die mit Zedernholz verkleideten Wände einen eher geschlossen Charakter vermitteln, wirken die großen Glasflächen, die den Blick auf das bewaldete Grundstück freigeben, sehr offen.

Selon les angles de vue, la maison semble plutôt fermée derrière son habillage de cèdre ou très ouverte par ses hauts panneaux de verre qui donnent sur le terrain boisé.

WINGÅRDHS

Wingårdh Arkitektkontor AB
Kungsgatan 10A
411 19 Göteborg
Sweden

Tel: +46 31 743 70 00
Fax: +46 31 711 98 38
E-mail: wingardhs@wingardhs.se
Web: www.wingardhs.se

Wingårdhs is one of the five largest architectural firms in Sweden. Founded in Göteborg in 1977, Wingårdhs has also had offices in Stockholm since 1985. Their staff numbers about 140. **GERT WINGÅRDH**, born in 1951 in Skövde, Sweden, is the owner, CEO, and manager of the firm. Wingårdh received his M.Arch degree from the Chalmers University of Technology (Göteborg, 1975). The office works on a variety of projects ranging from product development (Volvo stands at international car shows) to interior design (Filippa K store "Ease" in Grev Turgatan, Stockholm, 2006), city planning (Havneholmen in Copenhagen, Denmark), and large structures (Hyllie Center, Malmö, 2011). They completed the Swedish Embassy in Berlin (Germany, 1999) and have undertaken other projects such as a new 85-meter-high control tower at Stockholm Arlanda Airport (Runway 3 Project, Stockholm, 2001) and the Piano Pavilion (Lahti, Finland, 2007–08, published here).

Wingårdhs ist eins der fünf größten Architekturbüros in Schweden. Es wurde 1977 in Göteborg gegründet, hat seit 1985 auch eine Niederlassung in Stockholm und insgesamt etwa 140 Mitarbeiter. **GERT WINGÅRDH**, geboren 1951 in Skövde, Schweden, ist der Besitzer, Geschäftsführer und Manager der Firma. Er machte seinen Master in Architektur an der Technischen Hochschule Chalmers (Göteborg, 1975). Das Büro arbeitet an vielfältigen Projekten, die von Produktentwicklung (Volvo-Stände auf internationalen Autosalons) bis zu Innenausstattungen (Geschäft Filippa K „Ease" in Grev Turgatan, Stockholm, 2006), Stadtplanung (Havneholmen in Kopenhagen, Dänemark) und Großbauten (Hyllie Center, Malmö, 2011) reichen. Es baute die Schwedische Botschaft in Berlin (1999) und weitere wichtige Gebäude, z. B. einen 85 m hohen Kontrollturm auf dem Stockholmer Flughafen Arlanda (Projekt Startbahn 3, Stockholm, 2001) sowie den Piano-Pavillon (Lahti, Finnland, 2007–08, hier veröffentlicht).

Wingårdhs est l'une des cinq plus grandes agences d'architecture de Suède. Fondée à Göteborg en 1977, elle possède également des bureaux à Stockholm depuis 1985 et emploie environ 140 collaborateurs. **GERT WINGÅRDH**, né en 1951 à Skövde (Suède) en est le propriétaire, le président et le directeur général. Wingårdh a obtenu son M.Arch. à l'Université de technologie Chalmers (Göteborg, 1975). L'agence intervient sur des projets variés allant du développement de produits (stands pour Volvo dans les salons de l'automobile internationaux) à l'aménagement intérieur (magasin Filippa K « Ease » dans Grev Turgatan, Stockholm, 2006), en passant par l'urbanisme (Havneholmen à Copenhague) et de grandes réalisations architecturales (Hyllie Center, Malmö, 2011). Elle a réalisé l'ambassade de Suède à Berlin (1999) ; une tour de contrôle de 85 m de haut pour l'aéroport d'Arlanda à Stockholm (Projet piste 3, Stockholm, 2001) et le pavillon Piano (Lahti, Finlande, 2007–08, publié ici).

PIANO PAVILION

Lahti, Finland, 2007–08

Address: Börupinraitti 6, 15140 Lahti, Finland, +358 10 422 59 50, www.casseli.fi
Area: 147 m². Client: Wood in Culture Association. Cost: not disclosed

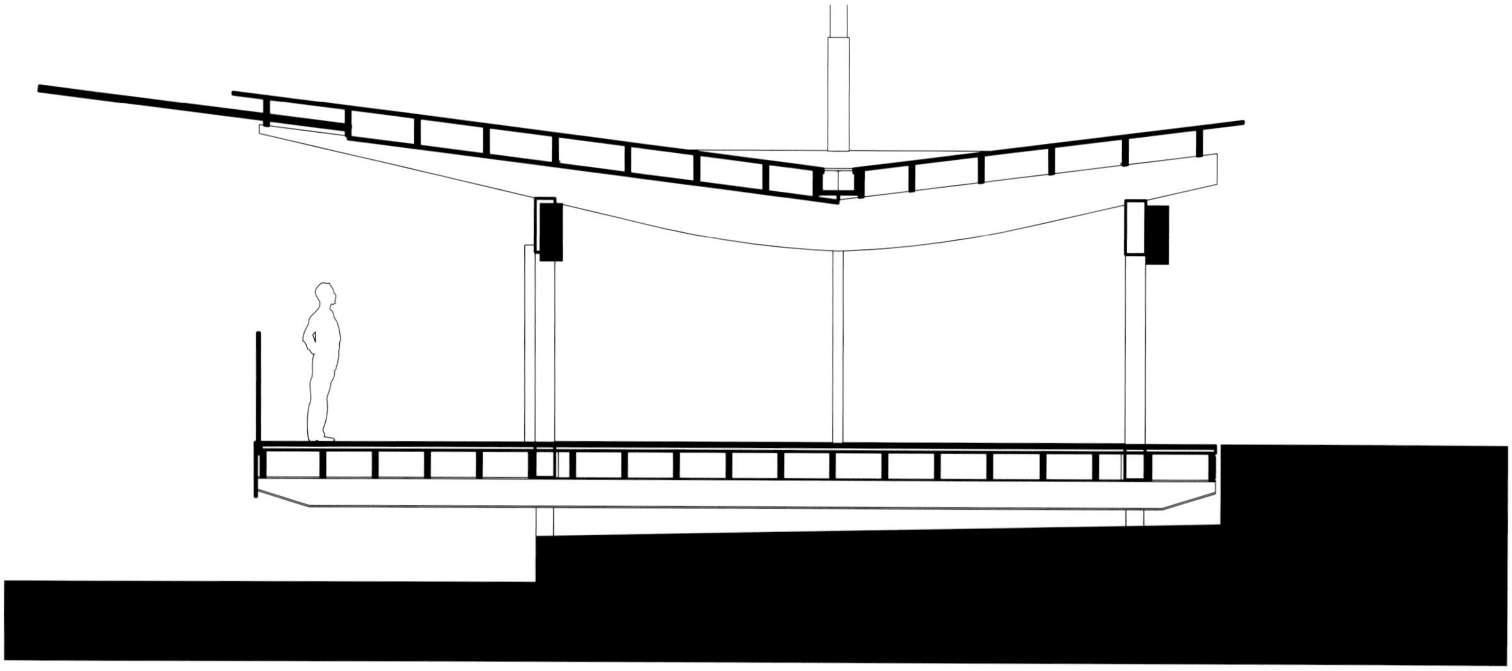

This Pavilion, commissioned by the Wood in Culture Association, is located near the Sibelius Hall in Lahti, Finland. Unexpectedly, the architect's firm declares of Gert Wingårdh: "His design echoes and celebrates the work of Italian Renzo Piano, recipient of the 2000 Spirit of Nature Wood Architecture Award." With steel foundation columns driven into the bedrock of the site, the structure has a glulam frame and steel beams. Glass walls give the impression that the roof is floating above the structure. The architect compares the building to a "ship about to be launched." Companies such as Finnforest supported the project, providing construction materials for example. The local UPM Lahti Mill provided the special plywood used for interior cladding, as they did the ProFi wood plastic composite employed for the terrace. Aspen staves used in the façade were trees felled in Artjärvi and Sysmä. Ash furniture in the café was designed by Tapio Anttila and manufactured at the joinery workshop of the ProPuu Association. The terrace furniture was designed by Kari Virtanen of Nikari Oy in Fiskars. In the summer, the **PIANO PAVILION** serves as a 60-seat café; in winter it can be reserved for meetings and private functions.

Dieser vom Verein Wood in Culture in Auftrag gegebene Pavillon steht neben der Sibelius-Halle in Lahti, Finnland. Das Architekturbüro berichtet spontan über Gert Wingårdh: „Sein Entwurf wurde inspiriert von Renzo Piano und ist eine Hommage an das Werk des Italieners, dem 2000 der Spirit of Nature Wood Architecture Award veliehen wurde." Das Gebäude mit Gründungspfeilern aus Stahl, die in den Felsboden getrieben wurden, hat ein Tragwerk aus Schichtholz und Stahlträgern. Glaswände vermitteln den Eindruck, als würde das Dach über dem Bauwerk schweben. Der Architekt vergleicht den Pavillon mit „einem Schiff, das vom Stapel gelassen wird". Firmen wie Finnforest haben das Projekt subventioniert, auch Baumaterial geliefert. Die Firma UPM Lahti Mill vor Ort lieferte das spezielle Furnier für die Innenverkleidung sowie ProFi-Holz-Kunststoff-Verbundmaterial für die Terrasse. Die für die Fassade verwendeten Espenstäbe stammen von Bäumen, die in Artjärvi und Sysmä gefällt wurden. Das Mobiliar aus Eschenholz im Café wurde von Tapio Anttila entworfen und in der Schreinerwerkstatt der Vereinigung ProPuu hergestellt. Die Möbel für die Terrasse gestaltete Kari Virtanen von Nikari Oy in Fiskars. Im Sommer dient der **PIANO-PAVILLON** als Café für bis zu 60 Besucher, im Winter kann er für Sitzungen und private Veranstaltungen genutzt werden.

Ce pavillon, commandité par l'Association du Bois dans la culture, se trouve près du Hall Sibelius à Lahti en Finlande. De façon qui étonne un peu, l'agence déclare : « Le projet [de Gert Wingårdh] rappelle et célèbre l'œuvre de l'architecte italien Renzo Piano, récipiendaire en 2000 du prix d'architecture Esprit de la nature. » Reposant sur des pieux de fondation en acier plantés dans l'assise rocheuse, la structure se compose d'une ossature en lamellé-collé et de poutres d'acier. Les murs de verre donnent l'impression que le toit flotte indépendamment. L'architecte le compare à un « bateau sur le point d'être lancé ». Des entreprises comme Finnforest soutiennent ce projet en fournissant par exemple les matériaux de construction. La scierie locale UPM de Lahti a offert le contreplaqué spécial utilisé pour l'habillage de l'intérieur ainsi que le matériau composite de bois et de plastique ProFi utilisé pour la terrasse. Les barreaux en peuplier proviennent d'arbres coupés à Artjärvi and Sysmä. Le mobilier en hêtre du café a été conçu par Tapio Anttila et fabriqué à l'atelier de menuiserie de l'association ProPuu. Celui de la terrasse a été conçu par Kari Virtanen de Nikari Oy à Fiskars. En été, le **PAVILLON PIANO** est aménagé en café de 60 places. En hiver, il est réservé à des réunions et des activités privées.

The Pavilion, with its asymmetric, upwardly inclined roof, is cantilevered over the water.

Der Pavillon mit seinem asymmetrischen, aufwärts gebogenen Dach kragt über das Wasser aus.

Le pavillon à toiture asymétrique en ailes de papillon se dresse en porte-à-faux au-dessus de l'eau.

The size of the roof allows for outdoor terraces to be fully covered. Full-height glazing allows patrons to view the harbor.

Aufgrund der Größe des Dachs sind die Außenterrassen voll überdeckt. Die Rundumverglasung bietet den Gästen Aussicht auf den Hafen.

Grâce à ses dimensions, le toit protège les terrasses. Les murs vitrés permettent aux clients de bénéficier de vues sur le port.

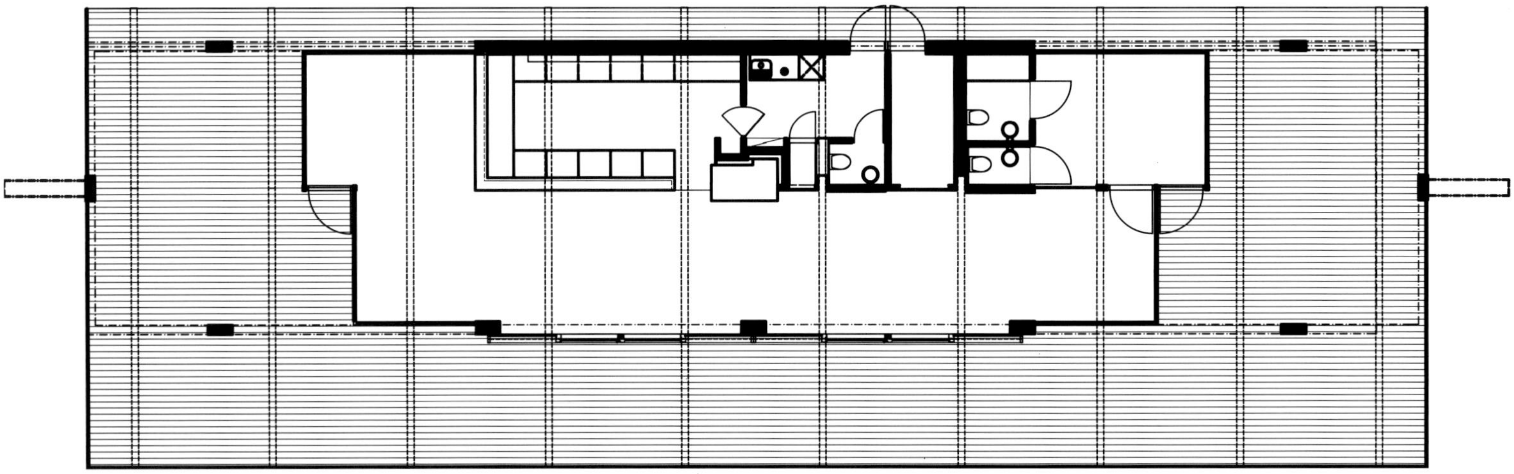

The terrace serves for outdoor seating when weather permits. Below, a drawing of the roof grid of the structure.

Wenn das Wetter es zulässt, kann auch die Terrasse genutzt werden. Unten: eine Aufsicht der Dachkonstruktion.

Des tables sont dressées sur la terrasse quand le temps le permet. Ci-dessous, un dessin de la trame de la structure du toit.

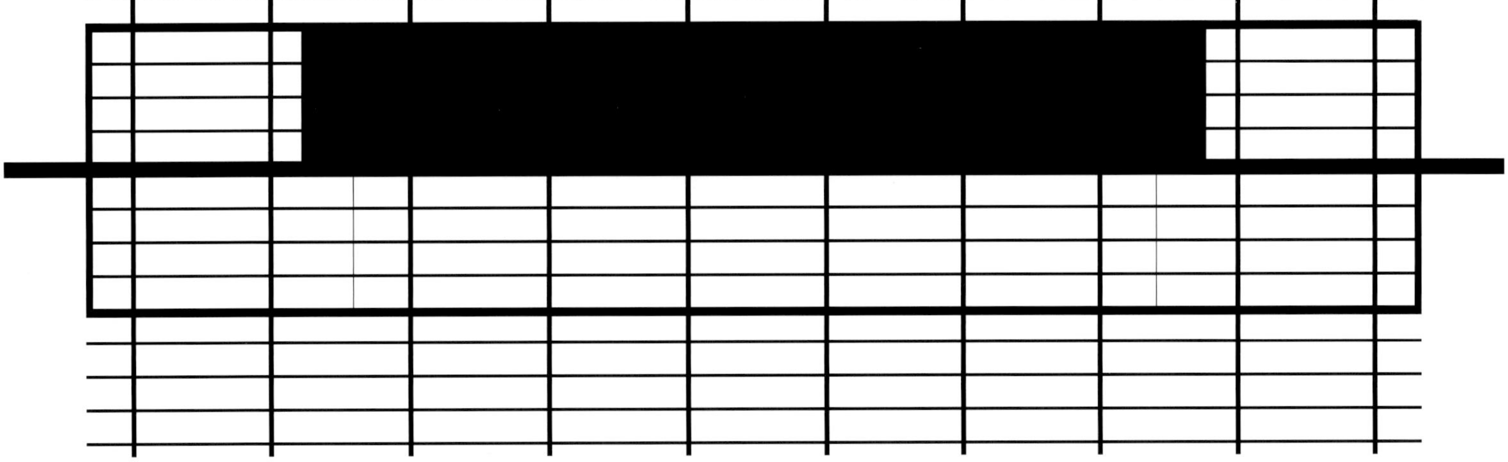

WMR

WMR Arquitectos
San Patricio 4150
Matanzas s/n Navidad
Santiago 7630287
Chile

Tel: +56 9744 2439
E-mail: info@wmraq.cl
Web: www.wmrarq.cl

FELIPE WEDELES TONDREAU was born in 1977. He obtained his degree in Architecture at the Finis Terrae University in Santiago (1994–2001). He was a founding Partner of the firm DAW (Santiago, 2001–03), and then cofounded WMR in 2005. **JORGE MANIEU BRICEÑO** was born in 1976. He also studied at the Finis Terrae University, obtaining his degree in Architecture in 1999. He worked with Manuel Casanueva and Felipe Assadi prior to cofounding WMR. **MACARENA RABAT ERRAZURIZ** was born in 1982, and also completed her architecture studies at Finis Terrae, before working at ZS arquitectos in Santiago and cofounding WMR. The acronym WMR is derived from the Partners' names—Wedeles Manieu Rabat. Their recent work includes the Hotel Surazo (Matanzas, 2008–10); Two Brothers Cabin (Matanzas, 2010); Mandakovic House (Navidad, Los Arcos, 2010, published here); Ingrid House (La Boca, 2010–11); Espinoza House (Matanzas, 2011); Cipres Surf Shop (Pichilemu, 2011–12); and Carlos Cortes House (Matanzas, 2011–12). They are currently working on the Awakova Hotel (Farellones, 2012–); and the La Sirena Hotel (Curanipe, 2012–), all in Chile.

FELIPE WEDELES TONDREAU wurde 1977 geboren. Sein Architekturdiplom erlangte er an der Universität Finis Terrae in Santiago (1994–2001). Er war Gründungspartner bei DAW (Santiago, 2001–03) und 2005 Mitbegründer von WMR. **JORGE MANIEU BRICEÑO**, Jahrgang 1976, studierte ebenfalls an der Universität Finis Terrae, wo er sein Architekturstudium 1999 abschloss. Vor der Gründung von WMR arbeitete er mit Manuel Casanueva und Felipe Assadi. Auch **MACARENA RABAT ERRAZURIZ**, geboren 1982, schloss ihr Architekturstudium an der Finis-Terrae-Universität ab und arbeitete vor der Gründung von WMR 2005 bei ZS arquitectos in Santiago. WMR steht für die Namen der Partner: Wedeles, Manieu, Rabat. In letzter Zeit entstanden das Hotel Surazo (Matanzas, 2008–10), eine Hütte für zwei Brüder (Matanzas, 2010), das Haus Mandakovic (Navidad, Los Arcos, 2010, hier veröffentlicht), das Haus Ingrid (La Boca, 2010–11), das Haus Espinoza (Matanzas, 2011), der Cipres Surf Shop (Pichilemu, 2011–12) und das Haus Carlos Cortes (Matanzas, 2011–12). Aktuelle Projekte sind das Hotel Awakova (Farellones, seit 2012) und das Hotel La Sirena (Curanipe, seit 2012), alle in Chile.

FELIPE WEDELES TONDREAU est né en 1977. Il a obtenu son diplôme en architecture à l'université Finis Terrae de Santiago (1994–2001). Il est l'un des partenaires fondateurs de l'agence DAW (Santiago, 2001–03) et a ensuite participé à la fondation de WMR en 2005. **JORGE MANIEU BRICEÑO** est né en 1976. Il a également fait ses études à l'université Finis Terrae et a obtenu son diplôme en architecture en 1999. Avant la fondation de WMR, il a travaillé avec Manuel Casanueva et Felipe Assadi. **MACARENA RABAT ERRAZURIZ** est née en 1982 et a elle aussi fait des études d'architecture à Finis Terrae avant de travailler à ZS arquitectos à Santiago et de participer à la fondation de WMR. L'acronyme WMR est tiré des noms des associés : Wedeles Manieu Rabat. Leurs réalisations récentes comprennent l'hôtel Surazo (Matanzas, 2008–10) ; la Cabane pour deux frères (Matanzas, 2010) ; la maison Mandakovic (Navidad, Los Arcos, 2010, publiée ici) ; la maison Ingrid (La Boca, 2010–11) ; la maison Espinoza (Matanzas, 2011) ; la boutique de surf Cipres (Pichilemu, 2011–12) et la maison Carlos Cortes (Matanzas, 2011–12). Ils travaillent actuellement à l'hôtel Awakova (Farellones, 2012–) et à l'hôtel La Sirena (Curanipe, 2012–), tous deux au Chili.

MANDAKOVIC HOUSE

Navidad, Los Arcos, Chile, 2010

Address: not disclosed. Area: 150 m²
Client: Carlos Cortes Simon. Cost: $160 000

The **MANDAKOVIC HOUSE** was built for a couple with two children. The two-story house was designed with timber, stone, and glass, and its plan is rectangular. A stairway divides the living room from the dining and kitchen area on the ground level. The bedrooms are above. The ground floor is a plinth made from local stone, with a line of glass above it, offering 180° views of the scenery. The shell of the house, made of wood, envelops the main volume and also serves to cover the forward terraces on the ocean side. It is difficult to imagine a more spectacular view of the Pacific, a fact that is the very basis for the architecture, which has been realized with an admirable economy of means.

Das **HAUS MANDAKOVIC** wurde für ein Paar mit zwei Kindern geplant. Der zweistöckige Entwurf mit rechteckigem Grundriss wurde aus Holz, Stein und Glas realisiert. Im Erdgeschoss gliedert eine Treppe Wohnbereich, Essbereich und Küche. Die Schlafzimmer sind im Obergeschoss untergebracht. Über einem Sockel aus lokalem Naturstein schließt sich ein Fensterband an, das 180°-Blicke in die Landschaft erlaubt. Die Gebäudehülle aus Holz umfängt nicht nur den Baukörper an sich, sondern überdacht auch die vordere Terrasse zum Meer. Ein spektakulärerer Blick auf den Pazifik lässt sich kaum vorstellen – eine Tatsache, die den eigentlichen Anlass zum Bau des Hauses gab, eine Architektur, die mit bewundernswert sparsamen Mitteln realisiert wurde.

La **MAISON MANDAKOVIC** a été construite pour un couple avec deux enfants. À deux étages, elle est construite en bois, pierre et verre selon un plan rectangulaire. Un escalier sépare le salon de l'espace salle à manger et cuisine au rez-de-chaussée. Les chambres à coucher sont à l'étage. Le rez-de-chaussée se compose d'un socle en pierre locale surmonté d'un bandeau de verre qui offre une vue à 180° du paysage. L'enveloppe de la maison, en bois, enrobe le volume principal et sert aussi à couvrir les terrasses à l'avant, côté océan. On peut difficilement imaginer une vue plus fantastique du Pacifique, elle constitue la base même de l'architecture qui a été réalisée avec des économies de moyens admirables.

A wood-clad box, the house is cantilevered in the direction of the cliff top and the ocean beyond. The wood shell continues outward to become a canopy for the terraces of the house. Right, section drawings.

Das Haus, ein kastenförmiger, holzverschalter Bau, kragt in Richtung Steilhang und Meer aus. Die Verkleidung aus Holz ist zum Terrassendach verlängert. Rechts Querschnittszeichnungen.

Cube revêtu de bois, la maison est en porte-à-faux vers le sommet de la falaise et l'océan en contrebas. La coque de bois se prolonge vers l'extérieur et forme un auvent pour les terrasses. À droite, dessins en coupe.

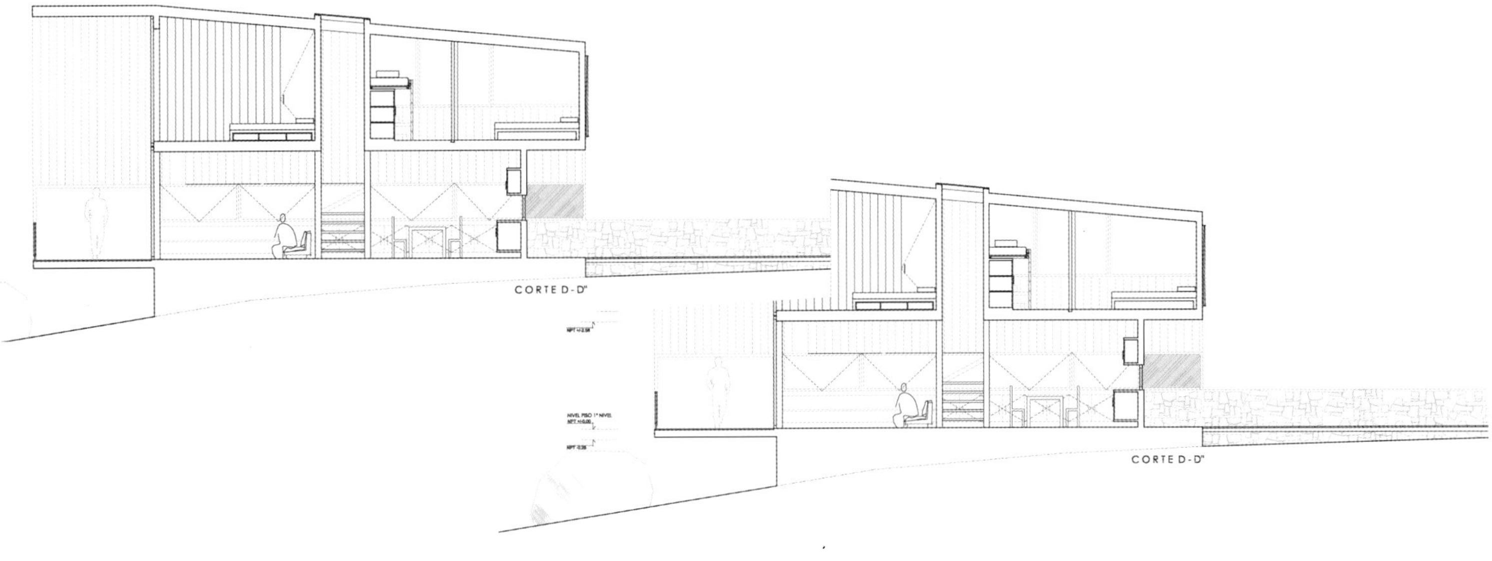
CORTE D-D'
CORTE D-D'

Wood is present everywhere in the house. Wooden floors, ceilings, and walls alternate here with full-height glazing and a steel staircase.

Holz ist überall im Haus zu finden. Holzböden, -decken und -wände wechseln sich hier mit raumhoher Verglasung und einer Stahltreppe ab.

Le bois est omniprésent dans toute la maison. Les sols, plafonds et murs en bois alternent avec le vitrage sur toute la hauteur de la pièce et un escalier en acier.

The relatively simple lines of the house (drawings below) translate into generous, open space with grand views of the ocean located just below the cliffside site (following double page).

Die schlichten Linien des Hauses (Zeichnungen unten) definieren großzügige, offene Räume mit großartigen Ausblicken auf den Ozean unterhalb des Hanggrundstücks (folgende Doppelseite).

Les lignes plutôt simples de la maison (schémas ci-dessous) donnent naissance à un espace ouvert et généreux avec une vue grandiose sur l'océan en bas de la falaise (double page suivante).

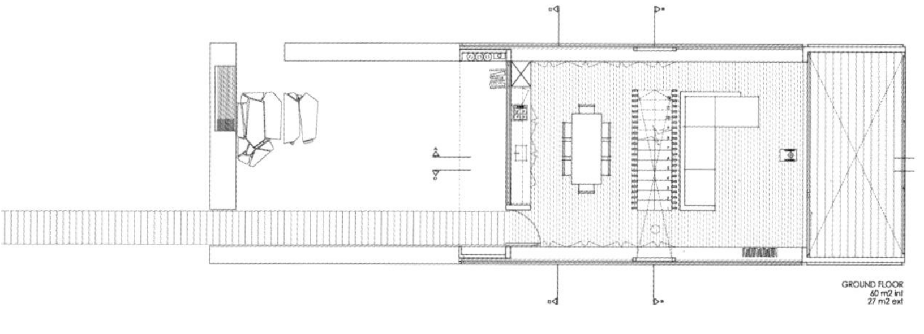

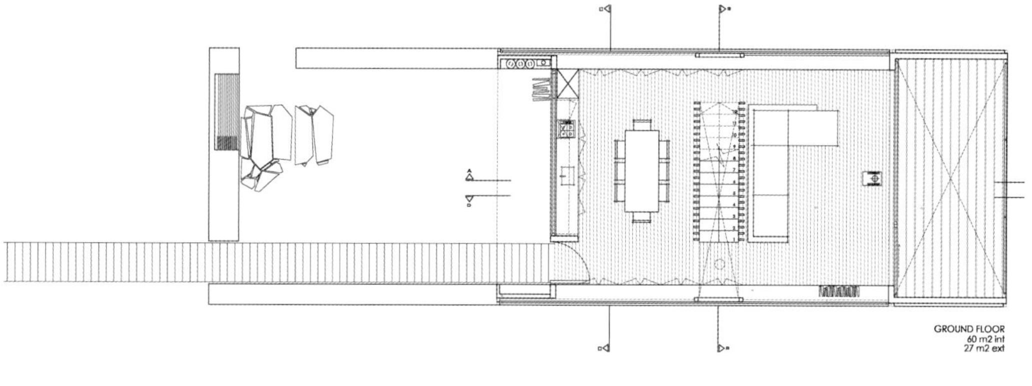

Casa Granero

CAZÚ ZEGERS

Cazú Zegers / arquitectura
Pedro de Villagra 2351
Vitacura
Santiago
Chile

Tel: +562 2952 7330
Fax: +562 2952 7288
E-mail: info@cazuzegers.cl
Web: www.cazuzegers.cl

Born in 1958, **CAZÚ ZEGERS** graduated in Architecture from the Universidad Católica de Valparaíso (Chile, 1984). Since 1990 she has worked on architectural projects, lamp design and furniture, urban planning, and cultural and territorial management. Her industrial design, interior architecture, architecture, residential buildings, and at least 33 single-family homes "highlight the search for new architectural forms generated through the relationship between poetry and architecture." Zegers concentrates on low-tech approaches. One of her most recent projects is the Tierra Patagonia Hotel (Torres del Paine, 2010–11, published here), for which she received a 2013 Wallpaper Design Award. Other recent work includes the Casa Granero (Pucon, 2004, also published here); Casa Soplo (Lo Barnechea, Santiago, 2011); and the Casa Esmeralda (Lo Barnechea, Santiago, 2013), all in Chile.

CAZÚ ZEGERS wurde 1958 geboren und schloss ihr Architekturstudium an der Universidad Católica de Valparaíso ab (Chile, 1984). Seit 1990 widmet sie sich außer der Architektur auch dem Design von Möbeln und Lampen, der Stadtplanung sowie dem Kulturmanagement und der Raumplanung. Ihre Industriedesign-, Inneneinrichtungs- und Architekturprojekte sowie ihre Wohngebäude und mindestens 33 Einfamilienhäuser zeigen „eine Suche nach neuen Formen des Bauens, die eine Beziehung zwischen Architektur und Poesie herstellen". Zegers konzentriert sich auf Lowtechverfahrensweisen. Für eines ihrer jüngsten Projekte, das Hotel Tierra Patagonia (Torres del Paine, 2010–11, hier vorgestellt), erhielt sie 2013 den Wallpaper Design Award. Weitere jüngere Arbeiten sind u. a. die Casa Granero (Pucon, 2004, ebenfalls hier vorgestellt), die Casa Soplo (Lo Barnechea, Santiago, 2011) und die Casa Esmeralda (Lo Barnechea, Santiago, 2013); alle in Chile.

Née en 1958, **CAZÚ ZEGERS** est diplômée en architecture de l'Université catholique de Valparaíso (Chile, 1984). Depuis 1990, elle a travaillé sur des projets d'architecture, de design de lampes et de mobilier, d'urbanisme et dans le domaine du management culturel et territorial. Son design industriel, son architecture intérieure, son architecture, ses bâtiments d'habitation et pas moins de 33 maisons individuelles « soulignent la recherche de nouvelles formes architecturales générées par la relation entre poésie et architecture ». Elle met l'accent sur une approche *low-tech*. L'un de ses derniers projets est l'hôtel Tierra Patagonia (Torres del Paine, 2010–11, publié ici) pour lequel elle a reçu en 2013 le prix de design Wallpaper. Parmi ses œuvres récentes figurent la Casa Granero (Pucon, 2004, également publiée ici) ; la Casa Soplo (Lo Barnechea, Santiago, 2011) et la Casa Esmeralda (Lo Barnechea, Santiago, 2013), toutes au Chili.

CASA GRANERO

Pucon, Chile, 2004

Address: not disclosed. Area: 116 m²
Client: Virginia Valdes. Cost: not disclosed

With its enveloping wood-plank skin, the structure sits lightly on the ground and fits in well with the wooded environment.

Das Gebäude verfügt über eine großflächige Holzverkleidung, steht leicht erhöht und fügt sich gut in die bewaldete Umgebung ein.

Avec son enveloppe en planches de bois, la structure repose légèrement sur le sol et s'intègre parfaitement dans son environnement boisé.

The barnlike shape of the house is clearly visible in the images on this page, but so, too, is the modern design with its extended wooden canopy and wall seen above.

Die Scheunenform des Hauses ist auf den Abbildungen dieser Seite deutlich zu erkennen, aber auch die moderne Formensprache mit Vordach und verlängerter Seitenwand (oben).

La forme de grange de la maison est bien visible sur les images de cette page, mais aussi son design moderne avec l'auvent en bois et le mur en avancée vus en haut.

The **CASA GRANERO** (Barn House) seeks to create a close relation between its wooden skin and the surrounding landscape. Cazú Zegers says: "It does not impose, but incorporates itself with the traditional type of construction typical of southern Chile." The architect's reference to the barn is in relation to her effort to create a contemporary representation of such agricultural buildings. Set slightly off the ground on a low concrete base, the house has horizontal wooden slats that cover its external surfaces aside from areas where generous glazing is present. The interior is also entirely in wood, with a stairway and mezzanine partially occupying the double-height space. The architecture manages to convey a feeling of rural roughness at the same time as it forms a sophisticated conceptualization of a specific building type.

Mit ihrer hölzernen Fassade steht die **CASA GRANERO** (Scheunenhaus) in einem engen Verhältnis zur landschaftlichen Umgebung. Cazú Zegers: „Das Haus mit seiner für den Süden Chiles typischen traditionellen Konstruktionsweise drängt sich nicht auf, sondern fügt sich ein." Dass Zegers als Referenz die Scheune aufgreift, rührt von ihrem Wunsch her, eine zeitgenössische Entsprechung für landwirtschaftliche Gebäudetypen zu schaffen. Das auf einem niedrigen Betonsockel leicht erhöht stehende Haus verfügt neben horizontal angebrachten Holzbrettern als Fassadenverkleidung auch über großzügige Glasflächen. Das Innere mit seiner Treppe und dem Mezzaningeschoss, das einen Teil der doppelten Raumhöhe einnimmt, ist ebenfalls vollständig holzverkleidet. Das Haus vermittelt ein Gefühl ländlicher Rustikalität und verkörpert zugleich die raffinierte Neuinterpretation eines spezifischen Gebäudetyps.

La **CASA GRANERO** (grange) cherche à établir une relation étroite entre l'enveloppe en bois et le paysage environnant. Cazú Zegers dit : « Elle ne s'impose pas, mais correspond au type de construction traditionnelle typique du sud du Chili. » La référence de l'architecte à la grange est liée à son effort de créer une représentation contemporaine de ces bâtiments agricoles. Légèrement surélevée sur un petit soubassement en béton, la maison présente des lames de bois horizontales qui recouvrent les surfaces extérieures à l'exception de zones dominées par de généreux vitrages. L'intérieur est lui aussi entièrement en bois avec un escalier et une mezzanine qui occupent une partie de l'espace à double hauteur. L'architecture parvient à transmettre une impression de rusticité tout en donnant forme à une conceptualisation sophistiquée d'un type de bâtiment spécifique.

The inside of the house is also inspired by the barnlike architecture of the exterior, with wood on almost every surface but the floor.

Auch die Innenräume des Hauses sind von der scheunenartigen Architektur des Äußeren inspiriert. Außer dem Boden bestehen hier nahezu alle Oberflächen aus Holz.

L'intérieur de la maison s'inspire également de l'architecture de grange, avec du bois sur presque toutes les surfaces à l'exception du sol.

TIERRA PATAGONIA HOTEL

Torres del Paine, Chile, 2010–11

Address: Torres del Paine National Park, Patagonia, Chile, +562 2370 5301, www.tierrapatagonia.com
Area: 4900 m². Client: Katari Inversiones. Cost: not disclosed
Collaboration: Roberto Benavente, Roderigo Ferrer (Associated Architects)

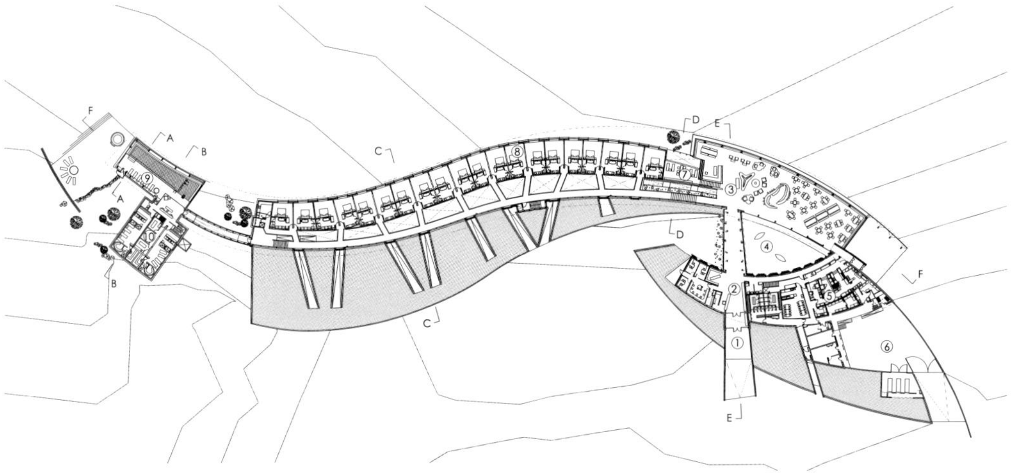

The gently curving wooden volume of the hotel—seen in plan to the left and in the images on these pages—appears to be in harmony with the low vegetation and nearby mountains.

Der sanft geschwungene Baukörper des Hotels – links als Grundriss und auf den Abbildungen dieser Doppelseite – harmoniert mit der niedrigen Vegetation und den Bergen im Umfeld.

Avec ses courbes souples, le volume en bois de l'hôtel – en plan à droite et en images sur cette double page – semble en parfaite harmonie avec la végétation basse et las montagnes voisines.

Also called Hotel of the Wind, this new structure is located at Sarmiento Lake at the entrance of the Torres del Paine National Park (XII Región). As the architect writes, the form of the hotel seeks to "merge with the metaphysical landscape, not to interrupt it." Inspired by the shape of an "old fossil, a prehistoric animal beached on the shore of the lake, not unlike those found and studied by Charles Darwin," the structure is also seen by its designer as having been carved by the wind. Washed Lenga wood paneling is used for all the exterior cladding, giving the building a silvery sheen. Cazú Zegers sought to create "warm and cozy spaces structured by internal pathways."

Dieses auch „Hotel des Windes" genannte Projekt liegt am Lago Sarmiento und damit am Eingang des Nationalparks Torres del Paine (XII Región). Der Architektin zufolge strebt die Form danach „mit der metaphysischen Landschaft zu verschmelzen, statt sie zu stören". Formal inspiriert von einem „uralten Fossil, einem prähistorischen Tier, das, ähnlich wie jene von Charles Darwin gefundenen und untersuchten Versteinerungen, am Ufer des Sees angespült wurde", erwecke das Gebäude den Eindruck, vom Wind geformt zu sein, so die Architektin. Das Hotel ist mit gewaschenem Lenga-Holz verkleidet, das ihm einen silberfarbenen Schimmer verleiht. Cazú Zegers Ziel war es, „warme und behagliche, von Gängen strukturierte Räumlichkeiten" schaffen.

Également appelé « Hôtel du vent », cette nouvelle structure est située au lac Sarmiento, à l'entrée du parc national Torres del Paine (XII Región). Comme l'écrit l'architecte, la forme de l'hôtel tente de « fusionner avec le paysage métaphysique, et non l'interrompre ». Inspirée par la forme d'un « vieux fossile, un animal préhistorique échoué au bord du lac, pas très différent de ceux découverts et étudiés par Charles Darwin », la structure semble, aux yeux du designer, avoir été sculptée par le vent. Des panneaux de lenga lavé font office de bardage extérieur et confèrent au bâtiment un aspect satiné argenté. Cazú Zegers tente de créer « des espaces chaleureux et cosy structurés par des sentiers intérieurs ».

Wood is also the main material inside the hotel, but broad glazed bands offer generous views of the area.

Auch im Inneren des Hotels ist Holz das Material erster Wahl. Großflächige Fensterbänder bieten eindrucksvolle Ausblicke.

Le bois est également le matériau principal à l'intérieur de l'hôtel, mais de larges bandes vitrées offrent de généreuses vues sur le site.

Below, sections drawings of the hotel volume show the curved roof. The broad, open interiors seen here are clearly designed with the broad natural expanses outside in mind.

Die Querschnittzeichnungen unten zeigen das kurvige Dach. Die hier abgebildeten großflächigen, offenen Innenräume sollen mit der Weite des Naturraums korrespondieren.

Ci-dessous, des coupes du volume de l'hôtel révèlent la toiture courbe. Les vastes intérieurs ouverts montrés ici ont à l'évidence été conçus en référence à l'immensité des espaces extérieurs.

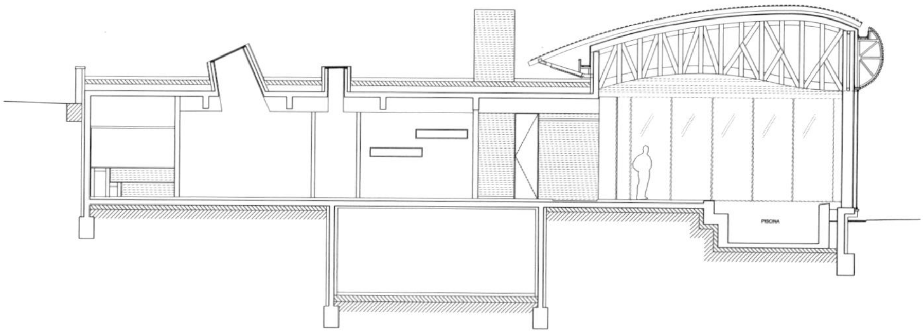

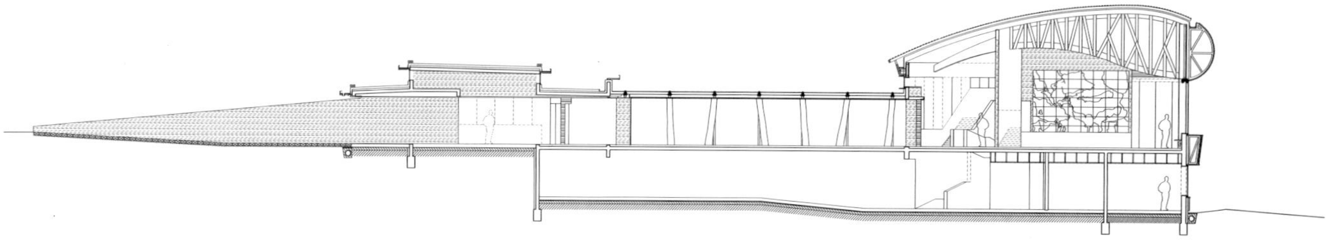

Cazú Zegers uses wood on nearly every surface that is not glazed, playing also on natural light and a relatively simple décor to continually make visitors aware of the natural setting.

Cazú Zegers verwendet für nahezu alle nicht verglasten Oberflächen Holz und setzt auf natürliches Licht und eine schlichte Ausstattung, um das Augenmerk auf die Natur zu lenken.

Cazú Zegers a recours au bois pour la quasi-totalité des surfaces non vitrées ; elle joue ainsi avec la lumière naturelle et un décor relativement sobre pour que les visiteurs soient sans cesse conscients du cadre naturel.

Reflections in a pool and views of a lake and mountains come together in the image above. Below, interior views where wood, the sky, and nature are brought together by the architect's talent.

Das Bild oben vereint die Spiegelungen im Pool mit dem See- und Bergpanorama. Mit feinem Gespür bringt die Architektin Holz, Himmel und Natur in Einklang, wie in den Innenansichten unten zu sehen ist.

L'image du haut rassemble les reflets dans la piscine et les vues sur un lac et des montagnes. Ci-dessous, des vues intérieures où le bois, le ciel et la nature sont réunis par le talent de l'architecte.

RENÉ VAN ZUUK

René van Zuuk Architekten b.v.
De Fantasie 9
1324 HZ Almere
The Netherlands

Tel: +31 36 537 91 39
Fax: +31 36 537 92 59
E-mail: info@renevanzuuk.nl
Web: www.renevanzuuk.nl

RENÉ VAN ZUUK received an M.Sc. degree from the Technical University of Eindhoven (1988), and created his own firm in 1993. He has a design staff of five people. Prior to 1993, he worked for Skidmore, Owings & Merrill in London and Chicago (1988–89), at Facilitair Bureau voor Bouwkunde Rotterdam, and at Hoogstad van Tilburg Architecten (1989–92). His notable completed projects include Eight Bridges (Nieuwsloten, 1993); Lock House "Oostersluis" (Groningen, 1995); Villa van Diepen (Almere, 1995); Four Canal Houses (Java Island, Amsterdam, 1997); Educational Farm "Griftsteede" (Utrecht, 1999); Center for Plastic Arts "CBK" (Alphen aan de Rijn, 2000); Art Pavilion "De Verbeelding" (Zeewolde, 2001); ARCAM Architectural Center (Amsterdam, 2003); Blok 16 housing and fitness complex (Almere, 2003); bridge for bicycles and pedestrians (Almere, 2003); Bridge Keeper's House (Middelburg, unbuilt); and "Zilverparkkade" Office Building (Lelystad, 2004). More recently, he has worked on a group of 20 houses (Bosrijk, Eindhoven, 2005); a 10-story apartment building (Dudok, Hilversum, 2006); a multifunctional first-aid post (Dordrecht, 2007); Project X (Almere, 2004–08); a villa in Wageningen (2008); and Roosendaal Pavilion (Roosendaal, 2006–09, published here), all in the Netherlands.

RENÉ VAN ZUUK erwarb 1988 seinen Master of Science an der Technischen Universität Eindhoven und gründete 1993 sein Büro. Er hat fünf Mitarbeiter. Vor 1993 war er für Skidmore, Owings & Merrill in London und Chicago (1988–89), am Facilitair Bureau voor Bouwkunde Rotterdam, Hoogstad, und für van Tilburg Architecten (1989–92) tätig. Zu seinen wichtigsten Projekten zählen acht Brücken (Nieuwsloten, 1993), das Schleusenhaus Oostersluis (Groningen, 1995), die Villa van Diepen (Almere, 1995), vier Kanalhäuser (Java Island, Amsterdam, 1997), der Kinderbauernhof Griftsteede (Utrecht, 1999), das Zentrum für bildende Künste CBK (Alphen aan de Rijn, 2000), der Kunstpavillon De Verbeelding (Zeewolde, 2001), das Architekturzentrum ARCAM (Amsterdam, 2003), Blok 16, ein Wohnkomplex mit Fitnesseinrichtungen (Almere, 2003), eine Radfahrer- und Fußgängerbrücke (Almere, 2003), ein Brückenwärterhaus (Middelburg, nicht gebaut) sowie das Bürohaus Zilverparkkade (Lelystad, 2004). In jüngster Zeit arbeitete van Zuuk an einer Gruppe von 20 Häusern (Bosrijk, Eindhoven, 2005), einem zehnstöckigen Apartmenthaus (Dudok, Hilversum, 2006), einer multifunktionalen Erste-Hilfe-Ambulanz (Dordrecht, 2007), am Projekt X (Almere, 2004–08), einer Villa in Wageningen (2008) und dem Roosendaal Pavillon (Roosendaal, 2006–09, hier vorgestellt), alle in den Niederlanden.

RENÉ VAN ZUUK obtient un master en sciences de l'Université de technologie d'Eindhoven (1988), et crée sa propre agence en 1993. Il emploie une équipe de création de cinq personnes. Avant 1993, il a travaillé pour Skidmore, Owings & Merrill à Londres et à Chicago (1988–89), au Facilitair Bureau voor Bouwkunde de Rotterdam, et chez Hoogstad van Tilburg Architecten (1989–92). Ses réalisations notables incluent huit ponts (Nieuwsloten, 1993) ; une maison éclusière « Oostersluis » (Groningue, 1995) ; la villa van Diepen (Almere, 1995) ; quatre maisons sur le canal (Java Eiland, Amsterdam, 1997) ; la ferme pour enfants « Griftsteede » (Utrecht, 1999) ; le Centre d'arts plastiques CBK (Alphen aan de Rijn, 2000) ; le pavillon d'art « De Verbeelding » (Zeewolde, 2001) ; le pavillon d'architecture ARCAM (Amsterdam, 2003) ; l'ensemble d'habitations Blok 16 et un centre de fitness (Almere, 2003) ; une passerelle cyclable et piétonnière (Almere, 2003) ; la maison du Gardien de pont (Middelburg, non construit) ; et l'immeuble de bureaux « Zilverparkkade » (Lelystad, 2004). Plus récemment, il a travaillé sur un lotissement de vingt maisons (Bosrijk, Eindhoven, 2005) ; un immeuble d'appartements de dix étages (Dudok, Hilversum, 2006) ; un poste d'urgence multifonctions (Dordrecht, 2007) ; la maison Project X (Almere, 2004–08) ; une villa à Wageningen (2008) ; et le pavillon de Roosendaal (Roosendaal, 2006–09, publié ici), tous situés aux Pays-Bas.

Rose d'Or
Rose d'Or
OUTLET SHOP

ROOSENDAAL PAVILION

Roosendaal, The Netherlands, 2006–09

Address: Nieuwe Markt 23, 4701 Roosendaal, The Netherlands
Area: 620 m². Client: City of Roosendaal. Cost: not disclosed
Collaboration: Jorrit Spel, Chimo Villa Belda (Design)

This project was the result of a staged process in which the municipality of Roosendaal in the southwest of the Netherlands decided in 2001 to remove automobile traffic from the New Market square in the city center and then to build a large two-story underground parking lot. An urban design firm called Quadrat was called on to imagine the new square. Their scheme called for the extensive use of brick, the planting of 15 trees, and the creation of a restaurant and coffee pavilion. René van Zuuk was brought into the process in 2005 and asked to design a pavilion in the square in a period of five weeks. This short design period led the architect to adopt the original positioning and form of the buildings proposed by Quadrat, but René van Zuuk decided to create a cantilevered, sloped structure clad in wood (sucupira amarela). The slope allows pedestrians to walk onto the roof, or to use it as a stage for live performances. Its form makes it part of the square rather than allowing it to become a dividing element. The building cantilevers above the entrance to the parking garage on the south side, allowing light to penetrate the lower levels. Convivial and practical, the structure, containing shops, a lunchroom, and the parking lot entrance, improves on the postwar architecture of the square and encourages meeting and activities.

Das Projekt entstand in einem mehrstufigen Planungsprozess: Ziel der Stadt Roosendaal in den südwestlichen Niederlanden war die Realisierung der 2001 beschlossenen autofreien Zone am Neumarkt im Stadtzentrum sowie der Bau eines großen zweigeschossigen unterirdischen Parkhauses. Das Stadtplanungsbüro Quadrat wurde mit der Neugestaltung des Marktplatzes beauftragt. Sein Konzept setzte insbesondere auf den Einsatz von Backstein, die Anpflanzung von 15 Bäumen sowie die Ansiedlung eines Restaurants und eines Cafépavillons. 2005 wurde René van Zuuk hinzugezogen und erhielt den Auftrag, in nur fünf Wochen einen Pavillon für den Marktplatz zu gestalten. Wegen der kurzen Entwurfsphase übernahm der Architekt die von Quadrat vorgesehene Platzierung und Form der Bauten, entwarf jedoch ein auskragendes, abgeschrägtes, mit Holz (Sucupira amarela) verkleidetes Gebäude. Dank der Abschrägung des Pavillons können Passanten das Dach des Baus besteigen oder als Bühne für Liveveranstaltungen nutzen. Durch seine Form wird der Bau zu einem Bestandteil des Platzes, statt ihn zu teilen. Über dem Parkhauseingang auf der Südseite kragt der Bau stark aus und lässt so Licht in die Untergeschosse einfallen. Der freundliche und praktische Pavillon beherbergt neben dem Parkhauseingang auch Läden und ein Café. Er trägt nachhaltig zur Belebung der Nachkriegsarchitektur am Platz bei und lädt zu Begegnungen und gemeinsamen Aktivitäten ein.

Ce projet est le résultat d'un processus par étapes, à l'initiative de la municipalité de Roosendaal, dans le sud-ouest des Pays-Bas, qui avait décidé en 2001 de supprimer le trafic automobile sur la place du Nouveau Marché située dans le centre-ville et de construire un vaste parking souterrain de deux étages. Le programme élaboré par le cabinet d'urbanisme Quadrat, auquel avait été confiée la conception de la nouvelle place, prévoyait un usage extensif de la brique, la plantation de quinze arbres, et la création d'un restaurant et d'un café. René van Zuuk est entré dans le projet en 2005, avec la mission de concevoir en cinq semaines un pavillon pour la place. Ce temps de conception très court a conduit l'architecte à adopter l'implantation et la forme des bâtiments initialement proposées par Quadrat, mais il a décidé de créer une structure en porte-à-faux inclinée, revêtue de bois (sucupira amarela). Grâce à sa pente, le toit est accessible aux piétons ou peut se transformer en scène de spectacle. Sa forme est plus perçue comme une portion de la place que comme un élément de partition. Le bâtiment en surplomb au-dessus de l'entrée du parking permet à la lumière de pénétrer dans les niveaux inférieurs. Convivial et pratique, le bâtiment, qui abrite des commerces, une cafétéria et l'entrée du parking, embellit l'architecture d'après-guerre de la place et favorise les rencontres et l'animation.

The cantilevered, sloping wood-clad building imagined by Rene van Zuuk is an unusual, but unprovocative presence in the town of Roosendaal. Pedestrians are seen on the roof of the building at nightfall (right).

Das auskragende, holzverschalte Gebäude mit seinem geneigten Dach, ein Entwurf von René van Zuuk, hat eine ungewöhnliche, wenn auch kaum provokante Präsenz in der Stadt Rosendaal. Rechts Fußgänger auf dem Dach bei Anbruch der Nacht.

Le bâtiment, revêtu de bois et en porte-à-faux incliné, imaginé par René van Zuuk, marque Rosendaal de sa présence originale, sans être provocante. À droite, des piétons sur le toit du bâtiment, la nuit.

Walkways allow the public to climb to the top of the roof of the building and to see the town from a new vantage point.

Rampen erlauben es Besuchern, das Dach bis zum höchsten Punkt hinaufzulaufen und die Stadt aus einer neuen Perspektive zu sehen.

Des allées permettent au public de grimper jusqu'au sommet du toit et de découvrir la ville depuis un nouveau point de vue.

INDEX OF BUILDINGS, NAMES, AND PLACES

CREDITS

PHOTO CREDITS — **2** © Dag Jenssen / **15** © Iwan Baan / **16** © Steven Heller / **17–21** © Leonardo Finotti / **22** © Ai Weiwei / **23** © Frank Schinki/documenta and Museum Fridericanium Veranstaltungs-GbmH / **24–25** © Ai Weiwei / **26** © Studio Aisslinger / **27, 31** © Hannes Meraner, Tom Nagy / **28–30** © Steffen Jänicke / **32** © Al Borde / **33–37** © Raed Gindeya M. / **38** © AND / **39–49** © Yongkwan Kim / **50** © Tadao Ando / **51–55** © Shigeo Ogawa / **56, 58, 60–61, 63–65, 67–69, 70 left** © Mitsuo Matsuoka / **57, 59, 62, 66, 70 right, 71** © Shinkenchiku-Sha / **72** © Atelier Bow-Wow / **73–79** © Iwan Baan / **80 top (a–d)** © Atelier Oslo / **80 bottom (a, b)** © AWP/photo F. Benzaquien / **80 bottom (c, d)** © AWP / **81–83 top** © The Lantern Atelier Oslo/AWP + Thomas Liu / **83 bottom** © The Lantern Atelier Oslo/AWP + Haakon Eikesdal / **84** © Shigeru Ban Architects / **85–89** © Didier Boy de la Tour / **90–95** © Hiroyuki Hirai / **96** © David Matthiessen / **97–101** © Roland Halbe / **102–111** © Belzberg Architects / **112** © Bernardes + Jacobsen Arquitetura / **113–117** © Leonardo Finotti / **118** © Jens Passoth / **119–123** © Jens Weber, Munich / **124** © Birk und Heilmeyer Architekten / **125–129** © Christian Richters / **130** © Bohlin Cywinski Jackson / **131–137** © Nic Lehoux / **138** © Agence Bernard Bühler / **139–143** © Vincent Monthier / **144** © Santiago Calatrava / **145–147** © Heinrich Helfenstein / **148–149** © Architekturphoto / **150–152** © Archiv Calatrava / **153** © Paolo Rosselli / **154** © Cannon Design / **155–159** © Nic Lehoux / **160** © Studio Arthur Casas SP / **161–163** © Leonardo Finotti / **164–171** © Centerbrook Architects and Planners / **172** © Claus en Kaan Architecten / **173, 175, 177** Sebastian van Damme © Claus en Kaan Architecten / **174, 176, 178–179** © Christian Richters/VIEW / **180** © Sebastian Yurjevic Z. / **181–187** © Aryeh Kornfeld K. / **188** © Dekleva Gregorič Arhitekti / **189–197** © Cristobal Palma / **198** © Djuric Tardio Architectes / **199–205** © Clément Guillaume / **206** © Established & Sons / **207–211** © Milo Keller & Julien Gallico / **212** © Estudio Nómada / **213–217** © Héctor Santos Díes/Bisimages / **218** © Terunobu Fujimori / **219–223** © Akihisa Masuda / **224** © David Vintiner Photography / **225–229** © Iwan Baan / **230** © General Design Co., Ltd. / **231–239** © Daici Ano / **240–249** © Earl Carter / **250** © GRAFT / **251–253** © Ricky Ridecos / **254** © Steven Holl Architects / **255–257** © Paul Warchol / **258** © Hudson Architects / **259–265** © James Brittain/VIEW / **266** © Hollwich Kushner / **267–271** © Michael Moran/OTTO / **272** © ICD/ITKE / **273–275** © Roland Halbe / **276–283** © Yosuke Inoue Architect & Associates / **284–289** © Jensen & Skodvin Architects / **290** © Johnsen Schmaling Architects / **291–297** © Doug Edmunds / **298** © Taiji Kawano Architects / **299–303** © Alessio Guarino / **304** © Esther Thorens / **305–309** © Roland Halbe / **310** © Kengo Kuma & Associates / **311–315** © Kengo Kuma & Associates for Glass Wood House / **316–319** © André Morin / **320** © Lassila Hirvilammi Architects Ltd. / **321–327** © Jussi Tiainen / **328–333** © Li Xiaodong / **334** © Bel Lobo & Bob Neri Arquitetos / **335–337** © Anna Kahn / **338** © Localarchitecture / **339–349** © Milo Keller / **350** © MacKay-Lyons Sweetapple / **351–355** © James Steeves/Atlantic Stock Images Inc. / **356** © MADA s.p.a.m. / **357–359, 360 bottom, 361** © Zhan Jin / **360 top** © Rong Huang / **362** © March Studio / **363–365** © Louis Baquiast / **366** © Sebstian Mariscal Studio / **367–371** © Paúl Rivera/archphoto / **372** © J. Mayer H. Architects / **373, 381** © David Franck / **374–380** © Fernando Alda / **382** © McBride Charles Ryan / **383–387** © John Gollings / **388** © Niall McLaughlin Architects / **389–393** © Nick Kane / **394** © Beatriz Meyer Arquitetura / **395–397** © Nelson Kon / **398** © SKM Architects / **399–401** © Yongkwan Kim / **402** © Marco Pietracupa / **403–411** © Günther Wett / **412–415** © Pete Nelson / **416** © Susanne Nobis / **417–421** © Roland Halbe / **422** © Pacific Environments NZ Ltd. Architects / **423–427** © Lucy Gauntlett / **428** © Renzo Piano Building Workshop / **429–435** © Hans Schlupp/architekturphoto / **436** © Plan:B + JPR/CR / **437** Sergio Gómez / **438–439 top, 441** © Iwan Baan / **439 bottom** © Carlos Mario Rodrigues / **440 top** © Felipe Mesa / **440 bottom** © Camilo Orozco / **442** © Antoine Predock / **443–447** © Robert Reck / **448** © Arne Quinze / **449–453** © Dave Bruel / **454–455** © Dave Bruel & Denis Decaluwe / **456–463** © Dag Jenssen / **464** © Benjamin Brolet / **465–469** © Eric Mairiaux / **470** © Hans-Jörg Ruch / **471–473** © Filippo Simonetti / **474** © Hiroshi Sambuichi Architects / **475–479** © Katsuhisa Kida/FOTOTECA / **480** © SARC Architects / **481–485** © Jussi Tiainen / **486** © Jan Lillebø/Bergens Tidende / **487–491** © Bent René Synnevåg / **492** © Rodrigo Sheward / **493–497** © Cristobal Palma / **498–503** © Shim-Sutcliffe Architects / **504** © Álvaro Siza / **505–511** © Duccio Malagamba / **512–517** © Germán del Sol, Architectos / **518** © Sotero Arquitetos / **519–523** © Leonardo Finotti / **524** © Studio of Cinematic Architecture / **525–527** © Charles Hosea / **528** © Peter Stutchbury / **529–535** © Michael Nicholson / **536–541** © Supersudaka / **542–547** © Tacklebox LLC / **548** © TAO / **549–553** © Shu He / **554** © Threefold Architects / **555–556, 560–561** © Nick Kane / **557–559** © Jon Holland / **562–565** © Charles Hosea / **566** © Martin Mai / **567–573** © Iwan Baan / **574** © UID architects / **575–581** © Hiroshi Ueda / **582–587** © Ulloa + Ding / **588** © Votrongnghia Co., Ltd. / **589–595** © Oki Hiroyuki / **596–601** © werk A architektur / **602** © White / **603–604, 605 bottom, 606–607** © Ole Haupt / **605 top** © Johan Elm for ERCO / **608–611** © Michael Moran / **612** © Wingårdh Arkitektkontor AB / **613–615** © Anders Adlercreutz / **616–617** Kimmo Räsinen / **618** © WMR arquitectos / **619–625** © Sergio Pirrone / **626** © Gonzalo Puga / **627–631** © Guy Wenborne / **632–639** © Tierra Hotels / **640** © René van Zuuk Architekten BV / **641–645** © Christian Richters

CREDITS FOR PLANS / DRAWINGS / CAD DOCUMENTS — **18, 21** © Adjaye Associates / **29, 31** © Studio Aisslinger / **35, 36** © Al Borde / **41–42, 47, 49** © AND / **53–54, 56, 59, 70** © Tadao Ando / **77** © Atelier Bow-Wow / **82** © Atelier Oslo/AWP / **86, 88, 90, 92, 95** © Shigeru Ban Architects / **99, 101** © Behnisch Architekten / **109** © Belzberg Architects / **117** © Bernardes + Jacobsen Arquitetura / **123** © Titus Bernhard / **127–128** © Birk und Heilmeyer Architekten / **133, 135** © Bohlin Cywinski Jackson / **141–142** © Agence Bernard Bühler / **152** © Santiago Calatrava / **159** © Cannon Design / **167–168, 171** © Centerbrook Architects and Planners / **175–176, 179** © Claus en Kaan Architecten / **183, 186–187** © Sebastian Yurjevic Z. / **191–192, 195** © Dekleva Gregorič Arhitekti / **201, 204** © Djuric Tardio Architectes / **209** © Sebastian Wrong / **215** © Estudio Nómada / **226** © Sou Fujimoto Architects / **232–233, 238** © General Design Co., Ltd. / **244, 249** © Sean Godsell Architects / **253** © GRAFT / **257** © Steven Holl Architects / **261–262** © Hudson Architects / **270–271** © Hollwich Kushner / **275** © ICD/ITKE / **278, 281** © Yosuke Inoue Architect & Associates / **287–288** © Jensen & Skodvin Architects / **292** © Johnsen Schmaling Architects / **300–301, 303** © Taiji Kawano Architects / **307–308** © bkarch / **312, 315, 317, 319** © Kengo Kuma & Associates / **322–324, 327** © Lassila Hirvilammi Architects Ltd. / **337, 338** © Li Xiaodong / **342** © Bel Lobo & Bob Neri Arquitetos / **347, 350, 355** © Localarchitecture / **361** © MacKay-Lyons Sweetapple / **365** © MADA s.p.a.m. / **371** © March Studio / **375, 377** © Sebstian Mariscal Studio / **381, 384, 386** © J. Mayer H. Architects / **390, 392–393** © McBride Charles Ryan / **397–398** © Niall McLaughlin Architects / **403** © Beatriz Meyer Arquitetura / **407** © SKM Architects / **410, 413, 417** © MODUS architects / **425, 427** © Susanne Nobis / **430–433** © Pacific Environments NZ Ltd. Architects / **437, 440–441** © Renzo Piano Building Workshop / **444, 446** © Plan:B + JPR/CR / **451, 453** © Antoine Predock / **461** © UTIL Structural Studies, Rolf Vansteenvegen / **447** © Studio Arne Quinze / **475** © Rotor / **478** © Hans-Jörg Ruch / **484** © Hiroshi Sambuichi Architects / **490–491** © SARC Architects / **495** © Todd Saunders Architechts / **502–503** © Rodrigo Sheward / **507** © Shim-Sutcliffe Architects / **514–515** © Álvaro Siza / **520** © Germán del Sol, Architectos / **545, 547** © Supersudaka / **556, 559** © TAO / **569** © Threefold Architects / **577–578** © Bernard Tschumi Architects / **583, 585** © UID architects / **591, 593** © Ulloa + Ding / **596, 600** © Votrongnghia Co., Ltd. / **605–606** © werk A architektur / **610** © White / **616** © Williams and Tsien / **620, 622–623** © Wingårdh Arkitektkontor AB / **627, 629** © WMR arquitectos / **638, 643** © Cazú Zegers

Cover:
Cazú Zegers, Casa Granero,
Pucon, Chile
Photo © Guy Wenborne

Back cover:
Susanne Nobis, Towards Landscape,
Lake Starnberg, Berg, Germany
Photo © Roland Halbe